FREE Study Skills Videos/DVD

Dear Customer,

Thank you for your purchase from Mometrix! We consider it an honor and a privilege that you have purchased our product and we want to ensure your satisfaction.

As part of our ongoing effort to meet the needs of test takers, we have developed a set of Study Skills Videos that we would like to give you for FREE. These videos cover our *best practices* for getting ready for your exam, from how to use our study materials to how to best prepare for the day of the test.

All that we ask is that you email us with feedback that would describe your experience so far with our product. Good, bad, or indifferent, we want to know what you think!

To get your FREE Study Skills Videos, you can use the **QR code** below, or send us an **email** at studyvideos@mometrix.com with *FREE VIDEOS* in the subject line and the following information in the body of the email:

- The name of the product you purchased.
- Your product rating on a scale of 1-5, with 5 being the highest rating.
- Your feedback. It can be long, short, or anything in between. We just want to know your impressions and experience so far with our product. (Good feedback might include how our study material met your needs and ways we might be able to make it even better. You could highlight features that you found helpful or features that you think we should add.)

If you have any questions or concerns, please don't hesitate to contact me directly.

Thanks again!

Sincerely,

Jay Willis
Vice President
jay.willis@mometrix.com
1-800-673-8175

Praxis 7001

Elementary Education Multiple Subjects Study Guide

Secrets Exam Prep

3 Full-Length Practice Tests

250+ Online Video Tutorials

Detailed Answer Explanations

DEAR FUTURE EXAM SUCCESS STORY

First of all, **THANK YOU** for purchasing Mometrix study materials!

Second, congratulations! You are one of the few determined test-takers who are committed to doing whatever it takes to excel on your exam. **You have come to the right place.** We developed these study materials with one goal in mind: to deliver you the information you need in a format that's concise and easy to use.

In addition to optimizing your guide for the content of the test, we've outlined our recommended steps for breaking down the preparation process into small, attainable goals so you can make sure you stay on track.

We've also analyzed the entire test-taking process, identifying the most common pitfalls and showing how you can overcome them and be ready for any curveball the test throws you.

Standardized testing is one of the biggest obstacles on your road to success, which only increases the importance of doing well in the high-pressure, high-stakes environment of test day. Your results on this test could have a significant impact on your future, and this guide provides the information and practical advice to help you achieve your full potential on test day.

Your success is our success

We would love to hear from you! If you would like to share the story of your exam success or if you have any questions or comments in regard to our products, please contact us at **800-673-8175** or **support@mometrix.com**.

Thanks again for your business and we wish you continued success!

Sincerely,
The Mometrix Test Preparation Team

> **Need more help? Check out our flashcards at:**
> http://MometrixFlashcards.com/PraxisII

TABLE OF CONTENTS

Introduction

Thank you for purchasing this resource! You have made the choice to prepare yourself for a test that could have a huge impact on your future, and this guide is designed to help you be fully ready for test day. Obviously, it's important to have a solid understanding of the test material, but you also need to be prepared for the unique environment and stressors of the test, so that you can perform to the best of your abilities.

For this purpose, the first section that appears in this guide is the **Secret Keys**. We've devoted countless hours to meticulously researching what works and what doesn't, and we've boiled down our findings to the five most impactful steps you can take to improve your performance on the test. We start at the beginning with study planning and move through the preparation process, all the way to the testing strategies that will help you get the most out of what you know when you're finally sitting in front of the test.

We recommend that you start preparing for your test as far in advance as possible. However, if you've bought this guide as a last-minute study resource and only have a few days before your test, we recommend that you skip over the first two Secret Keys since they address a long-term study plan.

If you struggle with **test anxiety**, we strongly encourage you to check out our recommendations for how you can overcome it. Test anxiety is a formidable foe, but it can be beaten, and we want to make sure you have the tools you need to defeat it.

Secret Key #1 – Plan Big, Study Small

There's a lot riding on your performance. If you want to ace this test, you're going to need to keep your skills sharp and the material fresh in your mind. You need a plan that lets you review everything you need to know while still fitting in your schedule. We'll break this strategy down into three categories.

Information Organization

Start with the information you already have: the official test outline. From this, you can make a complete list of all the concepts you need to cover before the test. Organize these concepts into groups that can be studied together, and create a list of any related vocabulary you need to learn so you can brush up on any difficult terms. You'll want to keep this vocabulary list handy once you actually start studying since you may need to add to it along the way.

Time Management

Once you have your set of study concepts, decide how to spread them out over the time you have left before the test. Break your study plan into small, clear goals so you have a manageable task for each day and know exactly what you're doing. Then just focus on one small step at a time. When you manage your time this way, you don't need to spend hours at a time studying. Studying a small block of content for a short period each day helps you retain information better and avoid stressing over how much you have left to do. You can relax knowing that you have a plan to cover everything in time. In order for this strategy to be effective though, you have to start studying early and stick to your schedule. Avoid the exhaustion and futility that comes from last-minute cramming!

Study Environment

The environment you study in has a big impact on your learning. Studying in a coffee shop, while probably more enjoyable, is not likely to be as fruitful as studying in a quiet room. It's important to keep distractions to a minimum. You're only planning to study for a short block of time, so make the most of it. Don't pause to check your phone or get up to find a snack. It's also important to **avoid multitasking**. Research has consistently shown that multitasking will make your studying dramatically less effective. Your study area should also be comfortable and well-lit so you don't have the distraction of straining your eyes or sitting on an uncomfortable chair.

The time of day you study is also important. You want to be rested and alert. Don't wait until just before bedtime. Study when you'll be most likely to comprehend and remember. Even better, if you know what time of day your test will be, set that time aside for study. That way your brain will be used to working on that subject at that specific time and you'll have a better chance of recalling information.

Finally, it can be helpful to team up with others who are studying for the same test. Your actual studying should be done in as isolated an environment as possible, but the work of organizing the information and setting up the study plan can be divided up. In between study sessions, you can discuss with your teammates the concepts that you're all studying and quiz each other on the details. Just be sure that your teammates are as serious about the test as you are. If you find that your study time is being replaced with social time, you might need to find a new team.

2

Secret Key #2 – Make Your Studying Count

You're devoting a lot of time and effort to preparing for this test, so you want to be absolutely certain it will pay off. This means doing more than just reading the content and hoping you can remember it on test day. It's important to make every minute of study count. There are two main areas you can focus on to make your studying count.

Retention

It doesn't matter how much time you study if you can't remember the material. You need to make sure you are retaining the concepts. To check your retention of the information you're learning, try recalling it at later times with minimal prompting. Try carrying around flashcards and glance at one or two from time to time or ask a friend who's also studying for the test to quiz you.

To enhance your retention, look for ways to put the information into practice so that you can apply it rather than simply recalling it. If you're using the information in practical ways, it will be much easier to remember. Similarly, it helps to solidify a concept in your mind if you're not only reading it to yourself but also explaining it to someone else. Ask a friend to let you teach them about a concept you're a little shaky on (or speak aloud to an imaginary audience if necessary). As you try to summarize, define, give examples, and answer your friend's questions, you'll understand the concepts better and they will stay with you longer. Finally, step back for a big picture view and ask yourself how each piece of information fits with the whole subject. When you link the different concepts together and see them working together as a whole, it's easier to remember the individual components.

Finally, practice showing your work on any multi-step problems, even if you're just studying. Writing out each step you take to solve a problem will help solidify the process in your mind, and you'll be more likely to remember it during the test.

Modality

Modality simply refers to the means or method by which you study. Choosing a study modality that fits your own individual learning style is crucial. No two people learn best in exactly the same way, so it's important to know your strengths and use them to your advantage.

For example, if you learn best by visualization, focus on visualizing a concept in your mind and draw an image or a diagram. Try color-coding your notes, illustrating them, or creating symbols that will trigger your mind to recall a learned concept. If you learn best by hearing or discussing information, find a study partner who learns the same way or read aloud to yourself. Think about how to put the information in your own words. Imagine that you are giving a lecture on the topic and record yourself so you can listen to it later.

For any learning style, flashcards can be helpful. Organize the information so you can take advantage of spare moments to review. Underline key words or phrases. Use different colors for different categories. Mnemonic devices (such as creating a short list in which every item starts with the same letter) can also help with retention. Find what works best for you and use it to store the information in your mind most effectively and easily.

Secret Key #3 – Practice the Right Way

Your success on test day depends not only on how many hours you put into preparing, but also on whether you prepared the right way. It's good to check along the way to see if your studying is paying off. One of the most effective ways to do this is by taking practice tests to evaluate your progress. Practice tests are useful because they show exactly where you need to improve. Every time you take a practice test, pay special attention to these three groups of questions:

- The questions you got wrong
- The questions you had to guess on, even if you guessed right
- The questions you found difficult or slow to work through

This will show you exactly what your weak areas are, and where you need to devote more study time. Ask yourself why each of these questions gave you trouble. Was it because you didn't understand the material? Was it because you didn't remember the vocabulary? Do you need more repetitions on this type of question to build speed and confidence? Dig into those questions and figure out how you can strengthen your weak areas as you go back to review the material.

Additionally, many practice tests have a section explaining the answer choices. It can be tempting to read the explanation and think that you now have a good understanding of the concept. However, an explanation likely only covers part of the question's broader context. Even if the explanation makes perfect sense, **go back and investigate** every concept related to the question until you're positive you have a thorough understanding.

As you go along, keep in mind that the practice test is just that: practice. Memorizing these questions and answers will not be very helpful on the actual test because it is unlikely to have any of the same exact questions. If you only know the right answers to the sample questions, you won't be prepared for the real thing. **Study the concepts** until you understand them fully, and then you'll be able to answer any question that shows up on the test.

It's important to wait on the practice tests until you're ready. If you take a test on your first day of study, you may be overwhelmed by the amount of material covered and how much you need to learn. Work up to it gradually.

On test day, you'll need to be prepared for answering questions, managing your time, and using the test-taking strategies you've learned. It's a lot to balance, like a mental marathon that will have a big impact on your future. Like training for a marathon, you'll need to start slowly and work your way up. When test day arrives, you'll be ready.

Start with the strategies you've read in the first two Secret Keys—plan your course and study in the way that works best for you. If you have time, consider using multiple study resources to get different approaches to the same concepts. It can be helpful to see difficult concepts from more than one angle. Then find a good source for practice tests. Many times, the test website will suggest potential study resources or provide sample tests.

4

Practice Test Strategy

If you're able to find at least three practice tests, we recommend this strategy:

UNTIMED AND OPEN-BOOK PRACTICE

Take the first test with no time constraints and with your notes and study guide handy. Take your time and focus on applying the strategies you've learned.

TIMED AND OPEN-BOOK PRACTICE

Take the second practice test open-book as well, but set a timer and practice pacing yourself to finish in time.

TIMED AND CLOSED-BOOK PRACTICE

Take any other practice tests as if it were test day. Set a timer and put away your study materials. Sit at a table or desk in a quiet room, imagine yourself at the testing center, and answer questions as quickly and accurately as possible.

Keep repeating timed and closed-book tests on a regular basis until you run out of practice tests or it's time for the actual test. Your mind will be ready for the schedule and stress of test day, and you'll be able to focus on recalling the material you've learned.

Secret Key #4 – Pace Yourself

Once you're fully prepared for the material on the test, your biggest challenge on test day will be managing your time. Just knowing that the clock is ticking can make you panic even if you have plenty of time left. Work on pacing yourself so you can build confidence against the time constraints of the exam. Pacing is a difficult skill to master, especially in a high-pressure environment, so **practice is vital**.

Set time expectations for your pace based on how much time is available. For example, if a section has 60 questions and the time limit is 30 minutes, you know you have to average 30 seconds or less per question in order to answer them all. Although 30 seconds is the hard limit, set 25 seconds per question as your goal, so you reserve extra time to spend on harder questions. When you budget extra time for the harder questions, you no longer have any reason to stress when those questions take longer to answer.

Don't let this time expectation distract you from working through the test at a calm, steady pace, but keep it in mind so you don't spend too much time on any one question. Recognize that taking extra time on one question you don't understand may keep you from answering two that you do understand later in the test. If your time limit for a question is up and you're still not sure of the answer, mark it and move on, and come back to it later if the time and the test format allow. If the testing format doesn't allow you to return to earlier questions, just make an educated guess; then put it out of your mind and move on.

On the easier questions, be careful not to rush. It may seem wise to hurry through them so you have more time for the challenging ones, but it's not worth missing one if you know the concept and just didn't take the time to read the question fully. Work efficiently but make sure you understand the question and have looked at all of the answer choices, since more than one may seem right at first.

Even if you're paying attention to the time, you may find yourself a little behind at some point. You should speed up to get back on track, but do so wisely. Don't panic; just take a few seconds less on each question until you're caught up. Don't guess without thinking, but do look through the answer choices and eliminate any you know are wrong. If you can get down to two choices, it is often worthwhile to guess from those. Once you've chosen an answer, move on and don't dwell on any that you skipped or had to hurry through. If a question was taking too long, chances are it was one of the harder ones, so you weren't as likely to get it right anyway.

On the other hand, if you find yourself getting ahead of schedule, it may be beneficial to slow down a little. The more quickly you work, the more likely you are to make a careless mistake that will affect your score. You've budgeted time for each question, so don't be afraid to spend that time. Practice an efficient but careful pace to get the most out of the time you have.

Secret Key #5 – Have a Plan for Guessing

When you're taking the test, you may find yourself stuck on a question. Some of the answer choices seem better than others, but you don't see the one answer choice that is obviously correct. What do you do?

The scenario described above is very common, yet most test takers have not effectively prepared for it. Developing and practicing a plan for guessing may be one of the single most effective uses of your time as you get ready for the exam.

In developing your plan for guessing, there are three questions to address:

- When should you start the guessing process?
- How should you narrow down the choices?
- Which answer should you choose?

When to Start the Guessing Process

Unless your plan for guessing is to select C every time (which, despite its merits, is not what we recommend), you need to leave yourself enough time to apply your answer elimination strategies. Since you have a limited amount of time for each question, that means that if you're going to give yourself the best shot at guessing correctly, you have to decide quickly whether or not you will guess.

Of course, the best-case scenario is that you don't have to guess at all, so first, see if you can answer the question based on your knowledge of the subject and basic reasoning skills. Focus on the key words in the question and try to jog your memory of related topics. Give yourself a chance to bring the knowledge to mind, but once you realize that you don't have (or you can't access) the knowledge you need to answer the question, it's time to start the guessing process.

It's almost always better to start the guessing process too early than too late. It only takes a few seconds to remember something and answer the question from knowledge. Carefully eliminating wrong answer choices takes longer. Plus, going through the process of eliminating answer choices can actually help jog your memory.

Summary: Start the guessing process as soon as you decide that you can't answer the question based on your knowledge.

How to Narrow Down the Choices

The next chapter in this book (**Test-Taking Strategies**) includes a wide range of strategies for how to approach questions and how to look for answer choices to eliminate. You will definitely want to read those carefully, practice them, and figure out which ones work best for you. Here though, we're going to address a mindset rather than a particular strategy.

Your odds of guessing an answer correctly depend on how many options you are choosing from.

Number of options left	5	4	3	2	1
Odds of guessing correctly	20%	25%	33%	50%	100%

You can see from this chart just how valuable it is to be able to eliminate incorrect answers and make an educated guess, but there are two things that many test takers do that cause them to miss out on the benefits of guessing:

- Accidentally eliminating the correct answer
- Selecting an answer based on an impression

We'll look at the first one here, and the second one in the next section.

To avoid accidentally eliminating the correct answer, we recommend a thought exercise called **the $5 challenge**. In this challenge, you only eliminate an answer choice from contention if you are willing to bet $5 on it being wrong. Why $5? Five dollars is a small but not insignificant amount of money. It's an amount you could afford to lose but wouldn't want to throw away. And while losing $5 once might not hurt too much, doing it twenty times will set you back $100. In the same way, each small decision you make—eliminating a choice here, guessing on a question there—won't by itself impact your score very much, but when you put them all together, they can make a big difference. By holding each answer choice elimination decision to a higher standard, you can reduce the risk of accidentally eliminating the correct answer.

The $5 challenge can also be applied in a positive sense: If you are willing to bet $5 that an answer choice *is* correct, go ahead and mark it as correct.

Summary: Only eliminate an answer choice if you are willing to bet $5 that it is wrong.

8

Which Answer to Choose

You're taking the test. You've run into a hard question and decided you'll have to guess. You've eliminated all the answer choices you're willing to bet $5 on. Now you have to pick an answer. Why do we even need to talk about this? Why can't you just pick whichever one you feel like when the time comes?

The answer to these questions is that if you don't come into the test with a plan, you'll rely on your impression to select an answer choice, and if you do that, you risk falling into a trap. The test writers know that everyone who takes their test will be guessing on some of the questions, so they intentionally write wrong answer choices to seem plausible. You still have to pick an answer though, and if the wrong answer choices are designed to look right, how can you ever be sure that you're not falling for their trap? The best solution we've found to this dilemma is to take the decision out of your hands entirely. Here is the process we recommend:

Once you've eliminated any choices that you are confident (willing to bet $5) are wrong, select the first remaining choice as your answer.

Whether you choose to select the first remaining choice, the second, or the last, the important thing is that you use some preselected standard. Using this approach guarantees that you will not be enticed into selecting an answer choice that looks right, because you are not basing your decision on how the answer choices look.

This is not meant to make you question your knowledge. Instead, it is to help you recognize the difference between your knowledge and your impressions. There's a huge difference between thinking an answer is right because of what you know, and thinking an answer is right because it looks or sounds like it should be right.

Summary: To ensure that your selection is appropriately random, make a predetermined selection from among all answer choices you have not eliminated.

Test-Taking Strategies

This section contains a list of test-taking strategies that you may find helpful as you work through the test. By taking what you know and applying logical thought, you can maximize your chances of answering any question correctly!

It is very important to realize that every question is different and every person is different: no single strategy will work on every question, and no single strategy will work for every person. That's why we've included all of them here, so you can try them out and determine which ones work best for different types of questions and which ones work best for you.

Question Strategies

☑ READ CAREFULLY

Read the question and the answer choices carefully. Don't miss the question because you misread the terms. You have plenty of time to read each question thoroughly and make sure you understand what is being asked. Yet a happy medium must be attained, so don't waste too much time. You must read carefully and efficiently.

☑ CONTEXTUAL CLUES

Look for contextual clues. If the question includes a word you are not familiar with, look at the immediate context for some indication of what the word might mean. Contextual clues can often give you all the information you need to decipher the meaning of an unfamiliar word. Even if you can't determine the meaning, you may be able to narrow down the possibilities enough to make a solid guess at the answer to the question.

☑ PREFIXES

If you're having trouble with a word in the question or answer choices, try dissecting it. Take advantage of every clue that the word might include. Prefixes can be a huge help. Usually, they allow you to determine a basic meaning. *Pre-* means before, *post-* means after, *pro-* is positive, *de-* is negative. From prefixes, you can get an idea of the general meaning of the word and try to put it into context.

☑ HEDGE WORDS

Watch out for critical hedge words, such as *likely, may, can, sometimes, often, almost, mostly, usually, generally, rarely,* and *sometimes.* Question writers insert these hedge phrases to cover every possibility. Often an answer choice will be wrong simply because it leaves no room for exception. Be on guard for answer choices that have definitive words such as *exactly* and *always.*

☑ SWITCHBACK WORDS

Stay alert for *switchbacks.* These are the words and phrases frequently used to alert you to shifts in thought. The most common switchback words are *but, although,* and *however.* Others include *nevertheless, on the other hand, even though, while, in spite of, despite,* and *regardless of.* Switchback words are important to catch because they can change the direction of the question or an answer choice.

☑ FACE VALUE

When in doubt, use common sense. Accept the situation in the problem at face value. Don't read too much into it. These problems will not require you to make wild assumptions. If you have to go beyond creativity and warp time or space in order to have an answer choice fit the question, then you should move on and consider the other answer choices. These are normal problems rooted in reality. The applicable relationship or explanation may not be readily apparent, but it is there for you to figure out. Use your common sense to interpret anything that isn't clear.

10

Answer Choice Strategies

⊘ ANSWER SELECTION

The most thorough way to pick an answer choice is to identify and eliminate wrong answers until only one is left, then confirm it is the correct answer. Sometimes an answer choice may immediately seem right, but be careful. The test writers will usually put more than one reasonable answer choice on each question, so take a second to read all of them and make sure that the other choices are not equally obvious. As long as you have time left, it is better to read every answer choice than to pick the first one that looks right without checking the others.

⊘ ANSWER CHOICE FAMILIES

An answer choice family consists of two (in rare cases, three) answer choices that are very similar in construction and cannot all be true at the same time. If you see two answer choices that are direct opposites or parallels, one of them is usually the correct answer. For instance, if one answer choice says that quantity x increases and another either says that quantity x decreases (opposite) or says that quantity y increases (parallel), then those answer choices would fall into the same family. An answer choice that doesn't match the construction of the answer choice family is more likely to be incorrect. Most questions will not have answer choice families, but when they do appear, you should be prepared to recognize them.

⊘ ELIMINATE ANSWERS

Eliminate answer choices as soon as you realize they are wrong, but make sure you consider all possibilities. If you are eliminating answer choices and realize that the last one you are left with is also wrong, don't panic. Start over and consider each choice again. There may be something you missed the first time that you will realize on the second pass.

⊘ AVOID FACT TRAPS

Don't be distracted by an answer choice that is factually true but doesn't answer the question. You are looking for the choice that answers the question. Stay focused on what the question is asking for so you don't accidentally pick an answer that is true but incorrect. Always go back to the question and make sure the answer choice you've selected actually answers the question and is not merely a true statement.

⊘ EXTREME STATEMENTS

In general, you should avoid answers that put forth extreme actions as standard practice or proclaim controversial ideas as established fact. An answer choice that states the "process should be used in certain situations, if…" is much more likely to be correct than one that states the "process should be discontinued completely." The first is a calm rational statement and doesn't even make a definitive, uncompromising stance, using a hedge word *if* to provide wiggle room, whereas the second choice is far more extreme.

⊘ BENCHMARK

As you read through the answer choices and you come across one that seems to answer the question well, mentally select that answer choice. This is not your final answer, but it's the one that will help you evaluate the other answer choices. The one that you selected is your benchmark or standard for judging each of the other answer choices. Every other answer choice must be compared to your benchmark. That choice is correct until proven otherwise by another answer choice beating it. If you find a better answer, then that one becomes your new benchmark. Once you've decided that no other choice answers the question as well as your benchmark, you have your final answer.

⊘ PREDICT THE ANSWER

Before you even start looking at the answer choices, it is often best to try to predict the answer. When you come up with the answer on your own, it is easier to avoid distractions and traps because you will know exactly what to look for. The right answer choice is unlikely to be word-for-word what you came up with, but it should be a close match. Even if you are confident that you have the right answer, you should still take the time to read each option before moving on.

General Strategies

⊘ TOUGH QUESTIONS

If you are stumped on a problem or it appears too hard or too difficult, don't waste time. Move on! Remember though, if you can quickly check for obviously incorrect answer choices, your chances of guessing correctly are greatly improved. Before you completely give up, at least try to knock out a couple of possible answers. Eliminate what you can and then guess at the remaining answer choices before moving on.

⊘ CHECK YOUR WORK

Since you will probably not know every term listed and the answer to every question, it is important that you get credit for the ones that you do know. Don't miss any questions through careless mistakes. If at all possible, try to take a second to look back over your answer selection and make sure you've selected the correct answer choice and haven't made a costly careless mistake (such as marking an answer choice that you didn't mean to mark). This quick double check should more than pay for itself in caught mistakes for the time it costs.

⊘ PACE YOURSELF

It's easy to be overwhelmed when you're looking at a page full of questions; your mind is confused and full of random thoughts, and the clock is ticking down faster than you would like. Calm down and maintain the pace that you have set for yourself. Especially as you get down to the last few minutes of the test, don't let the small numbers on the clock make you panic. As long as you are on track by monitoring your pace, you are guaranteed to have time for each question.

⊘ DON'T RUSH

It is very easy to make errors when you are in a hurry. Maintaining a fast pace in answering questions is pointless if it makes you miss questions that you would have gotten right otherwise. Test writers like to include distracting information and wrong answers that seem right. Taking a little extra time to avoid careless mistakes can make all the difference in your test score. Find a pace that allows you to be confident in the answers that you select.

⊘ KEEP MOVING

Panicking will not help you pass the test, so do your best to stay calm and keep moving. Taking deep breaths and going through the answer elimination steps you practiced can help to break through a stress barrier and keep your pace.

Final Notes

The combination of a solid foundation of content knowledge and the confidence that comes from practicing your plan for applying that knowledge is the key to maximizing your performance on test day. As your foundation of content knowledge is built up and strengthened, you'll find that the strategies included in this chapter become more and more effective in helping you quickly sift through the distractions and traps of the test to isolate the correct answer.

Now that you're preparing to move forward into the test content chapters of this book, be sure to keep your goal in mind. As you read, think about how you will be able to apply this information on the test. If you've already seen sample questions for the test and you have an idea of the question format and style, try to come up with questions of your own that you can answer based on what you're reading. This will give you valuable practice applying your knowledge in the same ways you can expect to on test day.

Good luck and good studying!

Teaching Reading

Transform passive reading into active learning! After immersing yourself in this chapter, put your comprehension to the test by taking a quiz. The insights you gained will stay with you longer this way. Scan the QR code to go directly to the chapter quiz interface for this study guide. If you're using a computer, simply visit the bonus page at **mometrix.com/bonus948/praxeems7001** and click the Chapter Quizzes link.

Phonological and Phonemic Awareness and Emergent Literacy

PHONETICS, PHONICS, AND PRINT CONCEPTS

BUILDING RAPID WORD IDENTIFICATION AND AUTOMATICITY

Rapid word identification and **automaticity** refer to the quick, effortless, and accurate recognition of individual words when reading. Speed and accuracy are strong predictors of comprehension, so the ability to identify words automatically plays an important role in reading development.

When readers come to unfamiliar words in texts, they pause to use reading strategies. This includes applying phonics skills and using semantic and syntactic clues. Using these strategies takes time, which may cause the reader to slow down. Applying strategies to decode words also requires significant processing in working memory, which is limited. This diverts attention away from comprehending the text, and comprehension may be negatively affected. When readers develop the ability to accurately and automatically identify words, they free up space in working memory to use for comprehension. This shift often occurs around second and third grade.

It is also important to remember that rapid word identification and automaticity are necessary for fluency but not sufficient on their own. Fluency also involves reading with appropriate phrasing and intonation.

USING INSTRUCTIONAL STRATEGIES TO BUILD AUTOMATIC RECOGNITION OF HIGH-FREQUENCY SIGHT WORDS

Readers need several opportunities to see words before they can automatically recognize them. Therefore, providing opportunities for repeated exposure to high-frequency sight words is an important goal of reading instruction and should be included along with explicit phonics instruction.

Sight words are commonly introduced to students a few at a time. The most frequently used words, such as *a*, *you*, and *the*, are typically introduced first. Some reading programs coordinate sight word lists with weekly texts, ensuring that students will have frequent exposure to each set of words as they are introduced.

There are several types of activities that can be done to build sight word recognition. Having students go on "word hunts" to locate and circle sight words in texts is one activity. Sight words can be built using magnetic letters or spelled in the air with fingers or wands. Activities that require students to read, build, and write each word are also commonly used. Additionally, flash card drills can be incorporated into the school day.

TYPICAL PROGRESSION OF PHONOLOGICAL AWARENESS SKILLS

One of the earliest phonological awareness skills children develop is the ability to recognize rhyming words. After recognizing rhyming words heard in stories, songs, and poems, children begin to produce their own sets of rhyming words. Alliteration, or identifying and producing words with the same initial sounds, is another early phonological awareness skill.

Later, children develop awareness of syllables. This involves both the ability to blend syllables to form whole words and the ability to break whole words into syllables. They also develop the ability to blend and segment onsets and rimes. **Onsets** are composed of the initial consonants or consonant blends in syllables, whereas **rimes** consist of the vowels and remaining consonants that follow. For example, in the word *star*, /st/ is the onset, and /ar/ is the rime. Phonemic awareness is the most advanced phonological awareness skill, and it is usually developed after the others.

RELATIONSHIP BETWEEN PHONOLOGICAL AWARENESS AND PHONEMIC AWARENESS

Although they are often used interchangeably, phonological awareness and phonemic awareness are distinct terms. **Phonological awareness** is a broader term that refers to the ability to identify and manipulate sounds in spoken language. This can refer to identifying and manipulating sounds at the word, syllable, or phoneme level. Example activities include rhyming, alliteration, breaking words into syllables, dividing syllables into onsets and rimes, and blending and segmenting phonemes.

Phonemic awareness is one specific component of phonological awareness. It focuses on the ability to identify and manipulate sounds at the phoneme level only. Phonemes are the smallest units of speech, and phonemic awareness is therefore the most advanced component of phonological awareness. It usually develops after other phonological awareness skills.

> **Review Video: Phonological and Phonemic Awareness, and Phonics**
> Visit mometrix.com/academy and enter code: 197017

PHONEMIC AWARENESS SKILLS

One early phonemic awareness skill is **phoneme isolation**, which is the ability to identify specific phonemes in spoken words. This includes identifying beginning (initial), middle (medial), and ending (final) sounds. Another skill is **phoneme identification**, which involves identifying the common sound in a list of words that have either the same beginning, middle, or ending sound. In **phoneme characterization**, students are given a set of words in which all but one have the same beginning, middle, or ending phoneme, and they must identify the word that doesn't belong.

In **blending**, a more complex skill, students are given the phonemes that make up a word in isolation. They must then identify the whole word formed by putting the phonemes together. In **segmentation**, students are given a whole word and must identify the individual phonemes that make up that word. **Phoneme deletion** involves removing one phoneme from a word and identifying what new word was formed. **Phoneme substitution** involves changing one phoneme in a word and identifying what new word was formed.

ACTIVITIES USED TO TEACH PHONEME BLENDING AND SEGMENTATION

Children often benefit from a multisensory approach to phonemic blending and segmentation. **Elkonin boxes** are one tool that can be used. Elkonin boxes consist of a series of connected boxes on paper. Students listen to a word and slide a penny or other token into a box each time they hear a new sound. For example, while listening to the word *cat*, students would slide three pennies into the boxes.

Students can also be given strings of beads, and they can move one bead for every sound, or phoneme, they hear. They can slide the beads back together as they blend the sounds to form the whole words again. Rubber bands can be used in a similar manner. Students can say whole words with the rubber bands un-stretched and then slowly stretch the bands as they segment the sounds. They can then push the rubber bands back together again as they blend the sounds to form the whole words.

PHONICS

Phonics refers to the relationship between letters and the sounds they make. After children learn to identify letter names, they learn that each letter makes a predictable sound. They later learn that groups of letters, such as consonant blends and digraphs, make predictable sounds as well. This understanding of letter-sound relationships is known as phonics.

Understanding the predictable relationship between letters and the sounds they make is important for the development of both decoding and encoding skills. When early readers come across unfamiliar words, they use knowledge of letter-sound relationships to decode the words as one common reading strategy. For early readers, this is especially helpful for unknown words that follow predictable spelling patterns, such as CVC words. When children are engaging in early writing activities, they use knowledge of letter-sound relationships to write words, which is known as **encoding**.

PHONEMIC AWARENESS VS. PHONICS

Phonemic awareness and phonics are commonly confused terms, but they are not the same. **Phonemic awareness** refers to identifying and manipulating phonemes in spoken language. **Phonics** refers to the relationship between letters and the sounds they make. A key question to ask when deciding if an activity is related to phonemic awareness or phonics is whether or not any letters are involved. If letters and their sounds are involved, the activity is related to phonics rather than phonemic awareness.

For example, asking students what sounds they hear in the word *cat* is a phonemic awareness activity because they are identifying sounds in a spoken word. However, asking students to decode the word *cat* when it is written in a text is a phonics activity because students must use their understanding of letter-sound relationships to successfully decode the word. Students are also using phonics skills if they write the word *cat* by identifying the sounds that they hear and writing the letters that make those sounds.

FLUENCY

Fluency is defined as reading accurately with the appropriate speed and intonation. Beginning readers typically have to stop and decode unknown words frequently, which affects both speed and intonation. Over time, as readers develop rapid word recognition, their reading speed increases. Appropriate intonation is also developed through frequent shared and guided reading experiences.

RELATIONSHIP BETWEEN FLUENCY AND COMPREHENSION

Research has shown that reading fluency is one major predictor of reading comprehension. Non-fluent readers burden their working memories with decoding. Sentences are read in a fragmented way, making it difficult for the brain to organize and make sense of what was read. After expending the energy to decode difficult words, they may forget what they have previously read. Fluent readers are free to use working memory for comprehending the text. They read using smooth, continuous phrasing, making it easier for the brain to make sense of what has been read.

USING SYNTACTIC AND SEMANTIC CUES TO FIGURE OUT UNKNOWN WORDS AND MAKING MEANING FROM TEXTS

Readers can use multiple cueing systems to figure out unknown words and make meaning from texts. When readers use **syntactic cues**, they use knowledge about correct oral language structures and the ways sentences are put together to decode and make meaning. For example, readers may use knowledge about subject-verb agreement and word order to decode new words and make meaning from sentences. When readers use **semantic cues**, they use prior knowledge from personal experiences along with meaning contained in the text and pictures to make sense of what they are reading. When they are stuck on unknown words, they consider what they already know about the topic or look to context clues or pictures for hints. While many readers still will use cueing systems to help them read unknown words, the best practice is to teach students to decode words using systematic and explicit phonics instruction rather than cueing systems.

DECODING VS. ENCODING

Decoding refers to the process of translating print to speech, which is done by translating graphemes into phonemes. **Graphemes** are letters or groups of letters that represent a single sound, and phonemes are the smallest units of sound in language. When a reader uses strategies to read the printed word *chair*, he or she is decoding the word.

Encoding refers to the process of translating sounds to print using knowledge of letter-sound relationships. This is done by translating phonemes to graphemes. When a writer uses knowledge of the sounds letters make to write the word *hop*, he or she is encoding the word.

> **Review Video: Phonics (Encoding and Decoding)**
> Visit mometrix.com/academy and enter code: 821361

Observing how a developing writer spells can be used to assess phonics knowledge. It can provide information about the writer's understanding of when to apply certain spelling patterns. By observing the writer's work over time, a teacher can determine which phonics strategies the writer has mastered and which are still developing. This information can be used to plan individualized phonics instruction. For example, if a writer frequently spells CVCe words without the e at the end, the teacher may focus on this spelling pattern during guided reading lessons with the student.

> **Review Video: Print Awareness and Alphabet Knowledge**
> Visit mometrix.com/academy and enter code: 541069

INSTRUCTIONAL STRATEGIES USED TO TEACH DECODING OF COMMON SPELLING PATTERNS

Blending is a common strategy to teach decoding of CVC words. Students say the sound represented by each letter in the word and then state the whole word they made. To increase fluency, students can be encouraged to increase the speed of blending over time. Once CVC words have been mastered and students have been introduced to consonant blends and digraphs, they can use the same blending process with CVCC words.

For CVVC and CVCe words that cannot be decoded using blending, students can be introduced to the sounds made by each spelling pattern. They can then build and explore word families that contain the same spelling pattern, changing the initial sounds to build new, related words. For example, after identifying the sound that /ake/ makes, students can build *rake*, *cake*, and *lake* using letter tiles or magnetic letters.

INSTRUCTIONAL STRATEGIES USED TO TEACH DECODING OF MULTISYLLABIC WORDS

Although decoding instruction typically tapers off around second grade, it is at this point that students begin reading texts with more complex, multisyllabic words. Therefore, it is important to teach specific strategies that readers can use to decode these types of words.

One strategy is to teach students to identify the different syllables present in a word. This can be done by clapping each syllable or saying the word while looking in a mirror and observing how many times the mouth opens. Students can then be taught to recognize common syllable spelling patterns and the sounds that they make. These common syllable spelling patterns include the following:

- closed syllables, which end in a consonant and usually have a short vowel sound (e.g., rabbit)
- open syllables, which end in a vowel and usually have a long vowel sound (e.g., bagel)
- r-controlled vowels (e.g., carpet)
- vowel digraph pairs (e.g., detain)
- vowel-consonant-silent-e syllables, which usually have a long vowel sound (e.g., athlete)
- consonant-le words, which are usually found at the end of a word (e.g., maple)

Readers can also be taught to look for known parts of words, such as known prefixes and suffixes.

CONSONANT BLENDS AND CONSONANT DIGRAPHS

A **consonant blend** is a group of two or three consonants that blend together to make a sound, but each individual letter sound is still heard. Examples include *bl*, *fr*, and *sw*. Blends are typically introduced after readers have learned to decode basic CVC words, and they are introduced in groups according to the second consonant they contain. Blends containing two consonants are usually introduced before blends containing three consonants. When introducing each blend, the teacher shows students how the sounds of each consonant are blended together to form the new sound. Common words containing the blend can be listed, and students can go on word hunts to find additional examples of words containing the blend. Students can also sort cards containing pictures of objects whose names are spelled with consonant blends.

A **consonant digraph** is a group of two consonants that form a new consonant sound when combined. Examples include *th*, *sh*, and *ch*. Digraphs are also typically introduced a few at a time, with beginning digraphs introduced before ending digraphs. Creating lists of example words, going on word hunts, and completing matching and sorting activities can also be used to teach digraphs.

R-CONTROLLED VOWELS

R-controlled vowels are vowels that appear before the letter r in a word. Words containing this spelling pattern are sometimes referred to as bossy-r words, because the letter r changes the sound of the vowel. The r-controlled vowel pairs are *ar*, *er*, *ir*, *or*, and *er*.

To teach decoding of words containing r-controlled vowels, teachers can model blending of simple words containing these spelling patterns by sliding their fingers along the words as they blend them. For each word, they can point out that the vowel and r together make one sound, and they can generate a list of other words containing the same letter pair and sound. Students can also be given word or picture cards to sort according to which r-controlled vowel sound they contain. Another strategy is to provide a picture of an object that contains an r-controlled vowel in its name. The word can be written below the picture, with the r-controlled vowel omitted. Students can be asked to provide the missing letters to complete the word.

BENEFITS OF EXPLICIT PHONICS INSTRUCTION

Research has shown that early readers benefit from an explicit and systematic approach to phonics instruction. Developing readers who receive explicit and systematic phonics instruction at an early age often show increased ability to decode and spell, along with increased reading comprehension skills when older.

Explicit instruction means that phonics lessons are purposely planned to address specific skills rather than waiting until problems arise with decoding words while reading. For example, a teacher may plan to focus on a set of consonant blends during one week of reading instruction. Systematic instruction means that the lessons follow a carefully planned scope and sequence, with phonics lessons progressing from basic to advanced. Early phonics lessons for kindergarteners may focus on letter-sound relationships, whereas first grade students may focus on decoding different spelling patterns.

ROLE OF PHONOLOGICAL AWARENESS AND PHONICS SKILLS IN READING DEVELOPMENT
ENGLISH LANGUAGE LEARNERS

For English language learners (ELLs), research has shown that **phonological awareness** in a reader's first language is a **strong predictor** of his or her ability to learn to read in a second language. This is especially true when the native language is closely related to English. Despite the fact that phonological awareness in the native language can be beneficial when learning English, it may lead to **overgeneralization** of rules of the native language. Continued language experiences in the native language along with language scaffolding can be beneficial to ELLs as they learn English.

Some ELLs may also speak native languages in which there is not a **one-to-one correspondence** between letters and phonemes. They may also speak languages that use the same alphabet as English but where the letters represent different sounds. It is important for teachers to understand their ELLs' prior knowledge and consider this when planning appropriate phonics instruction.

Additionally, some English phonemes may not be used in other languages. Introducing English vocabulary words that contain these phonemes helps give these sounds a meaningful context. Using poems and songs with repetition and rhyme can also be helpful.

STRUGGLING AND PROFICIENT STUDENTS

Research has shown that phonological awareness and phonics skills are important predictors of reading success. For struggling readers, daily phonological awareness and phonics practice are important. Explicit and systematic instruction should be tailored to the individual needs of each student and based upon observation and assessment data. Once a teacher has determined which skills the student needs to improve, instruction should be regularly included to target these skills until mastered. Ongoing reading assessments and flexible groupings can help make sure that struggling readers' individual needs are consistently met.

Phonological awareness and phonics assessments are important for proficient readers as well. Some proficient readers have developed strong rapid word identification skills without mastering the underlying phonological awareness and phonics skills. When they get into older grade levels and more frequently encounter unfamiliar vocabulary, they will have difficulty decoding the text. Assessment data can be used to identify specific skills to practice in small-group instruction with these proficient readers.

ROLE OF NATURAL EXPOSURE TO PHONICS IN EARLY READING DEVELOPMENT

Like explicit phonics instruction, natural exposure to phonics also plays a role in early reading development. This exposure occurs when children are involved in natural reading experiences, and they come across words they are unable to decode. Phonics instruction is provided in the moment to address the unknown words.

This type of phonics instruction is known as **implicit** instruction. It differs from explicit instruction, which progresses from part (letter sounds) to whole (whole words). Implicit instruction progresses from whole (unknown words encountered in text) to part (breaking down the words in order to decode them).

Implicit phonics instruction has some benefits. Because it occurs during natural reading experiences, the phonics skills are taught **in context** rather than in isolation. Readers are motivated to learn the skills needed to decode the unknown words and continue reading. Teachers can allow time to address unknown words while reading aloud or listening to students reading independently. However, research has shown that it is still important to schedule time for explicit and systematic phonics instruction as well.

STRATEGIES TO TEACH LETTER IDENTIFICATION

Most reading programs introduce letters gradually. Some suggest introducing letters that have high value to learners first, such as the first letters of their names. Others focus on letters that play prominent roles in the books they are reading for the week, whereas others sequence letters by physical characteristics. In general, it is best to avoid teaching commonly confused letter pairs simultaneously, such as b and d.

To develop **letter recognition**, students can be given texts and instructed to circle certain letters. They can play alphabet bingo and cover specific letters when they are called. They can sing the alphabet song while pointing to each letter. Additionally, they can go on letter hunts, where they search the classroom or building to find examples of specific letters in environmental print. To practice recognizing capital and lowercase forms of letters, students can play memory and find matches consisting of both letter forms.

STRATEGIES TO TEACH LETTER FORMATION

To teach letter formation, students can be given letter stencils to trace with pencils. They can also be provided cutout letters made from different materials, such as felt and sandpaper, to trace with their fingers. Later, they can attempt to write letters independently on writing paper following the school's selected handwriting program guidelines.

To practice letter formation using a **multisensory approach**, students can write letters with shaving cream or fingerpaint. They can also write letters in containers filled with salt or sand. Wax craft sticks, modeling dough, and pipe cleaners can be used to construct letter models. Large-sized letters can also be drawn using sidewalk chalk, and students can hop along the letter shapes to trace them. They can also trace letter shapes in the air with their fingers or toy wands. Additionally, students can be given outlines of letters, which they can fill in with buttons, dried beans, or other common objects.

STRATEGIES TO TEACH LETTER-SOUND RELATIONSHIPS

Once students understand that letters are combined to form words that convey meaning in print, they begin learning that each letter makes a predictable sound. This is known as the **alphabetic principle**. Although different reading programs introduce the letters and sounds in different orders, most introduce the letter-sound relationships gradually.

In some reading programs, each letter has a song, poem, or chant that incorporates repetition of the letter name and sound. In others, a letter character or visual is produced, which includes a hint about the sound it makes. The visual often includes a picture of a common object that starts with the letter. Students can also be encouraged to find objects beginning with the letter sound they are learning. Tactile activities, such as building letters out of wax craft sticks or writing them in shaving cream while repeating the names and sounds, are also commonly used. Bingo and other similar games that require matching letters to their sounds can also be used.

CONCEPTS OF PRINT THAT COLLECTIVELY FORM A FOUNDATION FOR EARLY READING INSTRUCTION

Concepts of print are the conventions used to convey meaning in printed text. Children begin developing an understanding of these concepts from an early age through shared reading experiences with others and interactions with printed materials.

Understanding concepts of print includes recognizing the front cover, back cover, and title of a book. It also includes recognizing that the print, rather than the pictures, carries the message. Additionally, it includes directionality concepts, such as knowing that you read from left to right and from the top of the page to the bottom, with a return sweep at the end of each line of text. One-to-one correspondence between written and spoken words is another concept of print. Letter concepts are also important, such as knowing that words are made up of individual letters, identifying letter names, and identifying both capital and lowercase letters. Identifying the names and purposes of common punctuation marks used to end sentences is also a key concept of print.

STRATEGIES TO TEACH PRINT AWARENESS

Starting at an early age, caregivers and teachers can begin introducing children to concepts of print. While reading storybooks and big books aloud, they can model how to hold the books, where the front and back covers and titles are located, and where to begin reading. They can also model directionality by following the text with their fingers as they read, showing the left-to-right movement and return sweep. They can point out different text features, such as capital letters and punctuation marks, and discuss their purposes.

When students are interacting with texts independently, teachers can ask them questions regarding concepts of print. For example, they can instruct students to follow the text with their fingers and pause after encountering punctuation marks at the ends of sentences. Teachers can also point out text features in environmental print, such as hallway signs.

READING DEVELOPMENT
TYPICAL PROGRESSION OF READING DEVELOPMENT

Readers typically progress through four stages of reading development. The first stage of reading development is known as **emergent reading**. It is the stage in which readers develop pre-reading behaviors and begin understanding concepts of print. The second stage is called **early reading**. Early readers begin to use a combination of reading strategies and cueing systems to decode and comprehend simple texts. The third stage is called **transitional reading**. Transitional readers use a wide range of reading strategies to support comprehension of more complex texts. Rapid word recognition combined with effective use of strategies allows readers to read at an increased pace. **Fluent reading** is the last stage of reading development. Fluent readers confidently read and comprehend a wide range of complex texts independently.

Students' individual differences and prior experiences can affect at what ages and rates they progress through the stages.

> **Review Video: Stages of Reading Development**
> Visit mometrix.com/academy and enter code: 121184

CHARACTERISTICS OF THE EMERGENT STAGE OF READING

Emergent reading skills are strong predictors of future reading success. In the emergent stage, readers display **pre-reading behaviors**. They begin interacting with texts without actually reading the words. They learn the concepts of print, such as learning how to correctly hold books and understanding that print holds meaning. They begin to identify capital and lowercase letters, and they understand the predictable relationships between letters and sounds. They begin to understand that letters are combined to form words and words are combined to form sentences.

Readers in the **emergent stage** also develop oral language skills. This includes phonological awareness skills, such as rhyming and alliteration. They develop phonemic awareness skills, including the ability to blend, segment, and manipulate phonemes within words.

Emergent readers enjoy having others read to them. They respond to texts that are read aloud by making predictions, retelling events, and other activities. They react to illustrations and use them to make sense of the texts.

INSTRUCTIONAL STRATEGIES USED IN THE EMERGENT STAGE

Teachers should read aloud to students in the emergent stage often, choosing from a range of genres. When reading, teachers should model concepts of print and how to make predictions, retell story events, and other reading strategies. Concepts of print should be explored in environmental print within the classrooms and the schools. Teachers should create print-rich environments containing several different types of texts for students to explore. Students should be given multiple opportunities to interact with different types of texts daily, both with others and independently.

Teachers should also plan **explicit instruction** on letter identification and letter-sound correspondence and give readers opportunities to practice recognizing and forming both capital and lowercase letters.

Additionally, teachers should plan classroom activities to build emergent readers' phonological awareness and phonemic awareness skills. This includes opportunities to practice rhyming, alliteration, onset and rime manipulation, and phoneme manipulation.

CHARACTERISTICS OF TEXTS DESIGNED FOR EMERGENT READERS

Texts designed for emergent readers should have **pictures** or **illustrations** that strongly support the print. They should have a limited amount of text on each page and use **repetitive words** and phrases. They should include several high-frequency and easily decodable words, and the text should be placed in predictable places on each page. Simple sentence structure should be used.

Additionally, books for emergent readers should be focused on familiar objects and topics that will activate readers' prior knowledge. This assists readers with comprehension and making connections and allows them to focus on print concepts. The vocabulary should also be familiar. Print should be large and contain wide spaces between letters and lines of text.

Some emergent texts follow a pattern in which only the last word in each sentence changes. For example, each page of a text might say, "I like to ____." The missing word could be easily guessed based upon picture support.

CHARACTERISTICS OF THE EARLY READING STAGE OF READING DEVELOPMENT

In the early reading stage of development, readers increasingly use strategies to figure out unknown words and make meaning from texts. They begin to self-monitor their reading and self-correct if they realize that errors have been made. They expand their vocabularies and their automatic recognition of high-frequency words. They use picture clues, knowledge of letter-sound relationships, and repetition to decode unknown words in longer and more complex texts.

Early readers also continue developing comprehension strategies, such as predicting and summarizing. They use a combination of these comprehension strategies to make meaning from what they have read. They begin to read silently and no longer need to point to each word while reading.

CHARACTERISTICS OF TEXTS FOR READERS IN THE EARLY READING STAGE

Texts for **early readers** contain more print than those for emergent readers. They include longer sentences, more sentences per page, and more pages per book. The texts also contain more complex and **varied sentence structure**. There is less reliance on picture clues than in books for emergent readers, with the print carrying most of the meaning. More complex and content-specific vocabulary words are included. Multiple spelling patterns are used, requiring readers to use a combination of decoding strategies. There is less repetition, or longer and more complex phrases are repeated than those in emergent texts.

Texts for early readers also frequently focus on more complex story lines. Descriptive language is often included. The content of these books is still typically familiar to readers.

Readers in the early stage understand a variety of genres and purposes for reading. Therefore, texts for this stage are varied in genre and purpose.

INSTRUCTIONAL STRATEGIES USED WITH READERS IN THE EARLY READING STAGE

Students in the early reading stage are beginning to increase their reading rates and build fluency. Teachers need to provide systematic and explicit phonics instruction during this time. Teachers can provide decodable text based off phonics instruction that has already been taught. Teachers can also provide students with opportunities to frequently read and reread favorite books, which will help them build fluency. Teachers can prompt students to decode words using previously taught phonics instruction.

Early readers also benefit from activities that focus on advanced phonemic awareness skills, such as phoneme substitution. Additionally, students benefit from instruction on complex vocabulary words and spelling patterns. Teachers can also provide students with frequent opportunities to read varied text types and genres that incorporate more sophisticated vocabulary words and sentence structures than emergent texts.

CHARACTERISTICS OF READERS IN THE TRANSITIONAL STAGE OF READING DEVELOPMENT

Readers in the transitional stage of reading development are able to engage in sustained, quiet reading for extended periods of time. They are able to read and comprehend longer, more advanced texts and can automatically identify a large number of high-frequency words. They have knowledge of complex spelling patterns, which they use to independently decode most unknown words, including multisyllabic words. They are also continuing to increase their fluency and reading rates.

Transitional readers utilize more strategies to assist with comprehension than early readers. They have an awareness of text structures and can gather and synthesize information from multiple text features, including print, graphs, charts, and sidebars. They rely more on the print than the pictures for meaning and can identify story elements, such as characters, setting, problem, and solution. Additionally, they develop higher-level comprehension skills, such as making inferences and drawing conclusions.

CHARACTERISTICS OF TEXTS FOR READERS IN THE TRANSITIONAL READING STAGE

Students in the transitional reading phase are able to read more difficult texts than early readers. This includes both fiction and nonfiction texts covering a wide range of genres. It also includes both beginning chapter books and challenging picture books. Nonfiction texts may utilize multiple text structures and include features like graphs, charts, photographs, sidebars, and more. The topics may be either familiar or unfamiliar to readers. Some challenging and unknown vocabulary words may be included along with many high-frequency words. Story elements may be described in detail, using descriptive words and phrases. There are numerous chapter book series designed for transitional readers.

Books written for transitional readers have several lines of text per page. Some pages may be composed entirely of text, as in chapter books. The books have many pages with clearly defined spaces between lines of text.

INSTRUCTIONAL STRATEGIES USED WITH READERS IN THE TRANSITIONAL STAGE

Because **transitional readers** are beginning to read more complicated texts of different genres, it is helpful to teach about text structures. Understanding text structures and where to look for main ideas can assist transitional readers with comprehension. Teachers can also teach strategies to determine the meanings of **unknown vocabulary** words by analyzing word morphology. This includes recognizing and analyzing both affixes and roots.

Teachers can plan several opportunities for students to build reading fluency by rereading texts for meaningful purposes. They can also model advanced analysis and comprehension strategies during shared reading experiences, such as making inferences and drawing conclusions. They can provide students with tools like graphic organizers to assist with comprehension during independent reading. Additionally, they can encourage readers to support responses with text evidence.

Teachers can also assist transitional readers with selecting appropriately challenging texts for independent reading.

CHARACTERISTICS OF READERS IN THE FLUENT STAGE OF READING DEVELOPMENT

Readers in the **fluent stage** of reading development read complex texts both **quickly** and **accurately**. They read with appropriate expression. They automatically recognize high-frequency words and efficiently use multiple strategies to determine unknown words they encounter. These strategies include using cueing systems, context clues, and substitutions.

Fluent readers are able to comprehend a wide range of complex fiction and nonfiction texts. They understand content-specific and technical vocabulary words or use strategies and tools to determine their meanings. They have a strong understanding of different types of text structures and know how to efficiently use text features to locate key information. They understand multiple purposes for reading and writing and are able to understand texts from multiple points of view. Additionally, fluent readers use **high-level thinking skills** to comprehend what they have read. They are able to evaluate texts and argue points using text evidence for support.

CHARACTERISTICS OF TEXTS FOR READERS IN THE FLUENT READING STAGE

Texts for readers in the fluent reading stage are complex, varied, and sometimes abstract. Complex text structures are often used. For example, they may use flashbacks or weave back and forth while comparing and contrasting two things. Fictional texts for fluent readers contain highly developed plots and character development. They often use descriptive and figurative language. Additionally, these texts may have multiple themes or layers that require deep analysis. Content-specific and technical vocabulary words are commonly used. Topics may be either familiar or unfamiliar to readers.

Texts for fluent readers rely mostly on the print to convey meaning. Photos or illustrations are mainly included to convey important information that may be difficult to explain in print. For example, photographs of animals may be included in biology texts. Illustrations may be included in historical fiction texts where the settings or characters may be unfamiliar to readers.

INSTRUCTIONAL STRATEGIES USED WITH READERS IN THE FLUENT READING STAGE

Readers in the fluent stage often read texts about new and **unfamiliar topics**. Therefore, teachers can instruct them to activate related prior knowledge that may assist them with making sense of the new texts. They can also model how to efficiently use **research tools** to learn more about unfamiliar topics.

Teachers can also model and encourage readers to use close reading techniques to deeply analyze texts. This process includes rereading texts multiple times to analyze different layers each time. It also includes evaluating, comparing and contrasting, making connections, and using other high-level comprehension strategies. Teachers can encourage readers to analyze texts from multiple perspectives, using text evidence to support their responses.

Because readers in this stage will frequently encounter content-specific and technical vocabulary words, teachers can continue to model word analysis skills, such as analyzing affixes and roots.

WRITING DEVELOPMENT
RELATIONSHIP BETWEEN READING AND WRITING DEVELOPMENT

Reading and writing are **interrelated** and should be taught together. Students who read a lot tend to have stronger writing skills, and students who write a lot tend to have stronger reading comprehension skills.

When students read varied types of texts, they learn how authors convey meaning differently through tone, language use, and sentence structure. They learn about different types of genres. They often use the texts as models and experiment with these elements in their own writing. Students also increase their vocabularies through reading, and they develop automatic recognition of high-frequency words. Students may then integrate the new vocabulary words into their own writing and remember how to spell words they have seen repeatedly in texts.

When students learn to write, they learn about and use different sentence and text structures. Awareness of these structures can help students recognize and make sense of them when encountered in other texts. Additionally, when students write about texts they have read, it facilitates additional analysis and comprehension. For example, writing about whether or not they would recommend books to others requires students to evaluate the texts and provide support for their reasoning.

CHARACTERISTICS OF WRITERS IN THE PRELITERATE STAGE OF WRITING DEVELOPMENT

The earliest stage of children's writing development is **scribbling**. Children begin scribbling at random places on the pages and do not proceed in any consistent direction. They typically hold writing utensils, such as pencils or crayons, with their fists. Scribbling helps children improve their fine motor skills and sets the stage for the understanding that writing carries meaning.

Over time, scribbling begins to follow a left-to-right directionality across the pages. Drawings may be included to help convey meaning.

Eventually, strings of pretend, letter-like symbols are used. They are sometimes mixed with numbers. Students are able to explain the meanings they are trying to convey through their writing. This phase demonstrates a beginning awareness of concepts of print. Spacing between words is not initially included but develops over time. There is no evidence of letter-sound relationships in the writing at this stage.

CHARACTERISTICS OF WRITERS IN THE EMERGENT STAGE OF WRITING DEVELOPMENT

In the **emergent stage,** writers begin to form letters correctly. Initially, they often write using all capital letters. They also begin to use their understandings of letter-sound relationships to write words. Some sounds are correctly represented in words, typically starting with the initial sounds.

In this stage, writers also begin spelling some words correctly. The first written words typically hold high personal meaning to students, such as their names and words like *mom* and *dad*. They may also write words found in environmental print, such as the names of popular restaurants frequently seen on signs. Some high-frequency sight words begin to be spelled correctly.

Students in the emergent stage write with left-to-right directionality and begin using spacing to separate words. They also begin to use common punctuation marks to split their writing into sentences, although this skill is still developing. Because it requires a lot of energy to encode words at this stage, writing pieces are typically short.

CHARACTERISTICS OF WRITERS IN THE TRANSITIONAL STAGE OF WRITING DEVELOPMENT

In the **transitional stage** of writing development, students begin using a mixture of capital and lowercase letters appropriately. They also correctly use several different punctuation marks. Their writing includes a broader vocabulary than when they were in the emergent stage.

Transitional writers know how to automatically spell many high-frequency words, and they use multiple strategies to encode words they do not know how to spell. These strategies include considering letter-sound relationships to record the sounds they hear, considering known spelling patterns, and thinking of related, known words. Writing includes a mixture of conventionally spelled words and phonetically spelled words that are readable.

Because transitional writers are able to encode many words quickly, they have more available energy to focus on writing development. They focus more attention on developing story elements and including descriptive details. They write longer texts than they wrote in the emergent stage, and their writing includes a mixture of text structures and genres. Transitional writers also have the ability to reread and edit their work.

CHARACTERISTICS OF WRITERS IN THE FLUENT STAGE OF WRITING DEVELOPMENT

Fluent writers spell most words correctly and use capitalization and punctuation marks conventionally throughout their writing. They are able to edit and evaluate their own writing and provide constructive feedback to others.

With the ability to spell most words quickly and automatically, fluent writers are able to focus more on writing craft, such as using descriptive language and developing story elements. Author's voice begins to develop. Writing may span several pages. Fluent writers consider their audiences and purposes for writing and consider them during the planning process. They use multiple strategies to plan their writing, such as brainstorming and using graphic organizers. They are able to write texts in a wide range of genres and select

Teaching Reading

appropriate text structures to fit their purposes. Additionally, fluent writers are able to independently use tools like dictionaries and thesauri to improve their writing pieces.

Review Video: <u>Sensory Language</u>
Visit mometrix.com/academy and enter code: 177314

SPELLING DEVELOPMENT

STAGES OF SPELLING DEVELOPMENT

Students typically progress through a series of stages of spelling development. Researchers name the stages differently, but they contain common characteristics.

In the **pre-phonetic stage**, students spell using random letter and number strings. There are no letter-sound relationships evident in words. In the **semi-phonetic stage**, some letter-sound relationships are used to spell words. Students typically learn to correctly spell the beginning and ending sounds in words first, followed later by the medial sounds. In the **phonetic stage**, some simple words begin to be spelled correctly, such as CVC words. In addition to initial, medial, and final sounds, some more complex sounds are accurately represented. This includes some consonant blends and digraphs. In the transitional, or **word extension stage**, students learn to use syllable patterns to spell more complex words. Most words are spelled correctly in this stage. In the **derivational constancy stage**, students use knowledge of roots and affixes to spell related words. Most or all words in students' writing pieces are spelled correctly in this stage.

ORTHOGRAPHY

Orthography refers to the conventional spelling of words in a language. Because many words are spelled using the same patterns, studying orthography helps students increase the number of words they can spell correctly. Learning to apply orthographic patterns is an important part of any literacy program.

Word studies, or word work, should be regularly included in the school day. Word work should be sequential and built upon the knowledge of orthographic patterns that students already possess.

There are three layers of orthography that students can explore during word work. The **alphabet layer** refers to letter-sound relationships. Activities in which students combine letters or letter groups to form words will help them explore the alphabet layer. When students explore the **pattern layer**, they look for larger patterns that guide the spellings of words. Activities in which students build words within word families, such as CVCe words, help them explore the pattern layer. The **meaning layer** explores the relationships between word meanings and spellings. Sorting and writing words that contain the same Latin roots will help students explore the meaning layer of orthography.

Layers of English Orthography

PHONETIC SPELLING

Phonetic spelling is common in the early stages of writing development. When writing words, students consider what sounds they hear. They use knowledge of phonics rules to select letters or groups of letters to represent those sounds. For example, a student who is familiar with CVC words might write *love* as *luv*.

Parents are sometimes concerned with the amount of misspelled words in their children's writing. However, phonetic spelling plays a role in reading and writing development and is a stepping stone to conventional spelling.

At this stage, students know how to automatically spell a limited number of words. Using known phonics rules helps them efficiently encode words they do not know how to spell. If students are worried about spelling every word conventionally, they must continuously ask others for help. This slows the writing process and puts more emphasis on spelling than on recording ideas. Therefore, teachers typically tell students in this stage to write the sounds they hear and move on. This process also allows students to apply the phonics skills they use while reading.

Over time, students learn more complex spelling patterns and automatically remember how to spell more words. At this point, spelling becomes more conventional.

ROLE OF MEMORIZATION IN SPELLING DEVELOPMENT AND INSTRUCTION

There are some words that students cannot learn to spell by learning spelling patterns. These include many high-frequency words with irregular spelling patterns, such as the word *the*. Students should have frequent and repeated exposure to these words to memorize their spellings. Practice activities are helpful, such as building these words with letter tiles.

Some academic vocabulary words are also difficult for students to spell using knowledge of spelling patterns. For example, second graders may learn about camouflage as part of a science unit on animal adaptations. However, it would be difficult for students of this age to spell the word *camouflage* using knowledge of spelling patterns. Frequent exposure to these academic words in print will help students learn to spell them over time. Adding these words to word walls or classroom charts can serve as tools to assist with spelling initially. Being given numerous opportunities to write these words with scaffolding will assist with memorization.

Although memorization plays a role in spelling some words, its use as an instructional strategy should be balanced with explicit instruction in spelling patterns. When choosing weekly spelling lists, teachers should focus on patterns that can be applied to multiple words.

DIFFERENT APPROACHES TO TEACHING STUDENTS TO SPELL

There are many methods and commercial programs available to teach spelling. Although they vary in approach, the methods that are most effective share some common characteristics.

Effective spelling instruction should be explicit. Although students naturally learn to spell many words through frequent reading experiences, some explicit spelling instruction is still helpful to teach common spelling patterns and relationships among words. The instruction should be both incremental and sequential.

Teachers can introduce weekly spelling patterns, and students can complete activities to familiarize themselves with the patterns. Depending on the ages of the students, this may include word sorts, word hunts, and tracing. Multisensory activities are also helpful, such as building words with letter tiles and writing words in sand. Teachers may assess students' applications of the spelling patterns at the end of each week. Some teachers give students lists of words to study ahead of time. Other teachers assess students by asking them to spell new words that follow the patterns they have been studying.

ACADEMIC LITERACY

Academic literacy refers to the knowledge and skills necessary to communicate effectively in academic situations. It includes content-specific knowledge and vocabulary, such as mathematical terms. It also includes general knowledge and vocabulary used across all content areas, such as the terms *synthesize*, *summarize*, and *evaluate*. Additionally, it refers to the ability to communicate effectively in academic situations through reading, writing, listening, and speaking.

Academic literacy helps students flexibly adapt their use of reading strategies according to the types of text used and the purposes for reading. It helps them acquire content-specific vocabulary needed to comprehend academic texts and effectively communicate their learning using a variety of response types. It helps them summarize, evaluate, and make connections among content acquired from multiple sources and across content areas. Academic literacy also encourages students to effectively communicate and collaborate with others to construct meaning.

TYPES OF KNOWLEDGE COMMONLY USED IN EDUCATION

There are many types of knowledge commonly used in education.

- **Social** knowledge is knowledge about social conventions passed down within members of a community. It includes conventions related to expected greetings, manners, and conversational behavior.
- **Procedural** knowledge refers to the knowledge applied to carry out procedural tasks. An example is solving a complex math problem using a multistep algorithm.
- **Physical** knowledge refers to knowledge learned by observing the features of something. When students discuss the physical properties of rock samples, they are using physical knowledge.
- **Domain** knowledge refers to the knowledge and skills used by experts in a particular field. For example, a student explaining how she completed a division problem using the terms *dividend*, *divisor*, and *quotient* is using domain knowledge.
- **Empirical** knowledge refers to knowledge obtained from scientific experimentation and data collection. Determining the boiling points of different liquids as part of a science experiment is an example of empirical knowledge.

ROLE OF LITERACY IN THE DEVELOPMENT AND APPLICATION OF DIFFERENT TYPES OF KNOWLEDGE

Literacy plays a large role in the development and application of different types of knowledge in the classroom. Social knowledge is passed down through oral language and written texts. Students learn about social norms through the actions of characters in stories and through discussing texts with others. For example, children learn about solving conflict with friends by reading about characters who work through conflict. They also learn how to listen attentively and take turns through participation in literature circles.

- When students read nonfiction **procedural texts**, they develop procedural knowledge that can be used to accomplish tasks. Procedural texts also provide models of text structures students can use when explaining procedures to others.
- Reading texts containing **academic language** helps students develop and apply physical, domain, and empirical knowledge. Developing their academic vocabularies can assist students with expressing their observations and conclusions using academic language.

ACADEMIC READING VS. READING FOR ENTERTAINMENT

- **Academic reading** refers to thoughtfully reading and analyzing academic texts as part of content area studies. Readers usually have specific purposes in mind before beginning academic reading. For example, an entomology student may consult a field guide to correctly classify an insect found during a nature hike. Another student may read a social studies textbook to identify some major causes of the Revolutionary War for an essay assignment.
- **Reading for entertainment** refers to reading for fun. A student may select a fictional book from a favorite series to read on a rainy day.

When completing academic reading, readers often pay special attention to text structures and features to efficiently **locate needed information**. They may skim or skip around in the texts. They may stop to look up the meanings of **unfamiliar vocabulary words**. They may also read more slowly or reread passages multiple times to make sense of unfamiliar content.

When reading for entertainment, proficient readers still self-monitor their comprehension, but they have more freedom about which text elements they wish to respond to and analyze. They may also read at a quicker pace and choose to reread favorite parts for fun.

ASSESSMENT METHODOLOGY FOR LANGUAGE SKILLS

PURPOSES OF LITERACY ASSESSMENT

Literacy assessments can serve many purposes. Assessments can be used to monitor the progress of students toward achieving district and state benchmarks as well as individualized goals. They can identify specific skills that students have mastered as well as those that need additional practice. They can also identify if students are making adequate yearly progress.

Additionally, assessments can be used to guide teacher instruction. By analyzing assessment results, teachers can determine which topics they should focus on for whole-class, small-group, and individualized instruction. This helps ensure that too much instructional time is not spent on topics students have already mastered while ignoring topics that need additional practice.

Assessments can also be used to evaluate the effectiveness of reading programs. By analyzing students' assessment data over time, districts can look for trends in student achievement and progress toward closing achievement gaps.

ADVANTAGES AND DISADVANTAGES OF GROUP AND INDIVIDUAL LITERACY ASSESSMENTS

Group literacy assessments are administered to groups of students at one time. Teachers explain the directions and then instruct all students to begin working, while they observe and answer questions. Assessments are scored after students finish and submit them. Examples of group literacy assessments include state-mandated standardized reading and writing tests. Using the group approach to literacy assessments is more efficient than individualized assessment, freeing up more time for classroom instruction. It also assists teachers with classroom management because all students are being assessed at once.

Individualized assessments are given to one student at a time. Teachers may listen to students read, observe strategy usage, or ask students to retell stories they have read. Dynamic Indicators of Basic Early Literacy Skills (DIBELS) and Developmental Reading Assessment (DRA) are examples of individual assessments. This approach allows teachers to closely observe the strategies each student uses. However, it is more time intensive, and the remaining students in the class must be engaged in other activities.

USING PROGRESS MONITORING TO ASSESS STUDENTS AND GUIDE INSTRUCTION

Progress monitoring is used to track students' progress toward achieving certain performance goals over time. Teachers first identify students who may benefit from progress monitoring. This usually occurs as a result of assessment data. Students who score below expectations on certain components of criterion-referenced tests may be progressively monitored in those areas.

Teachers then set performance goals that can be measured and tracked over time. For example, if students are currently decoding five CVC words correctly in one minute, the goal may be for them to decode 15 words per minute. Interventions are put in place to help students with these skills. Teachers then repeat testing in these targeted areas on a regular basis, such as weekly or biweekly. Results are recorded, and teachers look for progress over time. Once students have mastered the initial goals, new goals are set, or progress monitoring is discontinued, depending on students' needs.

Progress monitoring can help teachers identify whether or not current interventions are successful or whether changes are needed. It can also help teachers identify when students have mastered certain skills.

TYPES OF FORMAL ASSESSMENTS USED TO ASSESS ORAL LANGUAGE AND READING SKILLS

There are several types of formal assessments designed to assess readers. Some assessments assess knowledge of concepts of print. These are typically performance assessments. Students are asked to locate titles and authors' names, identify letters and words, track the direction of print, and more. Teachers observe students and mark their responses on recording sheets containing scoring criteria. Other formal assessments ask students to identify letter names, apply phonological and phonemic awareness skills, and decode words. Portions of the DIBELS assessment are examples of this type. Data gained from these assessments can be used to group students, plan differentiated instruction, and develop interventions.

Other formal assessments evaluate students' decoding abilities and reading fluency. Students may be asked to read short texts while being timed. They may also be asked to retell stories or answer comprehension questions. Both DIBELS and DRA are two examples of this type of assessment. State standardized tests often require students to read passages and answer comprehension questions. In addition to helping teachers group students and differentiate instruction, these assessments can also help teachers select appropriately leveled texts. There are also formal assessments that specifically assess students' vocabulary knowledge.

FORMALLY ASSESSING WRITTEN LANGUAGE

Students' writing is often formally assessed using teacher-created, district-mandated, and state-mandated assessments. These assessments typically provide students with specific writing prompts indicating the topics and text structures they are expected to use. Sometimes prompts are based on reading passages that are also contained in the assessments. For example, students may be asked to read two related texts and write responses that explain the common theme they share.

Students' written responses on formal assessments are usually scored using either analytic or holistic rubrics. These rubrics should contain clear criteria that reflect the performance expectations for students. Common criteria include development, organization, language use, conventions, and following the writing process. By analyzing students' performances on different rubric criteria, teachers can plan individualized instruction and develop interventions for struggling students. For example, if students are struggling with language use, teachers can help students analyze mentor texts that contain strong examples.

31

INFORMALLY ASSESSING LITERACY DEVELOPMENT

One type of informal assessment is **miscue analysis**, which occurs when teachers listen to students as they read and analyze their miscues. By looking for patterns in the miscues, teachers can determine which strategies students are using and which are lacking. This information can be used to guide instruction.

- **Informal reading inventories** require students to read leveled texts while teachers note errors and fluency. Students then respond to comprehension questions about the texts. Information gained from informal reading inventories can be used to select leveled texts, group students, and plan appropriate instruction.
- **Portfolios** are another type of informal assessment. Portfolios consist of collections of student work, which can be used to show progress over time.
- **Performance assessments** can also be used to assess students' literacy development while allowing students to complete authentic tasks. For example, students may research nutritional guidelines and read food labels to create healthy weekly meal plans.
- **Informal assessment** can also occur when teachers observe students engaged in literacy activities, ask them to explain their thinking, and note performance on assignments and homework. These methods can provide valuable information about students' knowledge and skills, which can be used to guide instruction.

RUBRICS

Rubrics are evaluation tools used to assign scores to students' work. They explain the criteria used to assign scores for different levels of mastery. Rubrics can be given to students when projects are assigned to ensure they understand expectations. They can make evaluation more consistent because all students are evaluated using the same criteria. Rubrics can also be easily adapted to reflect different types of activities and assignments.

There are many ways rubrics can be used to evaluate literacy development. They can be used to assess students' reading fluency, with categories relating to speed, accuracy, and prosody. They can also be used to evaluate projects relating to analysis and comprehension.

Additionally, rubrics can be used to assess students' writing. Categories relating to development, use of language, conventions, and other topics can be included. The rubrics can be adapted to reflect the genres or text structures used.

ANALYTIC VS. HOLISTIC RUBRICS

Analytic rubrics assign separate scores for each criterion being evaluated. For example, if a writing rubric has criteria for development, use of language, and conventions, each of these areas receives its own score. These scores are then added together to determine the overall score for the assignment. Analytic rubrics provide targeted feedback and help students understand their strengths and weaknesses. However, they can be time-consuming to create and adapt.

Holistic rubrics provide one overall score for the assignment rather than evaluating each criterion separately. They list varying levels of performance, and each level describes the characteristics of assignments earning that score. For example, a writing assignment might be assigned a score ranging from 1 to 4. Assignments earning a score of 4 would be well developed, have effective use of language, and have few or no errors with conventions. Holistic rubrics can be faster for teachers to create and adapt for different assignments. However, the feedback is less targeted than it is when using analytic rubrics, which evaluate each criterion separately.

RUNNING RECORDS

Running records are tools used to record students' behaviors and use of strategies during reading. To administer running records, teachers provide students with books in their developmental reading levels and ask them to read the books aloud. While students are reading, teachers record the words read correctly with check marks. They also note errors by recording the actual words in the texts and the words students substituted for them. Word repetitions, omissions, and self-corrections are also noted using special symbols.

While running records used to be considered best practice, new research has since denounced this tool. Running records are not efficient, and they do not act as a reliable indication of fundamental literacy skills. Educators are encouraged to use universal screenings to gather data to compose homogeneous skill-based groups. Another useful tool is a **decodable running record**. This defers from a normal running record because it assesses phonic and phonemic skills using a decodable text; whereas, a running record based off level generally assess reading behaviors and the use of cueing systems.

ROLE OF PERFORMANCE-BASED ASSESSMENTS IN LITERACY ASSESSMENT

Performance-based assessments require students to solve real-world problems and accomplish authentic tasks by applying literacy skills and strategies. An example of a performance-based assessment is writing a letter to a government official in support of a new law, citing evidence-based reasons for the position. Depending on the types of tasks involved, performance-based assessments may require students to synthesize information from multiple sources, defend positions with text evidence, write texts following the writing process, and create materials to convey information to others.

Performance-based assessments are open ended and do not contain right or wrong answers. Typically, there are multiple ways that students can approach the tasks. The assessments are evaluated using rubrics, with clear criteria determined and shared with students in advance.

An advantage of performance-based assessments is that they allow students opportunities to solve real-world problems, thereby increasing learner engagement. They also require higher-level thinking skills, such as analysis, application, synthesis, and creation. Additionally, they often allow students some choices in how they present their learning. A disadvantage is that performance-based assessments may be time-consuming to create and implement. Grading can also be subjective.

ROLE OF PORTFOLIOS IN LITERACY ASSESSMENT

Portfolios are collections of students' projects and work gathered over time. They can serve many purposes in assessing literacy development. They can be used to track students' progress over time and check for mastery of certain skills, which is useful for planning differentiated instruction. Portfolios can also be passed along to students' future teachers, helping them determine students' instructional levels. Additionally, portfolios can be used to help students self-evaluate their own progress and set future goals.

If using portfolios, teachers must make several decisions. They must determine how the portfolios will be used, which will influence the criteria used to select portfolio entries. They also need to determine how entries will be selected. Will teachers or students select the entries, or will both play roles in the process? Teachers also need to decide if the portfolios will be graded. Checklists and rubrics are possible tools that can be used to grade portfolios.

Some advantages of portfolios include the ability to see concrete evidence of student progress over time and the possibility of having students actively involved in assessing their own progress. However, evaluating portfolios is subjective, and teachers may be unsure of how to use them to guide instruction.

DETERMINING WHEN TO RESPOND TO STUDENT MISCUES IN READING

Even proficient readers make errors at times. Fluent readers often read texts rapidly and may occasionally omit or substitute words without changing the meanings of the texts. For example, they may substitute "her house" for "the house" in a text. These types of errors do not impact meaning and, if occasional, can be ignored. Stopping to correct these types of minor errors can interrupt fluency and comprehension.

Readers in the emergent and early stages of development may make frequent errors and become frustrated if corrected each time. Overcorrection may interfere with confidence and reading enjoyment. Teachers should

33

strategically choose which types of errors to respond to during each reading session. One approach is to focus on a single type of error each time, such as errors where syntax cues are ignored. Another approach is to intervene only when errors affect the meaning of the text. Minor errors can be ignored to build fluency and confidence.

INSTRUCTIONAL STRATEGIES TO SUPPORT READING SKILLS

SUPPORTING READING COMPREHENSION IN ELLS AND STRUGGLING READERS

It is helpful to build background knowledge before introducing new texts to English language learners (ELLs) and struggling readers. Readers can then draw upon this background knowledge to make meaning from the new texts. After assessing what students already know about the topics, background knowledge can be developed using other texts, charts, graphs, photographs, videos, discussions, and additional methods.

- ELLs and struggling readers can benefit from **previewing** new texts before reading them independently. This may include picture walks or receiving text outlines that identify the **main ideas** covered in each section.
- **Pre-teaching vocabulary** can also help ELLs and struggling readers comprehend new texts. Teachers can introduce the vocabulary words and use photos or real objects to help explain their meanings. The vocabulary words can be frequently incorporated into class discussions to familiarize students with them.
- Additionally, **graphic organizers** can be used to help ELLs and struggling readers identify and organize key parts of texts that assist with comprehension. To offer scaffolding, partially completed graphic organizers and/or sentence stems can be provided initially, and support can be gradually withdrawn over time.

SUPPORTING READING COMPREHENSION IN PROFICIENT READERS

Proficient readers can be encouraged to comprehend at the inferential and evaluative levels in addition to the literal level. They can analyze texts deeply and make inferences, draw conclusions, and form evaluations. They can also be encouraged to complete activities that require higher-level thinking skills. Rather than listing the main characters, for example, proficient readers can be asked to retell the stories from each character's point of view or evaluate the choices the characters made.

To **challenge proficient readers** and encourage them to be enthusiastic about reading, they can also be given choices about book selection. Teachers can guide students in expanding their text selections to include different topics and genres but allow them to make their own selections. Teachers can also encourage students to choose texts that are appropriately challenging. Proficient readers can benefit from ownership in reading-related activities. Teachers can create menus of challenging questions or projects that readers can choose from based on their interests.

ENGAGING IN COLLABORATIVE DISCUSSIONS ABOUT PRINT AND DIGITAL TEXTS

Engaging in **collaborative discussions** can have several benefits for readers. It allows them to learn from other people's experiences and perspectives, which may differ from their own. Readers may hear additional evidence that strengthens their own initial understandings and conclusions. Conversely, they may hear evidence that challenges their initial thoughts and requires them to make revisions. Readers also have to support their points with text evidence to explain their thoughts to classmates. Locating and analyzing text evidence can assist with comprehension.

Discussing texts with others also has broader social benefits. It gives students opportunities to be **active and social learners**. Sharing ideas and collaborating helps build a community of learners who are able to communicate and respect different points of view. It also allows students to experience different social roles within the group and develop conflict resolution skills.

INFLUENCE OF CULTURE ON READING COMPREHENSION

Culture affects the ways people view and interact with the world around them. As a result, readers of different cultural backgrounds may comprehend the same texts differently. Readers rely on prior knowledge and existing schemata to make sense of what was read. Texts that are culturally familiar and related to readers' existing cultural schemata are more easily comprehended than those that are unfamiliar. When reading culturally familiar topics, readers are better able to make predictions, inferences, and conclusions based on existing schemata.

Therefore, it is important for teachers to activate both students' content knowledge and cultural knowledge prior to reading. For example, students may read a text describing a birthday celebration. The teacher can activate students' knowledge about how birthdays are celebrated in different cultures.

Research has indicated that cultural differences in syntactic complexity are less likely to affect comprehension.

METHODS OF STRUCTURING COLLABORATIVE DISCUSSIONS ABOUT PRINT AND DIGITAL TEXTS

Literature circles are one way to structure collaborative discussions about print. **Literature circles** consist of small groups of students who lead discussions about shared texts, which may or may not have been self-selected. Students collaboratively analyze the texts, discussing topics such as character development and theme. In some classrooms, guiding questions are provided by the teachers, whereas discussion questions are student-generated in others. Sometimes students are assigned roles within the group, such as summarizer and discussion leader.

Other times, there may be whole-class collaborative discussions. These types of discussions may occur when the whole class is completing an author study, for example, and are comparing and contrasting the events of different texts. These discussions are typically teacher-led.

There may also be small-group, teacher-led, collaborative discussions about teacher-selected texts. For example, discussion time may be included during guided reading groups.

RECIPROCAL TEACHING STRATEGY

Reciprocal teaching is a strategy designed to assist students with reading comprehension. In reciprocal teaching, students and teachers **share the responsibilities** of leading small-group discussions about texts. Teachers initially take the lead and model using four main comprehension strategies, including generating questions, summarizing, clarifying, and predicting. They gradually share more responsibility with students, who eventually take over leading the groups in applying these strategies to analyze texts.

Reciprocal teaching has several benefits. It requires students to be actively engaged in the reading process, as they must understand and apply the reading strategies to guide their classmates. It encourages the use of higher-level reading strategies that can then be applied to other texts. It also encourages discussion and collaboration among class members. Additionally, reciprocal teaching can help build students' confidence in their abilities to independently read and analyze challenging texts.

ACTIVITIES PROMOTING READING COMPREHENSION

Before reading, teachers can set the purposes for reading and activate students' prior knowledge by making connections to what they already know. They can **preview** the texts and important vocabulary words and encourage students to make **predictions**.

During reading, teachers can model thinking aloud to demonstrate how they **monitor** their own understanding. They can check and revise predictions, make inferences, and form connections. They can provide students with guiding questions or graphic organizers to use as they read independently to encourage the same reading behaviors.

After reading, teachers can **model** summarizing, drawing conclusions, and evaluating the texts. They can also discuss how their thinking changed as they read and were presented with new evidence. They can encourage students to use the same strategies after reading independently by setting up literature circles, creating written response activities, and designing other reading response projects.

TYPES OF CONNECTIONS READERS CAN MAKE TO TEXTS

- Readers can make **text-to-text connections**. These are connections made between two or more different texts that have been read. Readers might make connections between the texts' events, characters, themes, or any other features. An example is when a reader identifies that characters in two different books both persisted to overcome challenges.
- **Text-to-self connections** refer to connections readers make between texts and their own personal experiences. An example is when a reader understands the sadness a character feels when losing a pet after having personally experienced the same thing.
- **Text-to-world connections** refer to connections readers make between events in texts and events that have happened in the real world. An example is when a reader makes connections between a text about an astronaut and news about a recent space launch.

To encourage readers to make these connections, teachers can model their own thinking during shared reading experiences. They can model thinking deeply about similarities rather than making surface connections. For example, rather than pointing out that two characters are both girls, they can compare their character traits. Teachers can also encourage the use of Venn diagrams to show the similarities and differences between two texts, people, or events.

BENEFITS OF COMPARING DIFFERENT BOOKS BY THE SAME AUTHOR

When students read and compare multiple books by the same author, they use several reading strategies important for comprehension. They compare and contrast story elements between texts, such as characters, settings, problems, and solutions; they make text-to-text connections. They also consider how the author's life experiences may impact his or her writing style and content.

After completing multiple author studies, readers may also begin to identify favorite authors. These authors can serve as **mentors** for students, providing models of how to use language and incorporate story elements in their own writing. The connections readers feel to their favorite authors can boost engagement with reading and encourage them to seek out additional texts. Students can learn about the authors' lives and the paths they have taken as writers. They may be inspired by learning that people similar to themselves have become published authors.

BENEFITS OF LEARNING ABOUT TOPICS USING DIFFERENT TEXTS AND/OR GENRES

Reading different texts on the same topic can give readers a more comprehensive understanding of the topic. Each text reflects the personal writing style and bias of the author. Reading multiple texts allows readers to hear different perspectives and form their own judgments.

Reading texts from **multiple genres** about the same topic is also beneficial. Each genre presents the information differently and serves unique purposes. Reading an **informational text** about the Civil War may provide readers with an understanding of the war's causes, events, and major figures. Reading a **historical fiction** book written from the perspective of a soldier may give readers a more personalized account of this period in time, engaging the readers and helping them form personal connections.

When reading multiple texts, readers also need to identify the important points from each and synthesize the information. They need to consider the authors' purposes for writing. These skills assist with reading comprehension.

PRINT-RICH LEARNING ENVIRONMENTS

CHARACTERISTICS OF LITERACY-RICH, CONTENT-AREA CLASSROOMS

Literacy-rich, content-area classrooms include frequent teacher modeling of academic behaviors. This includes teacher modeling of thinking aloud, use of reading and writing strategies, and incorporation of academic vocabulary into regular activities.

These classrooms also include daily reading, writing, listening, and speaking activities. Students are engaged in reading, writing, and discussing a range of different texts and media in both print in digital form. Depending on the content area, this may include lab reports, journal articles, maps, historical fiction, diaries, graphic organizers, narratives, and more.

Students in literacy-rich classrooms are encouraged to make connections between different sources and content areas. For example, readers may make connections between a historical fiction text about the Dust Bowl and what they have learned in science about weather patterns.

Additionally, teachers in literacy-rich classrooms encourage the respectful sharing of information and ideas among classmates.

CREATING LEARNING ENVIRONMENTS SUPPORTIVE OF CULTURAL AND LINGUISTIC DIFFERENCES

Classrooms should incorporate **culturally** and **linguistically diverse materials**, including those that represent the cultures of students. Reading materials, artwork, classroom labels, and posters are all examples of diverse materials that can be included. Students should also have opportunities to share items that are meaningful to them with other classmates.

Additionally, ELLs should not be punished for reluctance to participate in discussions. Instead, they should be offered **support** and **scaffolding** when needed. When ELLs are in the early stages of English language acquisition, teachers can also use simple sentence structures and provide visual clues to support students' comprehension.

Teachers should also work to create nonthreatening and supportive classroom environments by modeling accepting attitudes. They can model and explicitly teach how to compare and contrast different cultures respectfully. When studying historical and current events, teachers can help students explore the events from different perspectives and discuss how culture can affect people's experiences.

> **Review Video: <u>Importance of Promoting Literacy in the Home</u>**
> Visit mometrix.com/academy and enter code: 862347

USING WORD WALLS TO SUPPORT READING AND WRITING DEVELOPMENT

Word walls are collections of words that are prominently displayed in classrooms. Words selected for display on word walls should be meaningful for students. They might include high-frequency words that students need to read and write often or academic vocabulary words related to units of study. Word walls are flexible, and words may be added or removed throughout the year based on students' needs.

Teachers should model how to use word walls to locate and spell high-frequency words. Words may be attached using Velcro, magnets, or other methods that allow them to be removed. This allows students to take the words down while using them and return them to the wall when finished.

There are many ways to organize word walls. Words can be listed alphabetically under letter headings, helping young writers quickly locate them for spelling assistance. If focused on academic vocabulary, the words can be grouped by topic. Visuals can be included with vocabulary words to assist students with remembering meanings.

LEVELED BOOK ROOMS

Leveled book rooms are consolidated collections of leveled readers that can be checked out by all teachers within a school. Reading specialists often help organize and maintain leveled book rooms as part of their responsibilities. Because teachers frequently have students who read both well above and well below grade level, these types of book rooms ensure that all students have access to books within their instructional reading levels.

To implement successful leveled book rooms, books should be clearly organized and labeled according to level. The same leveling system used by classroom teachers should be used in the leveled book rooms for consistency. Books may also be organized in additional ways, such as by genre, topic, or author. Teachers should be taught the procedures for checking out and returning books. Records should be maintained in order to keep track of where all books are located.

INSTRUCTIONAL TECHNOLOGIES SUPPORTING LITERACY DEVELOPMENT

There are many ways that instructional technologies can be used to create classroom environments that support literacy development. Computer programs and apps can be used to practice and assess literacy skills, and there are many options that differentiate instruction based on students' existing skills. Many of these programs and apps also save and track students' progress, helping both students and teachers track progress toward goals.

- Projectors, document cameras, and interactive whiteboards can also be used to **magnify texts** so students can follow along during instruction. Interactive whiteboards also allow students to actively participate in literacy activities with classmates.
- **Digital texts** can be used to support listening development and assist students with reading texts that are too difficult for them to read independently. Interactive storybooks that display and track text for emergent and beginning readers can also be used.
- There are many **digital tools** and **software options** that can be used to create forms of media such as slideshow presentations, infographics, digital storybooks, and newsletters. Modern tools can also be used to help students collaborate on projects, even if they are working remotely.

Phonics and Decoding

MORPHOLOGY AND WORD ANALYSIS SKILLS

HOMOGRAPHS

Homographs are words that are spelled the same but may be pronounced differently and have different meanings. An example of a homograph pair is *bat* (baseball bat) and *bat* (the flying mammal).

After explaining the meaning of homographs, teachers can assist students with generating lists of homograph pairs. Teachers can provide sentences using homographs, and students can identify them and their meanings. Students can also look for homographs in texts and play matching games to find cards with two different definitions for the same word.

Homographs have different meanings, so it is important for readers to be able to identify which meanings are being used when they encounter homographs in texts. Readers can be encouraged to use context clues to assist with determining the meanings. Readers can also be encouraged to self-monitor their understanding of each homograph's meaning by asking themselves if what they have read makes sense. Because homograph pairs can also be pronounced differently, readers can be encouraged to try reading the sentences with each possible pronunciation and ask themselves which one sounds right.

Teaching Reading

COMPOUND WORDS

A **compound word** is formed by combining two or more words to form one word with a new, unique meaning. Examples of compound words include *houseboat*, *moonlight*, and *basketball*.

Identifying compound words rapidly can assist readers with decoding multisyllabic words. Identifying the smaller, known words contained in the compound words will help students decode the words quickly and maintain fluency.

To teach students to identify compound words, they can practice breaking them into parts. Compound words can be provided using letter tiles, magnetic letters, or in writing, and students can be asked to split them into the two smaller word parts. Puzzle cards can be created with which two smaller words join together to create a compound word. Readers can also be asked to find and mark compound words in texts. When students struggle to decode compound words while reading independently, teachers can ask what smaller, known words they see in the unknown words.

TYPES OF CONTEXT CLUES

- There are several different types of context clues that are often provided in sentences. One common type is a **definition clue**. In this type of clue, a definition for the unfamiliar word is provided somewhere within the same sentence; for example, *the precocious toddler surprised her parents by learning to read at a much earlier age than her peers.*
- Another type of context clue is an **antonym clue**. In this type of clue, an antonym or contrasting definition of the unfamiliar word is provided somewhere within the same sentence; for example, *unlike his amiable coworker, Mark was quite unfriendly when interacting with customers.*
- **Synonym clues** are a third type of context clue. In this type, a synonym for the unfamiliar word is provided somewhere within the same sentence; for example, *the altruistic donor was so selfless that she donated all of her lottery winnings to her favorite charity.*
- **Inference clues** are another type of context clue. With this type of clue, the unknown word's meaning is not explicitly given, and the reader must infer it from the context of the sentence; for example, *Sam was thirsty after hiking the three-mile trail, so he ordered a cold beverage at the café.*

AFFIXES

Affixes are letters or groups of letters that are added to root words. **Prefixes** and **suffixes** are two common types of **affixes**. Root words may have one or multiple affixes attached to them.

Learning to identify affixes and understand their meanings is important for both fluency and comprehension. Because the same affixes are used repeatedly in English, immediately recognizing them and knowing how they are pronounced can assist readers with decoding multisyllabic words. Decoding the words quickly will help the readers maintain fluency. Because affixes also have predictable meanings, understanding these meanings can help readers comprehend new words in texts and build vocabulary. For example, if readers encounter the word *declutter*, they may know that *de* means the opposite of something, and *clutter* means a messy collection of things. Using this knowledge, they can put the parts together and determine the meaning of *declutter*.

> **Review Video: Affixes**
> Visit mometrix.com/academy and enter code: 782422

PREFIXES

A **prefix** is a letter or group of letters added to the beginning of a root word. The prefix modifies the existing word's meaning, and a new word is formed. For example, the prefix *dis-* can be added to the word *respect* to form the new word *disrespect.*

Students need to understand the difference between a prefix and base word. It should be emphasized that the base is a whole word, whereas the prefix is a letter or group of letters that cannot stand alone. Examples of words containing prefixes can be provided, and students can practice identifying both the prefixes and root words. Non-examples can also be provided, such as the word *decal*. *De-* is not a prefix in this example because *cal* is not a word on its own.

The meanings of different prefixes can then be introduced. Root words can be presented, and their meanings discussed. Prefixes can then be added, and students can discuss how the meanings of the words change. They can list other words containing the same prefixes, along with their meanings.

Students can also be encouraged to find examples of words containing prefixes in texts independently and use clues to determine their meanings.

SUFFIXES

A **suffix** is a letter or group of letters added to the end of a root word. When added, it sometimes changes the meaning of the root word and forms a new word. It may also change the part of speech of the root word. An example of a suffix is *-ful*. When added to the end of the root word *thank*, it forms the word *thankful*, which means full of thanks.

To introduce the topic, students can be given lists of words containing suffixes and asked to identify what the words have in common. The suffixes can then be identified, and teachers can explain how the suffixes change the root words. Three-column charts can be created, with columns dedicated to suffixes, their meanings, and example words. Students can be given cards containing root words and suffixes, and they can experiment with pairing them. They can explain whether the combinations form real or nonsense words and define any real words they create. Students can be encouraged to find examples of words containing suffixes and identify their meanings based on context clues in the texts.

DERIVATIONAL VS. INFLECTIONAL AFFIXES

- **Derivational affixes** are letters or groups of letters added to root words to change the meanings of the words or the parts of speech.For example, if the affix *un-* is added to the root *kind*, the new word *unkind* is formed. Both the original and newly formed words are adjectives, but the meanings of the two words are different. However, if the affix *-ment* is added to the root word *fulfill*, the new word *fulfillment* is formed. The original word is a verb, and the newly formed word is a noun. Both of these examples demonstrate derivational affixes.
- **Inflectional affixes** do not change the part of speech of a word, but they do serve a grammatical function. Inflectional affixes include the suffixes *-s*, *-ed*, *-ing*, *-en*, *-'s*, *-er*, and *-est*. For example, adding an inflectional affix can change the word *walk* to *walked*. The part of speech does not change as both words are verbs. The affix only changes the tense of the verb. Inflectional affixes can indicate whether a noun is singular or plural, the verb tense, superlatives, or possessives.

RELATIONSHIP BETWEEN KNOWLEDGE OF ROOTS AND AFFIXES

Knowledge of roots and affixes and the use of **context clues** are closely related. Proficient readers use a combination of these strategies to determine the meanings of unknown words, check their initial guesses, and revise their guesses if necessary.

- When encountering an unknown multisyllabic word, a reader may first look for know**n parts** of the word. This may lead the reader to break the word down into the root and affixes. Using knowledge of what each of these components means, the reader may then guess the word's meaning.
- However, both roots and affixes can have multiple meanings. The reader's initial guess may not make sense in this particular context. Therefore, it is important for the reader to also consider **context clues** to check the conjectured meaning. If it does not fit the context, the reader may consider other meanings of the root and affixes that better fit the context clues.
- The reader may also begin by guessing the word's meaning using context clues and then use knowledge of the root and affixes to check the initial conjecture. Teachers should encourage readers to use both of these strategies to **check** and **self-correct** their deductions.

ORAL LANGUAGE AND NONVERBAL LANGUAGE DEVELOPMENT

STAGES OF FIRST LANGUAGE ACQUISITION

- Until about four to six months of age, babies are in the **cooing stage**. Babies in this stage commonly make vowel sounds, which represent their first attempts at oral language.
- From about four to six months until one year of age, babies are in the **babbling stage**. At first, they commonly make repeated consonant-vowel sounds, such as *ma-ma*. Over time, their babbling begins to show the expressive patterns they hear in the language around them. They repeat sounds that others respond to and reinforce.
- From about 12 to 24 months of age, children are in the **one-word stage**. In this stage, children begin referring to objects by consistent, one-word names. These words may be real or invented, and children begin to use language to convey meaning to others.
- From ages two to three, most children enter the **telegraphic stage**, when they string together words to convey meaning. The words that convey the most meaning in sentences are often included, whereas articles, conjunctions, and other words are omitted.
- After age three, most children enter the beginning **oral fluency stage**. They now use more complex sentences and begin using sentence structure and syntax appropriately. They use language for a variety of purposes.

Early milestones in language

STAGES OF SECOND LANGUAGE ACQUISITION

- In the **preproduction stage**, English language learners (ELLs) are listening and taking in the second language. Comprehension is minimal at this point. ELLs may not yet speak to others in the second language, and this stage is therefore sometimes referred to as the silent period. ELLs may communicate with gestures or single words.
- In the **early production stage**, comprehension is still limited. ELLs begin responding using one- or two-word answers. Vocabulary in the second language begins to grow.
- The **speech emergence stage** is marked by increased comprehension. ELLs begin speaking in longer sentences, but grammatical errors may be present. Vocabulary in the second language greatly increases.
- In the **intermediate proficiency stage**, ELLs are able to comprehend much of what they hear. They begin speaking in more complex sentences that contain fewer grammatical errors. They are able to fluently communicate with others in the second language for a variety of purposes.
- In the **advanced fluency stage**, ELLs understand academic vocabulary and need little support to participate actively in the classroom. Students in this stage speak with near-native English fluency.

COMPONENTS OF ORAL LANGUAGE DEVELOPMENT

- **Phonological skills** are one component of oral language development. These skills include the ability to recognize and manipulate sounds in spoken words. Rhyming and identifying syllables are examples of phonological skills.

- **Syntactic skills** are another component. Syntactic skills (syntax) include understanding grammatical rules and how to correctly arrange words in sentences. Children begin by using simple syntax, such as combining two words to express needs and wants. Over time, their sentence structure becomes more complex.
- **Oral language** also includes a semantic component, which refers to the ability to understand the meanings of words, phrases, sentences, and longer texts. The semantic component is vital for comprehension.
- **Morphological skills** are another component of oral language development. Morphological skills include understanding the meanings of word parts.
- Finally, **pragmatics** refers to understanding the social rules of language. Examples of pragmatics include knowing how to adjust the formality of language depending on the audience and knowing how to respond in certain social situations.

> **Review Video: Components of Oral Language Development**
> Visit mometrix.com/academy and enter code: 480589

RELATIONSHIP BETWEEN ORAL LANGUAGE DEVELOPMENT AND LITERACY DEVELOPMENT

Most children learn to speak through immersion in language-rich environments, with no formal speech instruction necessary. Starting at birth, these early language interactions help set the stage for later literacy development. Early language play, such as sharing songs, nursery rhymes, and poems, assists young children with the development of phonological awareness skills. Strong phonological awareness skills are a solid predictor of future reading success. Hearing spoken language also helps children understand syntax and how sounds and words are combined to form meaning.

- As children engage in frequent and varied oral language opportunities, they also increase their **vocabularies**. Opportunities to use both social and academic vocabulary during listening and speaking activities assists students with comprehending vocabulary words encountered in texts.
- **Oral language experiences** also help readers understand that language can be used for a variety of purposes, such as meeting needs, social interaction, and persuading others. This assists with recognizing an author's purpose. An understanding of cultural norms and nuances is also developed through oral language experiences.
- Additionally, comprehension requires the ability to combine literal meanings of words with prior knowledge and world experiences. Oral language activities, such as following directions, can assist with this.

ROLE THAT ORAL LANGUAGE PLAYS IN THE DEVELOPMENT OF CRITICAL THINKING SKILLS

Oral language leads to the development of other communication skills. Babies first listen to their caregivers and later say their first words before they learn to read and write. Through listening, children learn to evaluate the messages of others and make sense of newly learned information. Through speaking, they learn to organize and communicate their thoughts to others. All of these skills assist with the development of critical thinking skills.

Teachers can ask students to explain their thinking to others. They can also teach students to defend their answers using support and evidence. Students can also be explicitly taught to use strategic questioning when interacting with classmates. Strategic questions require higher-level thinking to answer, and questions with yes-or-no answers should be limited. For example, students explaining the results of science experiments might be asked to evaluate their processes and explain what they might do differently in the future. Additionally, students can respond to high-level questions about texts during class discussions and literature circles. For example, they can be asked to evaluate the ways that authors use persuasive techniques.

PROMOTING ORAL LANGUAGE SKILLS

When engaging in listening and speaking activities with students, it is recommended to use vocabulary words in context to promote comprehension later. Research has shown that identifying vocabulary words on flash cards and other similar types activities has **little effect** on later reading comprehension, whereas the ability to recognize and use words **in context** does.

Students should also have many opportunities to listen and speak for a **variety of purposes** to both peers and adults. Friendly conversations, academic discussions, formal presentations, and social interactions are all examples of different types of oral language activities. Varied activities will help students learn to change their language structures to fit the purposes of the interactions. Teachers can change their language structures throughout the school day. For example, they might chat informally with students about their interests during a morning meeting and switch to academic language when discussing a novel.

Additionally, students of all ages can benefit from reading and listening to a large variety of texts containing different types of sentence structure, language, and vocabulary. Young children can also benefit from word play and phonological awareness activities.

DEVELOPING LISTENING AND SPEAKING SKILLS

Like reading and writing, listening and speaking activities should be incorporated throughout all content areas rather than taught in isolation. Students should be given multiple opportunities each day to listen and speak for a variety of purposes.

Students can listen to texts in audio form, listen to teachers read aloud, or participate in paired reading activities in all content areas. Before beginning, they can be given specific purposes for listening to focus their attention. They can participate in role-playing scenarios to model common social situations and conflict resolution. They can be given frequent opportunities to present their learning to others using a variety of formats. Audience members can be instructed to ask specific and relevant questions, and presenters can be instructed to provide well-supported and evidence-based answers. Additionally, collaborative, problem-based learning activities can be planned, requiring all students to have roles within their groups.

For ELLs and students who struggle with speaking, partially completed scripts and/or sentence stems can be provided. These tools can assist students with outlining thoughts and organizing sentence structure before speaking.

TEACHING STUDENTS NONVERBAL COMMUNICATION SKILLS

Nonverbal communication, sometimes known as body language, includes gestures, facial expressions, and posture. Verbal and nonverbal communication work together to convey desired messages. If nonverbal communication is inappropriate for the audiences or purposes used, the meaning of the verbal communication may be lost or misconstrued. For example, a child may thank a grandparent for a gift. However, if the child has a disappointed look on his or her face while speaking, the grandparent may believe the child does not like the gift.

Additionally, certain types of nonverbal communication can be interpreted differently depending on culture. What is socially acceptable in one culture may be considered rude in another. Students should be aware of the messages their nonverbal communication sends to different audiences.

Teachers can engage students in discussions about what messages are sent by different types of nonverbal communication. They can role-play common scenarios and have other students evaluate the messages conveyed through both verbal and nonverbal communication. Students can also watch video clips of realistic situations, such as job interviews, and evaluate the nonverbal language of the participants. When giving presentations, teachers also provide checklists outlining expected nonverbal communication, such as eye contact with others and strong posture.

Vocabulary and Fluency

DEVELOPMENT OF READING FLUENCY
COMPONENTS OF FLUENCY

Reading fluency is made up of several elements including rate, accuracy, and prosody.

- **Rate** refers to reading speed. Proficient readers adjust their reading speed flexibly depending on their purposes for reading. For example, they may read scientific textbooks containing technical vocabulary more slowly than graphic novels they are reading for entertainment. Rate is important for comprehension. If readers read too slowly, they may forget what they have already read and lose the overall meanings of the texts. If readers read too quickly, important points may be overlooked.
- **Accuracy** is another component of fluency. It refers to decoding words correctly without errors. Fluent readers automatically recognize many high-frequency words and use multiple strategies to decode unknown words. Accuracy is important because frequent errors may affect comprehension, especially if errors are made on words central to the meaning of the text.
- **Prosody** is another component of fluency. It refers to reading expression, including phrasing and intonation. Prosody affects the ways texts are understood. For example, readers should pause appropriately at commas to emphasize certain phrases. Using the correct intonation associated with each punctuation mark affects the tone of the texts.

PROGRESSION OF FLUENCY DEVELOPMENT IN READERS

- **Early readers** devote most of their mental energy to decoding words. In this stage of reading, the focus is on developing reading accuracy, which is one component of fluency. Early readers practice high-frequency words and learn strategies to decode words with simple spelling patterns. Rate and prosody play lesser roles but are still practiced with scaffolding.
- In the **transitional reading stage**, readers automatically recognize many high-frequency words and more efficiently use strategies to decode unknown words. There is still a focus on accuracy as readers encounter more complex vocabulary and spelling patterns. However, transitional readers increase their reading rates and begin to read independently with prosody. As readers gain confidence with familiar texts, their fluency increases.
- By the time they reach the **fluent stage**, readers are able to flexibly adapt their reading rates based upon their purposes for reading. Automatic recognition of most words results in reading accuracy. Fluent readers read with prosody, and they appropriately match their expressions to the texts.

DEVELOPING FLUENCY IN EARLY READERS

When teaching early readers, the main focus is on developing **accuracy**. This is done through activities to develop automatic recognition of high-frequency sight words and explicit phonics instruction that teaches strategies to decode words with common spelling patterns.

To assist early readers with developing **speed and prosody**, teachers can encourage repeated readings of favorite texts. As readers develop more confidence with the texts through these repeated readings, their reading rates will increase. Because readers already know how to decode the words in these familiar texts, they have more energy available to focus on expression.

Teachers should frequently **model fluent reading**. This includes reading with appropriate speed, phrasing, and intonation. Teachers can also model disfluent reading, such as reading texts without expression, and ask students to explain the effects it has on comprehension. Choral reading of shared texts can also assist students with developing fluency.

Review Video: Fluency
Visit mometrix.com/academy and enter code: 531179

MAINTAINING FLUENCY IN ON-LEVEL READERS

Like struggling readers, on-level readers can benefit from frequent teacher modeling of fluent reading, choral reading, and opportunities to reread familiar texts. Additionally, they can benefit from partner reading. Partner reading allows students to hear fluent reading modeled by classmates and reread texts repeatedly while receiving feedback. Students should first be taught procedures for how to listen attentively to their partners' reading and provide effective and encouraging feedback. Teachers should always be mindful of individual needs when pairing students.

Reader's theater is another strategy to assist on-level readers with fluency. In **reader's theater**, students read scripts from appropriately leveled texts to perform for classmates. Through rehearsing and performing, students have multiple opportunities to reread the scripts. They must also practice reading with appropriate expression for their characters and reading with appropriate speeds so they can be understood by their audiences. Additionally, reader's theater allows students in the audience to hear models of fluent reading. In reader's theater, the focus is on the reading, and few or no props are used.

INTERVENTIONS TO USE ASSISTING READERS WHO ARE STRUGGLING WITH FLUENCY

Readers who are struggling with fluency can benefit from frequent modeling of fluent reading. As teachers reread familiar texts, students can join in and read chorally, matching their phrasing, speed, and expression to the teachers' reading. Students can also listen to audio recordings of texts.

Readers who struggle with fluency can also benefit from repeated readings of texts. After initial readings, teachers can give feedback to students and help them set goals for rereading. For example, they may encourage readers to pause at the periods between sentences. It is important that readers are given passages within their instructional reading levels. Reading texts far below their instructional levels will not challenge the readers. Reading texts that are too difficult will result in readers stopping frequently to decode unknown words, which interrupts fluency and causes frustration. Encouraging repeated readings of texts with rhyming and repetition, including poetry, can assist readers who are struggling with fluency.

Although teachers may monitor students' reading fluency over time, it is also important to create encouraging environments for readers. Continuously timing readers or forcing disfluent readers to read aloud in front of others may have negative effects.

SELECTING APPROPRIATELY-LEVELED TEXTS

SELECTING APPROPRIATE TEXTS TO SUPPORT THE BACKGROUNDS AND INTERESTS OF DIVERSE LEARNERS

When selecting appropriate texts to support diverse learners, teachers should take several factors into consideration. First, they should consider students' reading levels and stages of reading development to determine how much text support is needed. For emergent and early readers, teachers should consider how much picture support is present, how many words are printed on each page, and the predictability of the text. They should also consider how easily students will be able to decode the words based on spelling patterns, text clues, and use of high-frequency words.

For transitional and fluent readers, teachers should consider text complexity. This includes the vocabulary, language use, and sentence structure used in the texts. They should also consider how the texts relate to students' prior knowledge and interests and whether the content supports learning objectives. If topics are unfamiliar to students, some scaffolding or pre-teaching may be needed.

DETERMINING IF TEXTS ARE AT STUDENTS' INDEPENDENT READING LEVELS

When determining reading levels, teachers typically consider both accuracy rate and comprehension. Different reading programs vary slightly in their cutoff levels, but texts are generally considered to be at the independent level if they are read with 95% to 100% accuracy. Additionally, responding correctly to 90% to

100% of comprehension questions may indicate that texts are at students' independent levels. Texts at the independent reading level can be read by students with no assistance.

Texts that students can read independently are good candidates for free choice reading time. They also can be used when practicing comprehension strategies, such as inferring and drawing conclusions. Because students do not struggle to decode words in these texts, they have the mental energy available to do more complex analysis. Additionally, students can repeatedly read favorite books at their independent reading levels for fluency practice. They can also read these books to partners or family members.

DETERMINING IF TEXTS ARE AT STUDENTS' INSTRUCTIONAL READING LEVELS

Different reading programs vary slightly in their cutoff levels, but texts are generally considered to be at the instructional level if they are read with 90% to 94% accuracy. Additionally, responding correctly to 70% to 89% of comprehension questions may indicate that texts are at students' instructional levels. These books present some challenges for readers, but they can still be read without frustration.

Texts at the instructional level are appropriate for use in guided reading groups. Students are able to decode most words, yet a few miscues may occur that can be used as teaching points. Teachers may analyze student errors and use this information to plan mini-lessons. Additionally, students are able to apply comprehension strategies to analyze and discuss these texts. Texts at the instructional level allow students to have successful and positive experiences with reading while learning from their challenges.

DETERMINING IF TEXTS ARE AT STUDENTS' FRUSTRATION LEVELS

Different reading programs vary slightly in their cutoff levels, but texts are generally considered to be at the frustration level if they are read with less than 90% accuracy. Additionally, responding correctly to less than 70% of comprehension questions may indicate that texts are at students' frustration levels. These books are considered difficult for students to read.

Texts at the frustration level are not good candidates for students to read independently during guided reading groups, when teachers need to observe students' reading and help them apply strategies. Students may become frustrated with too many unknown words or lose the meanings of the texts.

However, these texts can be used in other beneficial ways. Students may enjoy exploring difficult texts on topics of interest, which may help them develop a love of reading. Because these texts can provide valuable information that students cannot access independently, teachers can also read these texts aloud or provide digital versions with audio. Teachers can model using reading strategies with these difficult texts during shared reading experiences. Additionally, students can be encouraged to read these texts with family members.

SYSTEMS USED TO LEVEL BOOKS

There are several different systems that are used to level books. **Lexile** measures consider both text complexity and word frequency to level books. Specialized assessments are used to determine students' Lexile levels, which can then be used to select appropriate books.

Irene Fountas and Gay Su Pinnell developed another system for leveling books based on their recommendations for guided reading groups. Their system, sometimes known as **guided reading levels**, considers several factors to assign book levels. These factors include word frequency, sentence complexity, vocabulary, and text features. Running records can help identify guided reading levels.

The **Developmental Reading Assessment (DRA)**, also provides a system for leveling books. Students can take the DRA to determine their instructional reading levels. Results can then be used to select books using the DRA system.

Because there are many different leveling systems, conversion charts are available online to help teachers and parents identify book levels using their preferred systems.

SUPPORTING VOCABULARY DEVELOPMENT

ENCOURAGING VOCABULARY ACQUISITION THROUGH READING AND WRITING ACTIVITIES

If a new text contains unfamiliar vocabulary words that are central to the meaning and/or may be difficult to decode, a teacher may **preview** the words with the group. After introducing the topic of the text, the teacher may flip to the words, show students their spellings, and ask students to share what the words may mean based on prior knowledge and picture clues. Exposure to these words before reading will build readers' confidence and help them recognize and decode the words faster, maintaining fluency. Knowing the meanings in advance will also assist with comprehension.

When reading aloud to students, teachers may pause at new vocabulary words and model how to use context clues, prior knowledge, and picture support to decode and comprehend the new words. Students can be encouraged to use these strategies when reading independently.

Readers need repeated exposure to vocabulary words to develop automatic recognition and comprehension. Teachers may display classroom charts containing vocabulary words and their meanings, possibly using picture clues for young readers.

Students can also be encouraged to incorporate vocabulary words in their own writing. Word walls or charts containing the words can assist students with spelling and remembering the meanings of the words.

HELPING READERS RECOGNIZE AND EXPLORE THE MEANINGS OF UNKNOWN VOCABULARY WORDS

First, it is important for students to identify unknown vocabulary words when reading. Readers who are not monitoring their own comprehension may decode the words and continue reading, even if they do not understand their meanings. Teachers can model how to stop when they reach words they don't understand, even if they can decode them, and encourage students to do the same.

Next, readers need to determine which unknown words are central to the meanings of the text and worth exploring further. This is important because there may be many unknown words and, if readers stop extensively at each one, fluency and comprehension may be interrupted. Therefore, students can be encouraged to consider whether or not they can comprehend the sentences and overall meanings of the texts without devoting more energy to these particular unknown words.

If readers determine that the unknown words are central to the meaning of the text, they can be encouraged to use strategies such as using context clues, looking for known roots or affixes, or consulting dictionaries. Overall, readers should be encouraged to monitor their own reading and comprehension and determine when to apply known strategies.

> **Review Video: Acknowledging the Unknown When Reading**
> Visit mometrix.com/academy and enter code: 712339

SUPPORTING VOCABULARY ACQUISITION AND USE THROUGH LISTENING AND SPEAKING

Young children begin their vocabulary development through listening well before they begin to read and write. Through listening to family members, caregivers, and others, children develop their meaning (oral) vocabularies. These are words that children understand when heard and eventually use in their own speech. These vocabularies can be developed by talking to the children frequently and for a variety of purposes, reading to them, exposing them to songs, rhymes, and poems, and many other language activities.

Children continue to build vocabulary through listening and speaking activities when they begin school. Teachers can read aloud to students often, varying the genres and purposes for listening. Engaging students in discussions about what was read aloud can give students a purpose for listening and opportunities to use text-related vocabulary in their own oral responses. Teachers can also incorporate key vocabulary words in class discussions.

Students should also have frequent opportunities to speak in the classroom. In addition to informal class discussions, students can present projects to classmates and explain their thinking during problem-solving. They should be encouraged to use content-specific vocabulary when appropriate.

TEACHING WORD ANALYSIS SKILLS AND VOCABULARY TO ENGLISH LANGUAGE LEARNERS

Focusing on cognates is one way to help build word analysis skills and vocabulary for English language learners (ELLs). Cognates are words in different languages that share the same roots. For example, the English word *directions* and the Spanish word *direcciones* are cognates. ELLs can be encouraged to look for known parts of unfamiliar words. They can then use knowledge about the meanings in their native languages to determine the meanings of the English words. This strategy builds upon ELLs' prior knowledge. Explicitly teaching common roots and affixes can help ELLs quickly increase their vocabularies as well.

Scaffolding should also be provided when introducing ELLs to new words. This can be done using visuals that help demonstrate the meanings of the words. Real objects, pictures, and gestures can all be used. Graphic organizers can also be used to show how new words are related and how they connect to specific topics.

TEACHING WORD ANALYSIS SKILLS TO STRUGGLING READERS

Struggling readers require consistent and explicit instruction, which often includes a combination of both whole-class instruction and targeted individual or small-group instruction daily. They also need frequent opportunities to manipulate words. Both building and breaking apart related words using letter tiles can help struggling readers develop understandings of patterns in the ways words are made.

Struggling readers can also benefit from explicit instruction on chunking words into component parts. Depending on the ages and prior knowledge of the students, this might include identifying syllable patterns, onsets and rimes, roots and affixes, or smaller sight words that are part of the larger words.

Struggling readers also need frequent opportunities to practice their word analysis skills using real texts. After explicit instruction on recognizing prefixes in words, for example, students can read texts that contain several prefixes. They can identify these words and their meanings. This will help them transfer their word analysis skills to realistic contexts. Scaffolding can be provided through anchor charts, graphic organizers, and teacher support during these independent reading experiences to provide reminders of known strategies.

TEACHING WORD ANALYSIS SKILLS TO HIGHLY PROFICIENT READERS

Proficient readers still have a need for differentiated reading instruction, even if they are meeting or exceeding grade-level expectations. They can benefit from developing the same word analysis skills as other readers, such as looking for known parts in unfamiliar vocabulary words, breaking words into components, and finding relationships between the meanings and spellings of different words. These strategies should be presented using materials and interactions that are both engaging and appropriately challenging for proficient readers. Use of texts that have some unfamiliar words will ensure that readers have opportunities to apply these strategies and continue to increase their vocabularies. Using assessments to determine reading levels or teaching readers to self-select appropriate texts can help ensure that the selected materials offer some challenges and learning opportunities for proficient readers.

Because proficient readers often devote less energy to decoding words than struggling readers, they are able to allocate more energy to reading comprehension, analysis, and reflection. Proficient readers can be asked to evaluate authors' word choices and discuss the effect that certain words have on the meaning or tone of the texts.

UNDERSTANDING GRAPHOPHONICS, SYNTAX, AND SEMANTICS READING STRATEGIES

Reading strategies can be used and applied to different situations as needed. The types of text a student reads may differ greatly in terms of vocabulary, quality of context clues, picture support, and connections to the reader's prior knowledge. Therefore, the strategies that work to determine an unknown word in any one sentence or text may not work as well in another. These strategies are often unreliable. Instead, teachers should encourage readers to use phonics knowledge to decode unknown words. Proficient and skilled readers do not rely on cues when identifying an unknown word.

While these reading strategies are not recommended for instructional purposes, it is important to know the difference between strategies a reader may be using. Decoding words using graphophonic clues is a strategy where readers consider the letter-sound relationships in the word. Another strategy is to consider syntax, or how the word sounds in the sentence and fits into the overall sentence structure. A third strategy is to consider semantics, or the meaning of the text, to guess the unknown word. Basically, the reader is trying to determine if the unknown word looks right (graphophonics), sounds right (syntax), and makes sense (semantics).

When it comes to reading unknown words, it is best practice for students to use phonetic knowledge to decode words. Students who lack a basic understanding of phonics may rely on cues while reading unknown words. Thus, explicit and systematic phonics instruction is necessary in order to develop proficient readers.

HELPING STUDENTS USE CONTEXT CLUES TO FIGURE OUT THE MEANINGS OF UNKNOWN WORDS

Teachers should explicitly introduce students to different types of context clues, including definition, antonym, synonym, and inference clues. Examples of sentences containing each type can be provided, and students can be asked to mark the clues, label each type, and explain the meanings of the unknown words. They can also be asked to find examples of each of these types of context clues in other texts. An anchor chart listing the different types of context clues and examples of each can also be posted in the classroom.

Students can also be given sets of words that are related in some way, such as pairs of synonyms or antonyms. They can be asked to write sentences that incorporate the word pairs, creating context clues for other readers. The students can then share their sentences with peers, asking them to identify the context clues and meanings of the unknown words.

> **Review Video: Reading Comprehension: Using Context Clues**
> Visit mometrix.com/academy and enter code: 613660

IMPORTANCE OF KNOWING LATIN AND GREEK ROOTS

Many English words are formed from Latin and Greek **roots**. Therefore, recognizing these roots and knowing their meanings can help readers with both decoding and comprehending.

When readers automatically recognize Latin and Greek roots, they will be able to quickly decode the main parts of words that contain them. If they automatically recognize the affixes as well, they will be able to break words into parts and decode them effortlessly. This will allow the readers to maintain speed and fluency while reading.

The roots also hold most of the meaning in words and form the bases of entire word families. Knowing the meanings of these roots will help readers quickly determine the meanings of many newly encountered words, especially if they also know the meanings of any attached affixes. For example, if readers know that the Latin root *port* means to carry, they will have clues about the meanings of the words *transport*, *transportation*, *import*, and *export* as well.

HELPING READERS IDENTIFY LATIN AND GREEK ROOTS IN UNFAMILIAR WORDS

When teaching readers about Latin and Greek roots in English words, one strategy is to help them see the relationships between words in the same word families. This can be done by creating charts or other visual representations of word families and their meanings. For example, a root and its meaning can be written in the middle of a web, and words containing the root and their meanings can be written in circles branching off from the root.

Another strategy is to create three sets of cards, including prefixes, suffixes, and roots. Students can experiment with combining the sets of cards to try to form real words. When real words are created, students can explain their meanings. Students can also be given words containing prefixes, roots, and suffixes. They can be asked to break the words into their components and identify the meanings of each part.

Additionally, students can be encouraged to locate words containing Latin and Greek roots in the texts they read independently. They can use their knowledge of the roots to define the words.

APPROACHES TO VOCABULARY LEARNING

- A **definitional approach** to vocabulary learning is the most traditional. Students are either provided definitions of words or look them up in a dictionary, and they are drilled until they commit the meanings to memory.
- A **structural approach** to vocabulary learning emphasizes the morphological features of words—the roots, prefixes, and suffixes. Once students learn the recurring morphemes in English, they can deduce the meaning of a word in isolation without relying on its context.
- A **contextual approach** to vocabulary learning provides the students with multiple examples of a word used in realistic contexts, allowing them to infer the meaning without resorting to a dictionary or an explicit definition.
- A **categorical approach** to vocabulary learning groups words into categories based on a semantic similarity. For example, a student might be given a list of words associated with driving a car, such as "steering wheel," "to brake," "to accelerate," and "gear shift."
- A **mnemonic approach** to vocabulary learning builds associations between target words and mental images so that hearing a target word evokes the image, facilitating recall of the word's meaning.

> **Review Video: Types of Vocabulary Learning (Broad and Specific)**
> Visit mometrix.com/academy and enter code: 258753

ROLE OF NON-CONTEXTUAL STRATEGIES IN VOCABULARY DEVELOPMENT

Non-contextual strategies are used when new vocabulary is learned without seeing or hearing the words in context. For example, teachers may give students lists of new vocabulary words they have not yet encountered in texts. The teachers may ask students to define the words, use them in sentences, and memorize them. Quizzes may then be given in which students must match the words to their definitions or provide examples of the terms.

There are times teachers may use non-contextual vocabulary strategies, such as when students are learning content-specific words that are not often found naturally in texts. When studying parts of speech, for example, teachers may have students memorize the definitions of *noun*, *verb*, and *adjective*. These words are important for students' understanding of sentence structure, yet students are not likely to encounter these words written in texts with contextual clues. However, it is recommended that teachers do use contextual strategies whenever possible.

Students can be taught to use tools such as dictionaries to define unknown words when contextual clues are not available. They can be prompted to draw pictures to explain word meanings or use graphic organizers to show the relationships among words.

ROLE OF CONTEXTUAL STRATEGIES IN VOCABULARY DEVELOPMENT

Contextual strategies are used to determine the meanings of unknown vocabulary words when they are encountered in context. The ability to use these strategies to quickly determine word meanings is important for both reading fluency and comprehension. Because words can have multiple meanings, readers also need to use contextual strategies to determine which meaning makes sense in a given sentence.

Teachers can explicitly teach students about the different types of contextual clues often found in sentences. They can encourage students to highlight the words and phrases that provide clues about meanings of the vocabulary words.

Contextual clues often include synonyms or antonyms for the unknown vocabulary words. Therefore, when introducing new words, teachers can assist students with creating lists of synonyms and antonyms. Teachers can also ask students to solve analogies or determine which word does not belong when given a group of related words. These activities will help students recognize synonyms and antonyms and understand relationships among words when they are encountered in context.

CRITERIA FOR SELECTING VOCABULARY WORDS FOR INSTRUCTION

Vocabulary words can be divided into three tiers. Teachers should consider these tiers when determining which words to focus on during instruction.

- **Tier one words** are common words used in everyday speech. They are typically learned by the early grades through normal conversation. Explicit instruction on the meanings of these words is seldom needed.
- **Tier two words** are found in both fiction and nonfiction texts and are common enough that readers will likely encounter them in multiple texts. Tier two words carry a lot of meaning and can negatively affect comprehension if they are not understood by readers. When deciding which tier two words to focus on, teachers should consider how the words affect the overall meanings of the texts and their morphologies. They should consider if students will be able to form connections between these words and other words, helping them understand unfamiliar words encountered in the future.
- **Tier three words** are mostly found in nonfiction texts and are domain-specific. These words are important for understanding the texts and their domains. Because students are unlikely to have encountered these words before, explicit instruction is needed. This often includes pre-teaching the words and analyzing them in context.

Comprehension of Literary and Informational Text

CULTURAL INFLUENCES ON LANGUAGE DEVELOPMENT AND USE
ROLE OF SOCIAL CONTEXT IN LANGUAGE DEVELOPMENT AND USAGE

Members of a group have a shared social identity that is formed by reading, writing, listening, and speaking with one another. Group members develop common expressions, mannerisms, and favorite stories that are understood by other members. For example, members of a professional group may use academic language specific to their field at conferences and work events. However, they will not likely use these terms while talking with people outside the field.

Additionally, **social context** plays a role in how people select the appropriate language to use. When asking a stranger for directions, a person would likely consider social norms and begin with an expression like "Excuse me." When talking with a good friend on the phone, a person might use an informal, joking tone. It is important for people to consider each situation and determine which approach to use.

Teachers can provide frequent opportunities for students to communicate with others for a variety of authentic purposes. This can include communicating with classmates, other students and adults within the school, family members, and community members.

ROLE OF CULTURAL CONTEXT IN LANGUAGE DEVELOPMENT AND USE

Language involves not only the words people say but also the ways in which these words are interpreted by recipients. Differing backgrounds and cultures can affect how messages are received, so it is important for people to consider that others may view communications differently. For example, in some cultures, students are encouraged to ask questions and initiate discussions in class. In others, students are expected to defer to their instructors and not speak unless they are directly questioned. A student who tells an instructor that something doesn't make sense may be praised for using metacognitive strategies in one class while perceived as being rude in another.

Cultural context also affects how nonverbal communications are interpreted. For example, different cultures have their own norms about making eye contact while speaking or the use of gestures during greetings.

Teachers should be sensitive to these cultural differences and consider the roles they may play in student participation and communication. Additionally, teachers should help students view situations from multiple perspectives and consider how their attempts at communication may be perceived by others in various situations.

INTERDEPENDENT RELATIONSHIP BETWEEN CULTURE AND LANGUAGE

The ways that people use language and interpret language directed toward them is related to their cultures. Additionally, as cultures change over time, so do languages. Existing words can take on new meanings, and new words may be added to languages. These changes sometimes occur as a result of popular culture, including television, video games, and music. As people with different cultural backgrounds interact, they must negotiate these differences to make meaning.

Because culture and language are so intertwined, understanding the cultural contexts in which language is used is an important part of learning any new language. English language learners should be taught English skills in context, helping them understand how the language is used in realistic social interactions. Additionally, it is important for teachers to understand the cultural backgrounds of ELLs and the roles their cultures may play in their language interactions and expectations. Teachers should incorporate a variety of teaching strategies and methods into their classrooms to meet the needs of all students.

COMPONENTS OF READING COMPREHENSION

READING COMPREHENSION

A basic definition of **reading comprehension** is understanding what has been read. However, reading comprehension is quite complex. It involves both taking meaning from the text and creating meaning by integrating the text with prior knowledge. It is an active process that requires the use of multiple skills and strategies, such as decoding, fluency, understanding word meanings, predicting, inferring, and more. It involves different levels of understanding, including comprehending both the literal meanings of the words and the unstated themes and implications of the text. Comprehension is one of the main goals of reading instruction.

Comprehension is essential to developing proficient readers. If readers are able to decode the words but cannot comprehend the messages, they won't make any meaning from the texts and will become easily frustrated. Because comprehension is an **active process**, it is also important for developing engaged readers who enjoy reading for a variety of purposes.

LITERAL COMPREHENSION

Literal comprehension refers to understanding the written meaning of a text. It involves a basic understanding of the text's vocabulary, events, main ideas, and other features. Literal comprehension is important because it is the foundation upon which deeper levels of comprehension are formed.

PROMOTING LITERAL COMPREHENSION

Answering **literal comprehension questions** using text evidence is one strategy to support development of this skill. This can be done through class discussions or written activities. Readers can be asked to identify the setting of the story, main characters, sequence of events, or other topics where the answers can be found directly in the text. Readers should be asked to provide text evidence for their answers, which might involve marking the sentences where the answers are found. Graphic organizers, such as story maps and problem/solution charts, can also help students develop literal comprehension skills.

To **scaffold** the development of literal comprehension, the teacher can begin by asking questions about a portion of the text immediately after it is read, using the same wording as the text. Over time, the wording can be varied and the teacher can wait for longer intervals before asking the questions.

INFERENTIAL COMPREHENSION

Inferential comprehension is a deeper level of understanding than literal comprehension. It requires inferring what the author meant. The answers to inferential comprehension questions are not found directly in the text. Readers must instead make inferences, draw conclusions, determine points of view, and make other informed decisions based upon the evidence provided in the text.

PROMOTING INFERENTIAL COMPREHENSION

To develop **inferential comprehension skills**, readers can be asked to make **predictions** or **inferences** and **draw conclusions**. This can be done using class discussions, written activities, or graphic organizers. For predictions, inferences, and conclusions, readers should be asked to provide text evidence to support their choices. This may involve marking parts of the text or recording relevant sentences. They should then be encouraged to evaluate their predictions, inferences, and conclusions as they continue reading. If new evidence conflicts with their initial predictions, inferences, or conclusions, readers should be encouraged to revise them as needed. Proficient readers self-monitor their comprehension and continually revise their understanding as additional evidence is gathered.

EVALUATIVE COMPREHENSION

Evaluative comprehension is a deeper level of understanding than literal comprehension and goes further than inferential comprehension. It requires readers to make judgments and share opinions about what they have read based upon evidence found in the text and prior knowledge. For example, evaluative comprehension questions might ask readers to consider if they would have handled an event in the text differently or explain whether they agree or disagree with the author's point of view.

PROMOTING EVALUATIVE COMPREHENSION

Because evaluative comprehension requires deeper thinking than literal comprehension, it is helpful for teachers to frequently model their thinking when responding to these types of questions. They can model how to identify relevant information within the text and draw upon prior experiences to form judgments about topics.

It is also helpful to provide readers with evaluative question stems they can reference when reading independently. These question stems can also be displayed on charts in the classroom.

SUMMARIZATION

Summarization refers to providing a concise description of the main idea and key details of a text. Summarization assists with comprehension by helping readers separate important information and vocabulary from unimportant information. It also helps readers remember what they have read.

Summarization is often a difficult skill for students to learn. Their initial summaries may provide too few or too many details from the text. Modeling and explicit instruction can help students learn to provide **effective summaries**. Students can be taught to reread a text and cross off unimportant or repetitive information. They can then be encouraged to locate and mark the main idea and key details that are essential to understanding the meaning of the text. Additionally, they can be encouraged to substitute general words for lists of related words in a category. For example, rather than listing all of the animals belonging to a character's family, students could use the word *pets* instead.

Readers can also complete **graphic organizers** to develop their summaries. One common type of graphic organizer asks students to complete the following sentence stems to form summaries: Someone, Wanted, But, So, Then.

ROLE OF PRIOR KNOWLEDGE IN READING COMPREHENSION

Research has shown that students learn best when they can relate new information to existing knowledge already stored in long-term memory. This helps them organize and make sense of the new information and apply it in future situations. When reading, prior knowledge can help students determine the meaning of unfamiliar vocabulary words, form predictions about what might happen next, make inferences, and make sense of story events. All of these skills are important for comprehension.

To activate students' prior knowledge, the teacher can ask what students already know about a topic when it is introduced. Students' contributions can be listed on a chart or graphic organizer. Know, want, and learned (KWL) charts can be completed, listing what students already know, want to know, and learned about the topic. The teacher can also ask students to make comparisons by asking how the new topic is similar to and different from something they have already learned.

DENOTATIVE VS. CONNOTATIVE MEANINGS

Words often have multiple meanings. **Denotative** meanings are the literal meanings of words. **Connotative** meanings are the secondary meanings of words and refer to the positive and negative associations that arise from them. For example, the denotative meaning of the word *heart* is a muscular organ in the circulatory system that pumps blood. A connotative meaning of the word *heart* is love.

There are several reference tools that can be used to locate the meanings of words. Dictionaries can be used to find the denotative and connotative meanings of words, along with other information like word origin and pronunciation. Thesauri can be used to find lists of synonyms for words, and antonyms are sometimes included as well. Glossaries list the definitions of important vocabulary words and are often found at the end of texts. All of these reference tools can be found in both print and digital forms.

HELPING LEARNERS RETELL FICTIONAL STORIES

There are specific steps teachers can take to focus readers' attention on key parts of stories to assist with retelling. Teachers can preview the stories with students and point out the key events they should listen for before they begin reading. During reading, they can pause and ask students to summarize the key events they have heard in the stories so far. After reading, teachers can lead students in shared retellings or ask students to retell the stories independently.

Students can fill out graphic organizers or create flip books that describe what happened in the beginning, middle, and end. They can also draw or act out the main story events. Additionally, students can be given sentence strips containing the main story events in a mixed-up order and asked to sequence them. Story ropes can also be used, where students tell story events in order as they move their hands along sets of beads or knots on ropes.

Mometrix

Retelling is important for story comprehension because it requires readers to identify and sequence the main story events. Readers must also consider other story elements, such as characters, setting, and plot, during retellings.

PURPOSES FOR READING

One purpose of reading is for entertainment, which is known as **aesthetic reading**. Sometimes readers select texts because they look interesting to read, and they read them just for fun. Selecting a fairy tale from the library for silent reading time and choosing a bedtime story are examples of times students read for entertainment.

Additionally, sometimes people read for information. This is known as **efferent reading**. It occurs when readers select nonfiction texts to learn something new. This might include learning new facts about a topic or learning the steps needed to accomplish a task. Selecting a book about whales while studying ocean life is an example of reading for information. Reading a recipe to prepare dinner is also an example of reading for information.

Reading to learn opinions is another purpose for reading. This type of reading occurs when people are trying to make decisions about things and look to others for advice. Reading online reviews before purchasing a product is an example of reading for opinions.

ASSISTING WITH COMPREHENSION BY RECOGNIZING THE AUTHOR'S PURPOSE

Recognizing the author's purpose can assist with comprehension in multiple ways. First, it can offer the readers clues about the text structures and features they are likely to encounter. If readers recognize that the author is writing to inform, they will know to look for features of informational texts, such as headings and content-specific vocabulary words. If readers recognize that the author is writing to entertain, they will know to pay attention to character traits, plot development, and other features of entertaining texts.

Additionally, knowing the **author's purpose** can help the reader evaluate the text more effectively. If readers recognize that the author is trying to persuade them, they will know to think critically about any claims that the author makes rather than accepting them at face value.

Knowing the author's purpose can also assist readers with determining if texts will meet their needs. For example, students may need to gather factual background information for a science experiment they are completing. They may preview a text and recognize that it is written for entertainment. They may then decide that the text is not suited to meet their needs in this circumstance.

> **Review Video: Understanding the Author's Intent**
> Visit mometrix.com/academy and enter code: 511819

TEACHING READERS TO RECOGNIZE AN AUTHOR'S PURPOSE

The author's purpose may be stated either explicitly or implicitly in a text. Readers can be taught to recognize text structures and features that help identify the author's purpose. Texts that are written to entertain often contain interesting characters and engaging plots. They may contain entertaining phrases and humor, and illustrations may be present.

Texts written to persuade usually contain evidence to support the author's points of view. This may include statistics, facts, and/or personal opinions. Readers can be asked if the authors appear to be for or against something to determine if texts are written to persuade.

Texts written to inform often include facts, which may be stated using text, charts, graphs, or other features. These texts may contain captioned photographs to provide additional information about the topics. Content-specific vocabulary words are often present. Readers can be asked if the authors appear to be trying to teach them about something to determine if texts are written for this purpose.

It is also important for readers to recognize that authors may have multiple purposes for writing. Readers may recognize text structures and features characteristic of two or more purposes within one text.

MAKING PREDICTIONS

When making predictions, readers gather evidence from the text and pictures to make inferences. They sequence story events and make connections between the text and prior experiences to predict what might happen next. Continually making and revising predictions also helps keep readers engaged. All of these activities support reading comprehension.

To help learners make predictions before shared reading experiences, teachers can conduct picture walks of texts. While showing the pictures, teachers can provide brief overviews of the stories, asking students to contribute their predictions about what each section might be about. During reading, teachers can pause to ask students to summarize what has happened so far and predict what might happen next. Teachers can model using prior experiences, picture and context clues, and memories of similar texts when making predictions.

Readers should be taught to evaluate their predictions to determine if they were correct. They should also be taught to look for additional information that might cause them to revise their original predictions. Readers can fill out charts listing their predictions, the evidence used to support these predictions, and what actually happened in the texts.

> **Review Video: Predictive Reading**
> Visit mometrix.com/academy and enter code: 437248

INFERRING

Authors sometimes provide clues in their writing rather than stating things explicitly. When this occurs, readers must make **inferences** or draw conclusions based on facts, prior knowledge, or text evidence rather than explicit statements. For example, an author might state that a character marched off and slammed the door. Although the author did not state it directly, readers may infer that the character is angry based on his actions.

- Making **inferences** is important for comprehension because much of the meaning in a text can be stated indirectly. If readers comprehend only direct statements, they may miss out on major themes or events in the story.
- Because **prior knowledge** can be used to make inferences, it is helpful for teachers to activate students' prior knowledge before reading through previewing and discussing what is known about the topic. Providing students with frequent opportunities to read varied texts can also build prior knowledge that will assist with inferring.
- Teachers can also show **pictures** to students and ask what inferences they can make based upon picture clues. Additionally, teachers can model **thinking aloud** while reading, discussing what inferences they are making and what prior knowledge, facts, or text clues they are using as evidence.

> **Review Video: Inference**
> Visit mometrix.com/academy and enter code: 379203

DRAWING CONCLUSIONS

Drawing conclusions is important for reading comprehension because it helps readers understand important events or concepts in a text that are not directly stated. Drawing conclusions about an author's purpose for writing can also help readers better evaluate the text because they will be aware of potential bias.

To help readers learn to draw conclusions, teachers can provide students with several supporting details about common topics and ask what conclusions they can draw. For example, they could describe a house with balloons, streamers, presents, and a cake in the kitchen, leading to a conclusion that it is somebody's birthday.

A graphic organizer can be used to organize this information, with the conclusion in the middle and the supporting details branching off from this conclusion. This process can then be repeated using details found in texts. This will show readers how they can use prior knowledge and text evidence to form conclusions when they read independently.

METACOGNITION

Metacognition is when readers think about their own thinking. Proficient readers continuously self-monitor their own reading. They ensure that they are making meaning from the text. If things do not make sense, they use strategies to self-correct the issues. Metacognitive strategies are important for reading comprehension because they ensure that readers are actively engaged while reading and that they understand what they have read. Modeling these strategies by thinking aloud is an important way to help students learn and apply these strategies in their independent reading.

Metacognitive strategies before reading include previewing the text, making predictions, and setting a purpose for reading. Metacognitive strategies during reading include visualizing, making connections, rereading to clarify confusion, and asking self-monitoring questions. Readers also utilize text features to locate and make sense of key information. Metacognitive strategies after reading include summarizing, drawing conclusions, and determining if any unanswered questions remain that need additional clarification.

COMPARING AND CONTRASTING

Readers can **compare and contrast** many things when reading, such as characters, settings, story events, multiple texts, and more. This supports comprehension because readers must recall details and find text evidence to compare and contrast. Comparing and contrasting also requires higher-level thinking skills, can help readers organize information, and can clarify confusion between two things.

Venn diagrams are a common way to help readers **compare and contrast** information. Text evidence and prior knowledge can be used to identify features that are the same and different between two things, and they can then be listed in the appropriate sections of the diagram.

Students can also be taught to identify key words that signal whether two things in a text are the same or different. Word such as *similarly* and *like* signal that two things are the same, whereas words and phrases such as *although* and *on the other hand* signal that two things are different. A chart that lists these key words and phrases can be displayed in the classroom as a reminder for students to use when reading.

> **Review Video: <u>Compare and Contrast</u>**
> Visit mometrix.com/academy and enter code: 798319

RECOGNIZING MAIN IDEAS AND DETAILS

The ability to recognize the main ideas and supporting details of texts assists with comprehension. Main ideas and supporting details help readers identify what the texts are covering and determine what message an author is trying to send.

Understanding paragraph structure can help readers locate the main idea and supporting details. Readers can be taught that the main idea is typically located in either the first or last sentence of the paragraph.

Readers can be encouraged to locate the main idea and mark it and then locate all supporting details and mark them in a different way. Main ideas and details can also be written on webs or other graphic organizers to help readers comprehend what they have read. Scaffolding can be provided when readers are first learning to complete these graphic organizers and then gradually withdrawn.

Prereading activities, such as discussing the title and previewing the pictures, can also help readers form initial thoughts about the main idea of a text. They can revise their initial thoughts as they read.

DISTINGUISHING BETWEEN FACTS AND OPINIONS

Facts are statements that can be proven to be true. For example, stating that George Washington was the first president of the United States is a fact. **Opinions** are statements that cannot be proven true or false. They represent people's judgements or views of something. Stating that cats are easier to take care of than dogs is an opinion.

It is important for readers to distinguish between facts and opinions. Recognizing when statements are opinions can help readers identify any biases the authors may have and recognize that the authors may be trying to persuade them. Distinguishing between facts and opinions is important when reading any text, but it necessitates special consideration when using digital sources. Anyone can post information online, and readers must be able to evaluate the sources effectively to determine if they are based on fact or opinion.

To teach students to identify facts and opinions, teachers can introduce the terms and provide examples of each. Students can be asked to mark examples of facts and opinions in texts using different colors. They can also be encouraged to look for key words that signal opinions, such as *think*, *believe*, *feel*, *best*, and *favorite*.

> **Review Video: <u>Distinguishing Fact and Opinion</u>**
> Visit mometrix.com/academy and enter code: 870899

ANALYZING AND INTERPRETING AN AUTHOR'S CRAFT AND STRUCTURE

An **author's craft** refers to an author's style of writing. It includes all of the choices an author makes when writing a text, such as word choice, text structure, point of view, use of literary elements, message, tone, and more. When focusing on an author's craft, readers analyze all of these choices and consider the effects they have on readers.

Analyzing and interpreting an author's craft and structure helps readers reach a deeper level of comprehension than surface comprehension. It aids them in understanding how different elements of the text work together to convey a certain meaning and tone. It helps them recognize that authors make several deliberate choices throughout the writing process about how to convey their messages most effectively, which will assist readers with making choices in their own writing. Additionally, it encourages active engagement with the text because readers are continuously analyzing and interpreting while they read. Comparing and contrasting an author's craft using different texts and other authors can also help readers make connections.

CLOSE READING

Close reading refers to reading and analyzing a text in a thoughtful manner to develop a deep understanding of its meaning, theme, use of language, and other elements. When close reading, readers first read through the text to determine the general meaning. They then reread the text to analyze the use of language and theme. They also make connections between the text and themselves, other texts, or real-world events and form evaluations. The goal of close reading is to develop independent readers who are able to gather deep meaning from texts with little or no scaffolding. Therefore, close reading activities do not involve previewing, picture walks, or other prereading activities.

Not all texts are ideal for close reading activities. Teachers should choose texts with deep meaning and multiple elements to discuss and analyze. They should consider the **complexity** of vocabulary, syntax, and meaning when choosing appropriate texts for close reading. Teachers should also consider the complexity of text features and structures.

Teachers can model how to reread texts and analyze different elements each time. They can guide students in this process by asking questions that require increasingly higher-level thinking skills after each reading of the text.

IMPORTANCE OF BEING ABLE TO SYNTHESIZE

Synthesis is the ability to gather information from multiple sources and combine it to make meaning. It is important because it requires readers to think critically about which parts of texts hold key information. Synthesis also requires readers to summarize and put ideas into their own words rather than repeat the texts verbatim. All of these skills assist with comprehension. Synthesis is also important when readers need to gather information about topics from multiple sources. The sources may differ in format and viewpoint, and readers must be able to find and combine the important points from each.

To teach students to **synthesize**, teachers can model tracking their thinking throughout the reading of a text and explain how it changes as new information is gathered. They can use phrases such as, "I used to think ____, but now I think ____. My thinking changed because____." Text evidence can be cited to explain the changes.

Readers can also be given **graphic organizers** to fill out as they read, recording key points in their own words. After compiling the key points, students can explain the main ideas they learned from the texts and how their thinking changed as they read.

READING VARIOUS TYPES OF TEXTS

GENRES OF FICTION

Realistic fiction stories are about events that could happen in real life. The characters and settings are realistic. **Historical** fiction stories also contain realistic characters, settings, and events, but they take place in the past—often during important times in history. **Mysteries** contain crimes or puzzling events that the characters must solve. **Fantasies** contain story elements that are unrealistic, such as talking animals or magic. **Science-fiction** stories focus on imagining life with advanced science or technological capabilities and other theorized situations, such as the existence of extraterrestrial life.

Folktales are another type of fiction. They are popular stories that are passed down from generation to generation, often by word of mouth. Fairy tales are one type of folktale. They often contain magical events and creatures, take place in enchanted places, have happy endings, and have good characters battling evil characters. There are often multiple versions of fairy tales. Cinderella is one example. Tall tales are folktales that are portrayed as if they were realistic but include characters with superhuman traits and exaggerated events. Paul Bunyan is an example of a tall tale.

> **Review Video: <u>Best Tips for Effectively Reading Fiction</u>**
> Visit mometrix.com/academy and enter code: 391411
>
> **Review Video: <u>Myths, Fables, Legends, and Fairy Tales</u>**
> Visit mometrix.com/academy and enter code: 347199

IMPORTANCE OF BEING ABLE TO RECOGNIZE DIFFERENT GENRES OF FICTION

Understanding the characteristics of different genres and being able to correctly classify texts by type is beneficial to readers for many reasons. Knowledge of the typical text structures of each genre assists readers with making predictions. For example, knowing that fairy tales typically end with good overcoming evil can help readers predict how stories will end. It also helps readers analyze texts deeply and incorporate characteristics of the genres in their own writing.

There are different approaches that can be used to teach about genres. One approach is to complete genre studies in which genres are explored in detail one at a time. Teachers may begin by providing explicit instruction on the characteristics of each genre and then give students opportunities to analyze examples. Teachers may also begin by sharing multiple texts of the same genre and asking students to identify common characteristics on their own. Another approach is to present multiple genres at once using a compare-and-contrast approach. No matter which approach is used, readers should have opportunities to explore many texts of each type of genre to develop an understanding of their common characteristics and text structures.

FICTIONAL STORY ELEMENTS

Fictional texts contain characters. There are both **primary characters**, who are central to the conflicts and resolutions of the stories, and **secondary characters**, who play smaller roles. The settings of the stories are another feature. The **settings** include both the times in history and the geographical locations where the stories occur. Fictional stories also contain problems or conflicts. The **conflicts** are usually introduced early in the stories to hook readers and encourage them to continue reading. The **plots** contain the main events of the stories, when the characters work to resolve the problems. The **solutions** contain the resolutions to the problems, which typically occur toward the ends of the stories. Fictional texts also typically contain **themes**, which are the underlying messages the authors are trying to convey to readers.

It is important for readers to understand that not all fictional texts contain every element. However, recognizing the common features will assist readers with making predictions and comprehending the texts.

> **Review Video: <u>Determining Relationships in a Story</u>**
> Visit mometrix.com/academy and enter code: 929925
>
> **Review Video: <u>How to Make a Story Map</u>**
> Visit mometrix.com/academy and enter code: 261719

TEACHING STUDENTS TO IDENTIFY FICTIONAL STORY ELEMENTS

A common way for teachers to introduce students to fictional story elements is modeling their thinking during shared reading experiences. For example, teachers may pause their reading when evidence is provided about the story's settings. The teachers may explain what they have gathered about the settings and show students which textual clues they used to make these determinations.

Graphic organizers, including story maps, are commonly used tools that help students locate and record story elements. These story maps typically ask students to locate the characters, settings, problems, events, and solutions in stories. Foldables or flip books can also be used to record these elements. These elements can be recorded using a combination of pictures and text depending on the ages and needs of the students. Students can also fill out these graphic organizers as prewriting activities when outlining their own stories.

Teachers should ask guiding questions to focus students' attention on story elements before reading. For example, they can ask students to listen for the problem in the story before they begin reading.

TYPES OF CHARACTERS FOUND IN FICTIONAL STORIES

There are several common types of characters found in fictional stories. However, not all fictional stories contain all types of characters.

- **Protagonists** are the main characters in fictional stories that readers can relate to and want to succeed. Protagonists can be complex characters with both positive and negative traits. Although readers empathize with protagonists, these characters do not always demonstrate admirable behavior.
- **Antagonists** are characters who stand in the way of protagonists accomplishing their goals. Antagonists are not necessarily bad characters and can also have both positive and negative traits.
- **Flat characters** do not change over time. Their actions and personalities are consistent throughout the stories. They are sometimes known as static characters.
- **Dynamic characters** change over time, usually as a result of experiencing the events in the narrative. Readers can identify changes in these characters as the story progresses. Dynamic characters change over time, usually as a result of experiencing the events in the stories. Readers can identify changes in these characters as the stories progress.

> **Review Video: <u>Definition of a Character in a Story</u>**
> Visit mometrix.com/academy and enter code: 429493

ANALYZING CHARACTER DEVELOPMENT

Authors of fictional texts present a variety of information about their characters. They describe the characters' physical characteristics, personality traits, hobbies, dreams and goals, and approaches to solving problems. After reading the stories, readers get to know the characters and develop the ability to predict how the characters might react to different types of situations. They also identify the roles that the characters play in the stories, such as being the protagonists or antagonists. Additionally, they determine whether or not any characters have changed as the stories progressed, and they identify reasons for these changes. All of these steps are part of analyzing **character development**.

Students can be asked to discuss character traits and complete character maps using text evidence from the stories. They can be asked to predict how characters would likely react in other situations, based upon their actions in the stories. Students can also be asked to describe how characters have changed from the beginnings of the stories to the ends, using text clues for support. They can compare and contrast characters from different texts or the same characters during different periods of time.

ROLE THAT THE SETTING PLAYS IN A STORY

Setting plays an important role in a story. It describes both the geographical location where the story takes place and the time in history when it occurs. A well-described setting also has the power to set the mood for the story. It can help readers visualize the story's events and imagine that they are present. This can assist readers with comprehension and increase engagement with the text.

To recognize setting, readers can be asked to identify both where and when the story takes place as well as to locate key words within the story that signal the answers to these questions. To explore setting more deeply, readers can be asked to identify how the story evokes their five senses. Using a graphic organizer, they can explore what the characters see, hear, taste, smell, and feel in the story. They can discuss how the use of these details helps readers visualize the setting, and they can be encouraged to use similar details in their own writing.

Teachers can also find examples of mentor texts with detailed settings. Students can explore the ways that the authors describe the settings and discuss how these details affect readers.

ELEMENTS OF POETRY

Discussing and analyzing poetry is a common part of literacy instruction. As part of this instruction, teachers can help students learn to recognize common elements in poetry and use the appropriate terminology to describe them.

There are several elements of poetry. A **verse** is a single line of poetry. Verses can be grouped together to form **stanzas**. The **rhythm** in a poem is developed from patterns of stressed and unstressed syllables. **Meter** refers to a poem's rhythmic structure. Some poems incorporate rhyme, which occurs when words end with the same sounds. **Rhymes** are often found at the ends of verses. Poetry can also use other literary elements, such as alliteration, similes, and metaphors.

Students can learn much about elements of poetry by exploring different types of poems. Students can be asked what they like or dislike about each poem, and these observations can be used to introduce the elements that are used. Students can also compare and contrast different types of poems to see how the elements can be used in different ways. While discussing these observations, teachers can also introduce the correct terminology and provide additional examples to explain how the elements are used by different poets.

> **Review Video: Structural Elements of Poetry**
> Visit mometrix.com/academy and enter code: 265216

HELPING STUDENTS DEVELOP AN APPRECIATION OF POETRY

There are many ways teachers can make learning about poetry fun and engaging for students. Early childhood and elementary students can be introduced to poetry during read-alouds and shared reading experiences. They can be encouraged to participate by clapping, making hand motions, and joining in the reading. As students get older, they can participate by highlighting and annotating poems and presenting them aloud to others.

Students can also be encouraged to explore different types of poetry to find styles that appeal to them. Free verse, sonnets, limericks, haikus, villanelles, and sestinas are just some examples of the many types of poetry. Students can also be encouraged to experiment with writing their own examples of different types of poetry.

Additionally, teachers can design poetry challenges for students. For example, students can be given magnetic words or print media that can be cut apart. Students can then explore rearranging the words into verses and stanzas to create different types of poems—seeing how the rhythm, meter, and other elements change. Students can also explore poetic elements in their favorite songs.

ENCOURAGING STUDENTS TO LOCATE AND USE EVIDENCE FROM NONFICTION TEXTS

Students can use T-charts while reading nonfiction texts. On the left side, they can record opinions, predictions, inferences, and similar thoughts made while reading. On the right side of the T-chart, students can record the **text evidence** used to support these thoughts.

Students can also complete scavenger hunts to find text evidence. Teachers can ask students **broad questions** that require higher-level thinking skills and instruct them to search nonfiction texts to find the answers. Information in the texts that are used to answer the questions can be highlighted or recorded on graphic organizers.

Teachers can also **model** this process for students. They can begin shared reading experiences by identifying what questions they want to answer by reading the texts. They can then model stopping when they reach evidence that answers the questions and making annotations as they go. Possible annotations include strong evidence presented by the author and additional questions that have arisen.

PROMOTING CLOSE READING OF NONFICTION TEXTS

Close reading activities are designed to help students deeply analyze texts. In all close reading activities, students begin reading without first completing any pre-reading activities. They reread the text multiple times, analyzing different layers each time.

The first time that students read the text, they can be encouraged to determine the overall main idea and supporting details. The second time they read the text, they can be encouraged to analyze the author's craft and the text structure. This might include determining which text structure the author used, identifying the key vocabulary words and their meanings, locating nonfiction text features, and establishing the author's purpose for writing. The third time that students read, they can be encouraged to evaluate the text, draw conclusions, and make connections to other texts, personal experiences, or real-world events.

Teachers can model this process for students during shared reading experiences. They can also provide students with graphic organizers to help them record information during each reading. Additionally, they can encourage students to highlight or make notes in the text to label key information.

ROLE READING FLUENCY PLAYS IN THE COMPREHENSION OF NONFICTION TEXTS

Fluency is important in comprehending any type of text. When readers are able to recognize words quickly and accurately, their working memories are available to focus on comprehension. Additionally, their thinking is not interrupted by stopping frequently to decode words.

Nonfiction texts present some special considerations for readers because they can utilize many types of structures. They also may contain several **content-specific vocabulary** words. Readers who are unfamiliar with these text structures and words may have difficulty locating key information and predicting what will come next, impeding comprehension.

Therefore, it is important to expose readers of all ages to a variety of text genres and structures. When practicing fluency passages, a combination of fiction and nonfiction texts should be included. Teachers should also model reading nonfiction texts so students will recognize what fluent reading sounds like.

PROMOTING COMPREHENSION OF NONFICTION TEXTS WITH WRITING ACTIVITIES

Writing can assist students with comprehension of nonfiction texts in many ways. Students often read nonfiction texts to learn new information or figure out how to accomplish tasks. They can create lists of questions they would like to have answered by the texts and record their answers as they read. They can also add additional questions that are generated by reading the texts.

Readers can **take notes** to record the main ideas and supporting details of nonfiction texts. There are many note-taking formats that can be used, such as outlining. Readers can also write text summaries or record the main concepts on semantic maps.

Additionally, there are many written response activities that can be used to encourage the use of **higher-level thinking skills**. Readers can write evaluations, compare and contrast essays, alternate endings, recommendations, and other similar responses.

APPLYING COMPREHENSION STRATEGIES TO DIGITAL TEXTS

Digital literacy includes the ability to make meaning from **digital texts**. Because the use of digital texts is now commonplace, teachers should give students opportunities to interact with both digital and print-based texts frequently.

Readers need to develop the ability to search **efficiently**. This includes generating lists of questions they want to have answered before they begin searching. It also includes selecting relevant search key words. Once search results are displayed, readers need to be able to scan the options and identify the links most likely to be relevant to their needs.

Digital texts are often nonlinear and contain multiple hyperlinks, so readers need the ability to break down the texts and **locate key information**. They can be taught to use note-taking strategies. This may involve using digital tools, like highlighting and annotation tools, or using graphic organizers.

Readers also need to develop the ability to identify author **bias** in digital sources. They should be encouraged to verify the sources and the validity of authors' claims.

Digital communications vary in **formality**. Readers should develop the ability to identify the **main points** in formal texts, like research articles, and informal texts, like blog posts.

PROMOTING COMPREHENSION BY BUILDING STUDENTS' ACADEMIC LANGUAGE

Academic language is language used in textbooks, class discussions, tests, and other school-related situations. It includes both vocabulary and syntax that differs from social language, which is less formal and structured.

Understanding the **vocabulary** of academic language is vital to understanding the authors' messages. If readers do not know the meanings of several key words, they will not understand the meanings of the texts and will be unable to analyze them deeply. Understanding academic syntax is also important because it helps students break down complex sentence structure to locate key information.

Students need **frequent exposure** to academic language and opportunities to use it across all content areas. For example, rather than asking students how texts are arranged, teachers can ask them to describe the *text structures*. Using these terms builds familiarity over time. Additionally, teachers can provide partial scripts that students can use to incorporate academic language when making presentations. To help students see the differences between social and academic language, teachers can also help students translate texts from one type to the other.

TYPES OF INFORMATIONAL TEXTS

- **Literary nonfiction** texts contain true information about topics but are presented using structures similar to fictional texts. They often include clear beginnings and endings and contain literary elements such as figurative language and imagery. Biographies, memoirs, and travel writing are examples of literary nonfiction.

- **Expository** texts are written to explain things using facts. They are structured differently than literary nonfiction texts.They often contain headings, tables of contents, glossaries, charts, graphs, and similar features. These text structures help readers navigate expository texts and locate specific information quickly. A science book explaining the water cycle is an example of an expository text.
- **Persuasive** texts are written to influence readers. They contain evidence to support the authors' claims. An advertisement urging readers to vote for a specific candidate is an example of a persuasive text.
- **Procedural** texts provide step-by-step directions for how to complete tasks. A manual describing how to complete office tasks using specific software is an example of a procedural text.

> **Review Video: Informational Text**
> Visit mometrix.com/academy and enter code: 924964

TEACHING READERS TO IDENTIFY DIFFERENT TYPES OF INFORMATIONAL TEXTS

Readers can look for specific features to identify types of informational texts. These features can be explicitly taught using example texts, and charts outlining each type of informational text and its features can be displayed in the classrooms.

- To identify **literary nonfiction** texts, readers can look for accurate and factual texts that are written using text structures commonly used in fiction. Although true, these texts read more like stories, with clear beginnings and endings. Literary elements such as figurative language and symbolism may also be included.
- To identify **expository texts**, readers can look for common expository text structures, including tables of contents, headings, sidebars, glossaries, charts, and other similar features. Readers should also be encouraged to check that the texts are factual because some fictional texts may contain these text features as well.
- To identify **persuasive texts**, readers can look for key phrases that signal opinions. These phrases include *I believe*, *you should*, and *in my opinion*. Readers can also look for details provided by the authors to support their viewpoints.
- To identify **procedural texts**, readers can look for clues that indicate sequence. This might include numbered steps or key words like *first*, *next*, and *finally.*

PURPOSES OF NONFICTION TEXTS

- One purpose of nonfiction texts is to **persuade**. In this type of text, authors try to convince readers to adopt their points of view using supporting statements. An article written by a doctor urging parents to limit their children's soda consumption is an example of a persuasive text.
- Another purpose is to **compare and contrast** two things. An essay comparing and contrasting the forms of government in two different countries is an example of this type.
- Other nonfiction texts are written to **inform**. These texts describe and explain topics using facts. A nonfiction book about characteristics of reptiles is an example of a text written to inform.
- Some nonfiction texts are written to **instruct**. These texts explain how to do something. A text about how to change a tire is an example of this type.
- Other nonfiction texts are written to **narrate** real-world events. These texts convey real information in entertaining and/or engaging ways. A personal narrative describing a funny event that occurred on a family vacation is an example of a text written for this purpose.

ADJUSTING READING STRATEGIES WHEN READING DIFFERENT TYPES OF TEXTS

It is important for students to self-monitor their reading and adjust their use of strategies depending upon the situation. This will help them focus their attention on key information. It will also ensure that they are comprehending the text and meeting their expected purposes for reading.

When students are reading fiction, they typically read from beginning to end rather than skipping around. This helps them understand the plot and correctly sequence story events. When reading nonfiction texts to answer specific questions, readers may utilize text features like the table of contents to jump to specific sections. This helps readers locate the desired information quickly.

When students are reading for entertainment, they may read the text at a faster rate than when they are reading to analyze specific literary elements or answer comprehension questions. Slowing the reading rate or rereading passages may allow for deeper interaction with the text.

FEATURES OF EXPOSITORY TEXTS

Expository texts often contain some common features. These features help readers locate and organize key information, and they also provide additional information about the content of the text.

The **table of contents** and **index** help readers know what information is presented in the text and on which pages to find certain topics. **Titles** and **headings** are used to separate content into sections of related information. Enlarged and/or **bolded print** is often used to draw attention to these titles and headings. Important vocabulary words are often highlighted or written in bold print to catch readers' attention. A **glossary** or set of sidebars is often included to provide definitions for these vocabulary words. Photographs or **illustrations** are used to convey information visually, and captions are used to explain their content. Charts, graphs, and tables are frequently used to present relevant data. Maps are also included to provide additional information about places discussed in the text.

HELPING READERS LOCATE AND IDENTIFY FEATURES OF EXPOSITORY TEXTS

There are many instructional strategies that can be used to help readers locate and identify features of expository texts. Leading students in feature walks is one common strategy. Using this strategy, teachers share informational and expository texts with students, previewing each section of the texts together. They point out each of the text's features, such as the titles, headings, table of contents, captions, and charts, and discuss the purposes of each. When reading the texts out loud, they model how to use the features to locate and make sense of key information.

To help readers locate and use these text features independently, charts listing the features and their functions can be posted in classrooms. Students can also be given blank charts they can use to record text features found while reading independently. Additionally, students can be given comprehension questions that require the use of text features to answer.

NONFICTION TEXT STRUCTURES

Some nonfiction texts use a **compare-and-contrast** structure. In this type of structure, both similarities and differences between two or more topics are explained. Sometimes the author presents each topic separately and then includes a discussion of similarities and differences. Other times, the author weaves back and forth between the two topics, comparing and contrasting different features along the way.

- **Cause and effect** is another nonfiction text structure. In this structure, the author describes an event and provides reasons why it happened.
- Another nonfiction text structure is **chronological order**. An author who retells the details of an event or period of time in the order that they happened is using this text structure.
- In the **problem/solution** text structure, a problem is introduced by the author. Possible solutions to the problem are then discussed.
- A **description** or **list** structure can also be used. In this type of structure, a topic is introduced. Descriptive details about the topic are then listed.

FAULTY REASONING IN NONFICTION TEXTS

Faulty reasoning occurs when conclusions are not supported by facts and evidence. The ability to recognize faulty reasoning is important because it helps readers evaluate the claims made in texts to determine if they are factual or not. It also helps readers identify potential author bias.

To assist readers with recognizing faulty reasoning, teachers can explicitly teach several different types and provide examples of how they are used in real texts. **Overgeneralizations** occur when authors draw conclusions based upon insufficient data. An example is stating that all fourth graders must like pizza because one fourth grader likes pizza. **Personal bias** occurs when authors base conclusions on personal opinions rather than factors or data. **Illogical conclusions** occur when authors draw conclusions about the relationships between things without data supporting the relationships. An example is stating that because someone was outside in the rain and later got a cold, the rain must have caused the cold.

Students can be encouraged to locate and share examples of faulty reasoning found during their independent reading experiences. They can also be encouraged to verify the sources used by authors to validate their claims and be wary of unsubstantiated online sources.

FIGURATIVE LANGUAGE
TYPES OF FIGURATIVE LANGUAGE

- **Similes** are one common type of figurative language used to compare two things using the terms *like* or *as*; for example, the child grew as fast as a weed.
- **Metaphors** are another common type of figurative language used to compare two things. Unlike similes, metaphors do not use the terms *like* or *as*. They simply state that one thing is another; for example, the star was a glistening diamond.
- **Personification** is a type of figurative language that gives human characteristics to nonhuman things, such as animals, objects in nature, or ideas; for example, the creek danced across the prairie.
- **Hyperbole** is a type of figurative language that uses exaggeration for effect. The exaggeration is so excessive that it is not intended to be taken literally; for example, if I don't eat now, I will starve to death.
- **Symbolism** is another type of figurative language. In symbolism, a writer uses a physical object as a representation of something other than its literal meaning. The symbol often represents something abstract, such as a feeling or idea; for example, diverging physical paths in a text can represent two people making different life choices.

> **Review Video: Figurative Language**
> Visit mometrix.com/academy and enter code: 584902

HELPING STUDENTS RECOGNIZE AND INTERPRET FIGURATIVE LANGUAGE

Some types of figurative language can be identified by recognizing **key words**. For example, students can be taught to recognize the words *like* and *as* in examples of similes. Students can be taught to recognize sound words, such as *buzz*, in examples of onomatopoeia. Charts displaying these key words can be displayed in the classroom.

Figurative language can also be explicitly taught, with teachers explaining each type and providing examples. Mentor texts can be used to provide examples of each type of figurative language, and students can be encouraged to locate additional examples on their own. When examples are identified, students can analyze the messages the authors are trying to convey through the use of figurative language.

Authors use figurative language to make their writing more descriptive and interesting. Because phrases containing figurative language cannot be literally translated, readers must have adequate background knowledge and/or use context clues to determine their meanings. The ability to recognize and interpret figurative language ensures that readers understand the authors' intended messages and are able to comprehend the depth of the story beyond the literal, surface meanings of the phrases.

ALLUSIONS

When authors use **allusions**, they refer to well-known people or events familiar to readers without describing them explicitly. For example, a character being warned to avoid opening Pandora's box is an example of an allusion. It refers to a commonly known story in Greek mythology, and readers are expected to know the meaning of the statement without any further explanation. Biblical, mythological, historical, and literary allusions are four common types. Allusions are commonly found in similes and metaphors.

To help readers recognize allusions, students can be asked to find examples of allusions in texts and discuss their types and meanings. Additionally, they can explore and evaluate the effects that allusions have on the meanings and tones of stories. Students can also be taught strategies for researching the meaning of unknown allusions they encounter while reading independently.

> **Review Video: <u>Allusions</u>**
> Visit mometrix.com/academy and enter code: 294065

IDIOMS

Idioms are a type of figurative language. They are expressions that have unique meanings that differ from the literal meanings of their component words. They are typically passed down within cultures. For example, "It's raining cats and dogs" is an idiom that means it is raining hard.

Idioms can be introduced to students a few at a time, with students contrasting the literal and figurative meanings. They can practice using context clues to determine the meanings of unknown idioms, and they can look for examples of idioms in texts. They can also explore the ways that idioms make writing interesting. For example, they can write a paragraph using the idiom, "It's raining cats and dogs." They can then rewrite the paragraph, substituting the words, "It's raining hard." They can compare the effects of each option on readers.

Special consideration should be given when using idioms with ELLs in the early stages of English language acquisition. Because vocabulary knowledge cannot be used to assist with comprehension of idioms, students may miss the meanings and become frustrated.

PROVERBS

Proverbs are short, well-known sayings that offer wisdom or advice. They are commonly passed down within cultures using oral language. An example of a proverb is: "Actions speak louder than words." Proverbs often use figurative language, and their literal meanings do not make sense. Therefore, students need to be taught to recognize proverbs and understand their figurative meanings to comprehend the overall messages of the texts containing them.

When introducing proverbs, teachers can help students understand the cultural and historical significance behind them. For example, the proverb "Don't look a gift horse in the mouth" refers to the historical practice of assessing a horse's teeth to determine its age. The proverb refers to being grateful for what you are given rather than assessing the worth of a gift. Teachers can help students research these proverbs to provide historical contexts for their meanings.

Students can write proverbs on graphic organizers and list both their literal and figurative meanings. They can analyze what the proverbs have in common, such as offering wisdom or advice about life. Additionally, when they are encountered in texts, readers can analyze how the meanings of the proverbs contribute to the meanings of the stories.

ROLE OF GRAMMAR IN READING COMPREHENSION

RELATIONSHIP BETWEEN UNDERSTANDING ENGLISH GRAMMAR/USAGE AND COMPREHENSION

There is evidence that having a strong understanding of English grammar and usage assists with reading comprehension. When readers are able to untangle complex sentences in texts and understand how the components work together to form meaning, they are better able to comprehend what was read. When answering comprehension questions, they are better able to locate key information within complex sentences. Readers are also better able to incorporate complex sentence structure in their own writing.

Understanding English grammar and usage includes knowledge of parts of speech, the roles that they play, and how they are arranged in English sentences. It also includes knowledge of how simple sentences can be combined to form complex sentences. Readers with strong syntactic knowledge are able to self-monitor their reading and recognize when something does not sound right due to decoding errors. The ability to self-monitor and make corrections when needed is important for comprehension.

> **Review Video: Grammar Skills and Reading Comprehension**
> Visit mometrix.com/academy and enter code: 411287

TEACHING ENGLISH GRAMMAR AND USAGE TO AID COMPREHENSION

One strategy to teach English grammar and usage to aid comprehension is to **break sentences apart** and analyze their components. Depending on the age and prior knowledge of the student, this may include **sentence diagramming**, dividing sentences into subjects and predicates, and splitting compound sentences into simple sentences. Students may also be asked to label sentence types—choosing from simple, compound, and complex sentences.

An alternative strategy is to combine words to form different types of sentences. Young readers may begin by combining only subjects and predicates to form the most basic types of sentences. As new parts of speech are learned, students can add additional words to form more complex sentences. Students can also be given word cards containing scrambled sentences. They can be asked to arrange the cards to form sentences, analyzing each attempt by asking if the sentences they have built sound right and make sense.

When given comprehension questions about texts, students can also highlight the parts of the sentences that contain the relevant information needed to respond.

SPOKEN VS. WRITTEN ENGLISH

Although there are some occasions for formal, scripted speech, most spoken English is informal and conversational in nature. Speech often includes a mixture of fragments and complete sentences and may include interrupting and switching between speakers. Grammar in spoken English tends to be less strict, and there is more flexibility in word order. There may be differences in pronunciation, pacing, and intonation among speakers, and listeners must adjust to these differences to comprehend what was said. Speakers can gauge the understanding of listeners and rephrase or re-explain when necessary. Unlike written text, there is no formal record of what was said to review later unless notes were taken or the speech was recorded. If speaking is part of an instructional lesson, listeners may benefit from being given overviews of the topics and guiding questions in advance to help focus their attention on key information.

On the other hand, written English allows for careful and deliberate organization. It is typically more formal and features more complex structures than spoken English. Word order is more rigid. Writers cannot gauge readers' understanding or re-explain if necessary, so the meaning needs to be clear. Readers are able to review the text later to further clarify information.

ROLE OF FREQUENT AND VARIED READING EXPERIENCES

Frequent and varied reading experiences allow readers to see diverse examples of how authors write. They can compare and contrast different writing styles and analyze how the audience, topic, and purpose of writing may affect formality and structure. For example, expository science texts will likely differ from graphic novels in formality. The science texts may also include more content-specific vocabulary words and use sentence patterns designed to present facts rather than resemble conversations. Additionally, readers can see vocabulary words and different parts of speech in context and observe how they work together to build meaning. They can also see the effects of different writers' word choices on the moods of the texts. Overall, frequent and varied reading experiences help readers become more comfortable with language.

Being exposed to varied texts also provides students with models of sentence structure and writing styles to emulate in their own writing. Students often consider examples of familiar texts that fit certain genres or themes, called mentor texts, when they write their own. Being exposed to a variety of reading experiences gives students more examples to draw upon when they are writing.

INDUCTIVE VS. DEDUCTIVE METHODS OF TEACHING GRAMMAR

- In **inductive** teaching, students read and analyze texts that contain similarities. They look for patterns and identify grammar rules by themselves. For example, a teacher might give students several compound sentences that contain semicolons to join the two component sentences. Students might be asked to determine what the sentences have in common, leading them to identify and discuss the use of semicolons to join two simple sentences. Benefits include active participation by students to determine the grammar rules and use of critical thinking skills.
- **Deductive** teaching is another method. In deductive teaching, students are explicitly told grammatical concepts and rules before being asked to apply them to their own reading and writing. For example, a teacher might present a lesson on using semicolons to create compound sentences and then ask students to look for examples of this rule during independent reading experiences. One benefit of this approach is that it can be quicker than inductive teaching. Some students may also be more accustomed to this teacher-centered type of approach.

Both methods of teaching grammar can be useful, and teachers often use a combination of both in their teaching.

Many teachers also use writing workshops to introduce grammar through mini-lessons and conferences with students. Using students' writing as informal assessment tools, teachers can determine which grammatical concepts and rules individual students need to practice.

ROLE OF GRAMMAR IN HELPING ELLS WITH COMPREHENSION

Understanding grammar can assist English language learners (ELLs) with reading comprehension. It helps them comprehend different types of sentences. Understanding punctuation marks and word order of different types of sentences helps ELLs determine if something is a statement, a command, or a question.

Additionally, discerning the functions of different **parts of speech** helps ELLs identify the parts of sentences that carry the most meaning. This aids in focusing their attention on the most important words in each sentence. Recognizing words and affixes that signal verb tense also helps ELLs determine when the action takes place. For example, an ELL might recognize that the verbs in a text end in *-ed* and realize that the story takes place in past tense.

Using **syntactic clues** is one important strategy readers use to make meaning from texts. To use syntactic clues, readers must have an understanding of what sounds right in English. When ELLs develop an understanding of English grammar and word order, they are better able to self-monitor their reading and determine if something sounds right. They are also better able to use context clues if they have an understanding of correct word order in English sentences.

TEACHING ELLs ENGLISH GRAMMAR AND USAGE

English language learners (ELLs) should be taught grammar and usage skills in realistic contexts rather than in isolation. It is also helpful to design grammar lessons around familiar topics and vocabulary so learners can focus on the grammar and usage concepts rather than trying to decipher the meaning.

Teachers should frequently **model** correct grammar and sentence structure through listening, reading, and speaking activities. One strategy is to read texts that model a specific grammar rule and ask ELLs to listen for examples of its use or apply it in their own writing. They can also be encouraged to look for patterns in grammar and usage, such as *-ed* and *-ing* endings.

Teachers need to carefully consider when and how to address grammatical and usage errors made by ELLs. Frequent and immediate corrections can cause **frustration**. However, if specific errors are not addressed over time, they may become **fossilized** and difficult to correct. One strategy is to note repeated errors and address them later in mini-lessons rather than at the time they are made. Teachers can also pick a small number of errors to focus on at any one time.

ENGLISH LANGUAGE PARTS OF SPEECH

The following are the eight parts of speech in the English language:

1. **Nouns** describe people, places, and things, for example, he ate a chocolate **cupcake**.
2. **Verbs** describe action or being; for example, the dog **chased** the squirrel around the yard.
3. **Pronouns** are words used in place of nouns, for example, **she** works in the office building downtown.
4. **Adjectives** describe nouns or pronouns. They usually describe which one, what kind, or how many of something, for example, the **yellow** house is located on the corner.
5. **Adverbs** describe verbs, adjectives, or other adverbs. They usually describe when, where, why, or how something happens, and they often end in *-ly*; for example, the fish swam **quickly** away from the shark.
6. **Prepositions** are words that relate nouns or pronouns to other words in the sentence; for example, the chef put the dough **in** the oven.
7. **Conjunctions** join words, phrases, or clauses; for example, the teacher **and** the principal attended the meeting.
8. **Interjections** show emotion in sentences; for example, **ouch**—I bumped my elbow.

When readers come across words whose meanings they do not know, knowing the parts of speech can help them determine the function of the words in the sentences. This will make it easier to guess the meanings using context clues.

> **Review Video: Parts of Speech**
> Visit mometrix.com/academy and enter code: 899611
>
> **Review Video: Nouns**
> Visit mometrix.com/academy and enter code: 344028

TEACHING STUDENTS TO RECOGNIZE DIFFERENT PARTS OF SPEECH

Parts of speech are typically introduced one or a few at a time. **Nouns** and **verbs** are often introduced first because they can be used as the building blocks of basic sentences. If an inductive method is used, students may be given a group of sentences with the same parts of speech highlighted and asked to determine what the words have in common. If a deductive method is used, teachers might explicitly teach what each part of speech does and provide examples.

Mini-lessons can also be used. A **mini-lesson** on nouns, for example, might include listing nouns that fit into the categories of people, places, and things. It might also include finding examples of nouns in texts or sorting words according to whether or not they are nouns. Teachers can also use shared reading and writing activities as opportunities to discuss parts of speech in context.

71

Sentence diagrams are pictorial representations that show how parts of speech work together to form sentences. Although sentence diagramming can help some students visualize sentence structure, it can be frustrating and tedious for others. Therefore, it can be considered as one component of grammar instruction as long as it fits the needs of the learners.

READING COMPREHENSION TOOLS AND STRATEGIES
GRAPHIC ORGANIZERS THAT PROMOTE READING COMPREHENSION AND ANALYSIS

Know, want, and learn (KWL) **charts** can be filled out before and after reading to identify what readers know, want to know, and learned about a topic. These charts help activate prior knowledge and give readers a purpose for reading. **Story maps** can be used to help readers identify the main elements of a story, such as characters, setting, problem, events, and solutions. **Character maps** can be used to describe traits of characters in the story.

Other graphic organizers can be used to help readers explain the relationships among events or ideas in a story. **Graphic organizers** can be used to help readers identify the problem and solution in a story, along with the events that led to the solution. Other graphic organizers can be used to record inferences and the text evidence used to make them. Graphic organizers like webs can be used to record the main idea and supporting details of a story. Venn diagrams can also be used to compare and contrast two stories, characters, or other elements.

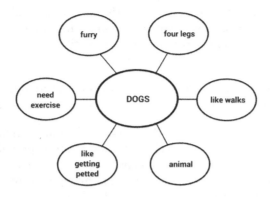

SQ3R READING STRATEGY

SQ3R is a strategy used to help students comprehend textbooks. The S stands for **survey**. In this step, students preview the text and note features like headings, graphs, and charts. They use this information to predict what the text is about. In the Q or **question** step, students reread the headings and convert them into questions. They then predict the answers to these questions. The first R stands for **reading**. In this step, students read the text and attempt to answer the questions they listed. They may also make annotations to note important points or additional questions. The second R stands for **recall**, and this step involves summarizing each section of the text immediately after it is read. The last R stands for **review**. Students attempt to answer their original questions without using the text. If they are unable to answer any questions from memory, they review the text and their notes for assistance.

The SQ3R strategy has several benefits. By surveying the text, students activate prior knowledge and set purposes for reading. Listing questions helps focus students' attention during reading. Annotating helps students analyze and make meaning from the text. Summarizing and reviewing help students remember key information.

Name: _____   Date: _____

SQ3R Chart

Title of Work: _____

Survey: Record important titles and subtitles from work.
_____
_____

Question: Write "Who, What, When, Where, and Why" questions from main topics.
_____
_____

Read: Write answers to questions from above.
_____
_____

Recite: Record key facts and phrases as needed for each question.
_____
_____

Review: Create a summary paragraph for each question.
_____
_____

TYPES OF LITERACIES

DIGITAL LITERACY

Digital literacy refers to the ability to communicate effectively using digital sources. It involves many component skills, such as locating, processing, analyzing, evaluating, and creating information in digital form. Information can be communicated digitally through websites, social media, apps, digital textbooks, multimedia presentations, emails, texts, and more.

The continually evolving nature of digital communication presents challenges for teachers. Tools, software, and equipment should be selected carefully based upon the ability to help students achieve learning objectives.

Teachers also need to help students locate and synthesize information from multiple sources and evaluate the sources for reliability. Students must also learn to share information responsibly and adhere to acceptable use policies. Additionally, students need to be taught to consider their audiences and purposes for communicating in digital environments, just as they do when communicating through speaking and writing. For example, different language and sentence structure will likely be used in business websites than in text messages. With global business and distance education now common, students also need to be taught how to use modern tools to collaborate with others.

MEDIA LITERACY

Media literacy refers to the ability to comprehend, evaluate, and create media. Media includes methods of communication, such as newspapers, magazines, videos, television, radio, and books.

Students need to critically evaluate the authors' messages and points of view to determine what biases may exist. They also need to determine whether the information presented is supported by reliable sources. Advertisements and testimonials may contain unsubstantiated information, for example.

Because there are many different types of media, students also need the ability to flexibly apply different comprehension strategies. For example, they may skim through newspaper articles to locate and highlight key information, whereas they may take notes during videos. Teachers should incorporate forms of media into classroom instruction and teach strategies for comprehending and evaluating each type.

Teachers can also allow students opportunities to present their learning using different forms of media, such as creating podcasts, writing newspaper articles, filming videos, and more. Students should be taught to consider which types of media will best convey their messages and reach their intended audiences. In addition to helping students develop media literacy, these project options will also accommodate students who prefer different learning modalities.

> **Review Video: Different Types of Media**
> Visit mometrix.com/academy and enter code: 785859

VISUAL LITERACY

Visual literacy refers to the ability to comprehend, evaluate, and create visuals. It includes all types of visuals, such as cartoons, photographs, illustrations, graphs, infographics, and maps.

Visual literacy is important from an early age. Before students can read words, they "read the pictures" to tell stories and make predictions. They are later presented with other visuals, such as graphs to explain data in nonfiction texts and infographics on websites.

As with all forms of media, students need to evaluate author bias and verify the sources used to create visuals. For example, they can be taught to consider where the data used to create graphs comes from. Students also need to extract key information from visuals by looking for clues, such as bolded print or use of color. Additionally, students need to be taught about the legal issues involved in creating visuals, including copyright issues. They also need to consider design and aesthetics issues.

Teachers can assist students with visual literacy by presenting information using a combination of print and visual forms and allowing students choices when completing assignments. For example, students can create posters to convince other classmates to read favorite books.

DATA LITERACY

Data literacy refers to the ability to comprehend, evaluate, gather, and organize data. With the increasing reliance on data analytics to drive business and education-related decisions, data literacy must be addressed in the classroom.

Students need to learn how to read and interpret **different representations of data**, such as charts, graphs, and tables. They also need to draw informed conclusions from the data and recognize potential author bias and data misuse.

Additionally, students must decide which types of data will be **useful** to answer specific questions and convey certain information. They need to determine the most effective ways to gather data and present it to others.

Teachers should incorporate data gathering and analysis into classroom activities across all subject areas. Students can gather data when completing science experiments and create tables and graphs to represent their findings. Teachers can conduct surveys with students and record their responses using poll-generating tools on the web. Mini-lessons can be focused on interpreting and evaluating data found in nonfiction texts.

FINANCIAL LITERACY

Financial literacy refers to making informed decisions about financial resources to prepare for a secure future. It includes skills such as saving and spending money, creating budgets, and paying bills. It also includes business-related terms like profit, expense, and revenue.

Although financial literacy is commonly linked to math skills like balancing checkbooks, it relates to traditional literacy as well. People must be able to read banking and billing statements and understand their terms and conditions. They must also critically evaluate financial offers, such as credit card deals, and consider authors' biases and underlying intentions. These skills are needed to make informed financial decisions.

While teaching about financial literacy, teachers should include a variety of realistic materials for students to read, analyze, and evaluate. They should be given opportunities to make and justify realistic financial decisions based on research and analysis.

INFORMATION LITERACY

Information literacy refers to the ability to locate, analyze, and evaluate information. It also refers to the ability to responsibly share information with others. Information can be obtained from a variety of sources, including websites, interviews, newspapers, books, and more.

Students first need to recognize when more information is needed. Teachers can encourage students to self-monitor their thinking and recognize when they need to learn more about topics before drawing conclusions. When planning a school garden, for example, students may recognize that they need to learn more about which plants grow well in their area. They may then consult gardening guides to select plants that are well suited for their climate and soil type.

Once information is located, it needs to be critically analyzed so students can comprehend it. They also need to consider author bias and reliability of sources. When sharing information, students need to ensure that they are using reliable sources and not misleading their audiences.

TECHNOLOGY LITERACY

Technology literacy involves the ability to use technological tools, equipment, and software to communicate effectively. It includes using technology to access, analyze, evaluate, and share information.

Technological tools are now commonly used in education, and teachers must dedicate instructional time to teaching students how to use them effectively and responsibly. Teachers can assist students with learning to use technology to locate information, such as teaching them to enter specific key words in search engines and skim the results for relevant matches. They can also teach students how to carefully select which technological tools they will use to accomplish specific tasks. For example, if students want to create visual representations of information for a class project, they may consider and evaluate the effectiveness of different infographic building tools.

Technology literacy also involves recognizing the possibilities and limitations of technology in accomplishing specific learning objectives. Additionally, it involves troubleshooting common technological problems and using technology in ethical and responsible ways.

MOTIVATING STUDENTS TO READ
CREATING SCHOOL ENVIRONMENTS THAT PROMOTE A LOVE OF READING

Helping students develop a lifelong love of reading is an important goal of literacy instruction. Teachers can model their own love of reading by talking about their favorite books and authors and modeling their own use of reading strategies. They can share stories of how reading has positively affected their own lives and opened up new opportunities.

- Teachers can also help develop **communities of readers** within their classrooms, making reading a social experience. Fun and interactive read-alouds and shared reading experiences can help create communities of readers, along with organizing literature circles and reader's theater activities. Favorite books can be reread multiple times, with students participating in the reading.
- Teachers can give students frequent opportunities to read **books of choice**. They can create classroom libraries containing multiple types of texts that students can access easily. Comfortable reading spaces, such as reading chairs and pillows, are also beneficial. Students should also have opportunities to visit their school libraries regularly.
- Additionally, teachers can guide students in completing **author studies**. Students may form connections to favorite authors and seek additional books they have written.

> **Review Video: Literacy-Rich Content-Area Classrooms**
> Visit mometrix.com/academy and enter code: 571455

PROMOTING SUCCESSFUL INDEPENDENT READING EXPERIENCES AT SCHOOL

Independent reading is beneficial for students' reading development and is sometimes necessary when teachers are working with other students. Therefore, some strategies can be used to make independent reading experiences successful.

It is important to teach students to select appropriate texts that will not lead to boredom or frustration. Some teachers instruct students to apply the five-finger rule. In this approach, students randomly select a single page of text to read. If they struggle to decode five or more words, the book is too difficult. Other teachers inform students of their reading levels and keep labeled boxes of leveled texts available. Students can also be encouraged to maintain personal book boxes that contain several appropriate books so that they are ready for independent reading time.

To remind students of decoding and comprehension strategies they can use during independent reading time, teachers can display posters in their classrooms. Students can also be given small, personalized copies of these strategies to use.

Additionally, students can be encouraged to analyze and discuss what they have read to build interest and engagement. They can maintain reader-response logs or join literature circles with others who have read the same texts.

MOTIVATING STUDENTS TO READ

One technique to motivate students to read is to make reading an enjoyable part of the daily routine. This includes designating daily time for reading, providing a comfortable, relaxed atmosphere, helping students select texts of interest, and showing genuine interest in discussing the texts together. This technique is easy to implement, and students who look forward to this reading time as children may continue reading for enjoyment in adulthood. A disadvantage is that some students may not respond to this approach.

Another technique is to use rewards and incentives for reading. Some programs reward students after they have read a certain number of books or for a certain number of minutes. Sometimes students are tested on the books they have read to assess comprehension. Read-athons are one example of this approach. Peer participation, competition, and opportunities to earn rewards may increase short-term motivation to read. Disadvantages include the costs of the incentives and the possibility that motivation will decrease once the rewards are removed.

Teachers frequently use a combination of these techniques by providing daily reading time while also incorporating some incentives for reading.

Written Expression

INSTRUCTIONAL ACTIVITIES THAT SUPPORT READING AND WRITING SKILLS
ACTIVITIES THAT SUPPORT READING, WRITING, LISTENING, AND SPEAKING DEVELOPMENT

Reading, writing, listening, and speaking are the four main components of English language development. All of these components are important and interdependent. They all play roles in making and conveying meaning, which are goals of literacy instruction.

These skills are sometimes practiced in isolation, such as when students listen to audio texts without any follow-up activities. However, when solving real-world problems, these skills are often used together. For example, doctors must listen to their patients' symptoms, make notes on the patients' charts, and then explain their treatment plans. Therefore, it is important for teachers to plan activities that integrate these four skills.

Project-based learning activities and performance assessments are useful for integrating these four skills. As an example, students could read about the benefits of recycling. They could then speak to the school principal to recommend implementing a school-wide recycling plan, listening and responding to the principal's concerns. They could then create posters to advertise the new program to other students.

CLOZE READING PROCEDURE

Cloze reading is an instructional strategy in which students read brief passages containing omitted words. They rely on background knowledge, semantic clues, and/or syntactic clues to determine the unknown words.

When designing cloze reading passages, teachers should consider a few key factors. The passages should be at the appropriate reading levels for the students. Students should be able to guess the omitted words by using reading strategies. If students need additional scaffolding to determine the missing words, word banks can be provided.

Cloze reading activities can be done independently or with partners. They can also be done as whole-class activities, with teachers reading the main passages and students supplying the missing words.

Cloze reading has several benefits. It requires students to use a variety of reading strategies, including using context clues, to determine the missing words. Students also cross-check their use of cueing systems to determine unknown words in cloze passages. If students read the passages multiple times to determine the missing words, it builds fluency as well.

LANGUAGE EXPERIENCE APPROACH TO READING INSTRUCTION

The **language experience approach** focuses on using students' own experiences as the topics of literacy experiences. Students think about experiences they would like to share. They dictate the experiences to teachers, who write the students' words down in front of them. The teachers then read the texts aloud while pointing to each word, modeling appropriate fluency. Students are then invited to join the teachers in rereading the texts.

The language experience approach can also be done as a whole-class activity, with classes writing about shared experiences together. For example, they could write about projects recently completed at school. Teachers help students generate ideas for what to include and list relevant vocabulary words that may be used. Students then dictate sentences to their teachers, who record them on chart paper. The classes then reread the texts multiple times.

A benefit of the language experience approach is that it involves reading, writing, listening, and speaking. It also builds upon students' prior knowledge and interests. If students are given multiple opportunities to reread the texts they have created, it also assists with fluency.

GUIDED READING AND SMALL GROUP READING INSTRUCTION

Guided reading is a term closely related to balanced literacy programs. Even though these programs are not considered to be best practice anymore, small groups should still be implemented in reading instruction. In guided reading, teachers arrange students in flexible groups and meet with each group separately. While meeting with each group, teachers provide leveled texts to each student, conduct picture walks, and focus on strategies that might be helpful when reading the texts. Instead of this, teachers should provide students with their own copies of decodable texts that are based off previously taught phonics skills. Before reading, teachers should review any irregular sight words that may appear and review previously taught phonics rules that will be helpful when reading the given texts. Teachers also should encourage the students to apply the rules they have learned to decode unknown words. Similarly to guided reading, students then read the texts independently in whisper voices while the teachers observe and make notes about students' reading. After students have read the texts independently, the teacher should conduct mini-lessons on skills that are targeted in the texts, such as specific phonics rules that are used a lot through the text. Students then take the texts to reread later, helping build fluency.

The flexible nature of reading groups ensures that students are always reading books within their instructional reading levels. Because the groups are small, teachers can target phonics skills that students within that specific group may still be struggling with. Teachers also have frequent opportunities to observe students' progress and determine which skills need additional practice.

SHARED READING EXPERIENCES

During **shared reading experiences**, teachers read aloud to students using materials like large print books, texts written on chart paper, and projected texts. Students follow along as teachers read and point to each word. Shared reading is an interactive experience, and teachers stop frequently to ask questions and model use of strategies. Depending on the ages and reading levels of the students, teachers focus on different teaching points. For example, kindergarten teachers may model and discuss concepts of print, whereas teachers of students in older grades may model and discuss comprehension strategies. Students may join the teachers in reading the texts as well.

Shared reading can be used across all subject areas and has several benefits. It allows students to see teachers modeling the use of reading strategies and practice using these strategies with scaffolding. It also allows students to participate in reading and discussing quality texts that they may not yet be able to read independently. Students learn about text features like punctuation marks and spelling patterns that they can incorporate into their own writing. They also have opportunities to hear examples of fluent reading.

Teaching Reading

READ-ALOUDS

During **read-alouds**, teachers read texts aloud to students. Depending on their purposes for reading, they may or may not pause to model the use of strategies or ask questions. Some read-alouds may be done strictly for entertainment purposes, whereas others may be done to provide background knowledge in content areas or allow for the modeling of reading strategies.

The key difference between read-alouds and shared reading experiences is that students do not have access to the texts during read-alouds. They listen as teachers read aloud, and they are sometimes shown the pictures. The focus is on listening to the texts and the teachers' use of strategies; students do not join in reading.

BENEFITS OF INDEPENDENT DAILY READING TIME

Independent daily reading has several benefits. Reading self-selected books can boost engagement with reading and help students develop a love of reading. When given opportunities to reread favorite texts, fluency may also increase. Independent reading also gives students opportunities to apply reading strategies to new texts autonomously.

Books for independent reading are usually self-selected. Students in the early stages of reading development who cannot read texts independently can be encouraged to "read the pictures." Teachers can model how to use prior knowledge and picture clues to tell the stories in their own words. Students who are able to read the words can be encouraged to select appropriate texts for independent reading time. Depending on the ages of the students, teachers may need to help readers build reading stamina. They can schedule a few minutes of daily independent reading time early in the school year and gradually add additional minutes. Teachers may schedule whole-class independent reading time or establish it as one station for students to complete during literacy stations.

Students can also be encouraged to have book boxes that contain several texts at the appropriate reading levels for use during independent reading time.

ROLE OF FLEXIBLE GROUPINGS IN EFFECTIVE READING INSTRUCTION

Flexible groupings are one way that teachers can differentiate instruction. When using **flexible grouping**, teachers strategically group students together to accomplish specific instructional goals. The groups may be large or small, and they vary depending on the activity. For example, a teacher may work with a small group of students who are all having difficulties with cause-and-effect relationships. The teacher is able to target instruction in this skill area to only the students who need extra practice. Guided reading groups are also flexible because students typically progress through instructional reading levels at different rates. Teachers can use both formal and informal assessment data to group students.

Flexible groupings have several benefits. They allow students to receive targeted instruction, often in small-group settings that allow for more teacher interaction. Students who have mastered these skills are able to work on other things, preventing them from becoming bored or frustrated. Additionally, students may feel more comfortable participating in small groups of their peers. Flexible groupings also mean that students will have opportunities to work with many other students throughout the year.

CONSIDERATIONS WHEN GROUPING STUDENTS FOR INSTRUCTIONAL PURPOSES

When determining when and how to group students for instructional purposes, teachers should take many factors into consideration. They should consider what instructional goals they want to accomplish. These goals are often based upon specific learning objectives.

Once teachers know what goals they want to accomplish, they can consider what types of groupings to use. Possibilities include partner learning as well as small or large group instruction. Teachers also need to consider the characteristics of the students in each group. For example, teachers may group students who need to practice specific skills together to target instruction. Other times, they may group students who have differing perspectives on topics to facilitate active discussion and sharing of viewpoints. These decisions should support the learning objectives. Teachers also need to consider what types of learning activities to use within the groups. Additionally, they need to consider what roles students will be assigned within their groups, if any. It is common for classrooms to use a variety of grouping arrangements throughout the year to accomplish different instructional goals.

CLASSROOM MANAGEMENT STRATEGIES FOR EFFECTIVE READING GROUPS

Reading groups are important components of literacy instruction because they allow students to receive differentiated, small-group instruction on a routine basis. However, they may be ineffective if frequent interruptions or classroom management issues occur. Clearly established and practiced routines can prevent these issues from occurring.

Students who are not working with their teachers in reading groups should be engaged in activities that they are able to successfully complete either independently or with the help of their peers. If center rotations are being used, students should know in what order to proceed through the centers and what the expectations are for each rotation.

Additionally, routines should be in place for how to solve problems without interrupting the reading groups. There should be clear criteria in place for when the teachers can be interrupted, such as in the case of emergencies. Students should be taught how to independently access any materials they may need to complete their activities. Hand signals or sign-out sheets may be utilized to minimize interruptions when students need permission to leave the classroom. Students can also be taught to ask a set number of classmates for assistance with problems before asking their teachers.

CHARACTERISTICS OF SHARED WRITING EXPERIENCES

During **shared writing experiences**, teachers and students collaboratively plan the content of shared writing pieces. Teachers assist their students with choosing topics, deciding which details to include, selecting words, and organizing text structure. Students are asked to share their ideas, and teachers help students organize their thoughts and put them into writing. Teachers control the writing instruments and put the words down on paper. Along the way, they may ask students for assistance with spelling words, determining how to punctuate, and other issues. Teachers model their thinking and use of writing strategies throughout the process. Once the drafting is finished, students may assist with revising, editing, and reading the texts aloud.

Shared writing experiences give students opportunities to be active participants in scaffolded versions of the writing process and work collaboratively to develop quality writing pieces. Additionally, they benefit from observing their teachers as they model the use of writing strategies.

CHARACTERISTICS OF INTERACTIVE WRITING EXPERIENCES

During **interactive writing experiences**, teachers and students work together to create shared writing pieces. With teacher guidance, students help plan writing topics, determine which details to include, and organize text structure. Students share the writing utensils with teachers and contribute to recording the words on paper. Teachers provide guidance along the way. For example, they may remind students of recently learned spelling patterns while students are spelling the words on paper. Classes may also work together to revise, edit, and read the writing pieces.

Giving students control over the writing utensils is what differentiates interactive writing from shared writing. In shared writing, teachers record the words on paper.

Interactive writing allows students to be active participants in the writing process while receiving scaffolding from teachers. It also allows students to collaboratively create quality writing pieces they are unable to produce independently at their current stages of writing development. Additionally, teachers can build targeted mini-lessons into the interactive writing process.

SUPPORTING THE DEVELOPMENT OF WRITING SKILLS
STAGES OF THE WRITING PROCESS

- In the **prewriting stage**, writers brainstorm ideas, decide on topics, and plan the structure of their writing. This may include brainstorming, using webs or other graphic organizers to map out main ideas and details, and creating outlines. Writers consider who their audiences will be and what their purposes are for writing.
- In the **drafting stage**, writers create their rough drafts. The focus of this stage is recording thoughts. Students are encouraged not to worry about spelling, grammar, and punctuation errors, which will be corrected later.
- In the **revising stage**, writers consider if any portions of their writing lack clarity or if any parts should be added or removed. They examine word choice and consider if there are ways to make the writing more descriptive. They also seek feedback from others about ways their writing could be improved.
- In the **editing stage**, writers carefully check their writing for spelling, capitalization, punctuation, and grammatical errors. They also ask others to edit their writing to ensure no errors are overlooked.
- In the **publishing stage**, writers share their writing with others. This may involve creating illustrated books, reading aloud in authors' circles, putting on plays, or presenting in other ways.

> **Review Video: The Recursive Writing Process**
> Visit mometrix.com/academy and enter code: 951611

TEACHING STUDENTS THE WRITING PROCESS

Modeling is an important strategy to help students become familiar with the writing process. Teachers can lead their classes in creating shared pieces of writing, going through each step as a group. Teachers can also share examples of their personal writing as they introduce each step of the process. Multiple examples that represent writing from various genres should be included to show students how the process can be applied to different types of writing.

Teachers can post charts outlining the **steps of the writing process** in their classrooms. Regular time should be set aside to work on writing so that, at the beginning of each session, students can identify which steps of the writing process they will focus on that day. This will help them establish goals for each session and maintain focus.

Teachers should also schedule time for frequent conferring with students to provide feedback and ensure they are staying focused on the process. Additionally, teachers can provide opportunities for students to reflect on the process and the changes they have made to improve their writing.

BENEFITS OF CONFERRING WITH STUDENTS DURING THE WRITING PROCESS

There are several benefits of conferring with students during the writing process. When writers know they will be frequently meeting with teachers, it increases accountability for following the writing process. It also gives teachers opportunities to provide timely feedback to students and personalize instruction based on their individual needs.

It is important for teachers to model the conference process for students before beginning. Students should be aware of the purposes of the conferences and the expectations for their roles. Additionally, students should practice routines for what to do while their teachers are conferring with others. This modeling and practice will increase the likelihood that conferences can be conducted without interruptions.

There are multiple ways that conferences can be conducted, but they typically include students sharing the progress they have made since their last conference and discussing any questions or concerns they have. Teachers usually pick a few points to focus on with each student, showing specific ways that improvements can be made using examples or mentor texts. Teachers should use the academic language of writing in their conferences. Additionally, conferences should be positive and motivating in nature to help students develop positive feelings about writing.

HELPING STUDENTS WRITE EFFECTIVELY FOR DIFFERENT AUDIENCES

As part of the prewriting process, writers should be encouraged to identify their **intended audience**. Once they have identified their audience, they should consider several factors. One factor is how much **prior knowledge** their audience has about the topics. This will affect what level of background information and detail the writers should go into to meet the **audience members' needs**. For example, writers who are explaining how to use computer programs will focus on different program capabilities depending on whether the audience members are beginners or advanced users. Another factor to consider is what type of relationship the writers have to their audience. This will affect the level of **formality** used in the writing. For example, a friendly letter to a classmate will be less formal than a letter written to a government representative.

Teachers should give students frequent opportunities to complete **authentic writing activities** for varied audiences rather than only submitting assignments for teacher evaluation. They can also provide opportunities for students to compare and contrast texts that are written about the same topics but written for different audiences.

HELPING STUDENTS EFFECTIVELY WRITE IN VARIOUS FORMS AND GENRES

Genre studies are one way to help students learn to effectively write in different genres. In **genre studies**, classes study one genre at a time, in detail, over the course of a few weeks. They read many different mentor texts in the genre and discuss common characteristics. Students can then be encouraged to complete their own writing activities within the genre, using the mentor texts as models.

A similar approach can be used to teach students to effectively write in different forms. For example, when learning to write friendly letters, students can explore many different examples. They can discuss common characteristics and use the examples as models when writing their own friendly letters.

Another strategy is to provide a mixture of **strong and weak examples** of a genre or writing form and ask students to evaluate their effectiveness. They can discuss which examples they think are the most effective and what characteristics these examples display that make them more successful. Similarly, they can discuss which features the weak examples contain or lack that make them less successful. They can then be encouraged to consider these findings during their own writing activities.

DEVELOPING WRITING SKILLS

Developing effective writing skills requires a multifaceted approach. Like reading, writing should be interwoven through the school day and all content areas rather than taught in isolation. It requires a combination of explicit skills instruction and opportunities to freely explore and experiment with writing. Skills instruction should include a wide range of topics, including spelling, grammar, language use, text structures, and more.

It is important to help students develop **positive attitudes** about writing. Building a community of writers where students can freely collaborate, share, and solicit feedback can help students feel safe and supported in the writing process. Students need to be explicitly taught how to solicit feedback from classmates and how to provide constructive and respectful feedback to others.

Because reading and writing are interrelated, students also need frequent opportunities to both read and write texts of different genres and purposes. They need to compare and contrast different texts and evaluate both their own writing and the writing of others. They should be explicitly taught how to participate in the five steps of the writing process, and they should receive frequent feedback on their writing. Feedback should provide specific suggestions for improvement in a positive and encouraging manner.

HELPING STUDENTS EFFECTIVELY COMPOSE WRITTEN TEXTS

While teaching the writing process, teachers should help students understand that quality writing takes time. They can model their own writing processes and share stories about the writing processes of favorite authors. Writing stamina can be developed gradually in younger students, with writing workshop time increasing as the year goes on.

- Although students need models of **quality writing**, they also benefit from seeing **weak examples**. Students can evaluate a range of writing samples and contrast their effectiveness. Comparing both strong and weak examples will help writers identify the characteristics of quality texts and consider them in their own writing.
- Students should also be encouraged to engage in **multiple rounds of revision**. Revisions should be based on feedback from both peers and teachers as well as personal reflection. Students should also be explicitly taught how to consider feedback critically and decide which suggestions to implement and which to disregard.
- Additionally, teachers should monitor students' writing through observation and conferences and plan mini-lessons based on the issues they notice. For writing that will be evaluated, **rubrics** should be given in advance. Students should be encouraged to consult the rubrics and **self-evaluate** their own writing at multiple stages throughout the process.

ASSISTING STUDENTS WITH THE REVISION PROCESS

Revising is often a difficult part of the writing process as students may struggle to see how they can improve their own writing pieces. First, it is important that students understand that the **focus of revision** is on improving clarity, detail, word choice, and other features rather than on the spelling and mechanical issues they will address during editing.

Modeling is often an effective way to help students understand the revision process. Teachers can share their own writing pieces and ask students to identify areas that do not make sense or could be explained in better detail. For example, teachers may ask students to close their eyes and visualize while they read one portion of their written pieces aloud. After asking students to share their visualizations, teachers may revise the writing to include more sensory details. Students can repeat the **visualization process** and note the differences. Teachers can also model writing sentences in multiple ways and ask which ways sound best. They may also help students identify descriptive words that can be used to replace commonly used words, such as replacing the word *nice* with *amiable*. These lists can be posted in classrooms for students to refer to when writing.

HELPING STUDENTS PRODUCE QUALITY WRITING IN THE CONTENT AREAS

In preparation for the workforce and independent living, students must be able to successfully write for a variety of purposes and audiences. This is essential because effective writing is required in many professions. For example, scientists publish research studies, sales professionals write sales reports, and marketing specialists create advertisements.

Going through the steps of the writing process helps students organize, synthesize, analyze, and evaluate complex information. They must make judgments about what information is relevant and which text structures should be used to best convey meaning. Putting content into their own words helps students comprehend difficult information and vocabulary. Therefore, writing in the content areas supports comprehension in these areas as well.

Teachers can provide varied types of texts to support learning in the content areas. This may include fiction books, journal articles, diaries, field guides, research studies, maps, interview transcripts, and more. Students should interact with various quality texts and discuss the roles they play in different professions.

HELPING STUDENTS RECOGNIZE AND USE ABBREVIATIONS AND ACRONYMS

Because there are numerous abbreviations and acronyms, teachers need to selectively choose which ones to focus on for instructional purposes. Therefore, teachers often address abbreviations and acronyms as they come up in students' reading and writing. For example, when writing letters, teachers can explain the abbreviations Dr., Mr., and Mrs. Teachers can also observe issues with abbreviations and acronyms as they occur in students' writing and address them through mini-lessons. Examples of abbreviations and acronyms can be pointed out in texts. Charts displaying common abbreviations and their long-form versions can also be displayed in classrooms to provide scaffolding before they are memorized.

In the age of digital communication and social media, it is also important to teach students when it is appropriate to use abbreviations and acronyms. Students need to consider their purpose for communication and their relationship with their audience. For example, informal acronyms may be appropriate for texts between friends but not for use in business letters.

PRINCIPLES OF EFFECTIVE WRITING

- **Clarity** and **brevity** are two related principles of effective writing. They require writers to include sufficient detail to convey their intended meanings while simultaneously omitting any extraneous or repetitive information. Students should be encouraged to consider the value that each word and sentence adds to their writing to determine whether or not it should be included. They should also consider the background knowledge of their intended audiences to ensure they go into the appropriate amount of detail to meet their needs.
- **Author's craft** and **voice** are also important principles of effective writing that draw readers in and compel them to read more. In fictional texts, they help readers identify with characters and make the stories seem realistic. These principles help maintain reader engagement with the texts.
- Additionally, careful **editing** is important for effective writing. If numerous errors are present, the meanings of the texts may be affected.

HELPING STUDENTS EDIT THEIR WRITING TO CORRECT ERRORS WITH MECHANICS

Frequent modeling is helpful when teaching students to edit. Teachers can model using editing checklists or rubrics to check for errors in their own work. The class can edit writing pieces they have composed together during shared writing experiences or edit texts containing errors written by other authors.

Teachers can also instruct students to **follow routines** when editing. This may include completing editing checklists or recalling mnemonic devices to ensure that all areas have been checked. CUPS is one mnemonic device that can be used to remind young writers to check for capitalization, usage, punctuation, and spelling. Because it can be difficult for students to recognize errors in their own writing, teachers can also encourage students to edit their own work first and then ask other students to edit it as well.

Additionally, students benefit from frequent, shared reading experiences using large print books, projected digital texts, or other means that allow them to follow along as teachers read. Teachers can stop to point out how authors use capital letters, punctuation marks, and other conventions. Frequently seeing these conventions in use will help students understand their purposes and notice when they are used incorrectly in other texts.

HELPING STUDENTS USE CORRECT PUNCTUATION IN THEIR WRITING

Teachers can explicitly teach students about each punctuation mark by introducing it, discussing its purpose, and demonstrating how to use it correctly in writing.

Students should also have frequent opportunities to explore how punctuation is used in context. They can be asked to find examples of certain punctuation marks in texts and examine the roles they play in the sentences. They can try reading the sentences with the given punctuation marks. They can then reread them with the punctuation marks omitted or substituted and discuss the differences in meaning and tone. For example, students could read a sentence in a book ending with a period, using appropriate intonation and pausing. They could then substitute the period for an exclamation point, adjusting their intonation. They could discuss how the meaning and tone of the sentence changed. Students can also edit their own writing by reading it aloud, using the intonation and phrasing suggested by the punctuation marks they included. They can ask themselves if any areas sound unclear, such as if sentences seem to blend together. They can also use punctuation checklists and ask other classmates to edit their work to double-check for errors.

> **Review Video: <u>Consistency in Punctuation</u>**
> Visit mometrix.com/academy and enter code: 169489

HELPING STUDENTS USE CORRECT CAPITALIZATION IN THEIR WRITING

One strategy to teach proper capitalization is to give students texts and ask them to circle all capital letters. Students can then be asked to identify what the words with capital letters have in common, leading to a discussion of capitalization rules. These rules can also be explicitly taught with examples provided.

- Posters can be displayed in classrooms as reminders of when to capitalize letters, such as at the beginnings of sentences, when using proper nouns, or when writing the word *I*.
- Additionally, students can be asked to edit texts, including their own writing pieces, to locate capitalization errors. Students should be reminded that errors may include both randomly capitalized letters and lowercase letters that should be capitalized.
- The ability to differentiate between common and proper nouns is needed to apply capitalization rules correctly. To assist with this skill, students can complete word sorts with common and proper nouns. They can also locate and circle examples of each type in texts.

> **Review Video: <u>Capitalization in Grammar</u>**
> Visit mometrix.com/academy and enter code: 369678

Chapter Quiz

Ready to see how well you retained what you just read? Scan the QR code to go directly to the chapter quiz interface for this study guide. If you're using a computer, simply visit the bonus page at **<u>mometrix.com/bonus948/praxeems7001</u>** and click the Chapter Quizzes link.

Mathematics

Numbers and Operations

NUMBER BASICS

CLASSIFICATIONS OF NUMBERS

Numbers are the basic building blocks of mathematics. Specific features of numbers are identified by the following terms:

Integer – any positive or negative whole number, including zero. Integers do not include fractions $\left(\frac{1}{3}\right)$, decimals (0.56), or mixed numbers $\left(7\frac{3}{4}\right)$.

Prime number – any whole number greater than 1 that has only two factors, itself and 1; that is, a number that can be divided evenly only by 1 and itself.

Composite number – any whole number greater than 1 that has more than two different factors; in other words, any whole number that is not a prime number. For example: The composite number 8 has the factors of 1, 2, 4, and 8.

Even number – any integer that can be divided by 2 without leaving a remainder. For example: 2, 4, 6, 8, and so on.

Odd number – any integer that cannot be divided evenly by 2. For example: 3, 5, 7, 9, and so on.

Decimal number – any number that uses a decimal point to show the part of the number that is less than one. Example: 1.234.

Decimal point – a symbol used to separate the ones place from the tenths place in decimals or dollars from cents in currency.

Decimal place – the position of a number to the right of the decimal point. In the decimal 0.123, the 1 is in the first place to the right of the decimal point, indicating tenths; the 2 is in the second place, indicating hundredths; and the 3 is in the third place, indicating thousandths.

The **decimal**, or base 10, system is a number system that uses ten different digits (0, 1, 2, 3, 4, 5, 6, 7, 8, 9). An example of a number system that uses something other than ten digits is the **binary**, or base 2, number system, used by computers, which uses only the numbers 0 and 1. It is thought that the decimal system originated because people had only their 10 fingers for counting.

Rational numbers include all integers, decimals, and fractions. Any terminating or repeating decimal number is a rational number.

Irrational numbers cannot be written as fractions or decimals because the number of decimal places is infinite and there is no recurring pattern of digits within the number. For example, pi (π) begins with 3.141592 and continues without terminating or repeating, so pi is an irrational number.

Real numbers are the set of all rational and irrational numbers.

> **Review Video: <u>Classification of Numbers</u>**
> Visit mometrix.com/academy and enter code: 461071
>
> **Review Video: <u>Prime and Composite Numbers</u>**
> Visit mometrix.com/academy and enter code: 565581

NUMBERS IN WORD FORM AND PLACE VALUE

When writing numbers out in word form or translating word form to numbers, it is essential to understand how a place value system works. In the decimal or base-10 system, each digit of a number represents how many of the corresponding place value—a specific factor of 10—are contained in the number being represented. To make reading numbers easier, every three digits to the left of the decimal place is preceded by a comma. The following table demonstrates some of the place values:

Power of 10	10^3	10^2	10^1	10^0	10^{-1}	10^{-2}	10^{-3}
Value	1,000	100	10	1	0.1	0.01	0.001
Place	thousands	hundreds	tens	ones	tenths	hundredths	thousandths

For example, consider the number 4,546.09, which can be separated into each place value like this:

> 4: thousands
> 5: hundreds
> 4: tens
> 6: ones
> 0: tenths
> 9: hundredths

This number in word form would be *four thousand five hundred forty-six and nine hundredths*.

> **Review Video: <u>Place Value</u>**
> Visit mometrix.com/academy and enter code: 205433

RATIONAL NUMBERS

The term **rational** means that the number can be expressed as a ratio or fraction. That is, a number, r, is rational if and only if it can be represented by a fraction $\frac{a}{b}$ where a and b are integers and b does not equal 0. The set of rational numbers includes integers and decimals. If there is no finite way to represent a value with a fraction of integers, then the number is **irrational**. Common examples of irrational numbers include: $\sqrt{5}$, $\left(1 + \sqrt{2}\right)$, and π.

> **Review Video: <u>Rational and Irrational Numbers</u>**
> Visit mometrix.com/academy and enter code: 280645
>
> **Review Video: <u>Ordering Rational Numbers</u>**
> Visit mometrix.com/academy and enter code: 419578

NUMBER LINES

A number line is a graph to see the distance between numbers. Basically, this graph shows the relationship between numbers. So a number line may have a point for zero and may show negative numbers on the left side

Mathematics

87

of the line. Any positive numbers are placed on the right side of the line. For example, consider the points labeled on the following number line:

We can use the dashed lines on the number line to identify each point. Each dashed line between two whole numbers is $\frac{1}{4}$. The line halfway between two numbers is $\frac{1}{2}$.

Review Video: <u>The Number Line</u>
Visit mometrix.com/academy and enter code: 816439

ABSOLUTE VALUE

A precursor to working with negative numbers is understanding what **absolute values** are. A number's absolute value is simply the distance away from zero a number is on the number line. The absolute value of a number is always positive and is written $|x|$. For example, the absolute value of 3, written as $|3|$, is 3 because the distance between 0 and 3 on a number line is three units. Likewise, the absolute value of –3, written as $|-3|$, is 3 because the distance between 0 and –3 on a number line is three units. So $|3| = |-3|$.

Review Video: <u>Absolute Value</u>
Visit mometrix.com/academy and enter code: 314669

OPERATIONS

An **operation** is simply a mathematical process that takes some value(s) as input(s) and produces an output. Elementary operations are often written in the following form: *value operation value*. For instance, in the expression $1 + 2$ the values are 1 and 2 and the operation is addition. Performing the operation gives the output of 3. In this way we can say that $1 + 2$ and 3 are equal, or $1 + 2 = 3$.

ADDITION

Addition increases the value of one quantity by the value of another quantity (both called **addends**). Example: $2 + 4 = 6$ or $8 + 9 = 17$. The result is called the **sum**. With addition, the order does not matter, $4 + 2 = 2 + 4$.

When adding signed numbers, if the signs are the same simply add the absolute values of the addends and apply the original sign to the sum. For example, $(+4) + (+8) = +12$ and $(-4) + (-8) = -12$. When the original signs are different, take the absolute values of the addends and subtract the smaller value from the larger value, then apply the original sign of the larger value to the difference. Example: $(+4) + (-8) = -4$ and $(-4) + (+8) = +4$.

Mathematics

SUBTRACTION

Subtraction is the opposite operation to addition; it decreases the value of one quantity (the **minuend**) by the value of another quantity (the **subtrahend**). For example, $6 - 4 = 2$ or $17 - 8 = 9$. The result is called the **difference**. Note that with subtraction, the order does matter, $6 - 4 \neq 4 - 6$.

For subtracting signed numbers, change the sign of the subtrahend and then follow the same rules used for addition. Example: $(+4) - (+8) = (+4) + (-8) = -4$

MULTIPLICATION

Multiplication can be thought of as repeated addition. One number (the **multiplier**) indicates how many times to add the other number (the **multiplicand**) to itself. Example: $3 \times 2 = 2 + 2 + 2 = 6$. With multiplication, the order does not matter, $2 \times 3 = 3 \times 2$ or $3 + 3 = 2 + 2 + 2$, either way the result (the **product**) is the same.

If the signs are the same, the product is positive when multiplying signed numbers. Example: $(+4) \times (+8) = +32$ and $(-4) \times (-8) = +32$. If the signs are opposite, the product is negative. Example: $(+4) \times (-8) = -32$ and $(-4) \times (+8) = -32$. When more than two factors are multiplied together, the sign of the product is determined by how many negative factors are present. If there are an odd number of negative factors then the product is negative, whereas an even number of negative factors indicates a positive product. Example: $(+4) \times (-8) \times (-2) = +64$ and $(-4) \times (-8) \times (-2) = -64$.

DIVISION

Division is the opposite operation to multiplication; one number (the **divisor**) tells us how many parts to divide the other number (the **dividend**) into. The result of division is called the **quotient**. Example: $20 \div 4 = 5$. If 20 is split into 4 equal parts, each part is 5. With division, the order of the numbers does matter, $20 \div 4 \neq 4 \div 20$.

The rules for dividing signed numbers are similar to multiplying signed numbers. If the dividend and divisor have the same sign, the quotient is positive. If the dividend and divisor have opposite signs, the quotient is negative. Example: $(-4) \div (+8) = -0.5$.

> **Review Video: Mathematical Operations**
> Visit mometrix.com/academy and enter code: 208095

PARENTHESES

Parentheses are used to designate which operations should be done first when there are multiple operations. Example: $4 - (2 + 1) = 1$; the parentheses tell us that we must add 2 and 1, and then subtract the sum from 4, rather than subtracting 2 from 4 and then adding 1 (this would give us an answer of 3).

> **Review Video: Mathematical Parentheses**
> Visit mometrix.com/academy and enter code: 978600

EXPONENTS

An **exponent** is a superscript number placed next to another number at the top right. It indicates how many times the base number is to be multiplied by itself. Exponents provide a shorthand way to write what would be a longer mathematical expression, Example: $2^4 = 2 \times 2 \times 2 \times 2$. A number with an exponent of 2 is said to be "squared," while a number with an exponent of 3 is said to be "cubed." The value of a number raised to an exponent is called its power. So 8^4 is read as "8 to the 4th power," or "8 raised to the power of 4."

> **Review Video: Exponents**
> Visit mometrix.com/academy and enter code: 600998

ROOTS

A **root**, such as a square root, is another way of writing a fractional exponent. Instead of using a superscript, roots use the radical symbol ($\sqrt{}$) to indicate the operation. A radical will have a number underneath the bar, and may sometimes have a number in the upper left: $\sqrt[n]{a}$, read as "the nth root of a." The relationship between radical notation and exponent notation can be described by this equation:

$$\sqrt[n]{a} = a^{\frac{1}{n}}$$

The two special cases of $n = 2$ and $n = 3$ are called square roots and cube roots. If there is no number to the upper left, the radical is understood to be a square root ($n = 2$). Nearly all of the roots you encounter will be square roots. A square root is the same as a number raised to the one-half power. When we say that a is the square root of b ($a = \sqrt{b}$), we mean that a multiplied by itself equals b: ($a \times a = b$).

A **perfect square** is a number that has an integer for its square root. There are 10 perfect squares from 1 to 100: 1, 4, 9, 16, 25, 36, 49, 64, 81, 100 (the squares of integers 1 through 10).

> **Review Video: Roots**
> Visit mometrix.com/academy and enter code: 795655
>
> **Review Video: Perfect Squares and Square Roots**
> Visit mometrix.com/academy and enter code: 648063

WORD PROBLEMS AND MATHEMATICAL SYMBOLS

When working on word problems, you must be able to translate verbal expressions or "math words" into math symbols. This chart contains several "math words" and their appropriate symbols:

Phrase	Symbol
equal, is, was, will be, has, costs, gets to, is the same as, becomes	=
times, of, multiplied by, product of, twice, doubles, halves, triples	×
divided by, per, ratio of/to, out of	÷
plus, added to, sum, combined, and, more than, totals of	+
subtracted from, less than, decreased by, minus, difference between	−
what, how much, original value, how many, a number, a variable	x, n, etc.

EXAMPLES OF TRANSLATED MATHEMATICAL PHRASES

- The phrase four more than twice a number can be written algebraically as $2x + 4$.
- The phrase half a number decreased by six can be written algebraically as $\frac{1}{2}x - 6$.
- The phrase the sum of a number and the product of five and that number can be written algebraically as $x + 5x$.
- You may see a test question that says, "Olivia is constructing a bookcase from seven boards. Two of them are for vertical supports and five are for shelves. The height of the bookcase is twice the width of the bookcase. If the seven boards total 36 feet in length, what will be the height of Olivia's bookcase?" You would need to make a sketch and then create the equation to determine the width of the shelves. The height can be represented as double the width. (If x represents the width of the shelves in feet, then the height of the bookcase is $2x$. Since the seven boards total 36 feet, $2x + 2x + x + x + x + x + x = 36$ or $9x = 36$; $x = 4$. The height is twice the width, or 8 feet.)

SUBTRACTION WITH REGROUPING

A great way to make use of some of the features built into the decimal system would be regrouping when attempting longform subtraction operations. When subtracting within a place value, sometimes the minuend is smaller than the subtrahend, **regrouping** enables you to 'borrow' a unit from a place value to the left in order to get a positive difference. For example, consider subtracting 189 from 525 with regrouping.

First, set up the subtraction problem in vertical form:

$$\begin{array}{r} 525 \\ -\ 189 \\ \hline \end{array}$$

Notice that the numbers in the ones and tens columns of 525 are smaller than the numbers in the ones and tens columns of 189. This means you will need to use regrouping to perform subtraction:

$$\begin{array}{r} 5 \quad 2 \quad 5 \\ -\ 1 \quad 8 \quad 9 \\ \hline \end{array}$$

To subtract 9 from 5 in the ones column you will need to borrow from the 2 in the tens columns:

$$\begin{array}{r} 5 \quad 1 \quad 15 \\ -\ 1 \quad 8 \quad 9 \\ \hline 6 \end{array}$$

Next, to subtract 8 from 1 in the tens column you will need to borrow from the 5 in the hundreds column:

$$\begin{array}{r} 4 \quad 11 \quad 15 \\ -\ 1 \quad 8 \quad 9 \\ \hline 3 \quad 6 \end{array}$$

Last, subtract the 1 from the 4 in the hundreds column:

$$\begin{array}{r} 4 \quad 11 \quad 15 \\ -\ 1 \quad 8 \quad 9 \\ \hline 3 \quad 3 \quad 6 \end{array}$$

> **Review Video: Subtracting Large Numbers**
> Visit mometrix.com/academy and enter code: 603350

ORDER OF OPERATIONS

The **order of operations** is a set of rules that dictates the order in which we must perform each operation in an expression so that we will evaluate it accurately. If we have an expression that includes multiple different operations, the order of operations tells us which operations to do first. The most common mnemonic for the order of operations is **PEMDAS**, or "Please Excuse My Dear Aunt Sally." PEMDAS stands for parentheses, exponents, multiplication, division, addition, and subtraction. It is important to understand that multiplication and division have equal precedence, as do addition and subtraction, so those pairs of operations are simply worked from left to right in order.

Mathematics

For example, evaluating the expression $5 + 20 \div 4 \times (2 + 3)^2 - 6$ using the correct order of operations would be done like this:

- **P:** Perform the operations inside the parentheses: $(2 + 3) = 5$
- **E:** Simplify the exponents: $(5)^2 = 5 \times 5 = 25$
  - The expression now looks like this: $5 + 20 \div 4 \times 25 - 6$
- **MD:** Perform multiplication and division from left to right: $20 \div 4 = 5$; then $5 \times 25 = 125$
  - The expression now looks like this: $5 + 125 - 6$
- **AS:** Perform addition and subtraction from left to right: $5 + 125 = 130$; then $130 - 6 = 124$

> **Review Video: Order of Operations**
> Visit mometrix.com/academy and enter code: 259675

PROPERTIES OF EXPONENTS

The properties of exponents are as follows:

Property	Description
$a^1 = a$	Any number to the power of 1 is equal to itself
$1^n = 1$	The number 1 raised to any power is equal to 1
$a^0 = 1$	Any number raised to the power of 0 is equal to 1
$a^n \times a^m = a^{n+m}$	Add exponents to multiply powers of the same base number
$a^n \div a^m = a^{n-m}$	Subtract exponents to divide powers of the same base number
$(a^n)^m = a^{n \times m}$	When a power is raised to a power, the exponents are multiplied
$(a \times b)^n = a^n \times b^n$ $(a \div b)^n = a^n \div b^n$	Multiplication and division operations inside parentheses can be raised to a power. This is the same as each term being raised to that power.
$a^{-n} = \dfrac{1}{a^n}$	A negative exponent is the same as the reciprocal of a positive exponent

Note that exponents do not have to be integers. Fractional or decimal exponents follow all the rules above as well. Example: $5^{\frac{1}{4}} \times 5^{\frac{3}{4}} = 5^{\frac{1}{4}+\frac{3}{4}} = 5^1 = 5$.

> **Review Video: Properties of Exponents**
> Visit mometrix.com/academy and enter code: 532558

FACTORS AND MULTIPLES

FACTORS AND GREATEST COMMON FACTOR

Factors are numbers that are multiplied together to obtain a **product**. For example, in the equation $2 \times 3 = 6$, the numbers 2 and 3 are factors. A **prime number** has only two factors (1 and itself), but other numbers can have many factors.

A **common factor** is a number that divides exactly into two or more other numbers. For example, the factors of 12 are 1, 2, 3, 4, 6, and 12, while the factors of 15 are 1, 3, 5, and 15. The common factors of 12 and 15 are 1 and 3.

A **prime factor** is also a prime number. Therefore, the prime factors of 12 are 2 and 3. For 15, the prime factors are 3 and 5.

The **greatest common factor** (**GCF**) is the largest number that is a factor of two or more numbers. For example, the factors of 15 are 1, 3, 5, and 15; the factors of 35 are 1, 5, 7, and 35. Therefore, the greatest common factor of 15 and 35 is 5.

> **Review Video: Factors**
> Visit mometrix.com/academy and enter code: 920086
>
> **Review Video: Prime Numbers and Factorization**
> Visit mometrix.com/academy and enter code: 760669
>
> **Review Video: Greatest Common Factor and Least Common Multiple**
> Visit mometrix.com/academy and enter code: 838699

MULTIPLES AND LEAST COMMON MULTIPLE

Often listed out in multiplication tables, **multiples** are integer increments of a given factor. In other words, dividing a multiple by the factor will result in an integer. For example, the multiples of 7 include: $1 \times 7 = 7$, $2 \times 7 = 14$, $3 \times 7 = 21$, $4 \times 7 = 28$, $5 \times 7 = 35$. Dividing 7, 14, 21, 28, or 35 by 7 will result in the integers 1, 2, 3, 4, and 5, respectively.

The least common multiple (**LCM**) is the smallest number that is a multiple of two or more numbers. For example, the multiples of 3 include 3, 6, 9, 12, 15, etc.; the multiples of 5 include 5, 10, 15, 20, etc. Therefore, the least common multiple of 3 and 5 is 15.

> **Review Video: Multiples**
> Visit mometrix.com/academy and enter code: 626738

FRACTIONS, DECIMALS, AND PERCENTAGES

FRACTIONS

A **fraction** is a number that is expressed as one integer written above another integer, with a dividing line between them $\left(\frac{x}{y}\right)$. It represents the **quotient** of the two numbers "x divided by y." It can also be thought of as x out of y equal parts.

The top number of a fraction is called the **numerator**, and it represents the number of parts under consideration. The 1 in $\frac{1}{4}$ means that 1 part out of the whole is being considered in the calculation. The bottom number of a fraction is called the **denominator**, and it represents the total number of equal parts. The 4 in $\frac{1}{4}$ means that the whole consists of 4 equal parts. A fraction cannot have a denominator of zero; this is referred to as "*undefined*."

Fractions can be manipulated, without changing the value of the fraction, by multiplying or dividing (but not adding or subtracting) both the numerator and denominator by the same number. If you divide both numbers by a common factor, you are **reducing** or simplifying the fraction. Two fractions that have the same value but are expressed differently are known as **equivalent fractions**. For example, $\frac{2}{10}$, $\frac{3}{15}$, $\frac{4}{20}$, and $\frac{5}{25}$ are all equivalent fractions. They can also all be reduced or simplified to $\frac{1}{5}$.

When two fractions are manipulated so that they have the same denominator, this is known as finding a **common denominator**. The number chosen to be that common denominator should be the least common multiple of the two original denominators. Example: $\frac{3}{4}$ and $\frac{5}{6}$; the least common multiple of 4 and 6 is 12. Manipulating to achieve the common denominator: $\frac{3}{4} = \frac{9}{12}$; $\frac{5}{6} = \frac{10}{12}$.

Review Video: <u>Overview of Fractions</u>
Visit mometrix.com/academy and enter code: 262335

PROPER FRACTIONS AND MIXED NUMBERS

A fraction whose denominator is greater than its numerator is known as a **proper fraction**, while a fraction whose numerator is greater than its denominator is known as an **improper fraction**. Proper fractions have values *less than one* and improper fractions have values *greater than one*.

A **mixed number** is a number that contains both an integer and a fraction. Any improper fraction can be rewritten as a mixed number. Example: $\frac{8}{3} = \frac{6}{3} + \frac{2}{3} = 2 + \frac{2}{3} = 2\frac{2}{3}$. Similarly, any mixed number can be rewritten as an improper fraction. Example: $1\frac{3}{5} = 1 + \frac{3}{5} = \frac{5}{5} + \frac{3}{5} = \frac{8}{5}$.

Review Video: <u>Proper and Improper Fractions and Mixed Numbers</u>
Visit mometrix.com/academy and enter code: 211077

ADDING AND SUBTRACTING FRACTIONS

If two fractions have a common denominator, they can be added or subtracted simply by adding or subtracting the two numerators and retaining the same denominator. If the two fractions do not already have the same denominator, one or both of them must be manipulated to achieve a common denominator before they can be added or subtracted. Example: $\frac{1}{2} + \frac{1}{4} = \frac{2}{4} + \frac{1}{4} = \frac{3}{4}$.

Review Video: <u>Adding and Subtracting Fractions</u>
Visit mometrix.com/academy and enter code: 378080

MULTIPLYING FRACTIONS

Two fractions can be multiplied by multiplying the two numerators to find the new numerator and the two denominators to find the new denominator. Example: $\frac{1}{3} \times \frac{2}{3} = \frac{1\times2}{3\times3} = \frac{2}{9}$.

DIVIDING FRACTIONS

Two fractions can be divided by flipping the numerator and denominator of the second fraction and then proceeding as though it were a multiplication problem. Example: $\frac{2}{3} \div \frac{3}{4} = \frac{2}{3} \times \frac{4}{3} = \frac{8}{9}$.

Review Video: <u>Multiplying and Dividing Fractions</u>
Visit mometrix.com/academy and enter code: 473632

MULTIPLYING A MIXED NUMBER BY A WHOLE NUMBER OR A DECIMAL

When multiplying a mixed number by something, it is usually best to convert it to an improper fraction first. Additionally, if the multiplicand is a decimal, it is most often simplest to convert it to a fraction. For instance, to multiply $4\frac{3}{8}$ by 3.5, begin by rewriting each quantity as a whole number plus a proper fraction. Remember, a mixed number is a fraction added to a whole number and a decimal is a representation of the sum of fractions, specifically tenths, hundredths, thousandths, and so on:

$$4\frac{3}{8} \times 3.5 = \left(4 + \frac{3}{8}\right) \times \left(3 + \frac{1}{2}\right)$$

Next, the quantities being added need to be expressed with the same denominator. This is achieved by multiplying and dividing the whole number by the denominator of the fraction. Recall that a whole number is equivalent to that number divided by 1:

$$= \left(\frac{4}{1} \times \frac{8}{8} + \frac{3}{8}\right) \times \left(\frac{3}{1} \times \frac{2}{2} + \frac{1}{2}\right)$$

When multiplying fractions, remember to multiply the numerators and denominators separately:

$$= \left(\frac{4 \times 8}{1 \times 8} + \frac{3}{8}\right) \times \left(\frac{3 \times 2}{1 \times 2} + \frac{1}{2}\right)$$
$$= \left(\frac{32}{8} + \frac{3}{8}\right) \times \left(\frac{6}{2} + \frac{1}{2}\right)$$

Now that the fractions have the same denominators, they can be added:

$$= \frac{35}{8} \times \frac{7}{2}$$

Finally, perform the last multiplication and then simplify:

$$= \frac{35 \times 7}{8 \times 2} = \frac{245}{16} = \frac{240}{16} + \frac{5}{16} = 15\frac{5}{16}$$

COMPARING FRACTIONS

It is important to master the ability to compare and order fractions. This skill is relevant to many real-world scenarios. For example, carpenters often compare fractional construction nail lengths when preparing for a project, and bakers often compare fractional measurements to have the correct ratio of ingredients. There are three commonly used strategies when comparing fractions. These strategies are referred to as the common denominator approach, the decimal approach, and the cross-multiplication approach.

USING A COMMON DENOMINATOR TO COMPARE FRACTIONS

The fractions $\frac{2}{3}$ and $\frac{4}{7}$ have different denominators. $\frac{2}{3}$ has a denominator of 3, and $\frac{4}{7}$ has a denominator of 7. In order to precisely compare these two fractions, it is necessary to use a common denominator. A common denominator is a common multiple that is shared by both denominators. In this case, the denominators 3 and 7 share a multiple of 21. In general, it is most efficient to select the least common multiple for the two denominators.

Rewrite each fraction with the common denominator of 21. Then, calculate the new numerators as illustrated below.

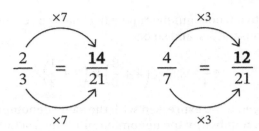

For $\frac{2}{3}$, multiply the numerator and denominator by 7. The result is $\frac{14}{21}$.

For $\frac{4}{7}$, multiply the numerator and denominator by 3. The result is $\frac{12}{21}$.

Now that both fractions have a denominator of 21, the fractions can accurately be compared by comparing the numerators. Since 14 is greater than 12, the fraction $\frac{14}{21}$ is greater than $\frac{12}{21}$. This means that $\frac{2}{3}$ is greater than $\frac{4}{7}$.

USING DECIMALS TO COMPARE FRACTIONS

Sometimes decimal values are easier to compare than fraction values. For example, $\frac{5}{8}$ is equivalent to 0.625 and $\frac{3}{5}$ is equivalent to 0.6. This means that the comparison of $\frac{5}{8}$ and $\frac{3}{5}$ can be determined by comparing the decimals 0.625 and 0.6. When both decimal values are extended to the thousandths place, they become 0.625 and 0.600, respectively. It becomes clear that 0.625 is greater than 0.600 because 625 thousandths is greater than 600 thousandths. In other words, $\frac{5}{8}$ is greater than $\frac{3}{5}$ because 0.625 is greater than 0.6.

USING CROSS-MULTIPLICATION TO COMPARE FRACTIONS

Cross-multiplication is an efficient strategy for comparing fractions. This is a shortcut for the common denominator strategy. Start by writing each fraction next to one another. Multiply the numerator of the fraction on the left by the denominator of the fraction on the right. Write down the result next to the fraction on the left. Now multiply the numerator of the fraction on the right by the denominator of the fraction on the left. Write down the result next to the fraction on the right. Compare both products. The fraction with the larger result is the larger fraction.

Consider the fractions $\frac{4}{7}$ and $\frac{5}{9}$.

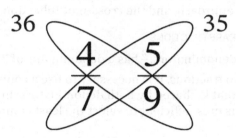

36 is greater than 35. Therefore, $\frac{4}{7}$ is greater than $\frac{5}{9}$.

DECIMALS

Decimals are one way to represent parts of a whole. Using the place value system, each digit to the right of a decimal point denotes the number of units of a corresponding *negative* power of ten. For example, consider the decimal 0.24. We can use a model to represent the decimal. Since a dime is worth one-tenth of a dollar and a penny is worth one-hundredth of a dollar, one possible model to represent this fraction is to have 2 dimes representing the 2 in the tenths place and 4 pennies representing the 4 in the hundredths place:

To write the decimal as a fraction, put the decimal in the numerator with 1 in the denominator. Multiply the numerator and denominator by tens until there are no more decimal places. Then simplify the fraction to lowest terms. For example, converting 0.24 to a fraction:

$$0.24 = \frac{0.24}{1} = \frac{0.24 \times 100}{1 \times 100} = \frac{24}{100} = \frac{6}{25}$$

> **Review Video: Decimals**
> Visit mometrix.com/academy and enter code: 837268

OPERATIONS WITH DECIMALS

ADDING AND SUBTRACTING DECIMALS

When adding and subtracting decimals, the decimal points must always be aligned. Adding decimals is just like adding regular whole numbers. Example: $4.5 + 2.0 = 6.5$.

If the problem-solver does not properly align the decimal points, an incorrect answer of 4.7 may result. An easy way to add decimals is to align all of the decimal points in a vertical column visually. This will allow you to see exactly where the decimal should be placed in the final answer. Begin adding from right to left. Add each column in turn, making sure to carry the number to the left if a column adds up to more than 9. The same rules apply to the subtraction of decimals.

> **Review Video: Adding and Subtracting Decimals**
> Visit mometrix.com/academy and enter code: 381101

MULTIPLYING DECIMALS

A simple multiplication problem has two components: a **multiplicand** and a **multiplier**. When multiplying decimals, work as though the numbers were whole rather than decimals. Once the final product is calculated, count the number of places to the right of the decimal in both the multiplicand and the multiplier. Then, count that number of places from the right of the product and place the decimal in that position.

For example, 12.3×2.56 has a total of three places to the right of the respective decimals. Multiply 123×256 to get 31,488. Now, beginning on the right, count three places to the left and insert the decimal. The final product will be 31.488.

> **Review Video: How to Multiply Decimals**
> Visit mometrix.com/academy and enter code: 731574

DIVIDING DECIMALS

Every division problem has a **divisor** and a **dividend**. The dividend is the number that is being divided. In the problem $14 \div 7$, 14 is the dividend and 7 is the divisor. In a division problem with decimals, the divisor must be converted into a whole number. Begin by moving the decimal in the divisor to the right until a whole number is created. Next, move the decimal in the dividend the same number of spaces to the right. For example, 4.9 into 24.5 would become 49 into 245. The decimal was moved one space to the right to create a whole number in the divisor, and then the same was done for the dividend. Once the whole numbers are created, the problem is carried out normally: $245 \div 49 = 5$.

Review Video: <u>Dividing Decimals</u>
Visit mometrix.com/academy and enter code: 560690

Review Video: <u>Dividing Decimals by Whole Numbers</u>
Visit mometrix.com/academy and enter code: 535669

PERCENTAGES

Percentages can be thought of as fractions that are based on a whole of 100; that is, one whole is equal to 100%. The word **percent** means "per hundred." Percentage problems are often presented in three main ways:

- Find what percentage of some number another number is.
  - Example: What percentage of 40 is 8?
- Find what number is some percentage of a given number.
  - Example: What number is 20% of 40?
- Find what number another number is a given percentage of.
  - Example: What number is 8 20% of?

There are three components in each of these cases: a **whole** (W), a **part** (P), and a **percentage** (%). These are related by the equation: $P = W \times \%$. This can easily be rearranged into other forms that may suit different questions better: $\% = \frac{P}{W}$ and $W = \frac{P}{\%}$. Percentage problems are often also word problems. As such, a large part of solving them is figuring out which quantities are what. For example, consider the following word problem:

In a school cafeteria, 7 students choose pizza, 9 choose hamburgers, and 4 choose tacos. What percentage of student choose tacos?

To find the whole, you must first add all of the parts: $7 + 9 + 4 = 20$. The percentage can then be found by dividing the part by the whole $\left(\% = \frac{P}{W} \right)$: $\frac{4}{20} = \frac{20}{100} = 20\%$.

Review Video: <u>Computation with Percentages</u>
Visit mometrix.com/academy and enter code: 693099

CONVERTING BETWEEN PERCENTAGES, FRACTIONS, AND DECIMALS

Converting decimals to percentages and percentages to decimals is as simple as moving the decimal point. To *convert from a decimal to a percentage*, move the decimal point **two places to the right**. To *convert from a percentage to a decimal*, move it **two places to the left**. It may be helpful to remember that the percentage number will always be larger than the equivalent decimal number. Example:

$$0.23 = 23\% \quad 5.34 = 534\% \quad 0.007 = 0.7\%$$
$$700\% = 7.00 \quad 86\% = 0.86 \quad 0.15\% = 0.0015$$

To convert a fraction to a decimal, simply divide the numerator by the denominator in the fraction. To convert a decimal to a fraction, put the decimal in the numerator with 1 in the denominator. Multiply the numerator and denominator by tens until there are no more decimal places. Then simplify the fraction to lowest terms. For example, converting 0.24 to a fraction:

$$0.24 = \frac{0.24}{1} = \frac{0.24 \times 100}{1 \times 100} = \frac{24}{100} = \frac{6}{25}$$

Fractions can be converted to a percentage by finding equivalent fractions with a denominator of 100. Example:

$$\frac{7}{10} = \frac{70}{100} = 70\% \quad \frac{1}{4} = \frac{25}{100} = 25\%$$

To convert a percentage to a fraction, divide the percentage number by 100 and reduce the fraction to its simplest possible terms. Example:

$$60\% = \frac{60}{100} = \frac{3}{5} \quad 96\% = \frac{96}{100} = \frac{24}{25}$$

> **Review Video: <u>Converting Fractions to Percentages and Decimals</u>**
> Visit mometrix.com/academy and enter code: 306233
>
> **Review Video: <u>Converting Percentages to Decimals and Fractions</u>**
> Visit mometrix.com/academy and enter code: 287297
>
> **Review Video: <u>Converting Decimals to Fractions and Percentages</u>**
> Visit mometrix.com/academy and enter code: 986765
>
> **Review Video: <u>Converting Decimals, Improper Fractions, and Mixed Numbers</u>**
> Visit mometrix.com/academy and enter code: 696924

PROPORTIONS AND RATIOS

PROPORTIONS

A proportion is a relationship between two quantities that dictates how one changes when the other changes. A **direct proportion** describes a relationship in which a quantity increases by a set amount for every increase in the other quantity, or decreases by that same amount for every decrease in the other quantity. Example: Assuming a constant driving speed, the time required for a car trip increases as the distance of the trip increases. The distance to be traveled and the time required to travel are directly proportional.

An **inverse proportion** is a relationship in which an increase in one quantity is accompanied by a decrease in the other, or vice versa. Example: the time required for a car trip decreases as the speed increases and increases as the speed decreases, so the time required is inversely proportional to the speed of the car.

> **Review Video: <u>Proportions</u>**
> Visit mometrix.com/academy and enter code: 505355

RATIOS

A **ratio** is a comparison of two quantities in a particular order. Example: If there are 14 computers in a lab, and the class has 20 students, there is a student to computer ratio of 20 to 14, commonly written as 20: 14. Ratios are normally reduced to their smallest whole number representation, so 20: 14 would be reduced to 10: 7 by dividing both sides by 2.

> **Review Video: <u>Ratios</u>**
> Visit mometrix.com/academy and enter code: 996914

CONSTANT OF PROPORTIONALITY

When two quantities have a proportional relationship, there exists a **constant of proportionality** between the quantities. The product of this constant and one of the quantities is equal to the other quantity. For example, if one lemon costs $0.25, two lemons cost $0.50, and three lemons cost $0.75, there is a proportional relationship between the total cost of lemons and the number of lemons purchased. The constant of proportionality is the **unit price**, namely $0.25/lemon. Notice that the total price of lemons, t, can be found by multiplying the unit price of lemons, p, and the number of lemons, n: $t = pn$.

WORK/UNIT RATE

Unit rate expresses a quantity of one thing in terms of one unit of another. For example, if you travel 30 miles every two hours, a unit rate expresses this comparison in terms of one hour: in one hour you travel 15 miles, so your unit rate is 15 miles per hour. Other examples are how much one ounce of food costs (price per ounce) or figuring out how much one egg costs out of the dozen (price per 1 egg, instead of price per 12 eggs). The denominator of a unit rate is always 1. Unit rates are used to compare different situations to solve problems. For example, to make sure you get the best deal when deciding which kind of soda to buy, you can find the unit rate of each. If soda #1 costs $1.50 for a 1-liter bottle, and soda #2 costs $2.75 for a 2-liter bottle, it would be a better deal to buy soda #2, because its unit rate is only $1.375 per 1-liter, which is cheaper than soda #1. Unit rates can also help determine the length of time a given event will take. For example, if you can paint 2 rooms in 4.5 hours, you can determine how long it will take you to paint 5 rooms by solving for the unit rate per room and then multiplying that by 5.

Review Video: **Rates and Unit Rates**
Visit mometrix.com/academy and enter code: 185363

Algebraic Thinking

LINEAR EXPRESSIONS

TERMS AND COEFFICIENTS

Mathematical expressions consist of a combination of one or more values arranged in terms that are added together. As such, an expression could be just a single number, including zero. A **variable term** is the product of a real number, also called a **coefficient**, and one or more variables, each of which may be raised to an exponent. Expressions may also include numbers without a variable, called **constants** or **constant terms**. The expression $6s^2$, for example, is a single term where the coefficient is the real number 6 and the variable term is s^2. Note that if a term is written as simply a variable to some exponent, like t^2, then the coefficient is 1, because $t^2 = 1t^2$.

LINEAR EXPRESSIONS

A **single variable linear expression** is the sum of a single variable term, where the variable has no exponent, and a constant, which may be zero. For instance, the expression $2w + 7$ has $2w$ as the variable term and 7 as the constant term. It is important to realize that terms are separated by addition or subtraction. Since an expression is a sum of terms, expressions such as $5x - 3$ can be written as $5x + (-3)$ to emphasize that the constant term is negative. A real-world example of a single variable linear expression is the perimeter of a square, four times the side length, often expressed: $4s$.

In general, a **linear expression** is the sum of any number of variable terms so long as none of the variables have an exponent. For example, $3m + 8n - \frac{1}{4}p + 5.5q - 1$ is a linear expression, but $3y^3$ is not. In the same way, the expression for the perimeter of a general triangle, the sum of the side lengths $(a + b + c)$ is considered to be linear, but the expression for the area of a square, the side length squared (s^2) is not.

SLOPE

On a graph with two points, (x_1, y_1) and (x_2, y_2), the **slope** is found with the formula $m = \frac{y_2 - y_1}{x_2 - x_1}$; where $x_1 \neq x_2$ and m stands for slope. If the value of the slope is **positive**, the line has an *upward direction* from left to right. If the value of the slope is **negative**, the line has a *downward direction* from left to right. Consider the following example:

A new book goes on sale in bookstores and online stores. In the first month, 5,000 copies of the book are sold. Over time, the book continues to grow in popularity. The data for the number of copies sold is in the table below.

# of Months on Sale	1	2	3	4	5
# of Copies Sold (In Thousands)	5	10	15	20	25

So, the number of copies that are sold and the time that the book is on sale is a proportional relationship. In this example, an equation can be used to show the data: $y = 5x$, where x is the number of months that the book is on sale. Also, y is the number of copies sold. So, the slope of the corresponding line is $\frac{\text{rise}}{\text{run}} = \frac{5}{1} = 5$.

> **Review Video: Finding the Slope of a Line**
> Visit mometrix.com/academy and enter code: 766664

LINEAR EQUATIONS

Equations that can be written as $ax + b = 0$, where $a \neq 0$, are referred to as **one variable linear equations**. A solution to such an equation is called a **root**. In the case where we have the equation $5x + 10 = 0$, if we solve for x we get a solution of $x = -2$. In other words, the root of the equation is –2. This is found by first subtracting 10 from both sides, which gives $5x = -10$. Next, simply divide both sides by the coefficient of the variable, in this case 5, to get $x = -2$. This can be checked by plugging –2 back into the original equation $(5)(-2) + 10 = -10 + 10 = 0$.

The **solution set** is the set of all solutions of an equation. In our example, the solution set would simply be –2. If there were more solutions (there usually are in multivariable equations) then they would also be included in the solution set. When an equation has no true solutions, it is referred to as an **empty set**. Equations with identical solution sets are **equivalent equations**. An **identity** is a term whose value or determinant is equal to 1.

Linear equations can be written many ways. Below is a list of some forms linear equations can take:

- **Standard Form**: $Ax + By = C$; the slope is $\frac{-A}{B}$ and the y-intercept is $\frac{C}{B}$
- **Slope Intercept Form**: $y = mx + b$, where m is the slope and b is the y-intercept
- **Point-Slope Form**: $y - y_1 = m(x - x_1)$, where m is the slope and (x_1, y_1) is a point on the line
- **Two-Point Form**: $\frac{y - y_1}{x - x_1} = \frac{y_2 - y_1}{x_2 - x_1}$, where (x_1, y_1) and (x_2, y_2) are two points on the given line
- **Intercept Form**: $\frac{x}{x_1} + \frac{y}{y_1} = 1$, where $(x_1, 0)$ is the point at which a line intersects the x-axis, and $(0, y_1)$ is the point at which the same line intersects the y-axis

> **Review Video: Slope-Intercept and Point-Slope Forms**
> Visit mometrix.com/academy and enter code: 113216
>
> **Review Video: Linear Equations Basics**
> Visit mometrix.com/academy and enter code: 793005

SOLVING EQUATIONS
SOLVING ONE-VARIABLE LINEAR EQUATIONS

Multiply all terms by the lowest common denominator to eliminate any fractions. Look for addition or subtraction to undo so you can isolate the variable on one side of the equal sign. Divide both sides by the coefficient of the variable. When you have a value for the variable, substitute this value into the original equation to make sure you have a true equation. Consider the following example:

Kim's savings are represented by the table below. Represent her savings, using an equation.

X (Months)	Y (Total Savings)
2	$1,300
5	$2,050
9	$3,050
11	$3,550
16	$4,800

The table shows a function with a constant rate of change, or slope, of 250. Given the points on the table, the slopes can be calculated as $\frac{(2,050-1300)}{(5-2)}$, $\frac{(3,050-2,050)}{(9-5)}$, $\frac{(3,550-3,050)}{(11-9)}$, and $\frac{(4,800-3,550)}{(16-11)}$, each of which equals 250.

Thus, the table shows a constant rate of change, indicating a linear function. The slope-intercept form of a linear equation is written as $y = mx + b$, where m represents the slope and b represents the y-intercept. Substituting the slope into this form gives $y = 250x + b$. Substituting corresponding x- and y-values from any point into this equation will give the y-intercept, or b. Using the point, (2, 1,300), gives $1,300 = 250(2) + b$, which simplifies as $b = 800$. Thus, her savings may be represented by the equation, $y = 250x + 800$.

RULES FOR MANIPULATING EQUATIONS
LIKE TERMS

Like terms are terms in an equation that have the same variable, regardless of whether or not they also have the same coefficient. This includes terms that *lack* a variable; all constants (i.e., numbers without variables) are considered like terms. If the equation involves terms with a variable raised to different powers, the like terms are those that have the variable raised to the same power.

For example, consider the equation $x^2 + 3x + 2 = 2x^2 + x - 7 + 2x$. In this equation, 2 and –7 are like terms; they are both constants. $3x$, x, and $2x$ are like terms, they all include the variable x raised to the first power. x^2 and $2x^2$ are like terms, they both include the variable x, raised to the second power. $2x$ and $2x^2$ are not like terms; although they both involve the variable x, the variable is not raised to the same power in both terms. The fact that they have the same coefficient, 2, is not relevant.

> **Review Video: Rules for Manipulating Equations**
> Visit mometrix.com/academy and enter code: 838871

CARRYING OUT THE SAME OPERATION ON BOTH SIDES OF AN EQUATION

When solving an equation, the general procedure is to carry out a series of operations on both sides of an equation, choosing operations that will tend to simplify the equation when doing so. The reason why the same operation must be carried out on both sides of the equation is because that leaves the meaning of the equation unchanged, and yields a result that is equivalent to the original equation. This would not be the case if we carried out an operation on one side of an equation and not the other. Consider what an equation means: it is a statement that two values or expressions are equal. If we carry out the same operation on both sides of the equation—add 3 to both sides, for example—then the two sides of the equation are changed in the same way, and so remain equal. If we do that to only one side of the equation—add 3 to one side but not the other—then that wouldn't be true; if we change one side of the equation but not the other then the two sides are no longer equal.

ADVANTAGE OF COMBINING LIKE TERMS

Combining like terms refers to adding or subtracting like terms—terms with the same variable—and therefore reducing sets of like terms to a single term. The main advantage of doing this is that it simplifies the equation. Often, combining like terms can be done as the first step in solving an equation, though it can also be done later, such as after distributing terms in a product.

For example, consider the equation $2(x + 3) + 3(2 + x + 3) = -4$. The 2 and the 3 in the second set of parentheses are like terms, and we can combine them, yielding $2(x + 3) + 3(x + 5) = -4$. Now we can carry out the multiplications implied by the parentheses, distributing the outer 2 and 3 accordingly: $2x + 6 + 3x + 15 = -4$. The $2x$ and the $3x$ are like terms, and we can add them together: $5x + 6 + 15 = -4$. Now, the constants 6, 15, and –4 are also like terms, and we can combine them as well: subtracting 6 and 15 from both sides of the equation, we get $5x = -4 - 6 - 15$, or $5x = -25$, which simplifies further to $x = -5$.

> **Review Video: Solving Equations by Combining Like Terms**
> Visit mometrix.com/academy and enter code: 668506

CANCELING TERMS ON OPPOSITE SIDES OF AN EQUATION

Two terms on opposite sides of an equation can be canceled if and only if they *exactly* match each other. They must have the same variable raised to the same power and the same coefficient. For example, in the equation $3x + 2x^2 + 6 = 2x^2 - 6$, $2x^2$ appears on both sides of the equation and can be canceled, leaving $3x + 6 = -6$. The 6 on each side of the equation *cannot* be canceled, because it is added on one side of the equation and subtracted on the other. While they cannot be canceled, however, the 6 and –6 are like terms and can be combined, yielding $3x = -12$, which simplifies further to $x = -4$.

It's also important to note that the terms to be canceled must be independent terms and cannot be part of a larger term. For example, consider the equation $2(x + 6) = 3(x + 4) + 1$. We cannot cancel the x's, because even though they match each other they are part of the larger terms $2(x + 6)$ and $3(x + 4)$. We must first distribute the 2 and 3, yielding $2x + 12 = 3x + 12 + 1$. Now we see that the terms with the x's do not match, but the 12s do, and can be canceled, leaving $2x = 3x + 1$, which simplifies to $x = -1$.

PROCESS FOR MANIPULATING EQUATIONS

ISOLATING VARIABLES

To **isolate a variable** means to manipulate the equation so that the variable appears by itself on one side of the equation, and does not appear at all on the other side. Generally, an equation or inequality is considered to be solved once the variable is isolated and the other side of the equation or inequality is simplified as much as possible. In the case of a two-variable equation or inequality, only one variable needs to be isolated; it will not usually be possible to simultaneously isolate both variables.

For a linear equation—an equation in which the variable only appears raised to the first power—isolating a variable can be done by first moving all the terms with the variable to one side of the equation and all other terms to the other side. (*Moving* a term really means adding the inverse of the term to both sides; when a term is *moved* to the other side of the equation its sign is flipped.) Then combine like terms on each side. Finally, divide both sides by the coefficient of the variable, if applicable. The steps need not necessarily be done in this order, but this order will always work.

> **Review Video: Solving One-Step Equations**
> Visit mometrix.com/academy and enter code: 777004

EQUATIONS WITH MORE THAN ONE SOLUTION

Some types of non-linear equations, such as equations involving squares of variables, may have more than one solution. For example, the equation $x^2 = 4$ has two solutions: 2 and –2. Equations with absolute values can also have multiple solutions: $|x| = 1$ has the solutions $x = 1$ and $x = -1$.

It is also possible for a linear equation to have more than one solution, but only if the equation is true regardless of the value of the variable. In this case, the equation is considered to have infinitely many solutions, because any possible value of the variable is a solution. We know a linear equation has infinitely many solutions if when we combine like terms the variables cancel, leaving a true statement. For example, consider the equation $2(3x + 5) = x + 5(x + 2)$. Distributing, we get $6x + 10 = x + 5x + 10$; combining like terms gives $6x + 10 = 6x + 10$, and the $6x$-terms cancel to leave $10 = 10$. This is clearly true, so the original equation is true for any value of x. We could also have canceled the 10s leaving $0 = 0$, but again this is clearly true—in general if both sides of the equation match exactly, it has infinitely many solutions.

EQUATIONS WITH NO SOLUTION

Some types of non-linear equations, such as equations involving squares of variables, may have no solution. For example, the equation $x^2 = -2$ has no solutions in the real numbers, because the square of any real number must be positive. Similarly, $|x| = -1$ has no solution, because the absolute value of a number is always positive.

It is also possible for an equation to have no solution even if does not involve any powers greater than one, absolute values, or other special functions. For example, the equation $2(x + 3) + x = 3x$ has no solution. We can see that if we try to solve it: first we distribute, leaving $2x + 6 + x = 3x$. But now if we try to combine all the terms with the variable, we find that they cancel: we have $3x$ on the left and $3x$ on the right, canceling to leave us with $6 = 0$. This is clearly false. In general, whenever the variable terms in an equation cancel leaving different constants on both sides, it means that the equation has no solution. (If we are left with the *same* constant on both sides, the equation has infinitely many solutions instead.)

FEATURES OF EQUATIONS THAT REQUIRE SPECIAL TREATMENT

LINEAR EQUATIONS

A linear equation is an equation in which variables only appear by themselves: not multiplied together, not with exponents other than one, and not inside absolute value signs or any other functions. For example, the equation $x + 1 - 3x = 5 - x$ is a linear equation; while x appears multiple times, it never appears with an exponent other than one, or inside any function. The two-variable equation $2x - 3y = 5 + 2x$ is also a linear equation. In contrast, the equation $x^2 - 5 = 3x$ is *not* a linear equation, because it involves the term x^2. $\sqrt{x} = 5$ is not a linear equation, because it involves a square root. $(x - 1)^2 = 4$ is not a linear equation because even though there's no exponent on the x directly, it appears as part of an expression that is squared. The two-variable equation $x + xy - y = 5$ is not a linear equation because it includes the term xy, where two variables are multiplied together.

Linear equations can always be solved (or shown to have no solution) by combining like terms and performing simple operations on both sides of the equation. Some non-linear equations can be solved by similar methods, but others may require more advanced methods of solution, if they can be solved analytically at all.

SOLVING EQUATIONS INVOLVING ROOTS

In an equation involving roots, the first step is to isolate the term with the root, if possible, and then raise both sides of the equation to the appropriate power to eliminate it. Consider an example equation, $2\sqrt{x + 1} - 1 = 3$. In this case, begin by adding 1 to both sides, yielding $2\sqrt{x + 1} = 4$, and then dividing both sides by 2, yielding $\sqrt{x + 1} = 2$. Now square both sides, yielding $x + 1 = 4$. Finally, subtracting 1 from both sides yields $x = 3$.

Squaring both sides of an equation may, however, yield a spurious solution—a solution to the squared equation that is *not* a solution of the original equation. It's therefore necessary to plug the solution back into the original equation to make sure it works. In this case, it does: $2\sqrt{3+1} - 1 = 2\sqrt{4} - 1 = 2(2) - 1 = 4 - 1 = 3$.

The same procedure applies for other roots as well. For example, given the equation $3 + \sqrt[3]{2x} = 5$, we can first subtract 3 from both sides, yielding $\sqrt[3]{2x} = 2$ and isolating the root. Raising both sides to the third power yields $2x = 2^3$; i.e., $2x = 8$. We can now divide both sides by 2 to get $x = 4$.

> **Review Video: Solving Equations Involving Roots**
> Visit mometrix.com/academy and enter code: 297670

SOLVING EQUATIONS WITH EXPONENTS

To solve an equation involving an exponent, the first step is to isolate the variable with the exponent. We can then take the appropriate root of both sides to eliminate the exponent. For instance, for the equation $2x^3 + 17 = 5x^3 - 7$, we can subtract $5x^3$ from both sides to get $-3x^3 + 17 = -7$, and then subtract 17 from both sides to get $-3x^3 = -24$. Finally, we can divide both sides by –3 to get $x^3 = 8$. Finally, we can take the cube root of both sides to get $x = \sqrt[3]{8} = 2$.

One important but often overlooked point is that equations with an exponent greater than 1 may have more than one answer. The solution to $x^2 = 9$ isn't simply $x = 3$; it's $x = \pm 3$ (that is, $x = 3$ or $x = -3$). For a slightly more complicated example, consider the equation $(x - 1)^2 - 1 = 3$. Adding 1 to both sides yields $(x - 1)^2 = 4$; taking the square root of both sides yields $x - 1 = 2$. We can then add 1 to both sides to get $x = 3$. However, there's a second solution. We also have the possibility that $x - 1 = -2$, in which case $x = -1$. Both $x = 3$ and $x = -1$ are valid solutions, as can be verified by substituting them both into the original equation.

> **Review Video: Solving Equations with Exponents**
> Visit mometrix.com/academy and enter code: 514557

SOLVING EQUATIONS WITH ABSOLUTE VALUES

When solving an equation with an absolute value, the first step is to isolate the absolute value term. We then consider two possibilities: when the expression inside the absolute value is positive or when it is negative. In the former case, the expression in the absolute value equals the expression on the other side of the equation; in the latter, it equals the additive inverse of that expression—the expression times negative one. We consider each case separately and finally check for spurious solutions.

For instance, consider solving $|2x - 1| + x = 5$ for x. We can first isolate the absolute value by moving the x to the other side: $|2x - 1| = -x + 5$. Now, we have two possibilities. First, that $2x - 1$ is positive, and hence $2x - 1 = -x + 5$. Rearranging and combining like terms yields $3x = 6$, and hence $x = 2$. The other possibility is that $2x - 1$ is negative, and hence $2x - 1 = -(-x + 5) = x - 5$. In this case, rearranging and combining like terms yields $x = -4$. Substituting $x = 2$ and $x = -4$ back into the original equation, we see that they are both valid solutions.

Note that the absolute value of a sum or difference applies to the sum or difference as a whole, not to the individual terms; in general, $|2x - 1|$ is not equal to $|2x + 1|$ or to $|2x| - 1$.

SPURIOUS SOLUTIONS

A **spurious solution** may arise when we square both sides of an equation as a step in solving it or under certain other operations on the equation. It is a solution to the squared or otherwise modified equation that is *not* a solution of the original equation. To identify a spurious solution, it's useful when you solve an equation involving roots or absolute values to plug the solution back into the original equation to make sure it's valid.

Mathematics

CHOOSING WHICH VARIABLE TO ISOLATE IN TWO-VARIABLE EQUATIONS

Similar to methods for a one-variable equation, solving a two-variable equation involves isolating a variable: manipulating the equation so that a variable appears by itself on one side of the equation, and not at all on the other side. However, in a two-variable equation, you will usually only be able to isolate one of the variables; the other variable may appear on the other side along with constant terms, or with exponents or other functions.

Often one variable will be much more easily isolated than the other, and therefore that's the variable you should choose. If one variable appears with various exponents, and the other is only raised to the first power, the latter variable is the one to isolate: given the equation $a^2 + 2b = a^3 + b + 3$, the b only appears to the first power, whereas a appears squared and cubed, so b is the variable that can be solved for: combining like terms and isolating the b on the left side of the equation, we get $b = a^3 - a^2 + 3$. If both variables are equally easy to isolate, then it's best to isolate the dependent variable, if one is defined; if the two variables are x and y, the convention is that y is the dependent variable.

> **Review Video: Solving Equations with Variables on Both Sides**
> Visit mometrix.com/academy and enter code: 402497

CROSS MULTIPLICATION
FINDING AN UNKNOWN IN EQUIVALENT EXPRESSIONS

It is often necessary to apply information given about a rate or proportion to a new scenario. For example, if you know that Jedha can run a marathon (26.2 miles) in 3 hours, how long would it take her to run 10 miles at the same pace? Start by setting up equivalent expressions:

$$\frac{26.2 \text{ mi}}{3 \text{ hr}} = \frac{10 \text{ mi}}{x \text{ hr}}$$

Now, cross multiply and solve for x:

$$26.2x = 30$$
$$x = \frac{30}{26.2} = \frac{15}{13.1}$$
$$x \approx 1.15 \text{ hrs } or \text{ 1 hr 9 min}$$

So, at this pace, Jedha could run 10 miles in about 1.15 hours or about 1 hour and 9 minutes.

> **Review Video: Cross Multiplying Fractions**
> Visit mometrix.com/academy and enter code: 893904

GRAPHING EQUATIONS
GRAPHICAL SOLUTIONS TO EQUATIONS

When equations are shown graphically, they are usually shown on a **Cartesian coordinate plane**. The Cartesian coordinate plane consists of two number lines placed perpendicular to each other and intersecting at the zero point, also known as the origin. The horizontal number line is known as the x-axis, with positive values to the right of the origin, and negative values to the left of the origin. The vertical number line is known as the y-axis, with positive values above the origin, and negative values below the origin. Any point on the plane can be identified by an ordered pair in the form (x, y), called coordinates. The x-value of the coordinate is called the abscissa, and the y-value of the coordinate is called the ordinate. The two number lines divide the plane into **four quadrants**: I, II, III, and IV.

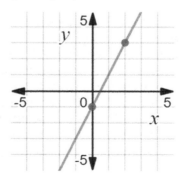

Note that in quadrant I $x > 0$ and $y > 0$, in quadrant II $x < 0$ and $y > 0$, in quadrant III $x < 0$ and $y < 0$, and in quadrant IV $x > 0$ and $y < 0$.

Recall that if the value of the slope of a line is positive, the line slopes upward from left to right. If the value of the slope is negative, the line slopes downward from left to right. If the y-coordinates are the same for two points on a line, the slope is 0 and the line is a **horizontal line**. If the x-coordinates are the same for two points on a line, there is no slope and the line is a **vertical line**. Two or more lines that have equivalent slopes are **parallel lines**. **Perpendicular lines** have slopes that are negative reciprocals of each other, such as $\frac{a}{b}$ and $\frac{-b}{a}$.

> **Review Video: Cartesian Coordinate Plane and Graphing**
> Visit mometrix.com/academy and enter code: 115173

GRAPHING EQUATIONS IN TWO VARIABLES

One way of graphing an equation in two variables is to plot enough points to get an idea for its shape and then draw the appropriate curve through those points. A point can be plotted by substituting in a value for one variable and solving for the other. If the equation is linear, we only need two points and can then draw a straight line between them.

For example, consider the equation $y = 2x - 1$. This is a linear equation—both variables only appear raised to the first power—so we only need two points. When $x = 0$, $y = 2(0) - 1 = -1$. When $x = 2$, $y = 2(2) - 1 = 3$. We can therefore choose the points $(0, -1)$ and $(2, 3)$, and draw a line between them:

INEQUALITIES
WORKING WITH INEQUALITIES

Commonly in algebra and other upper-level fields of math you find yourself working with mathematical expressions that do not equal each other. The statement comparing such expressions with symbols such as < (less than) or > (greater than) is called an *inequality*. An example of an inequality is $7x > 5$. To solve for x,

107

simply divide both sides by 7 and the solution is shown to be $x > \frac{5}{7}$. Graphs of the solution set of inequalities are represented on a number line. Open circles are used to show that an expression approaches a number but is never quite equal to that number.

Review Video: Solving Multi-Step Inequalities
Visit mometrix.com/academy and enter code: 347842

Review Video: Solving Inequalities Using All 4 Basic Operations
Visit mometrix.com/academy and enter code: 401111

Conditional inequalities are those with certain values for the variable that will make the condition true and other values for the variable where the condition will be false. **Absolute inequalities** can have any real number as the value for the variable to make the condition true, while there is no real number value for the variable that will make the condition false. Solving inequalities is done by following the same rules for solving equations with the exception that when multiplying or dividing by a negative number the direction of the inequality sign must be flipped or reversed. **Double inequalities** are situations where two inequality statements apply to the same variable expression. Example: $-c < ax + b < c$.

Review Video: Conditional and Absolute Inequalities
Visit mometrix.com/academy and enter code: 980164

DETERMINING SOLUTIONS TO INEQUALITIES

To determine whether a coordinate is a solution of an inequality, you can substitute the values of the coordinate into the inequality, simplify, and check whether the resulting statement holds true. For instance, to determine whether $(-2,4)$ is a solution of the inequality $y \geq -2x + 3$, substitute the values into the inequality, $4 \geq -2(-2) + 3$. Simplify the right side of the inequality and the result is $4 \geq 7$, which is a false statement. Therefore, the coordinate is not a solution of the inequality. You can also use this method to determine which part of the graph of an inequality is shaded. The graph of $y \geq -2x + 3$ includes the solid line $y = -2x + 3$ and, since it excludes the point $(-2,4)$ to the left of the line, it is shaded to the right of the line.

Review Video: Graphing Linear Inequalities
Visit mometrix.com/academy and enter code: 439421

FLIPPING INEQUALITY SIGNS

When given an inequality, we can always turn the entire inequality around, swapping the two sides of the inequality and changing the inequality sign. For instance, $x + 2 > 2x - 3$ is equivalent to $2x - 3 < x + 2$. Aside from that, normally the inequality does not change if we carry out the same operation on both sides of the inequality. There is, however, one principal exception: if we *multiply* or *divide* both sides of the inequality by a *negative number*, the inequality is flipped. For example, if we take the inequality $-2x < 6$ and divide both sides by –2, the inequality flips and we are left with $x > -3$. This *only* applies to multiplication and division, and only with negative numbers. Multiplying or dividing both sides by a positive number, or adding or subtracting any number regardless of sign, does not flip the inequality. Another special case that flips the inequality sign is when reciprocals are used. For instance, $3 > 2$ but the relation of the reciprocals is $\frac{1}{3} < \frac{1}{2}$.

COMPOUND INEQUALITIES

A **compound inequality** is an equality that consists of two inequalities combined with *and* or *or*. The two components of a proper compound inequality must be of opposite type: that is, one must be greater than (or greater than or equal to), the other less than (or less than or equal to). For instance, "$x + 1 < 2$ or $x + 1 > 3$" is a compound inequality, as is "$2x \geq 4$ and $2x \leq 6$." An *and* inequality can be written more compactly by having one inequality on each side of the common part: "$2x \geq 1$ and $2x \leq 6$," can also be written as $1 \leq 2x \leq 6$.

In order for the compound inequality to be meaningful, the two parts of an *and* inequality must overlap; otherwise, no numbers satisfy the inequality. On the other hand, if the two parts of an *or* inequality overlap, then *all* numbers satisfy the inequality and as such the inequality is usually not meaningful.

Solving a compound inequality requires solving each part separately. For example, given the compound inequality "$x + 1 < 2$ or $x + 1 > 3$," the first inequality, $x + 1 < 2$, reduces to $x < 1$, and the second part, $x + 1 > 3$, reduces to $x > 2$, so the whole compound inequality can be written as "$x < 1$ or $x > 2$." Similarly, $1 \leq 2x \leq 6$ can be solved by dividing each term by 2, yielding $\frac{1}{2} \leq x \leq 3$.

> **Review Video: Compound Inequalities**
> Visit mometrix.com/academy and enter code: 786318

SOLVING INEQUALITIES INVOLVING ABSOLUTE VALUES

To solve an inequality involving an absolute value, first isolate the term with the absolute value. Then proceed to treat the two cases separately as with an absolute value equation, but flipping the inequality in the case where the expression in the absolute value is negative (since that essentially involves multiplying both sides by –1.) The two cases are then combined into a compound inequality; if the absolute value is on the greater side of the inequality, then it is an *or* compound inequality, if on the lesser side, then it's an *and*.

Consider the inequality $2 + |x - 1| \geq 3$. We can isolate the absolute value term by subtracting 2 from both sides: $|x - 1| \geq 1$. Now, we're left with the two cases $x - 1 \geq 1$ or $x - 1 \leq -1$: note that in the latter, negative case, the inequality is flipped. $x - 1 \geq 1$ reduces to $x \geq 2$, and $x - 1 \leq -1$ reduces to $x \leq 0$. Since in the inequality $|x - 1| \geq 1$ the absolute value is on the greater side, the two cases combine into an *or* compound inequality, so the final, solved inequality is "$x \leq 0$ or $x \geq 2$."

> **Review Video: Solving Absolute Value Inequalities**
> Visit mometrix.com/academy and enter code: 997008

SOLVING INEQUALITIES INVOLVING SQUARE ROOTS

Solving an inequality with a square root involves two parts. First, we solve the inequality as if it were an equation, isolating the square root and then squaring both sides of the equation. Second, we restrict the solution to the set of values of x for which the value inside the square root sign is non-negative.

For example, in the inequality, $\sqrt{x - 2} + 1 < 5$, we can isolate the square root by subtracting 1 from both sides, yielding $\sqrt{x - 2} < 4$. Squaring both sides of the inequality yields $x - 2 < 16$, so $x < 18$. Since we can't take the square root of a negative number, we also require the part inside the square root to be non-negative. In this case, that means $x - 2 \geq 0$. Adding 2 to both sides of the inequality yields $x \geq 2$. Our final answer is a compound inequality combining the two simple inequalities: $x \geq 2$ and $x < 18$, or $2 \leq x < 18$.

Note that we only get a compound inequality if the two simple inequalities are in opposite directions; otherwise, we take the one that is more restrictive.

The same technique can be used for other even roots, such as fourth roots. It is *not*, however, used for cube roots or other odd roots—negative numbers *do* have cube roots, so the condition that the quantity inside the root sign cannot be negative does not apply.

> **Review Video: Solving Inequalities Involving Square Roots**
> Visit mometrix.com/academy and enter code: 800288

SPECIAL CIRCUMSTANCES

Sometimes an inequality involving an absolute value or an even exponent is true for all values of x, and we don't need to do any further work to solve it. This is true if the inequality, once the absolute value or exponent term is isolated, says that term is greater than a negative number (or greater than or equal to zero). Since an absolute value or a number raised to an even exponent is *always* non-negative, this inequality is always true.

GRAPHICAL SOLUTIONS TO INEQUALITIES

GRAPHING SIMPLE INEQUALITIES

To graph a simple inequality, we first mark on the number line the value that signifies the end point of the inequality. If the inequality is strict (involves a less than or greater than), we use a hollow circle; if it is not strict (less than or equal to or greater than or equal to), we use a solid circle. We then fill in the part of the number line that satisfies the inequality: to the left of the marked point for less than (or less than or equal to), to the right for greater than (or greater than or equal to).

For example, we would graph the inequality $x < 5$ by putting a hollow circle at 5 and filling in the part of the line to the left:

GRAPHING COMPOUND INEQUALITIES

To graph a compound inequality, we fill in both parts of the inequality for an *or* inequality, or the overlap between them for an *and* inequality. More specifically, we start by plotting the endpoints of each inequality on the number line. For an *or* inequality, we then fill in the appropriate side of the line for each inequality. Typically, the two component inequalities do not overlap, which means the shaded part is *outside* the two points. For an *and* inequality, we instead fill in the part of the line that meets both inequalities.

For the inequality "$x \leq -3$ or $x > 4$," we first put a solid circle at –3 and a hollow circle at 4. We then fill the parts of the line *outside* these circles:

GRAPHING INEQUALITIES INCLUDING ABSOLUTE VALUES

An inequality with an absolute value can be converted to a compound inequality. To graph the inequality, first convert it to a compound inequality, and then graph that normally. If the absolute value is on the greater side of the inequality, we end up with an *or* inequality; we plot the endpoints of the inequality on the number line and fill in the part of the line *outside* those points. If the absolute value is on the smaller side of the inequality, we end up with an *and* inequality; we plot the endpoints of the inequality on the number line and fill in the part of the line *between* those points.

For example, the inequality $|x + 1| \geq 4$ can be rewritten as $x \geq 3$ or $x \leq -5$. We place solid circles at the points 3 and –5 and fill in the part of the line *outside* them:

GRAPHING INEQUALITIES IN TWO VARIABLES

To graph an inequality in two variables, we first graph the border of the inequality. This means graphing the equation that we get if we replace the inequality sign with an equals sign. If the inequality is strict (> or <), we graph the border with a dashed or dotted line; if it is not strict (≥ or ≤), we use a solid line. We can then test any point not on the border to see if it satisfies the inequality. If it does, we shade in that side of the border; if not, we shade in the other side. As an example, consider $y > 2x + 2$. To graph this inequality, we first graph the

110

border, $y = 2x + 2$. Since it is a strict inequality, we use a dashed line. Then, we choose a test point. This can be any point not on the border; in this case, we will choose the origin, (0,0). (This makes the calculation easy and is generally a good choice unless the border passes through the origin.) Putting this into the original inequality, we get $0 > 2(0) + 2$, i.e., $0 > 2$. This is *not* true, so we shade in the side of the border that does *not* include the point (0,0):

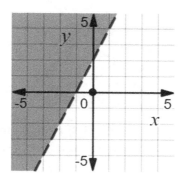

GRAPHING COMPOUND INEQUALITIES IN TWO VARIABLES

One way to graph a compound inequality in two variables is to first graph each of the component inequalities. For an *and* inequality, we then shade in only the parts where the two graphs overlap; for an *or* inequality, we shade in any region that pertains to either of the individual inequalities.

Consider the graph of "$y \geq x - 1$ and $y \leq -x$":

We first shade in the individual inequalities:

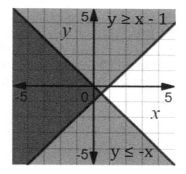

Now, since the compound inequality has an *and*, we only leave shaded the overlap—the part that pertains to *both* inequalities:

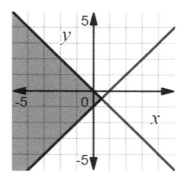

Mathematics

If instead the inequality had been "$y \geq x - 1$ or $y \leq -x$," our final graph would involve the *total* shaded area:

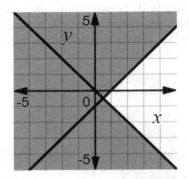

Review Video: **Graphing Solutions to Inequalities**
Visit mometrix.com/academy and enter code: 391281

SYSTEMS OF EQUATIONS
SOLVING SYSTEMS OF EQUATIONS

A **system of equations** is a set of simultaneous equations that all use the same variables. A solution to a system of equations must be true for each equation in the system. **Consistent systems** are those with at least one solution. **Inconsistent systems** are systems of equations that have no solution.

Review Video: **Solving Systems of Linear Equations**
Visit mometrix.com/academy and enter code: 746745

SUBSTITUTION

To solve a system of linear equations by **substitution**, start with the easier equation and solve for one of the variables. Express this variable in terms of the other variable. Substitute this expression in the other equation and solve for the other variable. The solution should be expressed in the form (x, y). Substitute the values into both of the original equations to check your answer. Consider the following system of equations:

$$x + 6y = 15$$
$$3x - 12y = 18$$

Solving the first equation for x: $x = 15 - 6y$

Substitute this value in place of x in the second equation, and solve for y:

$$3(15 - 6y) - 12y = 18$$
$$45 - 18y - 12y = 18$$
$$30y = 27$$
$$y = \frac{27}{30} = \frac{9}{10} = 0.9$$

Plug this value for y back into the first equation to solve for x:

$$x = 15 - 6(0.9) = 15 - 5.4 = 9.6$$

Check both equations if you have time:

$$9.6 + 6(0.9) = 15 \qquad\qquad 3(9.6) - 12(0.9) = 18$$
$$9.6 + 5.4 = 15 \qquad\qquad 28.8 - 10.8 = 18$$
$$15 = 15 \qquad\qquad 18 = 18$$

Therefore, the solution is (9.6,0.9).

Review Video: <u>The Substitution Method</u>
Visit mometrix.com/academy and enter code: 565151

Review Video: <u>Substitution and Elimination</u>
Visit mometrix.com/academy and enter code: 958611

<u>ELIMINATION</u>

To solve a system of equations using **elimination**, begin by rewriting both equations in standard form $Ax + By = C$. Check to see if the coefficients of one pair of like variables add to zero. If not, multiply one or both of the equations by a non-zero number to make one set of like variables add to zero. Add the two equations to solve for one of the variables. Substitute this value into one of the original equations to solve for the other variable. Check your work by substituting into the other equation. Now, let's look at solving the following system using the elimination method:

$$5x + 6y = 4$$
$$x + 2y = 4$$

If we multiply the second equation by -3, we can eliminate the y-terms:

$$5x + 6y = 4$$
$$-3x - 6y = -12$$

Add the equations together and solve for x:

$$2x = -8$$
$$x = \frac{-8}{2} = -4$$

Plug the value for x back in to either of the original equations and solve for y:

$$-4 + 2y = 4$$
$$y = \frac{4 + 4}{2} = 4$$

Check both equations if you have time:

$$5(-4) + 6(4) = 4 \qquad\qquad -4 + 2(4) = 4$$
$$-20 + 24 = 4 \qquad\qquad -4 + 8 = 4$$
$$4 = 4 \qquad\qquad 4 = 4$$

113

Mathematics

Therefore, the solution is $(-4, 4)$.

GRAPHICALLY

To solve a system of linear equations **graphically**, plot both equations on the same graph. The solution of the equations is the point where both lines cross. If the lines do not cross (are parallel), then there is **no solution**.

For example, consider the following system of equations:

$$y = 2x + 7$$
$$y = -x + 1$$

Since these equations are given in slope-intercept form, they are easy to graph; the y-intercepts of the lines are $(0,7)$ and $(0,1)$. The respective slopes are 2 and –1, thus the graphs look like this:

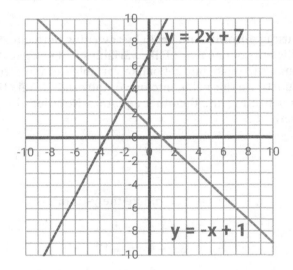

The two lines intersect at the point $(-2, 3)$, thus this is the solution to the system of equations.

Solving a system graphically is generally only practical if both coordinates of the solution are integers; otherwise the intersection will lie between gridlines on the graph and the coordinates will be difficult or impossible to determine exactly. It also helps if, as in this example, the equations are in slope-intercept form or some other form that makes them easy to graph. Otherwise, another method of solution (by substitution or elimination) is likely to be more useful.

SOLVING SYSTEMS OF EQUATIONS USING THE TRACE FEATURE

Using the trace feature on a calculator requires that you rewrite each equation, isolating the y-variable on one side of the equal sign. Enter both equations in the graphing calculator and plot the graphs simultaneously. Use the trace cursor to find where the two lines cross. Use the zoom feature if necessary to obtain more accurate results. Always check your answer by substituting into the original equations. The trace method is likely to be less accurate than other methods due to the resolution of graphing calculators but is a useful tool to provide an approximate answer.

ADVANCED SYSTEMS OF EQUATIONS
SOLVING A SYSTEM OF EQUATIONS CONSISTING OF A LINEAR EQUATION AND A QUADRATIC EQUATION
ALGEBRAICALLY

Generally, the simplest way to solve a system of equations consisting of a linear equation and a quadratic equation algebraically is through the method of substitution. One possible strategy is to solve the linear equation for y and then substitute that expression into the quadratic equation. After expansion and combining like terms, this will result in a new quadratic equation for x, which, like all quadratic equations, may have zero, one, or two solutions. Plugging each solution for x back into one of the original equations will then produce the corresponding value of y.

For example, consider the following system of equations:

$$x + y = 1$$
$$y = (x + 3)^2 - 2$$

We can solve the linear equation for y to yield $y = -x + 1$. Substituting this expression into the quadratic equation produces $-x + 1 = (x + 3)^2 - 2$. We can simplify this equation:

$$-x + 1 = (x + 3)^2 - 2$$
$$-x + 1 = x^2 + 6x + 9 - 2$$
$$-x + 1 = x^2 + 6x + 7$$
$$0 = x^2 + 7x + 6$$

This quadratic equation can be factored as $(x + 1)(x + 6) = 0$. It therefore has two solutions: $x_1 = -1$ and $x_2 = -6$. Plugging each of these back into the original linear equation yields $y_1 = -x_1 + 1 = -(-1) + 1 = 2$ and $y_2 = -x_2 + 1 = -(-6) + 1 = 7$. Thus, this system of equations has two solutions, $(-1, 2)$ and $(-6, 7)$.

It may help to check your work by putting each x- and y-value back into the original equations and verifying that they do provide a solution.

GRAPHICALLY

To solve a system of equations consisting of a linear equation and a quadratic equation graphically, plot both equations on the same graph. The linear equation will, of course, produce a straight line, while the quadratic equation will produce a parabola. These two graphs will intersect at zero, one, or two points; each point of intersection is a solution of the system.

For example, consider the following system of equations:

$$y = -2x + 2$$
$$y = -2x^2 + 4x + 2$$

The linear equation describes a line with a y-intercept of $(0, 2)$ and a slope of -2.

To graph the quadratic equation, we can first find the vertex of the parabola: the x-coordinate of the vertex is $h = -\frac{b}{2a} = -\frac{4}{2(-2)} = 1$, and the y-coordinate is $k = -2(1)^2 + 4(1) + 2 = 4$. Thus, the vertex lies at $(1, 4)$. To get a feel for the rest of the parabola, we can plug in a few more values of x to find more points; by putting in

Mathematics

115

$x = 2$ and $x = 3$ in the quadratic equation, we find that the points $(2,2)$ and $(3, -4)$ lie on the parabola; by symmetry, so must $(0, 2)$ and $(-1, -4)$. We can now plot both equations:

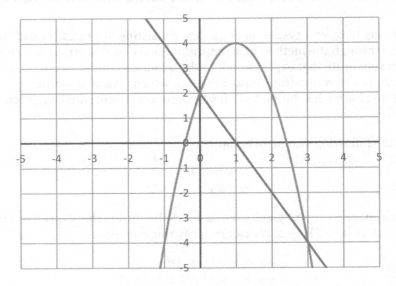

These two curves intersect at the points $(0,2)$ and $(3, -4)$, thus these are the solutions of the equation.

> **Review Video: Solving a System of Linear and Quadratic Equations**
> Visit mometrix.com/academy and enter code: 194870

CALCULATIONS USING POINTS

Sometimes you need to perform calculations using only points on a graph as input data. Using points, you can determine what the **midpoint** and **distance** are. If you know the equation for a line, you can calculate the distance between the line and the point.

To find the **midpoint** of two points (x_1, y_1) and (x_2, y_2), average the x-coordinates to get the x-coordinate of the midpoint, and average the y-coordinates to get the y-coordinate of the midpoint. The formula is: $\left(\frac{x_1+x_2}{2}, \frac{y_1+y_2}{2}\right)$.

The **distance** between two points is the same as the length of the hypotenuse of a right triangle with the two given points as endpoints, and the two sides of the right triangle parallel to the x-axis and y-axis, respectively. The length of the segment parallel to the x-axis is the difference between the x-coordinates of the two points. The length of the segment parallel to the y-axis is the difference between the y-coordinates of the two points. Use the Pythagorean theorem $a^2 + b^2 = c^2$ or $c = \sqrt{a^2 + b^2}$ to find the distance. The formula is $d = \sqrt{(x_2 - x_1)^2 + (y_2 - y_1)^2}$.

When a line is in the format $Ax + By + C = 0$, where A, B, and C are coefficients, you can use a point (x_1, y_1) not on the line and apply the formula $d = \frac{|Ax_1+By_1+C|}{\sqrt{A^2+B^2}}$ to find the distance between the line and the point (x_1, y_1).

> **Review Video: Calculations Using Points on a Graph**
> Visit mometrix.com/academy and enter code: 883228

POLYNOMIALS

MONOMIALS AND POLYNOMIALS

A **monomial** is a single constant, variable, or product of constants and variables, such as 7, x, $2x$, or x^3y. There will never be addition or subtraction symbols in a monomial. Like monomials have like variables, but they may have different coefficients. **Polynomials** are algebraic expressions that use addition and subtraction to combine two or more monomials. Two terms make a **binomial**, three terms make a **trinomial**, etc. The **degree of a monomial** is the sum of the exponents of the variables. The **degree of a polynomial** is the highest degree of any individual term.

> **Review Video: Polynomials**
> Visit mometrix.com/academy and enter code: 305005

SIMPLIFYING POLYNOMIALS

Simplifying polynomials requires combining like terms. The like terms in a polynomial expression are those that have the same variable raised to the same power. It is often helpful to connect the like terms with arrows or lines in order to separate them from the other monomials. Once you have determined the like terms, you can rearrange the polynomial by placing them together. Remember to include the sign that is in front of each term. Once the like terms are placed together, you can apply each operation and simplify. When adding and subtracting polynomials, only add and subtract the **coefficient**, or the number part; the variable and exponent stay the same.

ADD POLYNOMIALS

To add polynomials, you need to add like terms. These terms have the same variable part. An example is $4x^2$ and $3x^2$ have x^2 terms. To find the sum of like terms, find the sum of the coefficients. Then, keep the same variable part. You can use the distributive property to distribute the plus sign to each term of the polynomial. For example:

$$(4x^2 - 5x + 7) + (3x^2 + 2x + 1) =$$
$$(4x^2 - 5x + 7) + 3x^2 + 2x + 1 =$$
$$(4x^2 + 3x^2) + (-5x + 2x) + (7 + 1) =$$
$$7x^2 - 3x + 8$$

SUBTRACT POLYNOMIALS

To subtract polynomials, you need to subtract like terms. To find the difference of like terms, find the difference of the coefficients. Then, keep the same variable part. You can use the distributive property to distribute the minus sign to each term of the polynomial. For example:

$$(-2x^2 - x + 5) - (3x^2 - 4x + 1) =$$
$$(-2x^2 - x + 5) - 3x^2 + 4x - 1 =$$
$$(-2x^2 - 3x^2) + (-x + 4x) + (5 - 1) =$$
$$-5x^2 + 3x + 4$$

> **Review Video: Adding and Subtracting Polynomials**
> Visit mometrix.com/academy and enter code: 124088

MULTIPLYING POLYNOMIALS

In general, multiplying polynomials is done by multiplying each term in one polynomial by each term in the other and adding the results. In the specific case for multiplying binomials, there is a useful acronym, FOIL, that can help you make sure to cover each combination of terms. The **FOIL method** for $(Ax + By)(Cx + Dy)$ would be:

F   Multiply the *first* terms of each binomial $(\overbrace{Ax}^{first} + By)(\overbrace{Cx}^{first} + Dy)$ ACx^2

O   Multiply the *outer* terms $(\overbrace{Ax}^{outer} + By)(Cx + \overbrace{Dy}^{outer})$ $ADxy$

I   Multiply the *inner* terms $(Ax + \overbrace{By}^{inner})(\overbrace{Cx}^{inner} + Dy)$ $BCxy$

L   Multiply the *last* terms of each binomial $(Ax + \overbrace{By}^{last})(Cx + \overbrace{Dy}^{last})$ BDy^2

Then, add up the result of each and combine like terms: $ACx^2 + (AD + BC)xy + BDy^2$.

For example, using the FOIL method on binomials $(x + 2)$ and $(x - 3)$:

$$\text{First:} \quad (\boxed{x} + 2)(\boxed{x} + (-3)) \;\rightarrow\; (x)(x) = x^2$$
$$\text{Outer:} \quad (\boxed{x} + 2)(x + \boxed{(-3)}) \;\rightarrow\; (x)(-3) = -3x$$
$$\text{Inner:} \quad (x + \boxed{2})(\boxed{x} + (-3)) \;\rightarrow\; (2)(x) = 2x$$
$$\text{Last:} \quad (x + \boxed{2})(x + \boxed{(-3)}) \;\rightarrow\; (2)(-3) = -6$$

This results in: $(x^2) + (-3x) + (2x) + (-6)$

Combine like terms: $x^2 + (-3 + 2)x + (-6) = x^2 - x - 6$

> **Review Video: Multiplying Terms Using the FOIL Method**
> Visit mometrix.com/academy and enter code: 854792

DIVIDING POLYNOMIALS

Use long division to divide a polynomial by either a monomial or another polynomial of equal or lesser degree.

When **dividing by a monomial**, divide each term of the polynomial by the monomial.

When **dividing by a polynomial**, begin by arranging the terms of each polynomial in order of one variable. You may arrange in ascending or descending order, but be consistent with both polynomials. To get the first term of the quotient, divide the first term of the dividend by the first term of the divisor. Multiply the first term of the quotient by the entire divisor and subtract that product from the dividend. Repeat for the second and successive terms until you either get a remainder of zero or a remainder whose degree is less than the degree of the divisor. If the quotient has a remainder, write the answer as a mixed expression in the form:

$$\text{quotient} + \frac{\text{remainder}}{\text{divisor}}$$

For example, we can evaluate the following expression in the same way as long division:

$$\frac{x^3 - 3x^2 - 2x + 5}{x - 5}$$

$$
\begin{array}{r}
x^2 + 2x + 8 \\
x - 5 \overline{\smash{\big)}\, x^3 - 3x^2 - 2x + 5} \\
\underline{- (x^3 - 5x^2)} \\
2x^2 - 2x \\
\underline{-(2x^2 - 10x)} \\
8x + 5 \\
\underline{-(8x - 40)} \\
45
\end{array}
$$

$$\frac{x^3 - 3x^2 - 2x + 5}{x - 5} = x^2 + 2x + 8 + \frac{45}{x - 5}$$

When **factoring** a polynomial, first check for a common monomial factor, that is, look to see if each coefficient has a common factor or if each term has an x in it. If the factor is a trinomial but not a perfect trinomial square, look for a factorable form, such as one of these:

$$x^2 + (a + b)x + ab = (x + a)(x + b)$$
$$(ac)x^2 + (ad + bc)x + bd = (ax + b)(cx + d)$$

For factors with four terms, look for groups to factor. Once you have found the factors, write the original polynomial as the product of all the factors. Make sure all of the polynomial factors are prime. Monomial factors may be *prime* or *composite*. Check your work by multiplying the factors to make sure you get the original polynomial.

Below are patterns of some special products to remember to help make factoring easier:

- Perfect trinomial squares: $x^2 + 2xy + y^2 = (x + y)^2$ or $x^2 - 2xy + y^2 = (x - y)^2$
- Difference between two squares: $x^2 - y^2 = (x + y)(x - y)$
- Sum of two cubes: $x^3 + y^3 = (x + y)(x^2 - xy + y^2)$
  - Note: the second factor is *not* the same as a perfect trinomial square, so do not try to factor it further.
- Difference between two cubes: $x^3 - y^3 = (x - y)(x^2 + xy + y^2)$
  - Again, the second factor is *not* the same as a perfect trinomial square.
- Perfect cubes: $x^3 + 3x^2y + 3xy^2 + y^3 = (x + y)^3$ and $x^3 - 3x^2y + 3xy^2 - y^3 = (x - y)^3$

RATIONAL EXPRESSIONS

Rational expressions are fractions with polynomials in both the numerator and the denominator; the value of the polynomial in the denominator cannot be equal to zero. Be sure to keep track of values that make the denominator of the original expression zero as the final result inherits the same restrictions. For example, a denominator of $x - 3$ indicates that the expression is not defined when $x = 3$ and, as such, regardless of any operations done to the expression, it remains undefined there.

119

To **add or subtract** rational expressions, first find the common denominator, then rewrite each fraction as an equivalent fraction with the common denominator. Finally, add or subtract the numerators to get the numerator of the answer, and keep the common denominator as the denominator of the answer.

When **multiplying** rational expressions, factor each polynomial and cancel like factors (a factor which appears in both the numerator and the denominator). Then, multiply all remaining factors in the numerator to get the numerator of the product, and multiply the remaining factors in the denominator to get the denominator of the product. Remember: cancel entire factors, not individual terms.

To **divide** rational expressions, take the reciprocal of the divisor (the rational expression you are dividing by) and multiply by the dividend.

> **Review Video: Rational Expressions**
> Visit mometrix.com/academy and enter code: 415183

SIMPLIFYING RATIONAL EXPRESSIONS

To simplify a rational expression, factor the numerator and denominator completely. Factors that are the same and appear in the numerator and denominator have a ratio of 1. For example, look at the following expression:

$$\frac{x - 1}{1 - x^2}$$

The denominator, $(1 - x^2)$, is a difference of squares. It can be factored as $(1 - x)(1 + x)$. The factor $1 - x$ and the numerator $x - 1$ are opposites and have a ratio of –1. Rewrite the numerator as $-1(1 - x)$. So, the rational expression can be simplified as follows:

$$\frac{x - 1}{1 - x^2} = \frac{-1(1 - x)}{(1 - x)(1 + x)} = \frac{-1}{1 + x}$$

Note that since the original expression is only defined for $x \neq \{-1, 1\}$, the simplified expression has the same restrictions.

> **Review Video: Reducing Rational Expressions**
> Visit mometrix.com/academy and enter code: 788868

QUADRATICS
SOLVING QUADRATIC EQUATIONS

Quadratic equations are a special set of trinomials of the form $y = ax^2 + bx + c$ that occur commonly in math and real-world applications. The **roots** of a quadratic equation are the solutions that satisfy the equation when $y = 0$; in other words, where the graph touches the x-axis. There are several ways to determine these solutions including using the quadratic formula, factoring, completing the square, and graphing the function.

> **Review Video: Quadratic Equations Overview**
> Visit mometrix.com/academy and enter code: 476276
>
> **Review Video: Solutions of a Quadratic Equation on a Graph**
> Visit mometrix.com/academy and enter code: 328231

QUADRATIC FORMULA

The **quadratic formula** is used to solve quadratic equations when other methods are more difficult. To use the quadratic formula to solve a quadratic equation, begin by rewriting the equation in standard form $ax^2 + bx +$

$c = 0$, where a, b, and c are coefficients. Once you have identified the values of the coefficients, substitute those values into the quadratic formula

$$x = \frac{-b \pm \sqrt{b^2 - 4ac}}{2a}$$

Evaluate the equation and simplify the expression. Again, check each root by substituting into the original equation. In the quadratic formula, the portion of the formula under the radical ($b^2 - 4ac$) is called the **discriminant**. If the discriminant is zero, there is only one root: $-\frac{b}{2a}$. If the discriminant is positive, there are two different real roots. If the discriminant is negative, there are no real roots; you will instead find complex roots. Often these solutions don't make sense in context and are ignored.

> **Review Video: Using the Quadratic Formula**
> Visit mometrix.com/academy and enter code: 163102

FACTORING

To solve a quadratic equation by factoring, begin by rewriting the equation in standard form, $x^2 + bx + c = 0$. Remember that the goal of factoring is to find numbers f and g such that $(x + f)(x + g) = x^2 + (f + g)x + fg$, in other words $(f + g) = b$ and $fg = c$. This can be a really useful method when b and c are integers. Determine the factors of c and look for pairs that could sum to b.

For example, consider finding the roots of $x^2 + 6x - 16 = 0$. The factors of -16 include, -4 and 4, -8 and 2, -2 and 8, -1 and 16, and 1 and -16. The factors that sum to 6 are -2 and 8. Write these factors as the product of two binomials, $0 = (x - 2)(x + 8)$. Finally, since these binomials multiply together to equal zero, set them each equal to zero and solve each for x. This results in $x - 2 = 0$, which simplifies to $x = 2$ and $x + 8 = 0$, which simplifies to $x = -8$. Therefore, the roots of the equation are 2 and -8.

> **Review Video: Factoring Quadratic Equations**
> Visit mometrix.com/academy and enter code: 336566

COMPLETING THE SQUARE

One way to find the roots of a quadratic equation is to find a way to manipulate it such that it follows the form of a perfect square ($x^2 + 2px + p^2$) by adding and subtracting a constant. This process is called **completing the square**. In other words, if you are given a quadratic that is not a perfect square, $x^2 + bx + c = 0$, you can find a constant d that could be added in to make it a perfect square:

$$x^2 + bx + c + (d - d) = 0; \{\text{Let } b = 2p \text{ and } c + d = p^2\}$$

then:

$$x^2 + 2px + p^2 - d = 0 \text{ and } d = \frac{b^2}{4} - c$$

Once you have completed the square you can find the roots of the resulting equation:

$$x^2 + 2px + p^2 - d = 0$$
$$(x + p)^2 = d$$
$$x + p = \pm\sqrt{d}$$
$$x = -p \pm \sqrt{d}$$

It is worth noting that substituting the original expressions into this solution gives the same result as the quadratic formula where $a = 1$:

$$x = -p \pm \sqrt{d} = -\frac{b}{2} \pm \sqrt{\frac{b^2}{4} - c} = -\frac{b}{2} \pm \frac{\sqrt{b^2 - 4c}}{2} = \frac{-b \pm \sqrt{b^2 - 4c}}{2}$$

Completing the square can be seen as arranging block representations of each of the terms to be as close to a square as possible and then filling in the gaps. For example, consider the quadratic expression $x^2 + 6x + 2$:

$$x^2 + 6x + 2 \qquad\qquad = \qquad\qquad (x + 3)^2 - 7$$

Review Video: <u>Completing the Square</u>
Visit mometrix.com/academy and enter code: 982479

USING GIVEN ROOTS TO FIND QUADRATIC EQUATION

One way to find the roots of a quadratic equation is to factor the equation and use the **zero product property**, setting each factor of the equation equal to zero to find the corresponding root. We can use this technique in reverse to find an equation given its roots. Each root corresponds to a linear equation which in turn corresponds to a factor of the quadratic equation.

For example, we can find a quadratic equation whose roots are $x = 2$ and $x = -1$. The root $x = 2$ corresponds to the equation $x - 2 = 0$, and the root $x = -1$ corresponds to the equation $x + 1 = 0$.

These two equations correspond to the factors $(x - 2)$ and $(x + 1)$, from which we can derive the equation $(x - 2)(x + 1) = 0$, or $x^2 - x - 2 = 0$.

Any integer multiple of this entire equation will also yield the same roots, as the integer will simply cancel out when the equation is factored. For example, $2x^2 - 2x - 4 = 0$ factors as $2(x - 2)(x + 1) = 0$.

BASIC FUNCTIONS

FUNCTION AND RELATION

When expressing functional relationships, the **variables** x and y are typically used. These values are often written as the **coordinates** (x, y). The x-value is the independent variable and the y-value is the dependent variable. A **relation** is a set of data in which there is not a unique y-value for each x-value in the dataset. This means that there can be two of the same x-values assigned to different y-values. A relation is simply a relationship between the x- and y-values in each coordinate but does not apply to the relationship between the values of x and y in the data set. A **function** is a relation where one quantity depends on the other. For example, the amount of money that you make depends on the number of hours that you work. In a function, each x-value in the data set has one unique y-value because the y-value depends on the x-value.

FUNCTIONS

A function has exactly one value of **output variable** (dependent variable) for each value of the **input variable** (independent variable). The set of all values for the input variable (here assumed to be x) is the domain of the function, and the set of all corresponding values of the output variable (here assumed to be y) is the range of the function. When looking at a graph of an equation, the easiest way to determine if the equation is a function or not is to conduct the vertical line test. If a vertical line drawn through any value of x crosses the graph in more than one place, the equation is not a function.

DETERMINING A FUNCTION

You can determine whether an equation is a **function** by substituting different values into the equation for x. You can display and organize these numbers in a data table. A **data table** contains the values for x and y, which you can also list as coordinates. In order for a function to exist, the table cannot contain any repeating x-values that correspond with different y-values. If each x-coordinate has a unique y-coordinate, the table contains a function. However, there can be repeating y-values that correspond with different x-values. An example of this is when the function contains an exponent. Example: if $x^2 = y$, $2^2 = 4$, and $(-2)^2 = 4$.

> **Review Video: Definition of a Function**
> Visit mometrix.com/academy and enter code: 784611

FINDING THE DOMAIN AND RANGE OF A FUNCTION

The **domain** of a function $f(x)$ is the set of all input values for which the function is defined. The **range** of a function $f(x)$ is the set of all possible output values of the function—that is, of every possible value of $f(x)$, for any value of x in the function's domain. For a function expressed in a table, every input-output pair is given explicitly. To find the domain, we just list all the x-values and to find the range, we just list all the values of $f(x)$. Consider the following example:

x	−1	4	2	1	0	3	8	6
$f(x)$	3	0	3	−1	−1	2	4	6

In this case, the domain would be $\{-1, 4, 2, 1, 0, 3, 8, 6\}$ or, putting them in ascending order, $\{-1, 0, 1, 2, 3, 4, 6, 8\}$. (Putting the values in ascending order isn't strictly necessary, but generally makes the set easier to read.) The range would be $\{3, 0, 3, -1, -1, 2, 4, 6\}$. Note that some of these values appear more than once. This is entirely permissible for a function; while each value of x must be matched to a unique value of $f(x)$, the converse is not true. We don't need to list each value more than once, so eliminating duplicates, the range is $\{3, 0, -1, 2, 4, 6\}$, or, putting them in ascending order, $\{-1, 0, 2, 3, 4, 6\}$.

Note that by definition of a function, no input value can be matched to more than one output value. It is good to double-check to make sure that the data given follows this and is therefore actually a function.

> **Review Video: Domain and Range**
> Visit mometrix.com/academy and enter code: 778133
>
> **Review Video: Domain and Range of Quadratic Functions**
> Visit mometrix.com/academy and enter code: 331768

WRITING A FUNCTION RULE USING A TABLE

If given a set of data, place the corresponding x- and y-values into a table and analyze the relationship between them. Consider what you can do to each x-value to obtain the corresponding y-value. Try adding or subtracting different numbers to and from x and then try multiplying or dividing different numbers to and from x. If none of these **operations** give you the y-value, try combining the operations. Once you find a rule that works for one pair, make sure to try it with each additional set of ordered pairs in the table. If the same operation or combination of operations satisfies each set of coordinates, then the table contains a function. The rule is then used to write the equation of the function in "$y = f(x)$" form.

DIRECT AND INVERSE VARIATIONS OF VARIABLES

Variables that vary directly are those that either both increase at the same rate or both decrease at the same rate. For example, in the functions $y = kx$ or $y = kx^n$, where k and n are positive, the value of y increases as the value of x increases and decreases as the value of x decreases.

Variables that vary inversely are those where one increases while the other decreases. For example, in the functions $y = \frac{k}{x}$ or $y = \frac{k}{x^n}$ where k and n are positive, the value of y increases as the value of x decreases and decreases as the value of x increases.

In both cases, k is the constant of variation.

PROPERTIES OF FUNCTIONS

There are many different ways to classify functions based on their structure or behavior. Important features of functions include:

- **End behavior**: the behavior of the function at extreme values ($f(x)$ as $x \to \pm\infty$)
- **y-intercept**: the value of the function at $f(0)$
- **Roots**: the values of x where the function equals zero ($f(x) = 0$)
- **Extrema**: minimum or maximum values of the function or where the function changes direction ($f(x) \geq k$ or $f(x) \leq k$)

CLASSIFICATION OF FUNCTIONS

An **invertible function** is defined as a function, $f(x)$, for which there is another function, $f^{-1}(x)$, such that $f^{-1}(f(x)) = x$. For example, if $f(x) = 3x - 2$ the inverse function, $f^{-1}(x)$, can be found:

$$x = 3(f^{-1}(x)) - 2$$
$$\frac{x + 2}{3} = f^{-1}(x)$$

$$f^{-1}(f(x)) = \frac{3x - 2 + 2}{3}$$
$$= \frac{3x}{3}$$
$$= x$$

Note that $f^{-1}(x)$ is a valid function over all values of x.

In a **one-to-one function**, each value of x has exactly one value for y on the coordinate plane (this is the definition of a function) and each value of y has exactly one value for x. While the vertical line test will determine if a graph is that of a function, the horizontal line test will determine if a function is a one-to-one function. If a horizontal line drawn at any value of y intersects the graph in more than one place, the graph is not that of a one-to-one function. Do not make the mistake of using the horizontal line test exclusively in determining if a graph is that of a one-to-one function. A one-to-one function must pass both the vertical line test and the horizontal line test. As such, one-to-one functions are invertible functions.

A **many-to-one function** is a function whereby the relation is a function, but the inverse of the function is not a function. In other words, each element in the domain is mapped to one and only one element in the range. However, one or more elements in the range may be mapped to the same element in the domain. A graph of a many-to-one function would pass the vertical line test, but not the horizontal line test. This is why many-to-one functions are not invertible.

A **monotone function** is a function whose graph either constantly increases or constantly decreases. Examples include the functions $f(x) = x$, $f(x) = -x$, or $f(x) = x^3$.

124

An **even function** has a graph that is symmetric with respect to the y-axis and satisfies the equation $f(x) = f(-x)$. Examples include the functions $f(x) = x^2$ and $f(x) = ax^n$, where a is any real number and n is a positive even integer.

An **odd function** has a graph that is symmetric with respect to the origin and satisfies the equation $f(x) = -f(-x)$. Examples include the functions $f(x) = x^3$ and $f(x) = ax^n$, where a is any real number and n is a positive odd integer.

> **Review Video: Even and Odd Functions**
> Visit mometrix.com/academy and enter code: 278985

Constant functions are given by the equation $f(x) = b$, where b is a real number. There is no independent variable present in the equation, so the function has a constant value for all x. The graph of a constant function is a horizontal line of slope 0 that is positioned b units from the x-axis. If b is positive, the line is above the x-axis; if b is negative, the line is below the x-axis.

Identity functions are identified by the equation $f(x) = x$, where every value of the function is equal to its corresponding value of x. The only zero is the point $(0,0)$. The graph is a line with a slope of 1.

In **linear functions**, the value of the function changes in direct proportion to x. The rate of change, represented by the slope on its graph, is constant throughout. The standard form of a linear equation is $ax + cy = d$, where a, c, and d are real numbers. As a function, this equation is commonly in the form $y = mx + b$ or $f(x) = mx + b$ where $m = -\frac{a}{c}$ and $b = \frac{d}{c}$. This is known as the slope-intercept form, because the coefficients give the slope of the graphed function (m) and its y-intercept (b). Solve the equation $mx + b = 0$ for x to get $x = -\frac{b}{m}$, which is the only zero of the function. The domain and range are both the set of all real numbers.

> **Review Video: Graphing Linear Functions**
> Visit mometrix.com/academy and enter code: 699478

Algebraic functions are those that exclusively use polynomials and roots. These would include polynomial functions, rational functions, square root functions, and all combinations of these functions, such as polynomials as the radicand. These combinations may be joined by addition, subtraction, multiplication, or division, but may not include variables as exponents.

> **Review Video: Common Functions**
> Visit mometrix.com/academy and enter code: 629798

ABSOLUTE VALUE FUNCTIONS

An **absolute value function** is in the format $f(x) = |ax + b|$. Like other functions, the domain is the set of all real numbers. However, because absolute value indicates positive numbers, the range is limited to positive real numbers. To find the zero of an absolute value function, set the portion inside the absolute value sign equal to zero and solve for x. An absolute value function is also known as a piecewise function because it must be solved in pieces—one for if the value inside the absolute value sign is positive, and one for if the value is negative. The function can be expressed as:

$$f(x) = \begin{cases} ax + b \text{ if } ax + b \geq 0 \\ -(ax + b) \text{ if } ax + b < 0 \end{cases}$$

125

This will allow for an accurate statement of the range. The graph of an example absolute value function, $f(x) = |2x - 1|$, is below:

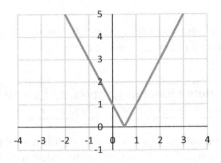

PIECEWISE FUNCTIONS

A **piecewise function** is a function that has different definitions on two or more different intervals. The following, for instance, is one example of a piecewise-defined function:

$$f(x) = \begin{cases} x^2, & x < 0 \\ x, & 0 \le x \le 2 \\ (x-2)^2, & x > 2 \end{cases}$$

To graph this function, you would simply graph each part separately in the appropriate domain. The final graph would look like this:

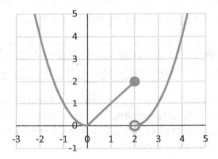

Note the filled and hollow dots at the discontinuity at $x = 2$. This is important to show which side of the graph that point corresponds to. Because $f(x) = x$ on the closed interval $0 \le x \le 2$, $f(2) = 2$. The point $(2, 2)$ is therefore marked with a filled circle, and the point $(2, 0)$, which is the endpoint of the rightmost $(x - 2)^2$ part of the graph but *not actually part of the function*, is marked with a hollow dot to indicate this.

> **Review Video: Piecewise Functions**
> Visit mometrix.com/academy and enter code: 707921

QUADRATIC FUNCTIONS

A **quadratic function** is a function in the form $y = ax^2 + bx + c$, where a does not equal 0. While a linear function forms a line, a quadratic function forms a **parabola**, which is a u-shaped figure that either opens upward or downward. A parabola that opens upward is said to be a **positive quadratic function,** and a parabola that opens downward is said to be a **negative quadratic function**. The shape of a parabola can differ, depending on the values of a, b, and c. All parabolas contain a **vertex**, which is the highest possible point, the **maximum**, or the lowest possible point, the **minimum**. This is the point where the graph begins moving in the opposite direction. A quadratic function can have zero, one, or two solutions, and therefore zero, one, or two x-intercepts. Recall that the x-intercepts are referred to as the zeros, or roots, of a function. A quadratic function will have only one y-intercept. Understanding the basic components of a quadratic function can give you an idea of the shape of its graph.

Example graph of a positive quadratic function, $x^2 + 2x - 3$:

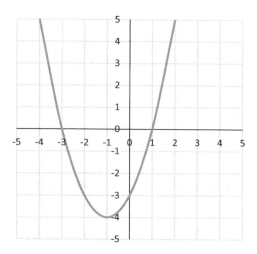

POLYNOMIAL FUNCTIONS

A **polynomial function** is a function with multiple terms and multiple powers of x, such as:

$$f(x) = a_n x^n + a_{n-1} x^{n-1} + a_{n-2} x^{n-2} + \cdots + a_1 x + a_0$$

where n is a non-negative integer that is the highest exponent in the polynomial and $a_n \neq 0$. The domain of a polynomial function is the set of all real numbers. If the greatest exponent in the polynomial is even, the polynomial is said to be of even degree and the range is the set of real numbers that satisfy the function. If the greatest exponent in the polynomial is odd, the polynomial is said to be odd and the range, like the domain, is the set of all real numbers.

RATIONAL FUNCTIONS

A **rational function** is a function that can be constructed as a ratio of two polynomial expressions: $f(x) = \frac{p(x)}{q(x)}$, where $p(x)$ and $q(x)$ are both polynomial expressions and $q(x) \neq 0$. The domain is the set of all real numbers, except any values for which $q(x) = 0$. The range is the set of real numbers that satisfies the function when the domain is applied. When you graph a rational function, you will have vertical asymptotes wherever $q(x) = 0$. If the polynomial in the numerator is of lesser degree than the polynomial in the denominator, the x-axis will also be a horizontal asymptote. If the numerator and denominator have equal degrees, there will be a horizontal asymptote not on the x-axis. If the degree of the numerator is exactly one greater than the degree of the denominator, the graph will have an oblique, or diagonal, asymptote. The asymptote will be along the line $y = \frac{p_n}{q_{n-1}} x + \frac{p_{n-1}}{q_{n-1}}$, where p_n and q_{n-1} are the coefficients of the highest degree terms in their respective polynomials.

SQUARE ROOT FUNCTIONS

A **square root function** is a function that contains a radical and is in the format $f(x) = \sqrt{ax + b}$. The domain is the set of all real numbers that yields a positive radicand or a radicand equal to zero. Because square root values are assumed to be positive unless otherwise identified, the range is all real numbers from zero to infinity. To find the zero of a square root function, set the radicand equal to zero and solve for x. The graph of a square root function is always to the right of the zero and always above the x-axis.

Example graph of a square root function, $f(x) = \sqrt{2x + 1}$:

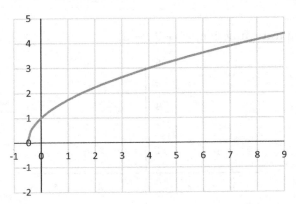

Geometry and Measurement

ROUNDING AND ESTIMATION

Rounding is reducing the digits in a number while still trying to keep the value similar. The result will be less accurate but in a simpler form and easier to use. Whole numbers can be rounded to the nearest ten, hundred, or thousand.

When you are asked to estimate the solution to a problem, you will need to provide only an approximate figure or **estimation** for your answer. In this situation, you will need to round each number in the calculation to the level indicated (nearest hundred, nearest thousand, etc.) or to a level that makes sense for the numbers involved. When estimating a sum **all numbers must be rounded to the same level**. You cannot round one number to the nearest thousand while rounding another to the nearest hundred.

> **Review Video: Rounding and Estimation**
> Visit mometrix.com/academy and enter code: 126243

SCIENTIFIC NOTATION

Scientific notation is a way of writing large numbers in a shorter form. The form $a \times 10^n$ is used in scientific notation, where a is greater than or equal to 1 but less than 10, and n is the number of places the decimal must move to get from the original number to a. Example: The number 230,400,000 is cumbersome to write. To write the value in scientific notation, place a decimal point between the first and second numbers, and include all digits through the last non-zero digit ($a = 2.304$). To find the appropriate power of 10, count the number of places the decimal point had to move ($n = 8$). The number is positive if the decimal moved to the left, and negative if it moved to the right. We can then write 230,400,000 as 2.304×10^8. If we look instead at the number 0.00002304, we have the same value for a, but this time the decimal moved 5 places to the right ($n = -5$). Thus, 0.00002304 can be written as 2.304×10^{-5}. Using this notation makes it simple to compare very large or very small numbers. By comparing exponents, it is easy to see that 3.28×10^4 is smaller than 1.51×10^5, because 4 is less than 5.

> **Review Video: Scientific Notation**
> Visit mometrix.com/academy and enter code: 976454

PRECISION, ACCURACY, AND ERROR

Precision: How reliable and repeatable a measurement is. The more consistent the data is with repeated testing, the more precise it is. For example, hitting a target consistently in the same spot, which may or may not be the center of the target, is precision.

Accuracy: How close the data is to the correct data. For example, hitting a target consistently in the center area of the target, whether or not the hits are all in the same spot, is accuracy.

Note: it is possible for data to be precise without being accurate. If a scale is off balance, the data will be precise, but will not be accurate. For data to have precision and accuracy, it must be repeatable and correct.

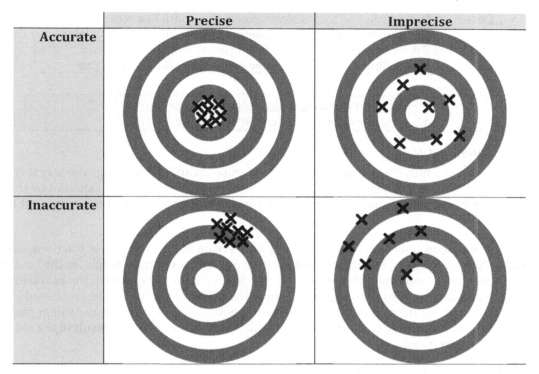

Approximate error: The amount of error in a physical measurement. Approximate error is often reported as the measurement, followed by the ± symbol and the amount of the approximate error.

Maximum possible error: Half the magnitude of the smallest unit used in the measurement. For example, if the unit of measurement is 1 centimeter, the maximum possible error is $\frac{1}{2}$ cm, written as ±0.5 cm following the measurement. It is important to apply significant figures in reporting maximum possible error. Do not make the answer appear more accurate than the least accurate of your measurements.

> **Review Video: Precision, Accuracy, and Error**
> Visit mometrix.com/academy and enter code: 520377

METRIC AND CUSTOMARY MEASUREMENTS

METRIC MEASUREMENT PREFIXES

Giga-	One billion	1 *giga*watt is one billion watts
Mega-	One million	1 *mega*hertz is one million hertz
Kilo-	One thousand	1 *kilo*gram is one thousand grams
Deci-	One-tenth	1 *deci*meter is one-tenth of a meter
Centi-	One-hundredth	1 *centi*meter is one-hundredth of a meter
Milli-	One-thousandth	1 *milli*liter is one-thousandth of a liter
Micro-	One-millionth	1 *micro*gram is one-millionth of a gram

---

Review Video: How the Metric System Works
Visit mometrix.com/academy and enter code: 163709

MEASUREMENT CONVERSION

When converting between units, the goal is to maintain the same meaning but change the way it is displayed. In order to go from a larger unit to a smaller unit, multiply the number of the known amount by the equivalent amount. When going from a smaller unit to a larger unit, divide the number of the known amount by the equivalent amount.

For complicated conversions, it may be helpful to set up conversion fractions. In these fractions, one fraction is the **conversion factor**. The other fraction has the unknown amount in the numerator. So, the known value is placed in the denominator. Sometimes, the second fraction has the known value from the problem in the numerator and the unknown in the denominator. Multiply the two fractions to get the converted measurement. Note that since the numerator and the denominator of the factor are equivalent, the value of the fraction is 1. That is why we can say that the result in the new units is equal to the result in the old units even though they have different numbers.

It can often be necessary to chain known conversion factors together. As an example, consider converting 512 square inches to square meters. We know that there are 2.54 centimeters in an inch and 100 centimeters in a meter, and we know we will need to square each of these factors to achieve the conversion we are looking for.

$$\frac{512 \text{ in}^2}{1} \times \left(\frac{2.54 \text{ cm}}{1 \text{ in}}\right)^2 \times \left(\frac{1 \text{ m}}{100 \text{ cm}}\right)^2 = \frac{512 \text{ in}^2}{1} \times \left(\frac{6.4516 \text{ cm}^2}{1 \text{ in}^2}\right) \times \left(\frac{1 \text{ m}^2}{10,000 \text{ cm}^2}\right) = 0.330 \text{ m}^2$$

Review Video: Measurement Conversions
Visit mometrix.com/academy and enter code: 316703

COMMON UNITS AND EQUIVALENTS
METRIC EQUIVALENTS

1000 µg (microgram)	1 mg
1000 mg (milligram)	1 g
1000 g (gram)	1 kg
1000 kg (kilogram)	1 metric ton
1000 mL (milliliter)	1 L
1000 µm (micrometer)	1 mm
1000 mm (millimeter)	1 m
100 cm (centimeter)	1 m
1000 m (meter)	1 km

DISTANCE AND AREA MEASUREMENT

Unit	Abbreviation	US equivalent	Metric equivalent
Inch	in	1 inch	2.54 centimeters
Foot	ft	12 inches	0.305 meters
Yard	yd	3 feet	0.914 meters
Mile	mi	5280 feet	1.609 kilometers
Acre	ac	4840 square yards	0.405 hectares
Square Mile	sq. mi. or mi.^{2}	640 acres	2.590 square kilometers

CAPACITY MEASUREMENTS

Unit	Abbreviation	US equivalent	Metric equivalent
Fluid Ounce	fl oz	8 fluid drams	29.573 milliliters
Cup	c	8 fluid ounces	0.237 liter
Pint	pt.	16 fluid ounces	0.473 liter
Quart	qt.	2 pints	0.946 liter
Gallon	gal.	4 quarts	3.785 liters
Teaspoon	t or tsp.	1 fluid dram	5 milliliters
Tablespoon	T or tbsp.	4 fluid drams	15 or 16 milliliters
Cubic Centimeter	cc or cm^3	0.271 drams	1 milliliter

WEIGHT MEASUREMENTS

Unit	Abbreviation	US equivalent	Metric equivalent
Ounce	oz	16 drams	28.35 grams
Pound	lb	16 ounces	453.6 grams
Ton	tn.	2,000 pounds	907.2 kilograms

VOLUME AND WEIGHT MEASUREMENT CLARIFICATIONS

Always be careful when using ounces and fluid ounces. They are not equivalent.

1 pint = 16 fluid ounces	1 fluid ounce ≠ 1 ounce
1 pound = 16 ounces	1 pint ≠ 1 pound

Having one pint of something does not mean you have one pound of it. In the same way, just because something weighs one pound does not mean that its volume is one pint.

In the United States, the word "ton" by itself refers to a short ton or a net ton. Do not confuse this with a long ton (also called a gross ton) or a metric ton (also spelled *tonne*), which have different measurement equivalents.

$$1 \text{ US ton} = 2000 \text{ pounds} \qquad \neq \qquad 1 \text{ metric ton} = 1000 \text{ kilograms}$$

Mathematics

131

POINTS, LINES, AND PLANES

POINTS AND LINES

A **point** is a fixed location in space, has no size or dimensions, and is commonly represented by a dot. A **line** is a set of points that extends infinitely in two opposite directions. It has length, but no width or depth. A line can be defined by any two distinct points that it contains. A **line segment** is a portion of a line that has definite endpoints. A **ray** is a portion of a line that extends from a single point on that line in one direction along the line. It has a definite beginning, but no ending.

Point   Line   Segment   Ray

INTERACTIONS BETWEEN LINES

Intersecting lines are lines that have exactly one point in common. **Concurrent lines** are multiple lines that intersect at a single point. **Perpendicular lines** are lines that intersect at right angles. They are represented by the symbol ⊥. The shortest distance from a line to a point not on the line is a perpendicular segment from the point to the line. **Parallel lines** are lines in the same plane that have no points in common and never meet. It is possible for lines to be in different planes, have no points in common, and never meet, but they are not parallel because they are in different planes.

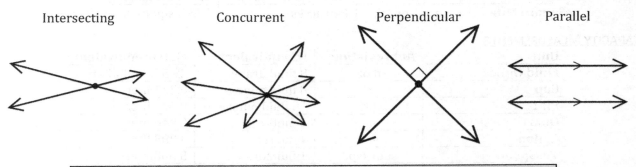

Intersecting   Concurrent   Perpendicular   Parallel

> **Review Video: Parallel and Perpendicular Lines**
> Visit mometrix.com/academy and enter code: 815923

A **transversal** is a line that intersects at least two other lines, which may or may not be parallel to one another. A transversal that intersects parallel lines is a common occurrence in geometry. A **bisector** is a line or line segment that divides another line segment into two equal lengths. A **perpendicular bisector** of a line segment is composed of points that are equidistant from the endpoints of the segment it is dividing.

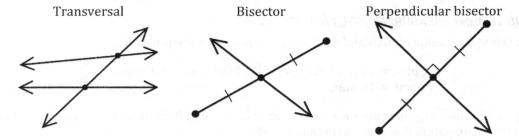

Transversal   Bisector   Perpendicular bisector

The **projection of a point on a line** is the point at which a perpendicular line drawn from the given point to the given line intersects the line. This is also the shortest distance from the given point to the line. The **projection of a segment on a line** is a segment whose endpoints are the points formed when perpendicular

132

lines are drawn from the endpoints of the given segment to the given line. This is similar to the length a diagonal line appears to be when viewed from above.

Projection of a point on a line

Projection of a segment on a line

PLANES

A **plane** is a two-dimensional flat surface defined by three non-collinear points. A plane extends an infinite distance in all directions in those two dimensions. It contains an infinite number of points, parallel lines and segments, intersecting lines and segments, as well as parallel or intersecting rays. A plane will never contain a three-dimensional figure or skew lines, which are lines that don't intersect and are not parallel. Two given planes are either parallel or they intersect at a line. A plane may intersect a circular conic surface to form **conic sections**, such as a parabola, hyperbola, circle or ellipse.

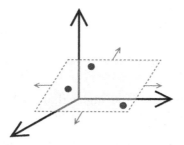

> **Review Video: Lines and Planes**
> Visit mometrix.com/academy and enter code: 554267

ANGLES

ANGLES AND VERTICES

An **angle** is formed when two lines or line segments meet at a common point. It may be a common starting point for a pair of segments or rays, or it may be the intersection of lines. Angles are represented by the symbol ∠.

The **vertex** is the point at which two segments or rays meet to form an angle. If the angle is formed by intersecting rays, lines, and/or line segments, the vertex is the point at which four angles are formed. The pairs of angles opposite one another are called vertical angles, and their measures are equal.

- An **acute** angle is an angle with a degree measure less than 90°.
- A **right** angle is an angle with a degree measure of exactly 90°.
- An **obtuse** angle is an angle with a degree measure greater than 90° but less than 180°.
- A **straight angle** is an angle with a degree measure of exactly 180°. This is also a semicircle.
- A **reflex angle** is an angle with a degree measure greater than 180° but less than 360°.
- A **full angle** is an angle with a degree measure of exactly 360°. This is also a circle.

> **Review Video: Angles**
> Visit mometrix.com/academy and enter code: 264624

133

RELATIONSHIPS BETWEEN ANGLES

Two angles whose sum is exactly 90° are said to be **complementary**. The two angles may or may not be adjacent. In a right triangle, the two acute angles are complementary.

Two angles whose sum is exactly 180° are said to be **supplementary**. The two angles may or may not be adjacent. Two intersecting lines always form two pairs of supplementary angles. Adjacent supplementary angles will always form a straight line.

Two angles that have the same vertex and share a side are said to be **adjacent**. Vertical angles are not adjacent because they share a vertex but no common side.

Review Video: <u>**Adjacent Angles**</u>
Visit mometrix.com/academy and enter code: 100375

Adjacent
Share vertex and side

Not adjacent
Share part of a side, but not vertex

When two parallel lines are cut by a transversal, the angles that are between the two parallel lines are **interior angles**. In the diagram below, angles 3, 4, 5, and 6 are interior angles.

When two parallel lines are cut by a transversal, the angles that are outside the parallel lines are **exterior angles**. In the diagram below, angles 1, 2, 7, and 8 are exterior angles.

When two parallel lines are cut by a transversal, the angles that are in the same position relative to the transversal and a parallel line are **corresponding angles**. The diagram below has four pairs of corresponding angles: angles 1 and 5, angles 2 and 6, angles 3 and 7, and angles 4 and 8. Corresponding angles formed by parallel lines are congruent.

When two parallel lines are cut by a transversal, the two interior angles that are on opposite sides of the transversal are called **alternate interior angles**. In the diagram below, there are two pairs of alternate interior angles: angles 3 and 6, and angles 4 and 5. Alternate interior angles formed by parallel lines are congruent.

When two parallel lines are cut by a transversal, the two exterior angles that are on opposite sides of the transversal are called **alternate exterior angles**.

In the diagram below, there are two pairs of alternate exterior angles: angles 1 and 8, and angles 2 and 7. Alternate exterior angles formed by parallel lines are congruent.

When two lines intersect, four angles are formed. The non-adjacent angles at this vertex are called vertical angles. Vertical angles are congruent. In the diagram, $\angle ABD \cong \angle CBE$ and $\angle ABC \cong \angle DBE$. The other pairs of angles, ($\angle ABC$, $\angle CBE$) and ($\angle ABD$, $\angle DBE$), are supplementary, meaning the pairs sum to 180°.

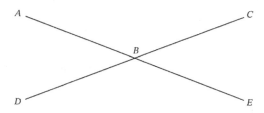

> **Review Video: Congruent Angles**
> Visit mometrix.com/academy and enter code: 642874

POLYGONS

A **polygon** is a closed, two-dimensional figure with three or more straight line segments called **sides**. The point at which two sides of a polygon intersect is called the **vertex**. In a polygon, the number of sides is always equal to the number of vertices. A polygon with all sides congruent and all angles equal is called a **regular polygon**. Common polygons are:

Triangle = 3 sides
Quadrilateral = 4 sides
Pentagon = 5 sides
Hexagon = 6 sides
Heptagon = 7 sides
Octagon = 8 sides
Nonagon = 9 sides
Decagon = 10 sides
Dodecagon = 12 sides

More generally, an n-gon is a polygon that has n angles and n sides.

> **Review Video: Intro to Polygons**
> Visit mometrix.com/academy and enter code: 271869

The sum of the interior angles of an n-sided polygon is $(n - 2) \times 180°$. For example, in a triangle $n = 3$. So the sum of the interior angles is $(3 - 2) \times 180° = 180°$. In a quadrilateral, $n = 4$, and the sum of the angles is $(4 - 2) \times 180° = 360°$.

Review Video: **Sum of Interior Angles**
Visit mometrix.com/academy and enter code: 984991

CONVEX AND CONCAVE POLYGONS

A **convex polygon** is a polygon whose diagonals all lie within the interior of the polygon. A **concave polygon** is a polygon with a least one diagonal that is outside the polygon. In the diagram below, quadrilateral $ABCD$ is concave because diagonal $\overline{AC}$ lies outside the polygon and quadrilateral $EFGH$ is convex because both diagonals lie inside the polygon.

APOTHEM AND RADIUS

A line segment from the center of a polygon that is perpendicular to a side of the polygon is called the **apothem**. A line segment from the center of a polygon to a vertex of the polygon is called a **radius**. In a regular polygon, the apothem can be used to find the area of the polygon using the formula $A = \frac{1}{2}ap$, where a is the apothem, and p is the perimeter.

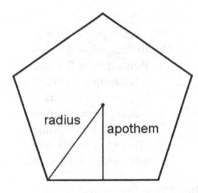

A **diagonal** is a line segment that joins two non-adjacent vertices of a polygon. The number of diagonals a polygon has can be found by using the formula:

$$\text{number of diagonals} = \frac{n(n - 3)}{2}$$

Note that n is the number of sides in the polygon. This formula works for all polygons, not just regular polygons.

CONGRUENCE AND SIMILARITY

Congruent figures are geometric figures that have the same size and shape. All corresponding angles are equal, and all corresponding sides are equal. Congruence is indicated by the symbol ≅.

Congruent polygons

Similar figures are geometric figures that have the same shape, but do not necessarily have the same size. All corresponding angles are equal, and all corresponding sides are proportional, but they do not have to be equal. It is indicated by the symbol ~.

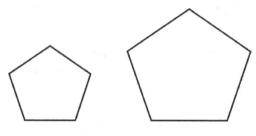

Similar polygons

Note that all congruent figures are also similar, but not all similar figures are congruent.

Review Video: Congruent Shapes
Visit mometrix.com/academy and enter code: 492281

LINE OF SYMMETRY

A line that divides a figure or object into congruent parts is called a **line of symmetry**. An object may have no lines of symmetry, one line of symmetry, or multiple (i.e., more than one) lines of symmetry.

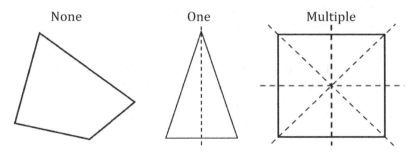

Review Video: Symmetry
Visit mometrix.com/academy and enter code: 528106

137

TRIANGLES

A triangle is a three-sided figure with the sum of its interior angles being 180°. The **perimeter of any triangle** is found by summing the three side lengths; $P = a + b + c$. For an equilateral triangle, this is the same as $P = 3a$, where a is any side length, since all three sides are the same length.

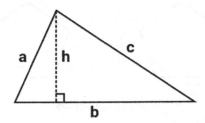

The **area of any triangle** can be found by taking half the product of one side length referred to as the base, often given the variable b and the perpendicular distance from that side to the opposite vertex called the altitude or height and given the variable h. In equation form that is $A = \frac{1}{2}bh$. Another formula that works for any triangle is $A = \sqrt{s(s-a)(s-b)(s-c)}$, where s is the semiperimeter: $\frac{a+b+c}{2}$, and a, b, and c are the lengths of the three sides. Special cases include isosceles triangles, $A = \frac{1}{2}b\sqrt{a^2 - \frac{b^2}{4}}$, where b is the unique side and a is the length of one of the two congruent sides, and equilateral triangles, $A = \frac{\sqrt{3}}{4}a^2$, where a is the length of a side.

PARTS OF A TRIANGLE

An **altitude** of a triangle is a line segment drawn from one vertex perpendicular to the opposite side. In the diagram that follows, $\overline{BE}$, $\overline{AD}$, and $\overline{CF}$ are altitudes. The length of an altitude is also called the height of the triangle. The three altitudes in a triangle are always concurrent. The point of concurrency of the altitudes of a triangle, O, is called the **orthocenter**. Note that in an obtuse triangle, the orthocenter will be outside the triangle, and in a right triangle, the orthocenter is the vertex of the right angle.

A **median** of a triangle is a line segment drawn from one vertex to the midpoint of the opposite side. In the diagram that follows, $\overline{BH}$, $\overline{AG}$, and $\overline{CI}$ are medians. This is not the same as the altitude, except the altitude to the base of an isosceles triangle and all three altitudes of an equilateral triangle. The point of concurrency of the medians of a triangle, T, is called the **centroid**. This is the same point as the orthocenter only in an equilateral triangle. Unlike the orthocenter, the centroid is always inside the triangle. The centroid can also be considered the exact center of the triangle. Any shape triangle can be perfectly balanced on a tip placed at the centroid. The centroid is also the point that is two-thirds the distance from the vertex to the opposite side.

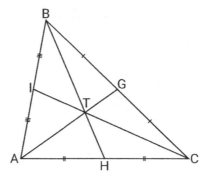

Review Video: <u>Centroid, Incenter, Circumcenter, and Orthocenter</u>
Visit mometrix.com/academy and enter code: 598260

TRIANGLE PROPERTIES
CLASSIFICATIONS OF TRIANGLES

A **scalene triangle** is a triangle with no congruent sides. A scalene triangle will also have three angles of different measures. The angle with the largest measure is opposite the longest side, and the angle with the smallest measure is opposite the shortest side. An **acute triangle** is a triangle whose three angles are all less than 90°. If two of the angles are equal, the acute triangle is also an **isosceles triangle**. An isosceles triangle will also have two congruent angles opposite the two congruent sides. If the three angles are all equal, the acute triangle is also an **equilateral triangle**. An equilateral triangle will also have three congruent angles, each 60°. All equilateral triangles are also acute triangles. An **obtuse triangle** is a triangle with exactly one angle greater than 90°. The other two angles may or may not be equal. If the two remaining angles are equal, the obtuse triangle is also an isosceles triangle. A **right triangle** is a triangle with exactly one angle equal to 90°. All right triangles follow the Pythagorean theorem. A right triangle can never be acute or obtuse.

The table below illustrates how each descriptor places a different restriction on the triangle:

Angles / Sides	Acute: All angles < 90°	Obtuse: One angle > 90°	Right: One angle = 90°
Scalene: No equal side lengths	$90° > \angle a > \angle b > \angle c$ $x > y > z$	$\angle a > 90° > \angle b > \angle c$ $x > y > z$	$90° = \angle a > \angle b > \angle c$ $x > y > z$
Isosceles: Two equal side lengths	$90° > \angle a, \angle b, \text{ or } \angle c$ $\angle b = \angle c, \quad y = z$	$\angle a > 90° > \angle b = \angle c$ $x > y = z$	$\angle a = 90°$ $\angle b = \angle c = 45°$ $x > y = z$
Equilateral: Three equal side lengths	$60° = \angle a = \angle b = \angle c$ $x = y = z$		

Review Video: Introduction to Types of Triangles
Visit mometrix.com/academy and enter code: 511711

GENERAL RULES FOR TRIANGLES

The **triangle inequality theorem** states that the sum of the measures of any two sides of a triangle is always greater than the measure of the third side. If the sum of the measures of two sides were equal to the third side, a triangle would be impossible because the two sides would lie flat across the third side and there would be no vertex. If the sum of the measures of two of the sides was less than the third side, a closed figure would be impossible because the two shortest sides would never meet. In other words, for a triangle with sides lengths A, B, and C: $A + B > C$, $B + C > A$, and $A + C > B$.

The sum of the measures of the interior angles of a triangle is always 180°. Therefore, a triangle can never have more than one angle greater than or equal to 90°.

In any triangle, the angles opposite congruent sides are congruent, and the sides opposite congruent angles are congruent. The largest angle is always opposite the longest side, and the smallest angle is always opposite the shortest side.

The line segment that joins the midpoints of any two sides of a triangle is always parallel to the third side and exactly half the length of the third side.

> **Review Video: General Rules (Triangle Inequality Theorem)**
> Visit mometrix.com/academy and enter code: 166488

SIMILARITY AND CONGRUENCE RULES

Similar triangles are triangles whose corresponding angles are equal and whose corresponding sides are proportional. Represented by AAA. Similar triangles whose corresponding sides are congruent are also congruent triangles.

Triangles can be shown to be **congruent** in 5 ways:

- **SSS**: Three sides of one triangle are congruent to the three corresponding sides of the second triangle.
- **SAS**: Two sides and the included angle (the angle formed by those two sides) of one triangle are congruent to the corresponding two sides and included angle of the second triangle.
- **ASA**: Two angles and the included side (the side that joins the two angles) of one triangle are congruent to the corresponding two angles and included side of the second triangle.
- **AAS**: Two angles and a non-included side of one triangle are congruent to the corresponding two angles and non-included side of the second triangle.
- **HL**: The hypotenuse and leg of one right triangle are congruent to the corresponding hypotenuse and leg of the second right triangle.

> **Review Video: Similar Triangles**
> Visit mometrix.com/academy and enter code: 398538

TRANSFORMATIONS

ROTATION

A **rotation** is a transformation that turns a figure around a point called the **center of rotation**, which can lie anywhere in the plane. If a line is drawn from a point on a figure to the center of rotation, and another line is drawn from the center to the rotated image of that point, the angle between the two lines is the **angle of rotation**. The vertex of the angle of rotation is the center of rotation.

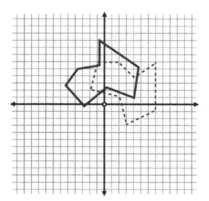

> **Review Video: Rotation**
> Visit mometrix.com/academy and enter code: 602600

TRANSLATION AND DILATION

A **translation** is a transformation which slides a figure from one position in the plane to another position in the plane. The original figure and the translated figure have the same size, shape, and orientation. A **dilation** is

141

a transformation which proportionally stretches or shrinks a figure by a **scale factor**. The dilated image is the same shape and orientation as the original image but a different size. A polygon and its dilated image are similar.

Translation

Dilation

Review Video: <u>Translation</u>
Visit mometrix.com/academy and enter code: 718628

Review Video: <u>Dilation</u>
Visit mometrix.com/academy and enter code: 471630

A **reflection of a figure over a line** (a "flip") creates a congruent image that is the same distance from the line as the original figure but on the opposite side. The **line of reflection** is the perpendicular bisector of any line segment drawn from a point on the original figure to its reflected image (unless the point and its reflected image happen to be the same point, which happens when a figure is reflected over one of its own sides). A **reflection of a figure over a point** (an inversion) in two dimensions is the same as the rotation of the figure 180° about that point. The image of the figure is congruent to the original figure. The **point of reflection** is the midpoint of a line segment which connects a point in the figure to its image (unless the point and its reflected image happen to be the same point, which happens when a figure is reflected in one of its own points).

Reflection of a figure over a line

Reflection of a figure over a point

Review Video: <u>Reflection</u>
Visit mometrix.com/academy and enter code: 955068

142

PYTHAGOREAN THEOREM

The side of a triangle opposite the right angle is called the **hypotenuse**. The other two sides are called the legs. The Pythagorean theorem states a relationship among the legs and hypotenuse of a right triangle: $(a^2 + b^2 = c^2)$, where a and b are the lengths of the legs of a right triangle, and c is the length of the hypotenuse. Note that this formula will only work with right triangles.

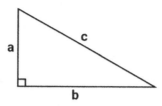

| **Review Video: Pythagorean Theorem** |
| Visit mometrix.com/academy and enter code: 906576 |

TRIGONOMETRIC FORMULAS

In the diagram below, angle C is the right angle, and side c is the hypotenuse. Side a is the side opposite to angle A and side b is the side opposite to angle B. Using ratios of side lengths as a means to calculate the sine, cosine, and tangent of an acute angle only works for right triangles.

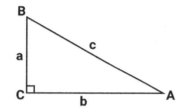

$$\sin A = \frac{\text{opposite side}}{\text{hypotenuse}} = \frac{a}{c} \qquad \csc A = \frac{1}{\sin A} = \frac{\text{hypotenuse}}{\text{opposite side}} = \frac{c}{a}$$

$$\cos A = \frac{\text{adjacent side}}{\text{hypotenuse}} = \frac{b}{c} \qquad \sec A = \frac{1}{\cos A} = \frac{\text{hypotenuse}}{\text{adjacent side}} = \frac{c}{b}$$

$$\tan A = \frac{\text{opposite side}}{\text{adjacent side}} = \frac{a}{b} \qquad \cot A = \frac{1}{\tan A} = \frac{\text{adjacent side}}{\text{opposite side}} = \frac{b}{a}$$

LAWS OF SINES AND COSINES

The **law of sines** states that $\frac{\sin A}{a} = \frac{\sin B}{b} = \frac{\sin C}{c}$, where A, B, and C are the angles of a triangle, and a, b, and c are the sides opposite their respective angles. This formula will work with all triangles, not just right triangles.

The **law of cosines** is given by the formula $c^2 = a^2 + b^2 - 2ab(\cos C)$, where a, b, and c are the sides of a triangle, and C is the angle opposite side c. This is a generalized form of the Pythagorean theorem that can be used on any triangle.

| **Review Video: Law of Sines** |
| Visit mometrix.com/academy and enter code: 206844 |
| **Review Video: Law of Cosines** |
| Visit mometrix.com/academy and enter code: 158911 |

QUADRILATERALS

A **quadrilateral** is a closed two-dimensional geometric figure that has four straight sides. The sum of the interior angles of any quadrilateral is 360°.

Review Video: <u>**Diagonals of Parallelograms, Rectangles, and Rhombi**</u>
Visit mometrix.com/academy and enter code: 320040

KITE

A **kite** is a quadrilateral with two pairs of adjacent sides that are congruent. A result of this is perpendicular diagonals. A kite can be concave or convex and has one line of symmetry.

TRAPEZOID

Trapezoid: A trapezoid is defined as a quadrilateral that has at least one pair of parallel sides. There are no rules for the second pair of sides. So, there are no rules for the diagonals and no lines of symmetry for a trapezoid.

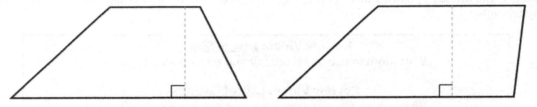

The **area of a trapezoid** is found by the formula $A = \frac{1}{2}h(b_1 + b_2)$, where h is the height (segment joining and perpendicular to the parallel bases), and b_1 and b_2 are the two parallel sides (bases). Do not use one of the other two sides as the height unless that side is also perpendicular to the parallel bases.

The **perimeter of a trapezoid** is found by the formula $P = a + b_1 + c + b_2$, where a, b_1, c, and b_2 are the four sides of the trapezoid.

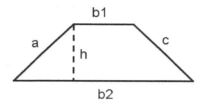

> **Review Video: Area and Perimeter of a Trapezoid**
> Visit mometrix.com/academy and enter code: 587523

Isosceles trapezoid: A trapezoid with equal base angles. This gives rise to other properties including: the two nonparallel sides have the same length, the two non-base angles are also equal, and there is one line of symmetry through the midpoints of the parallel sides.

PARALLELOGRAM

A **parallelogram** is a quadrilateral that has two pairs of opposite parallel sides. As such it is a special type of trapezoid. The sides that are parallel are also congruent. The opposite interior angles are always congruent, and the consecutive interior angles are supplementary. The diagonals of a parallelogram divide each other. Each diagonal divides the parallelogram into two congruent triangles. A parallelogram has no line of symmetry, but does have 180-degree rotational symmetry about the midpoint.

The **area of a parallelogram** is found by the formula $A = bh$, where b is the length of the base, and h is the height. Note that the base and height correspond to the length and width in a rectangle, so this formula would apply to rectangles as well. Do not confuse the height of a parallelogram with the length of the second side. The two are only the same measure in the case of a rectangle.

The **perimeter of a parallelogram** is found by the formula $P = 2a + 2b$ or $P = 2(a + b)$, where a and b are the lengths of the two sides.

> **Review Video: Area and Perimeter of a Parallelogram**
> Visit mometrix.com/academy and enter code: 718313

RECTANGLE

A **rectangle** is a quadrilateral with four right angles. All rectangles are parallelograms and trapezoids, but not all parallelograms or trapezoids are rectangles. The diagonals of a rectangle are congruent. Rectangles have two lines of symmetry (through each pair of opposing midpoints) and 180-degree rotational symmetry about the midpoint.

The **area of a rectangle** is found by the formula $A = lw$, where A is the area of the rectangle, l is the length (usually considered to be the longer side) and w is the width (usually considered to be the shorter side). The numbers for l and w are interchangeable.

The **perimeter of a rectangle** is found by the formula $P = 2l + 2w$ or $P = 2(l + w)$, where l is the length, and w is the width. It may be easier to add the length and width first and then double the result, as in the second formula.

RHOMBUS

A **rhombus** is a quadrilateral with four congruent sides. All rhombuses are parallelograms and kites; thus, they inherit all the properties of both types of quadrilaterals. The diagonals of a rhombus are perpendicular to each other. Rhombi have two lines of symmetry (along each of the diagonals) and 180° rotational symmetry. The **area of a rhombus** is half the product of the diagonals: $A = \frac{d_1 d_2}{2}$ and the perimeter of a rhombus is: $P = 2\sqrt{(d_1)^2 + (d_2)^2}$.

SQUARE

A **square** is a quadrilateral with four right angles and four congruent sides. Squares satisfy the criteria of all other types of quadrilaterals. The diagonals of a square are congruent and perpendicular to each other. Squares have four lines of symmetry (through each pair of opposing midpoints and along each of the diagonals) as well as 90° rotational symmetry about the midpoint.

The **area of a square** is found by using the formula $A = s^2$, where s is the length of one side. The **perimeter of a square** is found by using the formula $P = 4s$, where s is the length of one side. Because all four sides are equal in a square, it is faster to multiply the length of one side by 4 than to add the same number four times. You could use the formulas for rectangles and get the same answer.

> **Review Video: Area and Perimeter of Rectangles and Squares**
> Visit mometrix.com/academy and enter code: 428109

Mathematics

HIERARCHY OF QUADRILATERALS

The hierarchy of quadrilaterals is as follows:

148

CIRCLES

The **center** of a circle is the single point from which every point on the circle is **equidistant**. The **radius** is a line segment that joins the center of the circle and any one point on the circle. All radii of a circle are equal. Circles that have the same center but not the same length of radii are **concentric**. The **diameter** is a line segment that passes through the center of the circle and has both endpoints on the circle. The length of the diameter is exactly twice the length of the radius. Point O in the diagram below is the center of the circle, segments $\overline{OX}$, $\overline{OY}$, and $\overline{OZ}$ are radii; and segment $\overline{XZ}$ is a diameter.

> **Review Video: Points of a Circle**
> Visit mometrix.com/academy and enter code: 420746
>
> **Review Video: Diameter, Radius, and Circumference**
> Visit mometrix.com/academy and enter code: 448988

The **area of a circle** is found by the formula $A = \pi r^2$, where r is the length of the radius. If the diameter of the circle is given, remember to divide it in half to get the length of the radius before proceeding.

The **circumference** of a circle is found by the formula $C = 2\pi r$, where r is the radius. Again, remember to convert the diameter if you are given that measure rather than the radius.

> **Review Video: Area and Circumference of a Circle**
> Visit mometrix.com/academy and enter code: 243015

INSCRIBED AND CIRCUMSCRIBED FIGURES

These terms can both be used to describe a given arrangement of figures, depending on perspective. If each of the vertices of figure A lie on figure B, then it can be said that figure A is **inscribed** in figure B, but it can also be said that figure B is **circumscribed** about figure A. The following table and examples help to illustrate the concept. Note that the figures cannot both be circles, as they would be completely overlapping and neither would be inscribed or circumscribed.

Given	Description	Equivalent Description	Figures
Each of the sides of a pentagon is tangent to a circle	The circle is inscribed in the pentagon	The pentagon is circumscribed about the circle	
Each of the vertices of a pentagon lie on a circle	The pentagon is inscribed in the circle	The circle is circumscribed about the pentagon	

CIRCLE PROPERTIES
ARCS

An **arc** is a portion of a circle. Specifically, an arc is the set of points between and including two points on a circle. An arc does not contain any points inside the circle. When a segment is drawn from the endpoints of an arc to the center of the circle, a sector is formed. A **minor arc** is an arc that has a measure less than 180°. A **major arc** is an arc that has a measure of at least 180°. Every minor arc has a corresponding major arc that can be found by subtracting the measure of the minor arc from 360°. A **semicircle** is an arc whose endpoints are the endpoints of the diameter of a circle. A semicircle is exactly half of a circle.

Arc length is the length of that portion of the circumference between two points on the circle. The formula for arc length is $s = \frac{\pi r \theta}{180°}$, where s is the arc length, r is the length of the radius, and θ is the angular measure of the arc in degrees, or $s = r\theta$, where θ is the angular measure of the arc in radians (2π radians = 360 degrees).

ANGLES OF CIRCLES

A **central angle** is an angle whose vertex is the center of a circle and whose legs intercept an arc of the circle. The measure of a central angle is equal to the measure of the minor arc it intercepts.

An **inscribed angle** is an angle whose vertex lies on a circle and whose legs contain chords of that circle. The portion of the circle intercepted by the legs of the angle is called the intercepted arc. The measure of the intercepted arc is exactly twice the measure of the inscribed angle. In the following diagram, angle ABC is an inscribed angle. $\overset{\frown}{AC} = 2(\text{m}\angle ABC)$.

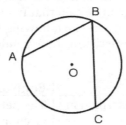

Any angle inscribed in a semicircle is a right angle. The intercepted arc is 180°, making the inscribed angle half that, or 90°. In the diagram below, angle ABC is inscribed in semicircle ABC, making angle ABC equal to 90°.

Review Video: <u>Arcs and Angles of Circles</u>
Visit mometrix.com/academy and enter code: 652838

SECANTS, CHORDS, AND TANGENTS

A **secant** is a line that intersects a circle in two points. The segment of a secant line that is contained within the circle is called a **chord**. Two secants may intersect inside the circle, on the circle, or outside the circle. When the two secants intersect on the circle, an inscribed angle is formed. When two secants intersect inside a circle, the measure of each of two vertical angles is equal to half the sum of the two intercepted arcs. Consider the following diagram where m∠AEB = $\frac{1}{2}(\widehat{AB} + \widehat{CD})$ and m∠BEC = $\frac{1}{2}(\widehat{BC} + \widehat{AD})$.

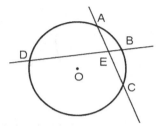

When two secants intersect outside a circle, the measure of the angle formed is equal to half the difference of the two arcs that lie between the two secants. In the diagram below, m∠AEB = $\frac{1}{2}(\widehat{AB} - \widehat{CD})$.

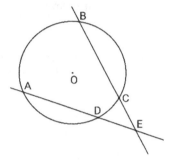

A **tangent** is a line in the same plane as a circle that touches the circle in exactly one point. The point at which a tangent touches a circle is called the **point of tangency**. While a line segment can be tangent to a circle as part of a line that is tangent, it is improper to say a tangent can be simply a line segment that touches the circle in exactly one point.

In the diagram below, $\overleftrightarrow{EB}$ is a secant and contains chord $\overline{EB}$, and $\overleftrightarrow{CD}$ is tangent to circle A. Notice that $\overline{FB}$ is not tangent to the circle. $\overline{FB}$ is a line segment that touches the circle in exactly one point, but if the segment were extended, it would touch the circle in a second point. In the diagram below, point B is the point of tangency.

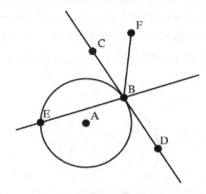

SECTORS

A **sector** is the portion of a circle formed by two radii and their intercepted arc. While the arc length is exclusively the points that are also on the circumference of the circle, the sector is the entire area bounded by the arc and the two radii.

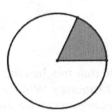

The **area of a sector** of a circle is found by the formula, $A = \frac{\theta r^2}{2}$, where A is the area, θ is the measure of the central angle in radians, and r is the radius. To find the area with the central angle in degrees, use the formula, $A = \frac{\theta \pi r^2}{360}$, where θ is the measure of the central angle and r is the radius.

3D Shapes

Solids

The **surface area of a solid object** is the area of all sides or exterior surfaces. For objects such as prisms and pyramids, a further distinction is made between base surface area (B) and lateral surface area (LA). For a prism, the total surface area (SA) is $SA = LA + 2B$. For a pyramid or cone, the total surface area is $SA = LA + B$.

The **surface area of a sphere** can be found by the formula $A = 4\pi r^2$, where r is the radius. The volume is given by the formula $V = \frac{4}{3}\pi r^3$, where r is the radius. Both quantities are generally given in terms of π.

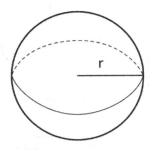

> **Review Video: Volume and Surface Area of a Sphere**
> Visit mometrix.com/academy and enter code: 786928
>
> **Review Video: How to Calculate the Volume of 3D Objects**
> Visit mometrix.com/academy and enter code: 163343

The **volume of any prism** is found by the formula $V = Bh$, where B is the area of the base, and h is the height (perpendicular distance between the bases). The surface area of any prism is the sum of the areas of both bases and all sides. It can be calculated as $SA = 2B + Ph$, where P is the perimeter of the base.

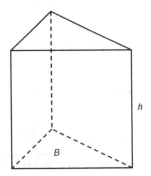

> **Review Video: Volume and Surface Area of a Prism**
> Visit mometrix.com/academy and enter code: 420158

For a **rectangular prism**, the volume can be found by the formula $V = lwh$, where V is the volume, l is the length, w is the width, and h is the height. The surface area can be calculated as $SA = 2lw + 2hl + 2wh$ or $SA = 2(lw + hl + wh)$.

Review Video: **Volume and Surface Area of a Rectangular Prism**
Visit mometrix.com/academy and enter code: 282814

The **volume of a cube** can be found by the formula $V = s^3$, where s is the length of a side. The surface area of a cube is calculated as $SA = 6s^2$, where SA is the total surface area and s is the length of a side. These formulas are the same as the ones used for the volume and surface area of a rectangular prism, but simplified since all three quantities (length, width, and height) are the same.

Review Video: **Volume and Surface Area of a Cube**
Visit mometrix.com/academy and enter code: 664455

The **volume of a cylinder** can be calculated by the formula $V = \pi r^2 h$, where r is the radius, and h is the height. The surface area of a cylinder can be found by the formula $SA = 2\pi r^2 + 2\pi rh$. The first term is the base area multiplied by two, and the second term is the perimeter of the base multiplied by the height.

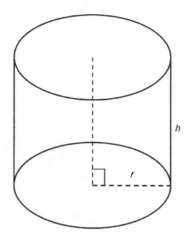

The **volume of a pyramid** is found by the formula $V = \frac{1}{3}Bh$, where B is the area of the base, and h is the height (perpendicular distance from the vertex to the base). Notice this formula is the same as $\frac{1}{3}$ times the volume of a prism. Like a prism, the base of a pyramid can be any shape.

Finding the **surface area of a pyramid** is not as simple as the other shapes we've looked at thus far. If the pyramid is a right pyramid, meaning the base is a regular polygon and the vertex is directly over the center of that polygon, the surface area can be calculated as $SA = B + \frac{1}{2}Ph_s$, where P is the perimeter of the base, and h_s is the slant height (distance from the vertex to the midpoint of one side of the base). If the pyramid is irregular, the area of each triangle side must be calculated individually and then summed, along with the base.

The **volume of a cone** is found by the formula $V = \frac{1}{3}\pi r^2 h$, where r is the radius, and h is the height. Notice this is the same as $\frac{1}{3}$ times the volume of a cylinder. The surface area can be calculated as $SA = \pi r^2 + \pi rs$, where s

is the slant height. The slant height can be calculated using the Pythagorean theorem to be $\sqrt{r^2 + h^2}$, so the surface area formula can also be written as $SA = \pi r^2 + \pi r \sqrt{r^2 + h^2}$.

Data, Statistics, and Probability

PROBABILITY

Probability is the likelihood of a certain outcome occurring for a given event. An **event** is any situation that produces a result. It could be something as simple as flipping a coin or as complex as launching a rocket. Determining the probability of an outcome for an event can be equally simple or complex. As such, there are specific terms used in the study of probability that need to be understood:

- **Compound event**—an event that involves two or more independent events (rolling a pair of dice and taking the sum)
- **Desired outcome** (or success)—an outcome that meets a particular set of criteria (a roll of 1 or 2 if we are looking for numbers less than 3)
- **Independent events**—two or more events whose outcomes do not affect one another (two coins tossed at the same time)
- **Dependent events**—two or more events whose outcomes affect one another (two cards drawn consecutively from the same deck)
- **Certain outcome**—probability of outcome is 100% or 1
- **Impossible outcome**—probability of outcome is 0% or 0
- **Mutually exclusive outcomes**—two or more outcomes whose criteria cannot all be satisfied in a single event (a coin coming up heads and tails on the same toss)
- **Random variable**—refers to all possible outcomes of a single event which may be discrete or continuous.

SAMPLE SPACE

The total set of all possible results of a test or experiment is called a **sample space**, or sometimes a universal sample space. The sample space, represented by one of the variables S, Ω, or U (for universal sample space) has individual elements called outcomes. Other terms for outcome that may be used interchangeably include elementary outcome, simple event, or sample point. The number of outcomes in a given sample space could be infinite or finite, and some tests may yield multiple unique sample sets. For example, tests conducted by drawing playing cards from a standard deck would have one sample space of the card values, another sample space of the card suits, and a third sample space of suit-denomination combinations. For most tests, the sample spaces considered will be finite.

An **event**, represented by the variable E, is a portion of a sample space. It may be one outcome or a group of outcomes from the same sample space. If an event occurs, then the test or experiment will generate an outcome that satisfies the requirement of that event. For example, given a standard deck of 52 playing cards as the sample space, and defining the event as the collection of face cards, then the event will occur if the card drawn is a J, Q, or K. If any other card is drawn, the event is said to have not occurred.

For every sample space, each possible outcome has a specific likelihood, or probability, that it will occur. The probability measure, also called the **distribution**, is a function that assigns a real number probability, from zero to one, to each outcome. For a probability measure to be accurate, every outcome must have a real number probability measure that is greater than or equal to zero and less than or equal to one. Also, the probability measure of the sample space must equal one, and the probability measure of the union of multiple outcomes must equal the sum of the individual probability measures.

Probabilities of events are expressed as real numbers from zero to one. They give a numerical value to the chance that a particular event will occur. The probability of an event occurring is the sum of the probabilities of the individual elements of that event. For example, in a standard deck of 52 playing cards as the sample space and the collection of face cards as the event, the probability of drawing a specific face card is $\frac{1}{52} = 0.019$, but the probability of drawing any one of the twelve face cards is $12(0.019) = 0.228$. Note that rounding of numbers can generate different results. If you multiplied 12 by the fraction $\frac{1}{52}$ before converting to a decimal, you would get the answer $\frac{12}{52} = 0.231$.

THEORETICAL AND EXPERIMENTAL PROBABILITY

Theoretical probability can usually be determined without actually performing the event. The likelihood of an outcome occurring, or the probability of an outcome occurring, is given by the formula:

$$P(A) = \frac{\text{Number of acceptable outcomes}}{\text{Number of possible outcomes}}$$

Note that $P(A)$ is the probability of an outcome A occurring, and each outcome is just as likely to occur as any other outcome. If each outcome has the same probability of occurring as every other possible outcome, the outcomes are said to be equally likely to occur. The total number of acceptable outcomes must be less than or equal to the total number of possible outcomes. If the two are equal, then the outcome is certain to occur and the probability is 1. If the number of acceptable outcomes is zero, then the outcome is impossible and the probability is 0. For example, if there are 20 marbles in a bag and 5 are red, then the theoretical probability of randomly selecting a red marble is 5 out of 20, $\left(\frac{5}{20} = \frac{1}{4}, 0.25, \text{ or } 25\%\right)$.

If the theoretical probability is unknown or too complicated to calculate, it can be estimated by an experimental probability. **Experimental probability**, also called empirical probability, is an estimate of the likelihood of a certain outcome based on repeated experiments or collected data. In other words, while theoretical probability is based on what *should* happen, experimental probability is based on what *has* happened. Experimental probability is calculated in the same way as theoretical probability, except that actual outcomes are used instead of possible outcomes. The more experiments performed or datapoints gathered, the better the estimate should be.

Theoretical and experimental probability do not always line up with one another. Theoretical probability says that out of 20 coin-tosses, 10 should be heads. However, if we were actually to toss 20 coins, we might record just 5 heads. This doesn't mean that our theoretical probability is incorrect; it just means that this particular experiment had results that were different from what was predicted. A practical application of empirical probability is the insurance industry. There are no set functions that define lifespan, health, or safety.

Insurance companies look at factors from hundreds of thousands of individuals to find patterns that they then use to set the formulas for insurance premiums.

> **Review Video: Empirical Probability**
> Visit mometrix.com/academy and enter code: 513468

OBJECTIVE AND SUBJECTIVE PROBABILITY

Objective probability is based on mathematical formulas and documented evidence. Examples of objective probability include raffles or lottery drawings where there is a pre-determined number of possible outcomes and a predetermined number of outcomes that correspond to an event. Other cases of objective probability include probabilities of rolling dice, flipping coins, or drawing cards. Most gambling games are based on objective probability.

In contrast, **subjective probability** is based on personal or professional feelings and judgments. Often, there is a lot of guesswork following extensive research. Areas where subjective probability is applicable include sales trends and business expenses. Attractions set admission prices based on subjective probabilities of attendance based on varying admission rates in an effort to maximize their profit.

COMPLEMENT OF AN EVENT

Sometimes it may be easier to calculate the possibility of something not happening, or the **complement of an event**. Represented by the symbol $\bar{A}$, the complement of A is the probability that event A does not happen. When you know the probability of event A occurring, you can use the formula $P(\bar{A}) = 1 - P(A)$, where $P(\bar{A})$ is the probability of event A not occurring, and $P(A)$ is the probability of event A occurring.

ADDITION RULE

The **addition rule** for probability is used for finding the probability of a compound event. Use the formula $P(A \cup B) = P(A) + P(B) - P(A \cap B)$, where $P(A \cap B)$ is the probability of both events occurring to find the probability of a compound event. The probability of both events occurring at the same time must be subtracted to eliminate any overlap in the first two probabilities.

CONDITIONAL PROBABILITY

Given two events A and B, the **conditional probability** $P(A|B)$ is the probability that event A will occur, given that event B has occurred. The conditional probability cannot be calculated simply from $P(A)$ and $P(B)$; these probabilities alone do not give sufficient information to determine the conditional probability. It can, however, be determined if you are also given the probability of the intersection of events A and B, $P(A \cap B)$, the probability that events A and B both occur. Specifically, $P(A|B) = \frac{P(A \cap B)}{P(B)}$. For instance, suppose you have a jar containing two red marbles and two blue marbles, and you draw two marbles at random. Consider event A being the event that the first marble drawn is red, and event B being the event that the second marble drawn is blue. If we want to find the probability that B occurs given that A occurred, $P(B|A)$, then we can compute it using the fact that $P(A)$ is $\frac{1}{2}$, and $P(A \cap B)$ is $\frac{1}{3}$. (The latter may not be obvious, but may be determined by finding the product of $\frac{1}{2}$ and $\frac{2}{3}$). Therefore $P(B|A) = \frac{P(A \cap B)}{P(A)} = \frac{1/3}{1/2} = \frac{2}{3}$.

CONDITIONAL PROBABILITY IN EVERYDAY SITUATIONS

Conditional probability often arises in everyday situations in, for example, estimating the risk or benefit of certain activities. The conditional probability of having a heart attack given that you exercise daily may be smaller than the overall probability of having a heart attack. The conditional probability of having lung cancer given that you are a smoker is larger than the overall probability of having lung cancer. Note that changing the order of the conditional probability changes the meaning: the conditional probability of having lung cancer given that you are a smoker is a very different thing from the probability of being a smoker given that you have lung cancer. In an extreme case, suppose that a certain rare disease is caused only by eating a certain food, but even then, it is unlikely. Then the conditional probability of having that disease given that you eat the dangerous food is nonzero but low, but the conditional probability of having eaten that food given that you have the disease is 100%!

> **Review Video: <u>Conditional Probability</u>**
> Visit mometrix.com/academy and enter code: 397924

INDEPENDENCE

The conditional probability $P(A|B)$ is the probability that event A will occur given that event B occurs. If the two events are independent, we do not expect that whether or not event B occurs should have any effect on whether or not event A occurs. In other words, we expect $P(A|B) = P(A)$.

This can be proven using the usual equations for conditional probability and the joint probability of independent events. The conditional probability $P(A|B) = \frac{P(A \cap B)}{P(B)}$. If A and B are independent, then $P(A \cap B) = P(A)P(B)$. So $P(A|B) = \frac{P(A)P(B)}{P(B)} = P(A)$. By similar reasoning, if A and B are independent then $P(B|A) = P(B)$.

MULTIPLICATION RULE

The **multiplication rule** can be used to find the probability of two independent events occurring using the formula $P(A \cap B) = P(A) \times P(B)$, where $P(A \cap B)$ is the probability of two independent events occurring, $P(A)$ is the probability of the first event occurring, and $P(B)$ is the probability of the second event occurring.

The multiplication rule can also be used to find the probability of two dependent events occurring using the formula $P(A \cap B) = P(A) \times P(B|A)$, where $P(A \cap B)$ is the probability of two dependent events occurring and $P(B|A)$ is the probability of the second event occurring after the first event has already occurred.

Use a **combination of the multiplication** rule and the rule of complements to find the probability that at least one outcome of the element will occur. This is given by the general formula $P(\text{at least one event occurring}) = 1 - P(\text{no outcomes occurring})$. For example, to find the probability that at least one even number will show when a pair of dice is rolled, find the probability that two odd numbers will be rolled (no even numbers) and subtract from one. You can always use a tree diagram or make a chart to list the possible outcomes when the sample space is small, such as in the dice-rolling example, but in most cases it will be much faster to use the multiplication and complement formulas.

> **Review Video: <u>Multiplication Rule</u>**
> Visit mometrix.com/academy and enter code: 782598

UNION AND INTERSECTION OF TWO SETS OF OUTCOMES

If A and B are each a set of elements or outcomes from an experiment, then the **union** (symbol $\cup$) of the two sets is the set of elements found in set A or set B. For example, if $A = \{2, 3, 4\}$ and $B = \{3, 4, 5\}$, $A \cup B = \{2, 3, 4, 5\}$. Note that the outcomes 3 and 4 appear only once in the union. For statistical events, the union is equivalent to "or"; $P(A \cup B)$ is the same thing as $P(A \text{ or } B)$. The **intersection** (symbol $\cap$) of two sets is the set of outcomes common to both sets. For the above sets A and B, $A \cap B = \{3, 4\}$. For statistical events, the intersection is equivalent to "and"; $P(A \cap B)$ is the same thing as $P(A \text{ and } B)$. It is important to note that union and intersection operations commute. That is:

$$A \cup B = B \cup A \text{ and } A \cap B = B \cap A$$

Mathematics

159

PERMUTATIONS AND COMBINATIONS IN PROBABILITY

When trying to calculate the probability of an event using the $\frac{\text{desired outcomes}}{\text{total outcomes}}$ formula, you may frequently find that there are too many outcomes to individually count them. **Permutation** and **combination formulas** offer a shortcut to counting outcomes. A permutation is an arrangement of a specific number of a set of objects in a specific order. The number of **permutations** of r items given a set of n items can be calculated as $_nP_r = \frac{n!}{(n-r)!}$.

Combinations are similar to permutations, except there are no restrictions regarding the order of the elements. While ABC is considered a different permutation than BCA, ABC and BCA are considered the same combination. The number of **combinations** of r items given a set of n items can be calculated as $_nC_r = \frac{n!}{r!(n-r)!}$ or $_nC_r = \frac{_nP_r}{r!}$.

Suppose you want to calculate how many different 5-card hands can be drawn from a deck of 52 cards. This is a combination since the order of the cards in a hand does not matter. There are 52 cards available, and 5 to be selected. Thus, the number of different hands is $_{52}C_5 = \frac{52!}{5! \times 47!} = 2,598,960$.

> **Review Video: Probability - Permutation and Combination**
> Visit mometrix.com/academy and enter code: 907664

TREE DIAGRAMS

For a simple sample space, possible outcomes may be determined by using a **tree diagram** or an organized chart. In either case, you can easily draw or list out the possible outcomes. For example, to determine all the possible ways three objects can be ordered, you can draw a tree diagram:

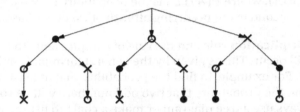

> **Review Video: Tree Diagrams**
> Visit mometrix.com/academy and enter code: 829158

You can also make a chart to list all the possibilities:

First object	Second object	Third object
●	x	o
●	o	x
o	●	x
o	x	●
x	●	o
x	o	●

Either way, you can easily see there are six possible ways the three objects can be ordered.

If two events have no outcomes in common, they are said to be **mutually exclusive**. For example, in a standard deck of 52 playing cards, the event of all card suits is mutually exclusive to the event of all card values. If two events have no bearing on each other so that one event occurring has no influence on the probability of another event occurring, the two events are said to be independent. For example, rolling a standard six-sided die multiple times does not change that probability that a particular number will be rolled from one roll to the next. If the outcome of one event does affect the probability of the second event, the two events are said to be dependent. For example, if cards are drawn from a deck, the probability of drawing an ace after an ace has been drawn is different than the probability of drawing an ace if no ace (or no other card, for that matter) has been drawn.

In probability, the **odds in favor of an event** are the number of times the event will occur compared to the number of times the event will not occur. To calculate the odds in favor of an event, use the formula $\frac{P(A)}{1-P(A)}$, where $P(A)$ is the probability that the event will occur. Many times, odds in favor is given as a ratio in the form $\frac{a}{b}$ or $a:b$, where a is the probability of the event occurring and b is the complement of the event, the probability of the event not occurring. If the odds in favor are given as 2:5, that means that you can expect the event to occur two times for every 5 times that it does not occur. In other words, the probability that the event will occur is $\frac{2}{2+5} = \frac{2}{7}$.

In probability, the **odds against an event** are the number of times the event will not occur compared to the number of times the event will occur. To calculate the odds against an event, use the formula $\frac{1-P(A)}{P(A)}$, where $P(A)$ is the probability that the event will occur. Many times, odds against is given as a ratio in the form $\frac{b}{a}$ or $b:a$, where b is the probability the event will not occur (the complement of the event) and a is the probability the event will occur. If the odds against an event are given as 3:1, that means that you can expect the event to not occur 3 times for every one time it does occur. In other words, 3 out of every 4 trials will fail.

TWO-WAY FREQUENCY TABLES

If we have a two-way frequency table, it is generally a straightforward matter to read off the probabilities of any two events A and B, as well as the joint probability of both events occurring, $P(A \cap B)$. We can then find the conditional probability $P(A|B)$ by calculating $P(A|B) = \frac{P(A \cap B)}{P(B)}$. We could also check whether or not events are independent by verifying whether $P(A)P(B) = P(A \cap B)$.

For example, a certain store's recent T-shirt sales:

	Small	Medium	Large	Total
Blue	25	40	35	100
White	27	25	22	74
Black	8	23	15	46
Total	60	88	72	220

Suppose we want to find the conditional probability that a customer buys a black shirt (event A), given that the shirt he buys is size small (event B). From the table, the probability $P(B)$ that a customer buys a small shirt is $\frac{60}{220} = \frac{3}{11}$. The probability $P(A \cap B)$ that he buys a small, black shirt is $\frac{8}{220} = \frac{2}{55}$. The conditional probability $P(A|B)$ that he buys a black shirt, given that he buys a small shirt, is therefore $P(A|B) = \frac{2/55}{3/11} = \frac{2}{15}$.

Similarly, if we want to check whether the event a customer buys a blue shirt, A, is independent of the event that a customer buys a medium shirt, B. From the table, $P(A) = \frac{100}{220} = \frac{5}{11}$ and $P(B) = \frac{88}{220} = \frac{4}{10}$. Also, $P(A \cap B) = \frac{40}{220} = \frac{2}{11}$. Since $\left(\frac{5}{11}\right)\left(\frac{4}{10}\right) = \frac{20}{110} = \frac{2}{11}$, $P(A)P(B) = P(A \cap B)$ and these two events are indeed independent.

EXPECTED VALUE

Expected value is a method of determining the expected outcome in a random situation. It is a sum of the weighted probabilities of the possible outcomes. Multiply the probability of an event occurring by the weight assigned to that probability (such as the amount of money won or lost). A practical application of the expected value is to determine whether a game of chance is really fair. If the sum of the weighted probabilities is equal to zero, the game is generally considered fair because the player has a fair chance to at least break even. If the expected value is less than zero, then players are expected to lose more than they win. For example, a lottery drawing might allow the player to choose any three-digit number, 000–999. The probability of choosing the winning number is 1:1000. If it costs \$1 to play, and a winning number receives \$500, the expected value is $\left(-\$1 \times \frac{999}{1,000}\right) + \left(\$499 \times \frac{1}{1,000}\right) = -\$0.50$. You can expect to lose on average 50 cents for every dollar you spend.

> **Review Video: Expected Value**
> Visit mometrix.com/academy and enter code: 643554

EXPECTED VALUE AND SIMULATORS

A die roll simulator will show the results of n rolls of a die. The result of each die roll may be recorded. For example, suppose a die is rolled 100 times. All results may be recorded. The numbers of 1s, 2s, 3s, 4s, 5s, and 6s, may be counted. The experimental probability of rolling each number will equal the ratio of the frequency of the rolled number to the total number of rolls. As the number of rolls increases, or approaches infinity, the experimental probability will approach the theoretical probability of $\frac{1}{6}$. Thus, the expected value for the roll of a die is shown to be $\left(1 \times \frac{1}{6}\right) + \left(2 \times \frac{1}{6}\right) + \left(3 \times \frac{1}{6}\right) + \left(4 \times \frac{1}{6}\right) + \left(5 \times \frac{1}{6}\right) + \left(6 \times \frac{1}{6}\right)$, or 3.5.

INTRODUCTION TO STATISTICS

Statistics is the branch of mathematics that deals with collecting, recording, interpreting, illustrating, and analyzing large amounts of **data**. The following terms are often used in the discussion of data and **statistics**:

- **Data** – the collective name for pieces of information (singular is datum)
- **Quantitative data** – measurements (such as length, mass, and speed) that provide information about quantities in numbers
- **Qualitative data** – information (such as colors, scents, tastes, and shapes) that cannot be measured using numbers
- **Discrete data** – information that can be expressed only by a specific value, such as whole or half numbers. (e.g., since people can be counted only in whole numbers, a population count would be discrete data.)
- **Continuous data** – information (such as time and temperature) that can be expressed by any value within a given range
- **Primary data** – information that has been collected directly from a survey, investigation, or experiment, such as a questionnaire or the recording of daily temperatures. (Primary data that has not yet been organized or analyzed is called **raw data**.)
- **Secondary data** – information that has been collected, sorted, and processed by the researcher
- **Ordinal data** – information that can be placed in numerical order, such as age or weight
- **Nominal data** – information that *cannot* be placed in numerical order, such as names or places

DATA COLLECTION
POPULATION

In statistics, the **population** is the entire collection of people, plants, etc., that data can be collected from. For example, a study to determine how well students in local schools perform on a standardized test would have a population of all the students enrolled in those schools, although a study may include just a small sample of students from each school. A **parameter** is a numerical value that gives information about the population, such as the mean, median, mode, or standard deviation. Remember that the symbol for the mean of a population is μ and the symbol for the standard deviation of a population is σ.

SAMPLE

A **sample** is a portion of the entire population. Whereas a parameter helped describe the population, a **statistic** is a numerical value that gives information about the sample, such as mean, median, mode, or standard deviation. Keep in mind that the symbols for mean and standard deviation are different when they are referring to a sample rather than the entire population. For a sample, the symbol for mean is $\bar{x}$ and the symbol for standard deviation is s. The mean and standard deviation of a sample may or may not be identical to that of the entire population due to a sample only being a subset of the population. However, if the sample is random and large enough, statistically significant values can be attained. Samples are generally used when the population is too large to justify including every element or when acquiring data for the entire population is impossible.

INFERENTIAL STATISTICS

Inferential statistics is the branch of statistics that uses samples to make predictions about an entire population. This type of statistic is often seen in political polls, where a sample of the population is questioned about a particular topic or politician to gain an understanding of the attitudes of the entire population of the country. Often, exit polls are conducted on election days using this method. Inferential statistics can have a large margin of error if you do not have a valid sample.

SAMPLING DISTRIBUTION

Statistical values calculated from various samples of the same size make up the **sampling distribution**. For example, if several samples of identical size are randomly selected from a large population and then the mean of each sample is calculated, the distribution of values of the means would be a sampling distribution.

The **sampling distribution of the mean** is the distribution of the sample mean, $\bar{x}$, derived from random samples of a given size. It has three important characteristics. First, the mean of the sampling distribution of the mean is equal to the mean of the population that was sampled. Second, assuming the standard deviation is non-zero, the standard deviation of the sampling distribution of the mean equals the standard deviation of the sampled population divided by the square root of the sample size. This is sometimes called the standard error. Finally, as the sample size gets larger, the sampling distribution of the mean gets closer to a normal distribution via the central limit theorem.

SURVEY STUDY

A **survey study** is a method of gathering information from a small group in an attempt to gain enough information to make accurate general assumptions about the population. Once a survey study is completed, the results are then put into a summary report.

Survey studies are generally in the format of surveys, interviews, or questionnaires as part of an effort to find opinions of a particular group or to find facts about a group.

It is important to note that the findings from a survey study are only as accurate as the sample chosen from the population.

Mathematics

CORRELATIONAL STUDIES

Correlational studies seek to determine how much one variable is affected by changes in a second variable. For example, correlational studies may look for a relationship between the amount of time a student spends studying for a test and the grade that student earned on the test or between student scores on college admissions tests and student grades in college.

It is important to note that correlational studies cannot show a cause and effect, but rather can show only that two variables are or are not potentially correlated.

EXPERIMENTAL STUDIES

Experimental studies take correlational studies one step farther, in that they attempt to prove or disprove a cause-and-effect relationship. These studies are performed by conducting a series of experiments to test the hypothesis. For a study to be scientifically accurate, it must have both an experimental group that receives the specified treatment and a control group that does not get the treatment. This is the type of study pharmaceutical companies do as part of drug trials for new medications. Experimental studies are only valid when the proper scientific method has been followed. In other words, the experiment must be well-planned and executed without bias in the testing process, all subjects must be selected at random, and the process of determining which subject is in which of the two groups must also be completely random.

OBSERVATIONAL STUDIES

Observational studies are the opposite of experimental studies. In observational studies, the tester cannot change or in any way control all of the variables in the test. For example, a study to determine which gender does better in math classes in school is strictly observational. You cannot change a person's gender, and you cannot change the subject being studied. The big downfall of observational studies is that you have no way of proving a cause-and-effect relationship because you cannot control outside influences. Events outside of school can influence a student's performance in school, and observational studies cannot take that into consideration.

RANDOM SAMPLES

For most studies, a **random sample** is necessary to produce valid results. Random samples should not have any particular influence to cause sampled subjects to behave one way or another. The goal is for the random sample to be a **representative sample**, or a sample whose characteristics give an accurate picture of the characteristics of the entire population. To accomplish this, you must make sure you have a proper **sample size**, or an appropriate number of elements in the sample.

BIASES

In statistical studies, biases must be avoided. **Bias** is an error that causes the study to favor one set of results over another. For example, if a survey to determine how the country views the president's job performance only speaks to registered voters in the president's party, the results will be skewed because a disproportionately large number of responders would tend to show approval, while a disproportionately large number of people in the opposite party would tend to express disapproval. **Extraneous variables** are, as the name implies, outside influences that can affect the outcome of a study. They are not always avoidable but could trigger bias in the result.

DATA ANALYSIS

DISPERSION

A **measure of dispersion** is a single value that helps to "interpret" the measure of central tendency by providing more information about how the data values in the set are distributed about the measure of central tendency. The measure of dispersion helps to eliminate or reduce the disadvantages of using the mean, median, or mode as a single measure of central tendency, and give a more accurate picture of the dataset as a whole. To have a measure of dispersion, you must know or calculate the range, standard deviation, or variance of the data set.

RANGE

The **range** of a set of data is the difference between the greatest and lowest values of the data in the set. To calculate the range, you must first make sure the units for all data values are the same, and then identify the greatest and lowest values. If there are multiple data values that are equal for the highest or lowest, just use one of the values in the formula. Write the answer with the same units as the data values you used to do the calculations.

> **Review Video: Statistical Range**
> Visit mometrix.com/academy and enter code: 778541

SAMPLE STANDARD DEVIATION

Standard deviation is a measure of dispersion that compares all the data values in the set to the mean of the set to give a more accurate picture. To find the **standard deviation of a sample**, use the formula

$$s = \sqrt{\frac{\sum_{i=1}^{n}(x_i - \bar{x})^2}{n-1}}$$

Note that s is the standard deviation of a sample, x_i represents the individual values in the data set, $\bar{x}$ is the mean of the data values in the set, and n is the number of data values in the set. The higher the value of the standard deviation is, the greater the variance of the data values from the mean. The units associated with the standard deviation are the same as the units of the data values.

> **Review Video: Standard Deviation**
> Visit mometrix.com/academy and enter code: 419469

SAMPLE VARIANCE

The **variance of a sample** is the square of the sample standard deviation (denoted s^2). While the mean of a set of data gives the average of the set and gives information about where a specific data value lies in relation to the average, the variance of the sample gives information about the degree to which the data values are spread out and tells you how close an individual value is to the average compared to the other values. The units associated with variance are the same as the units of the data values squared.

PERCENTILE

Percentiles and quartiles are other methods of describing data within a set. **Percentiles** tell what percentage of the data in the set fall below a specific point. For example, achievement test scores are often given in percentiles. A score at the 80th percentile is one which is equal to or higher than 80 percent of the scores in the set. In other words, 80 percent of the scores were lower than that score.

Quartiles are percentile groups that make up quarter sections of the data set. The first quartile is the 25th percentile. The second quartile is the 50th percentile; this is also the median of the dataset. The third quartile is the 75th percentile.

SKEWNESS

Skewness is a way to describe the symmetry or asymmetry of the distribution of values in a dataset. If the distribution of values is symmetrical, there is no skew. In general the closer the mean of a data set is to the median of the data set, the less skew there is. Generally, if the mean is to the right of the median, the data set is *positively skewed*, or right-skewed, and if the mean is to the left of the median, the data set is *negatively skewed*, or left-skewed. However, this rule of thumb is not infallible. When the data values are graphed on a curve, a set with no skew will be a perfect bell curve.

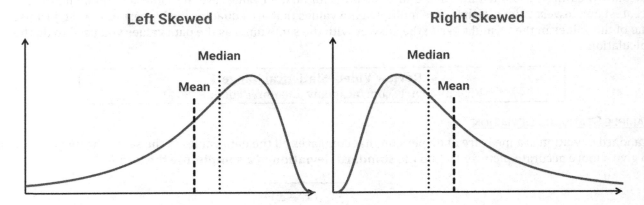

To estimate skew, use the formula:

$$\text{skew} = \frac{\sqrt{n(n-1)}}{n-2}\left(\frac{\frac{1}{n}\sum_{i=1}^{n}(x_i - \bar{x})^3}{\left(\frac{1}{n}\sum_{i=1}^{n}(x_i - \bar{x})^2\right)^{\frac{3}{2}}}\right)$$

Note that n is the datapoints in the set, x_i is the ith value in the set, and $\bar{x}$ is the mean of the set.

> **Review Video: Skew**
> Visit mometrix.com/academy and enter code: 661486

UNIMODAL VS. BIMODAL

If a distribution has a single peak, it would be considered **unimodal**. If it has two discernible peaks it would be considered **bimodal**. Bimodal distributions may be an indication that the set of data being considered is actually the combination of two sets of data with significant differences. A **uniform distribution** is a distribution in which there is *no distinct peak or variation* in the data. No values or ranges are particularly more common than any other values or ranges.

OUTLIER

An outlier is an extremely high or extremely low value in the data set. It may be the result of measurement error, in which case, the outlier is not a valid member of the data set. However, it may also be a valid member of the distribution. Unless a measurement error is identified, the experimenter cannot know for certain if an outlier is or is not a member of the distribution. There are arbitrary methods that can be employed to designate an extreme value as an outlier. One method designates an outlier (or possible outlier) to be any value less than $Q_1 - 1.5(IQR)$ or any value greater than $Q_3 + 1.5(IQR)$.

DATA ANALYSIS
SIMPLE REGRESSION

In statistics, **simple regression** is using an equation to represent a relation between independent and dependent variables. The independent variable is also referred to as the explanatory variable or the predictor and is generally represented by the variable x in the equation. The dependent variable, usually represented by the variable y, is also referred to as the response variable. The equation may be any type of function – linear, quadratic, exponential, etc. The best way to handle this task is to use the regression feature of your graphing calculator. This will easily give you the curve of best fit and provide you with the coefficients and other information you need to derive an equation.

LINE OF BEST FIT

In a scatter plot, the **line of best fit** is the line that best shows the trends of the data. The line of best fit is given by the equation $\hat{y} = ax + b$, where a and b are the regression coefficients. The regression coefficient a is also the slope of the line of best fit, and b is also the y-coordinate of the point at which the line of best fit crosses the y-axis. Not every point on the scatter plot will be on the line of best fit. The differences between the y-values of the points in the scatter plot and the corresponding y-values according to the equation of the line of best fit are the residuals. The line of best fit is also called the least-squares regression line because it is also the line that has the lowest sum of the squares of the residuals.

CORRELATION COEFFICIENT

The **correlation coefficient** is the numerical value that indicates how strong the relationship is between the two variables of a linear regression equation. A correlation coefficient of –1 is a perfect negative correlation. A correlation coefficient of +1 is a perfect positive correlation. Correlation coefficients close to –1 or +1 are very strong correlations. A correlation coefficient equal to zero indicates there is no correlation between the two variables. This test is a good indicator of whether or not the equation for the line of best fit is accurate. The formula for the correlation coefficient is

$$r = \frac{\sum_{i=1}^{n}(x_i - \bar{x})(y_i - \bar{y})}{\sqrt{\sum_{i=1}^{n}(x_i - \bar{x})^2}\sqrt{\sum_{i=1}^{n}(y_i - \bar{y})^2}}$$

where r is the correlation coefficient, n is the number of data values in the set, (x_i, y_i) is a point in the set, and $\bar{x}$ and $\bar{y}$ are the means.

Z-SCORE

A **z-score** is an indication of how many standard deviations a given value falls from the sample mean. To calculate a z-score, use the formula:

$$\frac{x - \bar{x}}{\sigma}$$

In this formula x is the data value, $\bar{x}$ is the mean of the sample data, and σ is the standard deviation of the population. If the z-score is positive, the data value lies above the mean. If the z-score is negative, the data value falls below the mean. These scores are useful in interpreting data such as standardized test scores, where every piece of data in the set has been counted, rather than just a small random sample. In cases where standard deviations are calculated from a random sample of the set, the z-scores will not be as accurate.

CENTRAL LIMIT THEOREM

According to the **central limit theorem**, regardless of what the original distribution of a sample is, the distribution of the means tends to get closer and closer to a normal distribution as the sample size gets larger and larger (this is necessary because the sample is becoming more all-encompassing of the elements of the population). As the sample size gets larger, the distribution of the sample mean will approach a normal distribution with a mean of the population mean and a variance of the population variance divided by the sample size.

MEASURES OF CENTRAL TENDENCY

A **measure of central tendency** is a statistical value that gives a reasonable estimate for the center of a group of data. There are several different ways of describing the measure of central tendency. Each one has a unique way it is calculated, and each one gives a slightly different perspective on the data set. Whenever you give a measure of central tendency, always make sure the units are the same. If the data has different units, such as hours, minutes, and seconds, convert all the data to the same unit, and use the same unit in the measure of central tendency. If no units are given in the data, do not give units for the measure of central tendency.

MEAN

The **statistical mean** of a group of data is the same as the arithmetic average of that group. To find the mean of a set of data, first convert each value to the same units, if necessary. Then find the sum of all the values, and count the total number of data values, making sure you take into consideration each individual value. If a value appears more than once, count it more than once. Divide the sum of the values by the total number of values and apply the units, if any. Note that the mean does not have to be one of the data values in the set, and may not divide evenly.

$$\text{mean} = \frac{\text{sum of the data values}}{\text{quantity of data values}}$$

For instance, the mean of the data set {88, 72, 61, 90, 97, 68, 88, 79, 86, 93, 97, 71, 80, 84, 89} would be the sum of the fifteen numbers divided by 15:

$$\frac{88 + 72 + 61 + 90 + 97 + 68 + 88 + 79 + 86 + 93 + 97 + 71 + 80 + 84 + 89}{15} = \frac{1242}{15}$$
$$= 82.8$$

While the mean is relatively easy to calculate and averages are understood by most people, the mean can be very misleading if it is used as the sole measure of central tendency. If the data set has outliers (data values that are unusually high or unusually low compared to the rest of the data values), the mean can be very distorted, especially if the data set has a small number of values. If unusually high values are countered with unusually low values, the mean is not affected as much. For example, if five of twenty students in a class get a 100 on a test, but the other 15 students have an average of 60 on the same test, the class average would appear as 70. Whenever the mean is skewed by outliers, it is always a good idea to include the median as an alternate measure of central tendency.

A **weighted mean**, or weighted average, is a mean that uses "weighted" values. The formula is weighted mean $= \frac{w_1x_1+w_2x_2+w_3x_3\dots+w_nx_n}{w_1+w_2+w_3+\dots+w_n}$. Weighted values, such as $w_1, w_2, w_3, \dots w_n$ are assigned to each member of the set $x_1, x_2, x_3, \dots x_n$. When calculating the weighted mean, make sure a weight value for each member of the set is used.

> **Review Video: All About Averages**
> Visit mometrix.com/academy and enter code: 176521

MEDIAN

The **statistical median** is the value in the middle of the set of data. To find the median, list all data values in order from smallest to largest or from largest to smallest. Any value that is repeated in the set must be listed the number of times it appears. If there are an odd number of data values, the median is the value in the middle of the list. If there is an even number of data values, the median is the arithmetic mean of the two middle values.

For example, the median of the data set {88, 72, 61, 90, 97, 68, 88, 79, 86, 93, 97, 71, 80, 84, 88} is 86 since the ordered set is {61, 68, 71, 72, 79, 80, 84, **86**, 88, 88, 88, 90, 93, 97, 97}.

The big disadvantage of using the median as a measure of central tendency is that is relies solely on a value's relative size as compared to the other values in the set. When the individual values in a set of data are evenly dispersed, the median can be an accurate tool. However, if there is a group of rather large values or a group of rather small values that are not offset by a different group of values, the information that can be inferred from the median may not be accurate because the distribution of values is skewed.

MODE

The **statistical mode** is the data value that occurs the greatest number of times in the data set. It is possible to have exactly one mode, more than one mode, or no mode. To find the mode of a set of data, arrange the data like you do to find the median (all values in order, listing all multiples of data values). Count the number of times each value appears in the data set. If all values appear an equal number of times, there is no mode. If one value appears more than any other value, that value is the mode. If two or more values appear the same number of times, but there are other values that appear fewer times and no values that appear more times, all of those values are the modes.

For example, the mode of the data set {**88**, 72, 61, 90, 97, 68, **88**, 79, 86, 93, 97, 71, 80, 84, **88**} is 88.

The main disadvantage of the mode is that the values of the other data in the set have no bearing on the mode. The mode may be the largest value, the smallest value, or a value anywhere in between in the set. The mode only tells which value or values, if any, occurred the greatest number of times. It does not give any suggestions about the remaining values in the set.

> **Review Video: Mean, Median, and Mode**
> Visit mometrix.com/academy and enter code: 286207

DISPLAYING INFORMATION

FREQUENCY TABLES

Frequency tables show how frequently each unique value appears in a set. A **relative frequency table** is one that shows the proportions of each unique value compared to the entire set. Relative frequencies are given as percentages; however, the total percent for a relative frequency table will not necessarily equal 100 percent due to rounding. An example of a frequency table with relative frequencies is below.

Favorite Color	Frequency	Relative Frequency
Blue	4	13%
Red	7	22%
Green	3	9%
Purple	6	19%
Cyan	12	38%

> **Review Video: Data Interpretation of Graphs**
> Visit mometrix.com/academy and enter code: 200439

CIRCLE GRAPHS

Circle graphs, also known as *pie charts*, provide a visual depiction of the relationship of each type of data compared to the whole set of data. The circle graph is divided into sections by drawing radii to create central angles whose percentage of the circle is equal to the individual data's percentage of the whole set. Each 1% of data is equal to 3.6° in the circle graph. Therefore, data represented by a 90° section of the circle graph makes up 25% of the whole. When complete, a circle graph often looks like a pie cut into uneven wedges. The pie chart below shows the data from the frequency table referenced earlier where people were asked their favorite color.

Favorite Color

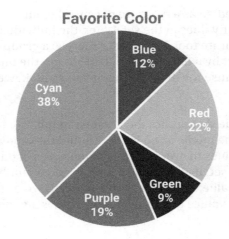

PICTOGRAPHS

A **pictograph** is a graph, generally in the horizontal orientation, that uses pictures or symbols to represent the data. Each pictograph must have a key that defines the picture or symbol and gives the quantity each picture or symbol represents. Pictures or symbols on a pictograph are not always shown as whole elements. In this case, the fraction of the picture or symbol shown represents the same fraction of the quantity a whole picture or symbol stands for. For example, a row with $3\frac{1}{2}$ ears of corn, where each ear of corn represents 100 stalks of corn in a field, would equal $3\frac{1}{2} \times 100 = 350$ stalks of corn in the field.

Name	Number of ears of corn eaten	Field	Number of stalks of corn
Michael	🌽 🌽 🌽 🌽 🌽	Field 1	🌽 🌽 🌽 🌽 🌽
Tara	🌽 🌽	Field 2	🌽 🌽 🌾
John	🌽 🌽 🌽 🌽	Field 3	🌽 🌽 🌽 🌽
Sara	🌽	Field 4	🌽
Jacob	🌽 🌽 🌽	Field 5	🌽 🌽 🌽 🌾

Each 🌽 represents 1 ear of corn eaten.   Each 🌽 represents 100 stalks of corn.

Review Video: Pictographs
Visit mometrix.com/academy and enter code: 147860

LINE GRAPHS

Line graphs have one or more lines of varying styles (solid or broken) to show the different values for a set of data. The individual data are represented as ordered pairs, much like on a Cartesian plane. In this case, the x- and y-axes are defined in terms of their units, such as dollars or time. The individual plotted points are joined

170

by line segments to show whether the value of the data is increasing (line sloping upward), decreasing (line sloping downward), or staying the same (horizontal line). Multiple sets of data can be graphed on the same line graph to give an easy visual comparison. An example of this would be graphing achievement test scores for different groups of students over the same time period to see which group had the greatest increase or decrease in performance from year to year (as shown below).

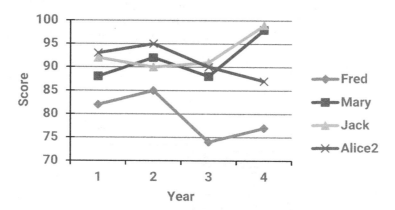

> **Review Video: How to Create a Line Graph**
> Visit mometrix.com/academy and enter code: 480147

LINE PLOTS

A **line plot**, also known as a *dot plot*, has plotted points that are not connected by line segments. In this graph, the horizontal axis lists the different possible values for the data, and the vertical axis lists the number of times the individual value occurs. A single dot is graphed for each value to show the number of times it occurs. This graph is more closely related to a bar graph than a line graph. Do not connect the dots in a line plot or it will misrepresent the data.

> **Review Video: Line Plot**
> Visit mometrix.com/academy and enter code: 754610

STEM AND LEAF PLOTS

A **stem and leaf plot** is useful for depicting groups of data that fall into a range of values. Each piece of data is separated into two parts: the first, or left, part is called the stem; the second, or right, part is called the leaf. Each stem is listed in a column from smallest to largest. Each leaf that has the common stem is listed in that stem's row from smallest to largest. For example, in a set of two-digit numbers, the digit in the tens place is the stem, and the digit in the ones place is the leaf. With a stem and leaf plot, you can easily see which subset of numbers (10s, 20s, 30s, etc.) is the largest. This information is also readily available by looking at a histogram, but a stem and leaf plot also allows you to look closer and see exactly which values fall in that range. Using a sample set of test scores $(82, 88, 92, 93, 85, 90, 92, 95, 74, 88, 90, 91, 78, 87, 98, 99)$, we can assemble a stem and leaf plot like the one below.

Test Scores

7	4	8							
8	2	5	7	8	8				
9	0	0	1	2	2	3	5	8	9

> **Review Video: Stem and Leaf Plots**
> Visit mometrix.com/academy and enter code: 302339

BAR GRAPHS

A **bar graph** is one of the few graphs that can be drawn correctly in two different configurations – both horizontally and vertically. A bar graph is similar to a line plot in the way the data is organized on the graph. Both axes must have their categories defined for the graph to be useful. Rather than placing a single dot to mark the point of the data's value, a bar, or thick line, is drawn from zero to the exact value of the data, whether it is a number, percentage, or other numerical value. Longer bar lengths correspond to greater data values. To read a bar graph, read the labels for the axes to find the units being reported. Then, look where the bars end in relation to the scale given on the corresponding axis and determine the associated value.

The bar chart below represents the responses from our favorite-color survey.

HISTOGRAMS

At first glance, a **histogram** looks like a vertical bar graph. The difference is that a bar graph has a separate bar for each piece of data and a histogram has one continuous bar for each *range* of data. For example, a histogram may have one bar for the range 0–9, one bar for 10–19, etc. While a bar graph has numerical values on one axis, a histogram has numerical values on both axes. Each range is of equal size, and they are ordered left to right from lowest to highest. The height of each column on a histogram represents the number of data values within that range. Like a stem and leaf plot, a histogram makes it easy to glance at the graph and quickly determine which range has the greatest quantity of values. A simple example of a histogram is below.

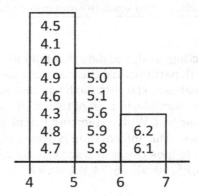

5-NUMBER SUMMARY

The **5-number summary** of a set of data gives a very informative picture of the set. The five numbers in the summary include the minimum value, maximum value, and the three quartiles. This information gives the reader the range and median of the set, as well as an indication of how the data is spread about the median.

BOX AND WHISKER PLOTS

A **box-and-whiskers plot** is a graphical representation of the 5-number summary. To draw a box-and-whiskers plot, plot the points of the 5-number summary on a number line. Draw a box whose ends are through the points for the first and third quartiles. Draw a vertical line in the box through the median to divide the box in half. Draw a line segment from the first quartile point to the minimum value, and from the third quartile point to the maximum value.

| **Review Video: Box and Whisker Plots** |
| Visit mometrix.com/academy and enter code: 810817 |

EXAMPLE

Given the following data (32, 28, 29, 26, 35, 27, 30, 31, 27, 32), we first sort it into numerical order: 26, 27, 27, 28, 29, 30, 31, 32, 32, 35. We can then find the median. Since there are ten values, we take the average of the 5th and 6th values to get 29.5. We find the lower quartile by taking the median of the data smaller than the median. Since there are five values, we take the 3rd value, which is 27. We find the upper quartile by taking the median of the data larger than the overall median, which is 32. Finally, we note our minimum and maximum, which are simply the smallest and largest values in the set: 26 and 35, respectively. Now we can create our box plot:

This plot is fairly "long" on the right whisker, showing one or more unusually high values (but not quite outliers). The other quartiles are similar in length, showing a fairly even distribution of data.

INTERQUARTILE RANGE

The **interquartile range, or IQR**, is the difference between the upper and lower quartiles. It measures how the data is dispersed: a high IQR means that the data is more spread out, while a low IQR means that the data is clustered more tightly around the median. To find the IQR, subtract the lower quartile value (Q_1) from the upper quartile value (Q_3).

EXAMPLE

To find the upper and lower quartiles, we first find the median and then take the median of all values above it and all values below it. In the following data set (16, 18, 13, 24, 16, 51, 32, 21, 27, 39), we first rearrange the values in numerical order: 13, 16, 16, 18, 21, 24, 27, 32, 39, 51. There are 10 values, so the median is the average of the 5th and 6th: $\frac{21+24}{2} = \frac{45}{2} = 22.5$. We do not actually need this value to find the upper and lower quartiles. We look at the set of numbers below the median: 13, 16, 16, 18, 21. There are five values, so the 3rd is the median (16), or the value of the lower quartile (Q_1). Then we look at the numbers above the median: 24, 27, 32, 39, 51. Again there are five values, so the 3rd is the median (32), or the value of the upper quartile (Q_3). We find the IQR by subtracting Q_1 from Q_3: $32 - 16 = 16$.

68-95-99.7 RULE

The **68–95–99.7 rule** describes how a normal distribution of data should appear when compared to the mean. This is also a description of a normal bell curve. According to this rule, 68 percent of the data values in a normally distributed set should fall within one standard deviation of the mean (34 percent above and 34 percent below the mean), 95 percent of the data values should fall within two standard deviations of the mean (47.5 percent above and 47.5 percent below the mean), and 99.7 percent of the data values should fall within three standard deviations of the mean, again, equally distributed on either side of the mean. This means that only 0.3 percent of all data values should fall more than three standard deviations from the mean. On the graph below, the normal curve is centered on the *y*-axis. The *x*-axis labels are how many standard deviations away from the center you are. Therefore, it is easy to see how the 68-95-99.7 rule can apply.

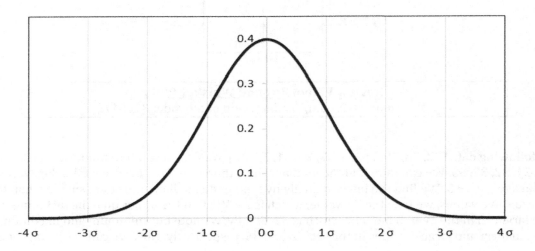

SCATTER PLOTS

BIVARIATE DATA

Bivariate data is simply data from two different variables. (The prefix *bi-* means *two.*) In a *scatter plot*, each value in the set of data is plotted on a grid similar to a Cartesian plane, where each axis represents one of the two variables. By looking at the pattern formed by the points on the grid, you can often determine whether or not there is a relationship between the two variables, and what that relationship is, if it exists. The variables may be directly proportionate, inversely proportionate, or show no proportion at all. It may also be possible to determine if the data is linear, and if so, to find an equation to relate the two variables. The following scatter plot shows the relationship between preference for brand "A" and the age of the consumers surveyed.

SCATTER PLOTS

Scatter plots are also useful in determining the type of function represented by the data and finding the simple regression. Linear scatter plots may be positive or negative. Nonlinear scatter plots are generally exponential or quadratic. Below are some common types of scatter plots:

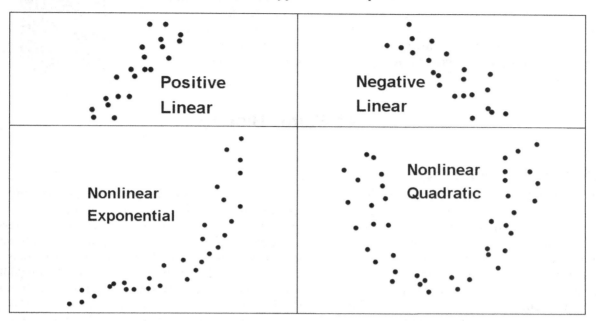

| **Review Video: Scatter Plot** |
| Visit mometrix.com/academy and enter code: 596526 |

175

Social Studies

Transform passive reading into active learning! After immersing yourself in this chapter, put your comprehension to the test by taking a quiz. The insights you gained will stay with you longer this way. Scan the QR code to go directly to the chapter quiz interface for this study guide. If you're using a computer, simply visit the bonus page at **mometrix.com/bonus948/praxeems7001** and click the Chapter Quizzes link.

United States History

US History
Colonial Period (1607-1765)

The **colonial period** describes a time in which several European countries attempted to settle and colonize the Americas to expand their territories. The earliest attempts to colonize were by Spain and France, who conquered and settled much of what are now the southern and central parts of the United States of America. In the process of colonizing the Americas, many Native American groups were displaced or killed by disease and territorial expansion. The main focus of the colonial period in what is now the United States is often placed on the **thirteen English colonies**, which were located on the east coast. The primary reasons for the English colonization in the Americas were in response to England's policy of mercantilism and colonists' desire to be free from **religious persecution**. **Mercantilism** in England required the colonies to provide raw materials to England to continue to grow and support the mother country while also limiting trade with other nations. The other primary motivation for settlement included escape from persecution by the Church of England toward Catholic and other religious groups.

The 13 Colonies

The **thirteen colonies** were a group of English colonies that were overtly similar in their political and religious beliefs. The thirteen colonies were comprised of:

New England Colonies:
- New Hampshire
- Massachusetts
- Rhode Island
- Connecticut

Chesapeake Bay Colonies:
- Virginia
- Maryland

> **Review Video: The English Colony of Virginia**
> Visit mometrix.com/academy and enter code: 537399

Middle Colonies:
- New York
- Pennsylvania
- New Jersey
- Delaware

Southern Colonies:
- North Carolina

176

- South Carolina
- Georgia

FRENCH AND INDIAN WAR

The **French and Indian War** was essentially a war over territory between the English colonies and the French colonies. Rising competition between the English and French empires brought more British military support into the colonies, which created a stronger feeling of unity between the colonies and England than ever before. In 1763, the **Treaty of Paris** brought an end to the war, as France relinquished some of its Eastern territory to England, including the territory east of modern-day Louisiana all the way to the Great Lakes. In the aftermath of the war, **tensions** rose between the colonies and England because of unequal investment in the war. British taxpayers had supplied the majority of funding for the war, while the colonists were forced to fight in a war that served the monarchy's interests rather than their own interests. These tensions, along with continued British occupation, were the foundation for the coming revolution.

AMERICAN REVOLUTION (1765-1783)
THE INTOLERABLE ACTS

Following the French and Indian War, Britain increased taxes and continued to impose quartering on the colonies. The most famous of these included the Stamp Acts, the Tea Acts, and the Quartering Acts. The purpose of these laws was to force the colonies to be dependent on Britain, and to help restore the British economy following the wars of the previous years. These laws were known to the British as the **Coercive Acts**. In America, they were called the **Intolerable Acts,** due to the offensive nature of England's attempt to control and stifle the colonies. As tensions rose, members of the colonies began organizing rebellious protests, such as the Boston Tea Party, in response to particular tax laws that were passed. These inciting reasons and protests led up to the official start of the **American Revolution.**

IMPORTANT EVENTS AND GROUPS LEADING UP TO AMERICAN REVOLUTION

Over several years, various events and groups contributed to the rebellion that became a revolution:

- **Sons of Liberty** – This was the protest group headed by Samuel Adams that incited the Revolution.
- **Boston Massacre** – On March 5, 1770, British soldiers fired on a crowd and killed five people.
- **Committees of Correspondence** – These were set up throughout the colonies to transmit revolutionary ideas and create a unified response.
- **The Boston Tea Party** – On December 6, 1773, the Sons of Liberty, dressed as Mohawks, dumped tea into the harbor from a British ship to protest the tea tax. The harsh British response further aggravated the situation.
- **First Continental Congress** – This was held in 1774 to list grievances and develop a response, including boycotts. It was attended by all the colonies with the exception of Georgia.
- **The Shot Heard Round the World** – In April, 1775, English soldiers on their way to confiscate arms in Concord passed through Lexington, Massachusetts and met the colonial militia called the Minutemen. A fight ensued. In Concord, a larger group of Minutemen forced the British to retreat.

ORIGINAL 13 COLONIES AND MAJOR TURNING POINTS OF THE REVOLUTION

The original **13 colonies** were: Connecticut, Delaware, Georgia, Maryland, Massachusetts, New Hampshire, New Jersey, New York, North Carolina, Pennsylvania, Rhode Island, South Carolina, and Virginia. Delaware was the first state to ratify the **constitution**.

The major turning points of the American Revolution were:

- The actions of the **Second Continental Congress** – This body established the Continental Army and chose George Washington as its commanding general. They allowed printing of money and created government offices.
- "**Common Sense**" – Published in 1776 by Thomas Paine, this pamphlet calling for independence was widely distributed.
- The **Declaration of Independence** – Written by Thomas Jefferson, it was ratified on July 4, 1776 by the Continental Congress assembled in Philadelphia.
- **Alliance with France** – Benjamin Franklin negotiated an agreement with France to fight with the Americans in 1778.
- **Treaty of Paris** – Signaled the official end of the war in 1782, granted independence to the colonies, and gave them generous territorial rights.

> **Review Video: Declaration of Independence**
> Visit mometrix.com/academy and enter code: 256838
>
> **Review Video: European Colonization of the Americas**
> Visit mometrix.com/academy and enter code: 438412

FOUNDING OF A NATION

Each of the colonies overthrew the British representation within their own colonies and established their own state constitutions. The newly formed 13 states, with the guidance and primary authorship of Thomas Jefferson, unanimously adopted the **Declaration of Independence,** which officially separated the colonies from British rule. Shortly thereafter, the **Second Continental Congress**, made up of state representatives, met together to ratify the **Articles of Confederation**, which was the original constitution for the United States of America, outlining how sovereignty would be shared among the states in the new country. With the assistance of the French, the Americans were able to fend off a large scale naval and military invasion from the British and secure their revolution.

> **Review Video: Founding Fathers and Mothers**
> Visit mometrix.com/academy and enter code: 704562

CONFEDERATION PERIOD

The **Confederation Period** (1783-1788) was the period in US history directly following the American Revolution. The Articles of Confederation held the states loosely, and the states were largely self-governing and did not have much political unity. In this format, the federal government was very weak, with no chief executive or judicial system. The weak federal government was bound to continue degrading in unity and would eventually fail if left without reform. In 1787, political leaders met to write a new constitution with more thoroughly written policies that would establish federal powers, while still sharing power with the state governments. This new constitution ended the confederation period and led the way into the Federalist Era.

FEDERALIST ERA (1788-1801)

The 1787 convention that wrote the new **Constitution of the United States of America** established three government branches, the **legislative** (making laws) the **executive** (enforcing laws), and the **judicial** (interpreting and judging laws). Having three branches with separate powers helped to provide what is known as **checks and balances** in government, so that no one branch will have too much power. This was meant to maintain liberty and state powers, while giving the federal government enough power to effectively govern the new country. The new constitution also established voting practices on the individual and state level, including the controversial topic of slavery and voting practices for states that did not abolish slavery. At this point, some northern states had made slavery illegal, but the constitution of the time allowed for the states to determine their own laws on the matter. The Federalist Era placed more power in the hands of the federal government, but also established a place for political parties to advocate for the rights of the people.

BILL OF RIGHTS AND AMENDMENTS

Over the next few years, the need for revision to the constitution was made clear. In 1789, congress adopted several **amendments** to the constitution, mostly dealing with individual rights, such as the right to freedom of speech, the right to bear arms, and several others. The first ten amendments are called "**The Bill of Rights.**" In the process of instituting these amendments, it was also laid out that any declarations (such as rights or laws) not specifically granted in the constitution or amendments to the constitution are reserved for the states or lower jurisdictions to establish.

JEFFERSONIAN ERA (1801-1817)

The **Jeffersonian Era** is defined by the influences of Thomas Jefferson and his political activism. In the Federalist Era, many of the political voices advocated for power going to those with wealth and property, rather than the equal rights of all people. Jefferson's political outlook was called **American Republicanism** (now the Democratic-Republican Party), which opposed aristocracy, elitism, and corruption in government. During Jefferson's presidency, he made significant strides toward a more inclusive voting system. He also managed to purchase Louisiana from France at an extremely reasonable price, thus roughly doubling the size of the United States at the time. From 1812-1815, a war ensued between the United Kingdom and the United States due to the British cutting off trade routes and fostering hostility between the Native Americans and the United States. The war concluded with no changes to boundaries, leading to the beginning of the **Era of Good Feelings.**

ERA OF GOOD FEELINGS AND THE JACKSONIAN ERA

The **Era of Good Feelings** (1817-1825) followed the Jeffersonian Era, and was marked by the collapse of the Federalist system. President James Monroe attempted to deter the partisan political system and prevent political parties from driving national politics. During the Era of Good Feelings, there was a **temporary sense of national security** and a **desire for unity** in America following the war of previous years. Following Monroe's presidency, votes were largely split between the two major parties of the time, the **Whigs** and the **Democrats**.

During the **Jacksonian Era** (1825-1849), **voting rights** were extended to most white men over 21 years old and revised other federal policies. The policy favored the idea of election by the "common man," which expanded voting rights, while continuing to deny rights to women, Native Americans and African Americans. This period also saw an increase in **expansionism**, encouraging territorial expansion to the west in the name of manifest destiny. During this period, issues of slavery were largely avoided at first, though they grew over the coming years, leading into the Civil War Era.

> **Review Video: Andrew Jackson – Key Events and Major Issues**
> Visit mometrix.com/academy and enter code: 739251

CIVIL WAR ERA (1850-1865)

The **Civil War Era** began with continued push from the northern states to expand democratic rights to Black people. The constitution of the time allowed for slavery to be a state's right to determine and enforce. Eleven states (with two to join later) determined to secede from the United States of America and become their own nation. In these eleven states, slavery was a major mode and means for the economy, and despite the overt ethical issues with slavery, these southern states were adamant about maintaining their way of life. The official Confederacy was formed in 1861 and continued until the end of the civil war in 1865.

> **Review Video: Overview of the American Civil War**
> Visit mometrix.com/academy and enter code: 239557

RECONSTRUCTION ERA (1865-1877) AND THE 13TH, 14TH, AND 15TH AMENDMENTS

Reconstruction was the period from 1865 to 1877, during which the South was under strict control of the US government. In March, 1867, all state governments of the former Confederacy were terminated, and **military occupation** began. Military commanders called for constitutional conventions to reconstruct the state governments, to which delegates were to be elected by universal male suffrage. After a state government was in operation and the state had **ratified the 14th Amendment**, its representatives were admitted to Congress. Three constitutional amendments from 1865 to 1870, which tried to rectify the problems caused by slavery, became part of the Reconstruction effort. The **13th Amendment** declared slavery illegal. The **14th Amendment** made all persons born or naturalized in the country US citizens, and forbade any state to interfere with their fundamental civil rights. The **15th Amendment** made it illegal to deny individuals the right to vote on the grounds of race. In his 1876 election campaign, President **Rutherford B. Hayes** promised to withdraw troops from the South, and did so in 1877.

> **Review Video: The Reconstruction Era**
> Visit mometrix.com/academy and enter code: 790561

MAJOR CHANGES IN INDUSTRY IN THE LATE 1800S

Important events during this time of enormous business growth and large-scale exploitation of natural resources include:

- **Industrialization** – Like the rest of the world, the United States' entry into the Industrial Age was marked by many new inventions and the mechanization of factories.
- **Railroad expansion** – The Transcontinental Railroad was built from 1865 to 1969. Railroad tracks stretched over 35,000 miles in 1865, but that distance reached 240,000 miles by 1910. The raw materials and manufactured goods needed for the railroads kept mines and factories very busy.
- **Gold and silver mining** – Mines brought many prospectors to the West from 1850 to about 1875, but mining corporations soon took over.
- **Cattle ranching** – This was a large-scale enterprise beginning in the late 1860s, but by the 1880s open ranges were being fenced and plowed for farming and pastures. Millions of farmers moved into the high plains, establishing the "Bread Basket," which was the major wheat growing area of the country.

GILDED AGE (1877-1895)

The **Gilded Age**, from the 1870s to 1890, was so named because of the enormous wealth and grossly opulent lifestyle enjoyed by a handful of powerful families. This was the time when huge mansions were built as summer "cottages" in Newport, Rhode Island, and great lodges were built in mountain areas for the pleasure of families such as the Vanderbilts, Ascots, and Rockefellers.

Control of the major industries was held largely by the following men:

- Jay Gould—railroads
- Andrew Carnegie—steel
- John D. Rockefeller Sr.—oil
- Philip Danforth Armour—meatpacking
- J. P. Morgan—banking
- John Jacob Astor—fur pelts
- Cornelius Vanderbilt—steamboat shipping

These men were were known as **Robber Barons** for their ruthless business practices and exploitation of workers. Of course, all of these heads of industry diversified and became involved in multiple business ventures. To curb cutthroat competition, particularly among the railroads, and to prohibit restrained trade, Congress created the **Interstate Commerce Commission** and the **Sherman Anti-Trust Act**. Neither of these, however, was enforced.

Review Video: The Gilded Age: An Overview
Visit mometrix.com/academy and enter code: 684770

Review Video: The Gilded Age: Chinese Immigration
Visit mometrix.com/academy and enter code: 624166

IMMIGRATION TRENDS IN LATE 1800S

The population of the United States doubled between 1860 and 1890, with the arrival of 10 million immigrants. Most lived in the north. Cities and their **slums** grew tremendously because of immigration and industrialization. While previous immigrants had come from Germany, Scandinavia, and Ireland, the 1880s saw a new wave of immigrants from Italy, Poland, Hungary, Bohemia, and Greece, as well as Jewish groups from central and eastern Europe, especially Russia. The Roman Catholic population grew from 1.6 million in 1850 to 12 million in 1900, a growth that ignited an anti-Catholic backlash from the anti-Catholic Know-Nothing Party of the 1880s and the Ku Klux Klan. Exploited immigrant workers started **labor protests** in the 1870s, and the **Knights of Labor** was formed in 1878, calling for sweeping social and economic reform. Its membership reached 700,000 by 1886. Eventually, this organization was replaced by the **American Federation of Labor**, headed by Samuel Gompers.

PROGRESSIVE ERA (1896–1916)

The **Progressive Era**, which was the time period from the 1890s to the 1920s, got its name from progressive, reform-minded political leaders who wanted to export a just and rational social order to the rest of the world while increasing trade with foreign markets. Consequently, the United States interfered in a dispute between Venezuela and Britain. America invoked the **Monroe Doctrine** and sided with Cuba in its struggle for independence from Spain. The latter resulted in the **Spanish-American Wars** in 1898 that ended with Cuba, Puerto Rico, the Philippines, and Guam becoming American protectorates at the same time the United States annexed Hawaii. In 1900, America declared an **Open Door policy** with China to support its independence and open markets. In 1903, Theodore Roosevelt helped Panama become independent of Colombia, and then secured the right to build the **Panama Canal**. Roosevelt also negotiated the peace treaty to end the Russo-Japanese War, which earned him the Nobel Peace prize. He then sent the American fleet on a world cruise to display his country's power.

Review Video: An Overview of American Imperialism
Visit mometrix.com/academy and enter code: 629170

DOMESTIC ACCOMPLISHMENTS OF THE PROGRESSIVE ERA

To the Progressives, promoting law and order meant cleaning up city governments to make them honest and efficient, bringing more democracy and humanity to state governments, and establishing a core of social workers to improve slum housing, health, and education. Also during the **Progressive Era**, the national government strengthened or created the following regulatory agencies, services, and acts to oversee business enterprises:

- Passed in 1906, the **Hepburn A**ct reinforced the Interstate Commerce Commission. In 1902, Roosevelt used the Justice Department and lawsuits to try to break monopolies and enforce the **Sherman Anti-Trust Act**. The **Clayton Anti-Trust Act** was added in 1914.
- From 1898 to 1910, the **Forest Service** guided lumber companies in the conservation and more efficient use of woodland resources under the direction of Gifford Pinchot.

- In 1906, the **Pure Food and Drug Act** was passed to protect consumers from fraudulent labeling and adulteration of products.
- In 1913, the **Federal Reserve System** was established to supervise banking and commerce. In 1914, the **Fair Trade Commission** was established to ensure fair competition.

WORLD WAR I (1917–1919)

When World War I broke out in 1914, America declared **neutrality**. The huge demand for war goods by the Allies broke a seven-year industrial stagnation and gave American factories full-time work. The country's sympathies lay mostly with the Allies, and before long American business and banking were heavily invested in an Allied victory. In 1916, **Woodrow Wilson** campaigned on the slogan "He kept us out of war." However, when the British ship the *Lusitania* was torpedoed in 1915 by a German submarine and many Americans were killed, the United States broke its neutrality and directly entered the war. Eventually, when it was proven that Germany was trying to incite Mexico and Japan into attacking the United States, Wilson declared war in 1917, even though America was unprepared. Nonetheless, America quickly armed and transferred sufficient troops to Europe, bringing the **Allies** to victory in 1918.

> **Review Video: WWI Overview**
> Visit mometrix.com/academy and enter code: 659767

ROARING TWENTIES AND THE GREAT DEPRESSION

The **Roaring Twenties** (1920–1929) refers to the economically successful period of time following World War I. New technologies such as automobiles, new forms of media such as films, and new communication technology became widely available. In the wake of industrial growth and revolution, culture shifted toward more modern sentiments, and moved toward a more **practical** approach to life. New forms of art and music were born and thrived during this period, and during this timeframe civil rights were expanded to allow **women to vote**. In 1929, the stock market crashed and caused the end of the Roaring Twenties and the beginning of the **Great Depression**, which lasted from 1930 until 1941. The Great Depression was characterized by high unemployment rates and a slow-moving market with little profit to be made. Many banks failed during this time, and there was no governmental protection against bank failures. As a result, many depositors withdrew their money from banks to protect themselves, removing much of the money from the economy in an effect called economic contraction.

> **Review Video: The 1920's**
> Visit mometrix.com/academy and enter code: 124996
>
> **Review Video: What Caused the Great Depression**
> Visit mometrix.com/academy and enter code: 635912

WORLD WAR II (1939–1945)

World War II began in 1939. As with World War I, the United States tried to stay out of World War II, even though the **Lend-Lease program** transferred munitions to Great Britain. However, on December 7, 1941, Japan attacked **Pearl Harbor** in Hawaii. Since Japan was an ally of Germany, the United States declared war on all the Axis powers. Although there was fighting in both Europe and the Pacific, the decision was made to concentrate on defeating Hitler first. Since it did not have combat within its borders, the United States became the great manufacturer of goods and munitions for the war effort. Women went to work in the factories, while the men entered the military. All facets of American life were centered on the war effort, including rationing, metal collections, and buying war bonds. The benefit of this production was an **end to the economic**

depression. The influx of American personnel and supplies eventually brought victory in Europe in April of 1945, and in Asia the following August.

> **Review Video: World War II**
> Visit mometrix.com/academy and enter code: 759402

MAJOR PROGRAMS AND EVENTS RESULTING FROM THE COLD WAR

After World War II, the Soviet Union kept control of Eastern Europe, including half of Germany. **Communism** spread around the world. Resulting fears led to:

- The **Truman Doctrine** (1947) – This was a policy designed to protect free peoples everywhere against oppression.
- The **Marshall Plan** (1948) – This devoted $12 billion to rebuild Western Europe and strengthen its defenses.
- The **Organization of American States** (1948) – This was established to bolster democratic relations in the Americas.
- The **Berlin Blockade** (1948-49) – The Soviets tried to starve out West Berlin, so the United States provided massive supply drops by air.
- The **North Atlantic Treaty Organization** (1949) – This was formed to militarily link the United States and western Europe so that an attack on one was an attack on both.
- The **Korean War** (1950-53) – This divided the country into the communist North and the democratic South.
- The **McCarthy era** (1950-54) – Senator Joseph McCarthy of Wisconsin held hearings on supposed Communist conspiracies that ruined innocent reputations and led to the blacklisting of suspected sympathizers in the government, Hollywood, and the media.

MAJOR EVENTS OF THE 1960S

The 1960s were a tumultuous time for the United States. Major events included:

- The **Cuban Missile Crisis** (1961) – This was a stand-off between the United States and the Soviet Union over a build-up of missiles in Cuba. Eventually, the Soviets stopped their shipments and a nuclear war was averted.
- The **assassinations** of President Kennedy (1963), Senator Robert Kennedy (1968), and Dr. Martin Luther King, Jr. (1968).
- The **Civil Rights Movement** – Protest marches were held across the nation to draw attention to the plight of Black citizens. From 1964 to 1968, race riots exploded in more than 100 cities.
- The **Vietnam War** (1964-73) – This resulted in a military draft. There was heavy involvement of American personnel and money. There were also protest demonstrations, particularly on college campuses. At Kent State, several students died after being shot by National Guardsmen.
- **Major legislation** – Legislation passed during this decade included the Civil Rights Act, the Clean Air Act, and the Water Quality Act. This decade also saw the creation of the Peace Corps, Medicare, and the War on Poverty, in which billions were appropriated for education, urban redevelopment, and public housing.

PRESIDENTS AND VICE PRESIDENTS FROM 1972 TO 1974

In a two-year time span, the United States had two presidents and two vice presidents. This situation resulted first from the resignation of Vice President **Spiro T. Agnew** in October of 1973 because of alleged kickbacks. President **Richard M. Nixon** then appointed House Minority Leader **Gerald R. Ford** to be vice president. This was accomplished through Senate ratification, a process that had been devised after Harry Truman succeeded to the presidency upon the death of Franklin Roosevelt and went through nearly four years of his presidency without a vice president. Nixon resigned the presidency in August of 1974 because some Republican party members broke into Democratic headquarters at the **Watergate** building in Washington, DC, and the president

Social Studies

183

participated in covering up the crime. Ford succeeded Nixon, and had to appoint another vice president. He chose **Nelson Rockefeller**, former governor of New York.

POST-WAR ERA AND THE CIVIL RIGHTS ERA

The **Post-War Era** (1945-1964) was a time of **economic recovery** and general growth in America. The wars of the past several decades inspired a more active foreign policy to deter such violent wars from occurring again. This largely focused on the Soviet Union and the expansion of Communism around the world. Several countries at this time participated in both a space race and an **arms race**, a rush to develop and accumulate more powerful weapons, particularly nuclear weapons, to become the world's strongest military power. The political differences and concerns over powerful armaments eventually led to the Cold War, Vietnam War, and Korean War. The 60s were also a major pivot-point for civil rights, leading into the **Civil Rights Era** (1965-1980). Due to the protesting and activism of several groups, including **Dr. Martin Luther King Jr**. and the **NAACP**, civil rights landmarks were made regarding racial equality, including laws dealing with **segregation**, **employment opportunity**, and **voting** rights.

REAGAN ERA (1981–1991)

The **Reagan Era** is an era largely describing the foreign policy of the United States during the 1980s and sometimes viewed as extending through the 1990s or early-2000s. During this period, conservative reforms worked to **increase military spending** while also **cutting taxes** and reducing or restricting the involvement of the national government. Ronald Reagan's financial policy revolved around the idea that if the government stepped back, the economy could grow, which would in turn help to reduce national debt.

1990S AND EARLY-2000S

The 1990s and early-2000s were characterized largely by new economic developments surrounding the availability of computers and the development of the internet, allowing new technology to drive the economy in new ways. The economy boomed in the late 1990s leading into the early 2000s. Amid all of the economic success, the United States faced attacks by terrorist groups such as al-Qaeda, which caused alarm and greater restriction to national security and border control. The most influential of these terror attacks was the September 11, 2001 airliner hijacking, where al-Qaeda members took over four airplanes and used them as weapons to crash into key governmental and trade buildings. These attacks triggered a focus of American attention on terrorist groups, and led to several wars in Afghanistan and Iraq.

2008 TO PRESENT

Following the economic success of the 1990s and 2000s, the housing industry collapsed, leading to what is known as the **Great Recession** in 2008. In 2008, President Barack Obama was elected as the country's first African-American president. The war on terror continued until 2011, when Obama announced the death of Osama bin Laden, the al-Qaeda leader of the time. Obama's primary focus during his presidency included large stimulus packages and reforms to health insurance programs, an attempt to make healthcare affordable and available to all Americans. In 2016, President Donald Trump took office. His campaigns centered around immigration laws and tax reforms. Other major trends within this time period include a new wave of social equality issues surrounding same-sex rights and racial tension issues within America.

United States Government and Citizenship

US GOVERNMENT AND CITIZENSHIP

PRINCIPLES OF THE CONSTITUTION

The six basic principles of the Constitution are:

1. **Popular Sovereignty** – The people establish government and give power to it; the government can function only with the consent of the people.
2. **Limited Government** – The Constitution specifies limits on government authority, and no official or entity is above the law.
3. **Separation of Powers** – Power is divided among three government branches: the legislative (Congress), the executive (President), and the judicial (federal courts).
4. **Checks and Balances** – This is a system that enforces the separation of powers and ensures that each branch has the authority and ability to restrain the powers of the other two branches, thus preventing tyranny.
5. **Judicial Review** – Judges in the federal courts ensure that no act of government is in violation of the Constitution. If an act is unconstitutional, the judicial branch has the power to nullify it.
6. **Federalism** – This is the division of power between the central government and local governments, which limits the power of the federal government and allows states to deal with local problems.

CLASSIC FORMS OF GOVERNMENT

Forms of government that have appeared throughout history include:

- **Feudalism** – This is based on the rule of local lords who are loyal to the king and control the lives and production of those who work on their land.
- **Classical republic** – This form is a representative democracy. Small groups of elected leaders represent the interests of the electorate.
- **Absolute monarchy** – A king or queen has complete control of the military and government.
- **Authoritarianism** – An individual or group has unlimited authority. There is no system in place to restrain the power of the government.
- **Dictatorship** – Those in power are not held responsible to the people.
- **Autocracy** – This is rule by one person (despot), not necessarily a monarch, who uses power tyrannically.
- **Oligarchy** – A small, usually self-appointed elite rules a region.
- **Liberal democracy** – This is a government based on the consent of the people that protects individual rights and freedoms from any intolerance by the majority.
- **Totalitarianism** – All facets of the citizens' lives are controlled by the government.

INFLUENCES OF PHILOSOPHERS ON POLITICAL STUDY

Ancient Greek philosophers **Aristotle** and **Plato** believed political science would lead to order in political matters, and that this scientifically organized order would create stable, just societies.

Thomas Aquinas adapted the ideas of Aristotle to a Christian perspective. His ideas stated that individuals have certain rights, but also certain duties, and that these rights and duties should determine the type and extent of government rule. In stating that laws should limit the role of government, he laid the groundwork for ideas that would eventually become modern constitutionalism.

Niccolò Machiavelli, author of *The Prince*, was a proponent of politics based solely on power.

Social Studies

PARLIAMENTARY AND DEMOCRATIC SYSTEMS OF GOVERNMENT

In a **parliamentary system**, government involves a legislature and a variety of political parties. The head of government, usually a Prime Minister, is typically the head of the dominant party. A head of state can be elected, or this position can be taken by a monarch, such as in Great Britain's constitutional monarchy system.

In a **democratic system** of government, the people elect their government representatives. The term democracy is a Greek term that means "for the rule of the people." There are two forms of democracy—direct and indirect. In a direct democracy, each issue or election is decided by a vote where each individual is counted separately. An indirect democracy employs a legislature that votes on issues that affect large number of people whom the legislative members represent. Democracy can exist as a Parliamentary system or a Presidential system. The US is a presidential, indirect democracy.

BILL OF RIGHTS

The **United States Bill of Rights** was based on principles established by the **Magna Carta** in 1215, the 1688 **English Bill of Rights**, and the 1776 **Virginia Bill of Rights**. In 1791, the federal government added 10 amendments to the United States Constitution that provided the following **protections**:

- Freedom of speech, religion, peaceful assembly, petition of the government, and petition of the press
- The right to keep and bear arms
- No quartering of soldiers on private property without the consent of the owner
- Regulations on government search and seizure
- Provisions concerning prosecution
- The right to a speedy, public trial and the calling of witnesses
- The right to trial by jury
- Freedom from excessive bail or cruel punishment
- These rights are not necessarily the only rights
- Powers not prohibited by the Constitution are reserved to the states

> **Review Video: Bill of Rights**
> Visit mometrix.com/academy and enter code: 585149

MAKING A FORMAL AMENDMENT TO THE CONSTITUTION

So far, there have been only **27 amendments** to the federal Constitution. There are four different ways to change the constitution: two methods for proposal and two methods for ratification:

1. An amendment is proposed by a two-thirds vote in each house of Congress and ratified by three-fourths of the state legislatures.
2. An amendment is proposed by a two-thirds vote in each house of Congress and ratified by three-fourths of the states in special conventions called for that purpose.
3. An amendment is proposed by a national convention that is called by Congress at the request of two-thirds of the state legislatures and ratified by three-fourths of the state legislatures.
4. An amendment is proposed by a national convention that is called by Congress at the request of two-thirds of the state legislatures and ratified by three-fourths of the states in special conventions called for that purpose.

DIVISION OF POWERS

The **division of powers** in the federal government system is as follows:

- **National** – This level can coin money, regulate interstate and foreign trade, raise and maintain armed forces, declare war, govern United States territories and admit new states, and conduct foreign relations.

- **Concurrent** – This level can levy and collect taxes, borrow money, establish courts, define crimes and set punishments, and claim private property for public use.
- **State** – This level can regulate trade and business within the state, establish public schools, pass license requirements for professionals, regulate alcoholic beverages, conduct elections, and establish local governments.

There are three types of **delegated powers** granted by the Constitution:

1. **Expressed or enumerated powers** – These are specifically spelled out in the Constitution.
2. **Implied** – These are not expressly stated, but are reasonably suggested by the expressed powers.
3. **Inherent** – These are powers not expressed by the Constitution but ones that national governments have historically possessed, such as granting diplomatic recognition.

Powers can also be classified as reserved or exclusive. **Reserved powers** are not granted to the national government, but not denied to the states. **Exclusive powers** are those reserved to the national government, including concurrent powers.

STAGES OF EXTENDING SUFFRAGE IN THE US

Originally, the Constitution of 1789 provided the right to vote only to white male property owners. Through the years, suffrage was extended through the following five stages.

1. In the early 1800s, states began to eliminate **property ownership** and **tax payment qualifications**.
2. By 1810, there were no more **religious tests** for voting. In the late 1800s, the 15th Amendment protected citizens from being denied the right to vote because of **race or color**.
3. In 1920, the 19th Amendment prohibited the denial of the right to vote because of **gender**, and women were given the right to vote.
4. Passed in 1961 and ratified in 1964, the 23rd Amendment added the voters of the **District of Columbia** to the presidential electorate and eliminated the poll tax as a condition for voting in federal elections. The **Voting Rights Act of 1965** prohibited disenfranchisement through literacy tests and various other means of discrimination.
5. In 1971, the 26th Amendment set the minimum voting age at **18 years of age**.

MAJOR SUPREME COURT CASES

Out of the many Supreme Court rulings, several have had critical historical importance. These include:

- **Marbury v. Madison** (1803) – This ruling established judicial review as a power of the Supreme Court.
- **Dred Scott v. Sandford** (1857) – This decision upheld property rights over human rights in the case of a slave who had been transported to a free state by his master, but was still considered a slave.
- **Brown v. Board of Education** (1954) – The Court ruled that segregation was a violation of the Equal Protection Clause and that the "separate but equal" practice in education was unconstitutional. This decision overturned the 1896 Plessy v. Ferguson ruling that permitted segregation if facilities were equal.

Social Studies

- **Miranda v. Arizona** (1966) – This ruling compelled the reading of Miranda rights to those arrested for crimes the law. It ensured that confessions could not be illegally obtained and that citizen rights to fair trials and protection under the law would be upheld.

> **Review Video: <u>Marbury vs. Madison</u>**
> Visit mometrix.com/academy and enter code: 573964

FAMOUS SPEECHES IN US HISTORY THAT DEFINED GOVERNMENT POLICY, FOREIGN RELATIONS, AND AMERICAN SPIRIT

Among the best-known speeches and famous lines known to modern Americans are the following:

- The **Gettysburg Address** – Made by Abraham Lincoln on November 19, 1863, it dedicated the Gettysburg battleground's cemetery.
- The **Fourteen Points** – Made by Woodrow Wilson on January 18, 1918, this outlined Wilson's plans for peace and the League of Nations.
- **Address to Congress** – Made by Franklin Roosevelt on December 8, 1941, it declared war on Japan and described the attack on Pearl Harbor as "a day which will live in infamy."
- **Inaugural Address** – Made by John F. Kennedy on January 20, 1961, it contained the famous line: "Ask not what your country can do for you, ask what you can do for your country."
- **Berlin Address** – Made by John F. Kennedy on June 26, 1963, it contained the famous line "Ich bin ein Berliner," which expressed empathy for West Berliners in their conflict with the Soviet Union.
- **"I Have a Dream"** and **"I See the Promised Land"** – Made by Martin Luther King, Jr. on August 28, 1963 and April 3, 1968, respectively, these speeches were hallmarks of the Civil Rights Movement.
- **Brandenburg Gate speech** – Made by Ronald Reagan on June 12, 1987, this speech was about the Berlin Wall and the end of the Cold War. It contained the famous line "Tear down this wall."

CLOSED AND OPEN PRIMARIES IN A DIRECT PRIMARY SYSTEM

The **direct primary system** is a means for members of a political party to participate in the selection of a candidate from their party to compete against the other party's candidate in a general election. A **closed primary** is a party nominating election in which only declared party members can vote. Party membership is usually established by registration. Currently, 26 states and the District of Columbia use this system. An **open primary** is a party nominating election in which any qualified voter can take part. The voter makes a public choice at the polling place about which primary to participate in, and the choice does not depend on any registration or previous choices. A **blanket primary**, which allowed voters to vote in the primaries of both parties, was used at various times by three states. The Supreme Court ruled against this practice in 2000.

IMPORTANT DOCUMENTS IN UNITED STATES HISTORY AND GOVERNMENT

The following are among the greatest **American documents** because of their impact on foreign and domestic policy:

- Declaration of Independence (1776)
- The Articles of Confederation (1777)
- The Constitution (1787) and the Bill of Rights (1791)
- The Northwest Ordinance (1787)
- The Federalist Papers (1787-88)
- George Washington's Inaugural Address (1789) and Farewell Address (1796)
- The Alien and Sedition Act (1798)
- The Louisiana Purchase Treaty (1803)
- The Monroe Doctrine (1823); The Missouri Compromise (1830)
- The Compromise of 1850
- The Kansas-Nebraska Act (1854)
- The Homestead Act (1862)

- The Emancipation Proclamation (1863)
- The agreement to purchase Alaska (1866)
- The Sherman Anti-Trust Act (1890)
- Theodore Roosevelt's Corollary to the Monroe Doctrine (1905)
- The Social Security Act (1935) and other acts of the New Deal in the 1930s; The Truman Doctrine (1947); The Marshall Plan (1948)
- The Civil Rights Act (1964)

FEDERAL TAXES

The four types of **federal taxes** are:

- **Income taxes on individuals** – This is a complex system because of demands for various exemptions and rates. Further, the schedule of rates can be lowered or raised according to economic conditions in order to stimulate or restrain economic activity. For example, a tax cut can provide an economic stimulus, while a tax increase can slow down the rate of inflation. Personal income tax generates about five times as much as corporate taxes. Rates are based on an individual's income, and range from 10 to 35 percent.
- **Income taxes on corporations** – The same complexity of exemptions and rates exists for corporations as individuals. Taxes can be raised or lowered according to the need to stimulate or restrain the economy.
- **Excise taxes** – These are taxes on specific goods such as tobacco, liquor, automobiles, gasoline, air travel, and luxury items, or on activities such as highway usage by trucks.
- **Customs duties** – These are taxes imposed on imported goods. They serve to regulate trade between the United States and other countries.

UNITED STATES CURRENCY SYSTEM

The Constitution of 1787 gave the United States Congress the central authority to **print or coin money** and to **regulate its value**. Before this time, states were permitted to maintain separate currencies. The currency system is based on a **modified gold standard**. There is an enormous store of gold to back up United States currency housed at Fort Knox, Kentucky. Paper money is actually **Federal Reserve notes** and coins. It is the job of the Bureau of Engraving and Printing in the Treasury Department to design plates, special types of paper, and other security measures for bills and bonds. This money is put into general circulation by the Treasury and Federal Reserve Banks, and is taken out of circulation when worn out. Coins are made at the Bureau of the Mint in Philadelphia, Denver, and San Francisco.

EMPLOYMENT ACT OF 1946

The **Employment Act of 1946** established the following entities to combat unemployment:

- The **Council of Economic Advisers** (CEA) – Composed of a chair and two other members appointed by the President and approved by the Senate, this council assists the President with the development and implementation of US economic policy. The Council members and their staff, located in the Executive Office, are professionals in economics and statistics who forecast economic trends and provide analysis based on evidence-based research.
- The **Economic Report of the President** – This is presented every January by the President to Congress. Based on the work of the Council, the report recommends a program for maximizing employment, and may also recommend legislation.
- **Joint Economic Committee** (JEC) – This is a committee composed of 10 members of the House and 10 members of the Senate that makes a report early each year on its continuous study of the economy. Study is conducted through hearings and research, and the report is made in response to the president's recommendations.

Social Studies

QUALIFICATIONS OF A US CITIZEN

Anyone born in the US, born abroad to a US citizen, or who has gone through a process of **naturalization** to become a citizen, is considered a **citizen** of the United States. It is possible to lose US citizenship as a result of conviction of certain crimes such as treason. Citizenship may also be lost if a citizen pledges an oath to another country or serves in the military of a country engaged in hostilities with the US. A US citizen can also choose to hold dual citizenship, work as an expatriate in another country without losing US citizenship, or even renounce citizenship if he or she so chooses.

RIGHTS, DUTIES, AND RESPONSIBILITIES GRANTED TO OR EXPECTED FROM US CITIZENS

Citizens are granted certain rights under the US government. The most important of these are defined in the **Bill of Rights**, and include freedom of speech, religion, assembly, and a variety of other rights the government is not allowed to remove.

Duties of a US citizen include:

- Paying taxes
- Loyalty to the government, though the US does not prosecute those who criticize or seek to change the government
- Support and defend the Constitution
- Serve in the Armed Forces as required by law
- Obeying laws as set forth by the various levels of government.

Responsibilities of a US citizen include:

- Voting in elections
- Respecting one another's rights and not infringing upon them
- Staying informed about various political and national issues
- Respecting one another's beliefs

UNITED STATES POLITICAL SYSTEMS

REPRESENTATIVE DEMOCRACY

In a system of government characterized as a representative democracy, voters elect **representatives** to act in their interests. Typically, a representative is elected by and responsible to a specific subset of the total population of eligible voters; this subset of the electorate is referred to as a representative's constituency. A **representative democracy** may foster a more powerful legislature than other forms of government systems; to compensate for a strong legislature, most constitutions stipulate that measures must be taken to balance the powers within government, such as the creation of a separate judicial branch. Representative democracy became popular in post-industrial nations where increasing numbers of people expressed an interest in politics, but where technology and census counts remained incompatible with systems of direct democracy. Today, the majority of the world's population resides in representative democracies, including constitutional monarchies that possess a strong representative branch.

DEMOCRACY

Democracy, or rule by the people, is a form of government in which power is vested in the people and in which policy decisions are made by the majority in a decision-making process such as an election that is open to all or most citizens. Definitions of democracy have become more generalized and include aspects of society and political culture in democratic societies that do not necessarily represent a form of government. What defines a democracy varies, but some of the characteristics of a democracy could include the presence of a middle class, the presence of a civil society, a free market, political pluralism, universal suffrage, and specific rights and freedoms. In practice however, democracies do have limits on specific freedoms, which are justified as being necessary to maintain democracy and ensure democratic freedoms. For example, freedom of association is limited in democracies for individuals and groups that pose a threat to government or to society.

190

PRESIDENTIAL/CONGRESSIONAL SYSTEM

In a **presidential system**, also referred to as a **congressional system**, the legislative branch and the executive branches are elected separately from one another. The features of a presidential system include a *president* who serves as both the head of state and the head of the government, who has no formal relationship with the legislative branch, who is not a voting member, who cannot introduce bills, and who has a fixed term of office. *Elections* are held at scheduled times. The president's *cabinet* carries out the policies of the executive branch and the legislative branch.

POLITICAL PARTIES

A **political party** is an organization that advocates a particular ideology and seeks to gain power within government. The tendency of members of political parties to support their party's policies and interests relative to those of other parties is referred to as partisanship. Often, a political party is comprised of members whose positions, interests and perspectives on policies vary, despite having shared interests in the general ideology of the party. As such, many political parties will have divisions within them that have differing opinions on policy. Political parties are often placed on a political spectrum, with one end of the spectrum representing conservative, traditional values and policies and the other end of the spectrum representing radical, progressive value and policies.

TYPES OF PARTY SYSTEMS

There is a variety of **party systems**, including single-party systems, dominant-party systems, and dual-party systems. In a **single-party system**, only one political party may hold power. In this type of system, minor parties may be permitted, but they must accept the leadership of the dominant party. **Dominant-party systems** allow for multiple parties in opposition of one another, however the dominant party is the only party considered to have power. A **two-party system**, such as in the United States, is one in which there are two dominant political parties. In such a system, it is very difficult for any other parties to win an election. In most two-party systems, there is typically one right wing party and one left wing party.

DEMOCRATIC PARTY

The **Democratic Party** was founded in 1792. In the United States, it is one of the two dominant political parties, along with the Republican Party. The Democratic Party is to the left of the Republican Party. The Democratic Party began as a conservative party in the mid-1800s, shifting to the left during the 1900s. There are many factions within the Democratic Party in the United States. The **Democratic National Committee (DNC)** is the official organization of the Democratic Party, and it develops and promotes the party's platform and coordinates fundraising and election strategies. There are Democratic committees in every US state and most US counties. The official symbol of the Democratic Party is the donkey.

REPUBLICAN PARTY

The **Republican Party** is often referred to as the **GOP**, which stands for *Grand Old Party*. The Republican Party is considered socially conservative and economically neoliberal relative to the Democratic Party. Like the Democratic Party, there are factions within the Republic Party that agree with the party's overall ideology, but disagree with the party's positions on specific issues. The official symbol of the Republican Party is the elephant. The **Republican National Committee (RNC)** is the official organization of the Republican Party, and it develops and promotes the party's platform and coordinates fundraising and election strategies. There are Republican committees in every US state and most US counties.

POLITICAL CAMPAIGNS

A **political campaign** is an organized attempt to influence the decisions of a particular group of people. Examples of campaigns could include elections or efforts to influence policy changes. One of the first steps in a campaign is to develop a **campaign message**. The message must then be delivered to the individuals and groups that the campaign is trying to reach and influence through a campaign plan. There are various ways for a campaign to communicate its message to the intended audience, including public media; paid media such as television, radio and newspaper ads, billboards and the internet; public events such as protests and rallies;

Social Studies

meetings with speakers; mailings; canvassing; fliers; and websites. Through these efforts, the campaign attempts to attract additional support and, ultimately, to reach the goal of the campaign.

VOTING

Voting is a method of decision making that allows people to express their opinion or preference for a candidate or for a proposed resolution of an issue. In a democratic system, voting typically takes place as part of an **election**. An individual participates in the voting process by casting a vote, or a **ballot**; ballots are produced by states A *secret ballot* can be used at polls to protect voters' privacy. Individuals can also vote via *absentee ballot*. In some states voters can write-in a name to cast a vote for a candidate that is not on the ballot. Some states also use *straight ticket voting*, allowing the voter to vote for one party for all the elected positions on the ballot.

US ELECTIONS

In the United States, **officials** are elected at the federal, state and local levels. The first two articles of the Constitution, as well as various amendments, establish how **federal elections** are to be held. The **President** is elected indirectly, by electors of an electoral college. Members of the electoral college nearly always vote along the lines of the popular vote of their respective states. Members of **Congress** are directly elected. At the state level, state law establishes most aspects of how elections are held. There are many elected offices at the state level, including a governor and state legislature. There are also elected offices at the local level.

VOTER ELIGIBILITY

The United States Constitution establishes that individual people are permitted to **vote** in elections if they are citizens of the United States and are at least eighteen years old. The **fifteenth** and **nineteenth amendments** of the United States Constitution stipulate that the right to vote cannot be denied to any United States citizen based on race or sex, respectively. States regulate voter eligibility beyond the minimum qualifications stipulated by the United States Constitution. Depending on the regulations of individual states, individuals may be denied the right to vote if they are convicted criminals.

ADVANTAGES AND DISADVANTAGES TO TWO-PARTY SYSTEM

Advocates of the **two-party system** argue that its advantages are that they are stable because they enable policies and government to change slowly rather than rapidly due to the relative lack of influence from small parties representing unconventional ideologies. In addition, they seem to drive voters toward a middle ground and are less susceptible to revolutions, coups, or civil wars. Among the critiques of the two-party system is the claim that stability in and of itself is not necessarily desirable, as it often comes at the expense of democracy. Critics also argue that the two-party system promotes negative political campaigns, in which candidates and their respective parties only take positions on issues that will differentiate themselves from their opponents, rather than focusing on policy issues that are of significance to citizens. Another concern is that if one of the two major parties becomes weak, a dominant-party system may develop.

CAMPAIGN MESSAGE

Political campaigns consist of three main elements, which are the campaign message, the money that is necessary to run the campaign, and the "machine," or the capital that is necessary to run the campaign. A campaign message is a succinct statement expressing why voters should support the campaign and the individual or policy associated with that campaign. The message is one of the most significant aspects of a political campaign, and a considerable amount of time, money and effort is invested in devising a successful campaign message, as it will be repeated throughout the campaign and will be one of the most identifying factors of the campaign.

MODERN ELECTION CAMPAIGNS IN THE US

Political campaigns in the US have changed and continue to change as advances in technology permit varied campaign methods. Campaigns represent a civic practice, and today they are a high profit industry. The US has an abundance of professional political consultants that employ highly sophisticated campaign management strategies and tools. The election process varies widely between the federal, state and local levels. Campaigns are typically controlled by individual candidates, rather than by the parties that they are associated with. Larger campaigns utilize a vast array of media to reach their targeted audiences, while smaller campaigns are typically limited to direct contact with voters, direct mailings and other forms of low-cost advertising to reach their audiences. In addition to fundraising and spending done by individual candidates, party committees and political action committees also raise money and spend it in ways that will advance the cause of the particular campaign they are associated with.

VOTER REGISTRATION

Individuals have the responsibility of **registering to vote**. Every state except North Dakota requires citizens to register to vote. In an effort to increase voter turnout, Congress passed the **National Voter Registration Act** in 1993. This Act is also known as "Motor Voter," because it required states to make the voter registration process easier by providing registration services through drivers' license registration centers, as well as through disability centers, schools, libraries, and mail-in registration. Some states are exempt because they permit same-day voter registration, which enables voters to register to vote on the day of the election.

PRESIDENTIAL ELECTIONS

The President of the United States is elected **indirectly**, by members of an **electoral college**. Members of the electoral college nearly always vote along the lines of the popular vote of their respective states. The winner of a presidential election is the candidate with at least 270 electoral college votes. It is possible for a candidate to win the electoral vote, and lose the popular vote. Incumbent Presidents and challengers typically prefer a balanced ticket, where the President and Vice President are elected together and generally balance one another with regard to geography, ideology, or experience working in government. The nominated Vice Presidential candidate is referred to as the President's *running mate*.

ELECTORAL COLLEGE

Electoral college votes are cast by state by a group of electors; each elector casts one electoral college vote. State law regulates how states cast their electoral college votes. In all states except Maine and Nebraska, the candidate winning the most votes receives all the state's electoral college votes. In Maine and Nebraska two electoral votes are awarded based on the winner of the statewide election, and the rest go to the highest vote-winner in each of the state's congressional districts. Critics of the electoral college argue that it is undemocratic because the President is elected indirectly as opposed to directly, and that it creates inequality between voters in different states because candidates focus attention on voters in swing states who could influence election results. Critics argue that the electoral college provides more representation for voters in small states than large states, where more voters are represented by a single electoral than in small states and discriminates against candidates that do not have support concentrated in a given state.

CONGRESSIONAL ELECTIONS

Congressional elections are every two years. Members of the **House of Representatives** are elected for a two year term and elections occur every two years on the first Tuesday after November 1st in even years. A Representative is elected from each of the 435 House districts in the US House elections usually occur in the same year as Presidential elections. Members of the **Senate** are elected to six year terms; one-third of the Senate is elected every two years. Per the Seventeenth Amendment to the Constitution, which was passed in 1913, Senators are elected by the electorate of states. The country is divided into **Congressional districts**. Critics argue that this division eliminates voter choice, sometimes creating areas in which Congressional races are uncontested. Every ten years **redistricting** of Congressional districts occurs. However, redistricting is often partisan and therefore reduces the number of competitive districts. The division of voting districts resulting in an unfair advantage to one party in elections is known as gerrymandering. Gerrymandering has been criticized as being undemocratic.

STATE AND LOCAL ELECTIONS

State elections are regulated by state laws and constitutions. In keeping with the ideal of separation of powers, the legislature and the executive are elected separately at the state level, as they are at the federal level. In each state, a **Governor** and a **Lieutenant Governor** are elected. In some states, the Governor and Lieutenant Governor are elected on a joint ticket, while in other states they are elected separately from one another. In some states, executive positions such as Attorney General and Secretary of State are also elected offices. All members of state legislatures are elected, including state senators and state representatives. Depending on the state, members of the state supreme court and other members of the state judiciary may be chosen in elections. Local government can include the governments of counties and cities. At this level, nearly all government offices are filled through an election process. Elected local offices may include sheriffs, county school boards, and city mayors.

CAMPAIGN FINANCE AND INDEPENDENT EXPENDITURES

An individual or group is legally permitted to make unlimited **independent expenditures** in association with federal elections. An independent expenditure is an expenditure that is made to pay for a form of communication that supports the election or defeat of a candidate; the expenditure must be made independently from the candidate's own campaign. To be considered independent, the communication may not be made with the cooperation or consultation with, or at the request or suggestion of, any candidate, any committees or political party associated with the candidate, or any agent that acts on behalf of the candidate. There are no restrictions on the amount that anyone may spend on an independent expenditure, however, any individual making an independent expenditure must report it and disclose the source of the funds they used.

CAMPAIGN FINANCE AND ACTIVITIES OF POLITICAL PARTIES

Political parties participate in federal elections at the local, state and national levels. Most **party committees** must register with the **Federal Election Committee** and file reports disclosing federal campaign activities. While party committees may contribute funds directly to federal candidates, the amounts that they contribute are restricted by the campaign finance contribution limits. National and state party committees are permitted to make additional **coordinated expenditures**, within limits, to assist their nominees in general elections. However, national party committees are not permitted to make unlimited **independent expenditures**, also known as soft money, to support or oppose federal candidates. State and local party committees are also not permitted to use soft money for the purpose of supporting or opposing federal candidates, but they are allowed to spend soft money, up to a limit of $10,000 per source, on voter registration and on efforts aimed at increasing voter participation. All party committees are required to register themselves and file disclosure reports with the Federal Election Committee once their federal election activities exceed specified monetary limits.

PUBLIC OPINION

Public opinion represents the collective attitudes of individual members of the adult population in the United States of America. There are many varied forces that may influence public opinion. These forces include *public relations efforts* on the part of political campaigns and political parties. Another force affecting political opinion is the *political media* and the *mass media*. Public opinion is very important during elections, particularly Presidential elections, as it is an indicator of how candidates are perceived by the public and of how well candidates are doing during their election campaigns. Public opinion is often measured and evaluated using survey sampling.

MASS MEDIA AND PUBLIC OPINION

The **mass media** is critical in developing public opinion. In the short term people generally evaluate information they receive relative to their own beliefs; in the long term the media may have a considerable impact on people's beliefs. Due to the impact of the media on an individual's beliefs, some experts consider the effects of the media on an individual's independence and autonomy to be negative. Others view the impact of the media on individuals as a positive one, because the media provides information that expands worldviews and enriches lives, and fosters the development of opinions that are informed by many sources of information.

A critical aspect of the relationship between the media and public opinion is who is in control of the knowledge and information that is disseminated through the media. Whoever controls the media can propagate their own agenda. The extent to which an individual interprets and evaluates information received through the media can influence behaviors such as voting patterns, consumer behavior, and social attitudes.

Geography, Anthropology, and Sociology

GEOGRAPHY

Geography involves learning about the world's primary **physical and cultural patterns** to help understand how the world functions as an interconnected and dynamic system. Combining information from different sources, geography teaches the basic patterns of climate, geology, vegetation, human settlement, migration, and commerce. Thus, geography is an **interdisciplinary** study of history, anthropology, and sociology. **History** incorporates geography in discussions of battle strategies, slavery (trade routes), ecological disasters (the Dust Bowl of the 1930s), and mass migrations. Geographic principles are useful when reading **literature** to help identify and visualize the setting, and also when studying **earth science**, **mathematics** (latitude, longitude, sun angle, and population statistics), and **fine arts** (song, art, and dance often reflect different cultures). Consequently, a good background in geography can help students succeed in other subjects as well.

THEMES OF GEOGRAPHY

The five themes of geography are:

- **Location** – This includes relative location (described in terms of surrounding geography such as a river, sea coast, or mountain) and absolute location (the specific point of latitude and longitude).
- **Place** – This includes physical characteristics (deserts, plains, mountains, and waterways) and human characteristics (features created by humans, such as architecture, roads, religion, industries, and food and folk practices).
- **Human-environmental interaction** – This includes human adaptation to the environment (using an umbrella when it rains), human modification of the environment (building terraces to prevent soil erosion), and human dependence on the environment for food, water, and natural resources.
- **Movement** –Interaction through trade, migration, communications, political boundaries, ideas, and fashions.
- **Regions** – This includes formal regions (a city, state, country, or other geographical organization as defined by political boundaries), functional regions (defined by a common function or connection, such as a school district), and vernacular regions (informal divisions determined by perceptions or one's mental image, such as the "Far East").

> **Review Video: Regional Geography**
> Visit mometrix.com/academy and enter code: 350378

AREAS COVERED BY GEOGRAPHY

Geography is connected to many issues and provides answers to many everyday questions. Some of the areas covered by geography include:

- Geography investigates global climates, landforms, economies, political systems, human cultures, and migration patterns.
- Geography answers questions not only about where something is located, but also why it is there, how it got there, and how it is related to other things around it.
- Geography explains why people move to certain regions (climate, availability of natural resources, arable land, etc.).
- Geography explains world trade routes and modes of transportation.
- Geography identifies where various animals live and where various crops and forests grow.

Social Studies

- Geography identifies and locates populations that follow certain religions.
- Geography provides statistics on population numbers and growth, which aids in economic and infrastructure planning for cities and countries.

PHYSICAL AND CULTURAL GEOGRAPHY AND PHYSICAL AND POLITICAL LOCATIONS

- **Physical geography** is the study of climate, water, and land and their relationships with each other and humans. Physical geography locates and identifies the earth's surface features and explores how humans thrive in various locations according to crop and goods production.
- **Cultural geography** is the study of the influence of the environment on human behaviors as well as the effect of human activities such as farming, building settlements, and grazing livestock on the environment. Cultural geography also identifies and compares the features of different cultures and how they influence interactions with other cultures and the earth.
- **Physical location** refers to the placement of the hemispheres and the continents.
- **Political location** refers to the divisions within continents that designate various countries. These divisions are made with borders, which are set according to boundary lines arrived at by legal agreements.

Both physical and political locations can be precisely determined by geographical surveys and by latitude and longitude.

SPATIAL ORGANIZATION

Spatial organization in geography refers to how things or people are grouped in a given space anywhere on earth. Spatial organization applies to the **placement of settlements**, whether hamlets, towns, or cities. These settlements are located to make the distribution of goods and services convenient. For example, in farm communities, people come to town to get groceries, to attend church and school, and to access medical services. It is more practical to provide these things to groups than to individuals. These settlements, historically, have been built close to water sources and agricultural areas. Lands that are topographically difficult, have few resources, or experience extreme temperatures do not have as many people as temperate zones and flat plains, where it is easier to live. Within settlements, a town or city will be organized into commercial and residential neighborhoods, with hospitals, fire stations, and shopping centers centrally located. All of these organizational considerations are spatial in nature.

IMPORTANT TERMS RELATED TO MAPS

The most important terms used when describing items on a map or globe are:

- **Latitude and longitude** – Latitude and longitude are the imaginary lines (horizontal and vertical, respectively) that divide the globe into a grid. Both are measured using the 360 degrees of a circle.
- **Coordinates** – These are the latitude and longitude measures for a place.
- **Absolute location** – This is the exact spot where coordinates meet. The grid system allows the location of every place on the planet to be identified.
- **Equator** – This is the line at 0° latitude that divides the earth into two equal halves called hemispheres.
- **Parallels** – This is another name for lines of latitude because they circle the earth in parallel lines that never meet.
- **Meridians** – This is another name for lines of longitude. The Prime Meridian is located at 0° longitude, and is the starting point for measuring distance (both east and west) around the globe. Meridians circle the earth and connect at the Poles.

> **Review Video: Elements of a Map**
> Visit mometrix.com/academy and enter code: 437727

TYPES OF MAPS

- A **physical map** is one that shows natural features such as mountains, rivers, lakes, deserts, and plains. Color is used to designate the different features.
- A **topographic map** is a type of physical map that shows the relief and configuration of a landscape, such as hills, valleys, fields, forest, roads, and settlements. It includes natural and human-made features.
- A **topological map** is one on which lines are stretched or straightened for the sake of clarity, but retain their essential geometric relationship. This type of map is used, for example, to show the routes of a subway system.
- A **political map** uses lines for state, county, and country boundaries; points or dots for cities and towns; and various other symbols for features such as airports and roads.

MAP STYLES

There are three basic styles of maps:

- **Base maps** – Created from aerial and field surveys, base maps serve as the starting point for topographic and thematic maps.
- **Topographic maps** – These show the natural and human-made surface features of the earth, including mountain elevations, river courses, roads, names of lakes and towns, and county and state lines.
- **Thematic maps** – These use a base or topographic map as the foundation for showing data based on a theme, such as population density, wildlife distribution, hill-slope stability, economic trends, etc.

Scale is the size of a map expressed as a ratio of the actual size of the land (for example, 1 inch on a map represents 1 mile on land). In other words, it is the proportion between a distance on the map and its corresponding distance on earth. The scale determines the level of detail on a map. **Small-scale maps** depict larger areas, but include fewer details. **Large-scale maps** depict smaller areas, but include more details.

TIME ZONES

Time is linked to **longitude** in that a complete rotation of the Earth, or 360° of longitude, occurs every 24 hours. Each hour of time is therefore equivalent to 15° of longitude, or 4 minutes for each 1° turn. By the agreement of 27 nations at the 1884 International Meridian Conference, the time zone system consists of **24 time zones** corresponding to the 24 hours in a day. Although high noon technically occurs when the sun is directly above a meridian, calculating time that way would result in 360 different times for the 360 meridians. Using the 24-hour system, the time is the same for all locations in a 15° zone. The 1884 conference established the meridian passing through Greenwich, England, as the zero point, or **prime meridian**. The halfway point is found at the 180th meridian, a half day from Greenwich. It is called the **International Date Line**, and serves as the place where each day begins and ends on earth.

CARTOGRAPHY

Cartography is the art and science of **mapmaking**. Maps of local areas were drawn by the Egyptians as early as 1300 BC, and the Greeks began making maps of the known world in the 6th century BC. Cartography eventually grew into the field of geography. The first step in modern mapmaking is a **survey**. This involves designating a few key sites of known elevation as benchmarks to allow for measurement of other sites. **Aerial photography** is then used to chart the area by taking photos in sequence. Overlapping photos show the same area from different positions along the flight line. When paired and examined through a stereoscope, the cartographer gets a three-dimensional view that can be made into a **topographical map**. In addition, a field survey (on the ground) is made to determine municipal borders and place names. The second step is to compile the information and **computer-draft** a map based on the collected data. The map is then reproduced or printed.

Social Studies

GLOBE AND MAP PROJECTIONS

A **globe** is the only accurate representation of the earth's size, shape, distance, and direction since it, like the earth, is **spherical**. The flat surface of a map distorts these elements. To counter this problem, mapmakers use a variety of "**map projections**," a system for representing the earth's curvatures on a flat surface through the use of a grid that corresponds to lines of latitude and longitude. Some distortions are still inevitable, though, so mapmakers make choices based on the map scale, the size of the area to be mapped, and what they want the map to show. Some projections can represent a true shape or area, while others may be based on the equator and therefore become less accurate as they near the poles. In summary, all maps have some distortion in terms of the shape or size of features of the spherical earth.

TYPES OF MAP PROJECTIONS

There are three main types of map projections:

- **Conical** – This type of projection superimposes a cone over the sphere of the earth, with two reference parallels secant to the globe and intersecting it. There is no distortion along the standard parallels, but distortion increases further from the chosen parallels. A Bonne projection is an example of a conical projection, in which the areas are accurately represented but the meridians are not on a true scale.
- **Cylindrical** – This is any projection in which meridians are mapped using equally spaced vertical lines and circles of latitude (parallels) are mapped using horizontal lines. A Mercator's projection is a modified cylindrical projection that is helpful to navigators because it allows them to maintain a constant compass direction between two points. However, it exaggerates areas in high latitudes.
- **Azimuthal** – This is a stereographic projection onto a plane centered so that a straight line from the center to any other point represents the shortest distance. This distance can be measured to scale.

> **Review Video: Map Projections**
> Visit mometrix.com/academy and enter code: 327303

HEMISPHERES AND PARALLELS ON THE WORLD MAP

The definitions for these terms are as follows:

- **Northern Hemisphere** – This is the area above, or north, of the equator.
- **Southern Hemisphere** – This is the area below, or south, of the equator.
- **Western Hemisphere** – This is the area between the North and South Poles. It extends west from the Prime Meridian to the International Date Line.
- **Eastern Hemisphere** – This is the area between the North and South Poles. It extends east from the Prime Meridian to the International Date Line.
- **North and South Poles** – Latitude is measured in terms of the number of degrees north and south from the equator. The North Pole is located at 90°N latitude, while the South Pole is located at 90°S latitude.
- **Tropic of Cancer** – This is the parallel, or latitude, 23½° north of the equator.
- **Tropic of Capricorn** – This is the parallel, or latitude, 23½° south of the equator. The region between these two parallels is the tropics. The subtropics is the area located between 23½° and 40° north and south of the equator.
- **Arctic Circle** – This is the parallel, or latitude, 66½° north of the equator.
- **Antarctic Circle** – This is the parallel, or latitude, 66½° south of the equator.

> **Review Video: Geographical Features**
> Visit mometrix.com/academy and enter code: 773539

GPS

Global Positioning System (GPS) is a system of satellites that orbit the Earth and communicate with mobile devices to pinpoint the mobile device's position. This is accomplished by determining the distance between the mobile device and at least three satellites. A mobile device might calculate a distance of 400 miles between it and the first satellite. The possible locations that are 400 miles from the first satellite and the mobile device will fall along a circle. The possible locations on Earth relative to the other two satellites will fall somewhere along different circles. The point on Earth at which these three circles intersect is the location of the mobile device. The process of determining position based on distance measurements from three satellites is called **trilateration**.

PHYSICAL AND CULTURAL FEATURES OF GEOGRAPHIC LOCATIONS AND COUNTRIES

PHYSICAL FEATURES

- **Vegetation zones, or biomes** – Forests, grasslands, deserts, and tundra are the four main types of vegetation zones.
- **Climate zones** – Tropical, dry, temperate, continental, and polar are the five different types of climate zones. Climate is the long-term average weather conditions of a place.

CULTURAL FEATURES

- **Population density** – This is the number of people living in each square mile or kilometer of a place. It is calculated by dividing population by area.
- **Religion** – This is the identification of the dominant religions of a place, whether Christianity, Hinduism, Judaism, Buddhism, Islam, Shinto, Taoism, or Confucianism. All of these originated in Asia.
- **Languages** – This is the identification of the dominant or official language of a place. There are 12 major language families. The Indo-European family (which includes English, Russian, German, French, and Spanish) is spoken over the widest geographic area, but Mandarin Chinese is spoken by the most people.

GEOMORPHOLOGY

The study of landforms is call **geomorphology** or physiography, a science that considers the relationships between *geological structures* and *surface landscape features*. It is also concerned with the processes that change these features, such as erosion, deposition, and plate tectonics. Biological factors can also affect landforms. Examples are when corals build a coral reef or when plants contribute to the development of a salt marsh or a sand dune. Rivers, coastlines, rock types, slope formation, ice, erosion, and weathering are all part of geomorphology. A **landform** is a landscape feature or geomorphological unit. These include hills, plateaus, mountains, deserts, deltas, canyons, mesas, marshes, swamps, and valleys. These units are categorized according to elevation, slope, orientation, stratification, rock exposure, and soil type. Landform elements include pits, peaks, channels, ridges, passes, pools, and plains. The highest order landforms are continents and oceans. Elementary landforms such as segments, facets, and relief units are the smallest homogenous divisions of a land surface at a given scale or resolution.

OCEANS, SEAS, LAKES, RIVERS, AND CANALS

- **Oceans** are the largest bodies of water on earth and cover nearly 71% of the earth's surface. There are five major oceans: Atlantic, Pacific (largest and deepest), Indian, Arctic, and Southern (surrounds Antarctica).
- **Seas** are smaller than oceans and are somewhat surrounded by land like a lake, but lakes are fresh water and seas are salt water. Seas include the Mediterranean, Baltic, Caspian, Caribbean, and Coral.
- **Lakes** are bodies of water in a depression on the earth's surface. Examples of lakes are the Great Lakes and Lake Victoria.
- **Rivers** are a channeled flow of water that start out as a spring or stream formed by runoff from rain or snow. Rivers flow from higher to lower ground, and usually empty into a sea or ocean. Great rivers of the world include the Amazon, Nile, Rhine, Mississippi, Ganges, Mekong, and Yangtze.

Social Studies

- **Canals** are artificial waterways constructed by humans to connect two larger water bodies. Examples of canals are the Panama and the Suez.

MOUNTAINS, HILLS, FOOTHILLS, VALLEYS, PLATEAUS, AND MESAS

The definitions for these geographical features are as follows:

- **Mountains** are elevated landforms that rise fairly steeply from the earth's surface to a summit of at least 1,000-2,000 feet (definitions vary) above sea level.
- **Hills** are elevated landforms that rise 500-2,000 feet above sea level.
- **Foothills** are a low series of hills found between a plain and a mountain range.
- **Valleys** are a long depression located between hills or mountains. They are usually products of river erosion. Valleys can vary in terms of width and depth, ranging from a few feet to thousands of feet.
- **Plateaus** are elevated landforms that are fairly flat on top. They may be as high as 10,000 feet above sea level and are usually next to mountains.
- **Mesas** are flat areas of upland. Their name is derived from the Spanish word for table. They are smaller than plateaus and often found in arid or semi-arid areas.

FORMATION OF MOUNTAINS

Mountains are formed by the movement of geologic plates, which are rigid slabs of rocks beneath the earth's crust that float on a layer of partially molten rock in the earth's upper mantle. As the plates collide, they push up the crust to form mountains. This process is called **orogeny**. There are three basic forms of orogeny:

- If the collision of continental plates causes the crust to buckle and fold, a chain of **folded mountains**, such as the Appalachians, the Alps, or the Himalayas, is formed.
- If the collision of the plates causes a denser oceanic plate to go under a continental plate, a process called **subduction**; strong horizontal forces lift and fold the margin of the continent. A mountain range like the Andes is the result.
- If an oceanic plate is driven under another oceanic plate, **volcanic mountains** such as those in Japan and the Philippines are formed.

CORAL REEFS

Coral reefs are formed from millions of tiny, tube-shaped **polyps**, an animal life form encased in tough limestone skeletons. Once anchored to a rocky surface, polyps eat plankton and miniscule shellfish caught with poisonous tentacles near their mouth. Polyps use calcium carbonate absorbed from chemicals given off by algae to harden their body armor and cement themselves together in fantastic shapes of many colors. Polyps reproduce through eggs and larvae, but the reef grows by branching out shoots of polyps. There are three types of coral reefs:

- **Fringing reefs** – These surround, or "fringe," an island.
- **Barrier reefs** – Over the centuries, a fringe reef grows so large that the island sinks down from the weight, and the reef becomes a barrier around the island. Water trapped between the island and the reef is called a lagoon.
- **Atolls** – Eventually, the sinking island goes under, leaving the coral reef around the lagoon.

PLAINS, DESERTS, DELTAS, AND BASINS

- **Plains** are extensive areas of low-lying, flat, or gently undulating land, and are usually lower than the landforms around them. Plains near the seacoast are called lowlands.
- **Deserts** are large, dry areas that receive less than 10 inches of rain per year. They are almost barren, containing only a few patches of vegetation.
- **Deltas** are accumulations of silt deposited at river mouths into the seabed. They are eventually converted into very fertile, stable ground by vegetation, becoming important crop-growing areas. Examples include the deltas of the Nile, Ganges, and Mississippi River.

- **Basins** come in various types. They may be low areas that catch water from rivers; large hollows that dip to a central point and are surrounded by higher ground, as in the Donets and Kuznetsk basins in Russia; or areas of inland drainage in a desert when the water can't reach the sea and flows into lakes or evaporates in salt flats as a result. An example is the Great Salt Lake in Utah.

MARSHES AND SWAMPS AND TUNDRA AND TAIGA

Marshes and swamps are both **wet lowlands**. The water can be fresh, brackish, or saline. Both host important ecological systems with unique wildlife. There are, however, some major differences. **Marshes** have no trees and are always wet because of frequent floods and poor drainage that leaves shallow water. Plants are mostly grasses, rushes, reeds, typhas, sedges, and herbs. **Swamps** have trees and dry periods. The water is very slow-moving, and is usually associated with adjacent rivers or lakes.

Both taiga and tundra regions have many plants and animals, but they have few humans or crops because of their harsh climates. **Taiga** has colder winters and hotter summers than tundra because of its distance from the Arctic Ocean. Taiga is the world's largest forest region, located just south of the tundra line. It contains huge mineral resources and fur-bearing animals. **Tundra** is a Russian word describing marshy plain in an area that has a very cold climate but receives little snow. The ground is usually frozen, but is quite spongy when it is not.

HUMID CONTINENTAL, PRAIRIE, SUBTROPICAL, AND MARINE CLIMATES

- A **humid continental climate** is one that has four seasons, including a cold winter and a hot summer, and sufficient rainfall for raising crops. Such climates can be found in the United States, Canada, and Russia. The best farmlands and mining areas are found in these countries.
- **Prairie climates**, or steppe regions, are found in the interiors of Asia and North America where there are dry flatlands (prairies that receive 10-20 inches of rain per year). These dry flatlands can be grasslands or deserts.
- **Subtropical climates** are very humid areas in the tropical areas of Japan, China, Australia, Africa, South America, and the United States. The moisture, carried by winds traveling over warm ocean currents, produces long summers and mild winters. It is possible to produce a continuous cycle of a variety of crops.
- A **marine climate** is one near or surrounded by water. Warm ocean winds bring moisture, mild temperatures year-round, and plentiful rain. These climates are found in Western Europe and parts of the United States, Canada, Chile, New Zealand, and Australia.

> **Review Video: Climates**
> Visit mometrix.com/academy and enter code: 991320

ADAPTATION TO ENVIRONMENTAL CONDITIONS

The environment influences the way people live. People **adapt** to **environmental conditions** in ways as simple as putting on warm clothing in a cold environment; finding means to cool their surroundings in an environment with high temperatures; building shelters from wind, rain, and temperature variations; and digging water wells if surface water is unavailable. More complex adaptations result from the physical diversity of the earth in terms of soil, climate, vegetation, and topography. Humans take advantage of opportunities and avoid or minimize limitations. Examples of environmental limitations are that rocky soils offer few opportunities for agriculture and rough terrain limits accessibility. Sometimes, **technology** allows humans to live in areas that were once uninhabitable or undesirable. For example, air conditioning allows people to live comfortably in hot climates; modern heating systems permit habitation in areas with extremely low temperatures, as is the case with research facilities in Antarctica; and airplanes have brought people to previously inaccessible places to establish settlements or industries.

NATURAL RESOURCES, RENEWABLE RESOURCES, NONRENEWABLE RESOURCES, AND COMMODITIES

Natural resources are things provided by nature that have commercial value to humans, such as minerals, energy, timber, fish, wildlife, and the landscape. **Renewable resources** are those that can be replenished, such as wind, solar radiation, tides, and water (with proper conservation and clean-up). Soil is renewable with proper conservation and management techniques, and timber can be replenished with replanting. Living resources such as fish and wildlife can replenish themselves if they are not over-harvested. **Nonrenewable resources** are those that cannot be replenished. These include fossil fuels such as oil and coal and metal ores. These cannot be replaced or reused once they have been burned, although some of their products can be recycled. **Commodities** are natural resources that have to be extracted and purified rather than created, such as mineral ores.

> **Review Video: <u>Renewable vs. Nonrenewable Resources</u>**
> Visit mometrix.com/academy and enter code: 840194

HARMFUL OR POTENTIALLY HARMFUL INTERACTION WITH ENVIRONMENT

Wherever humans have gone on the earth, they have made **changes** to their surroundings. Many are harmful or potentially harmful, depending on the extent of the alterations. Some of the changes and activities that can harm the **environment** include:

- Cutting into mountains by machine or blasting to build roads or construction sites
- Cutting down trees and clearing natural growth
- Building houses and cities
- Using grassland to graze herds
- Polluting water sources
- Polluting the ground with chemical and oil waste
- Wearing out fertile land and losing topsoil
- Placing communication lines cross country using poles and wires or underground cable
- Placing railway lines or paved roads cross country
- Building gas and oil pipelines cross country
- Draining wetlands
- Damming up or re-routing waterways
- Spraying fertilizers, pesticides, and defoliants
- Hunting animals to extinction or near extinction

CARRYING CAPACITY AND NATURAL HAZARDS

Carrying capacity is the maximum, sustained level of use of an environment can incur without sustaining significant environmental deterioration that would eventually lead to environmental destruction. Environments vary in terms of their carrying capacity, a concept humans need to learn to measure and respect before harm is done. Proper **assessment of environmental conditions** enables responsible decision making with respect to how much and in what ways the resources of a particular environment should be consumed. **Energy and water conservation** as well as recycling can extend an area's carrying capacity. In addition to carrying capacity limitations, the physical environment can also have occasional extremes that are costly to humans. **Natural hazards** such as hurricanes, tornadoes, earthquakes, volcanoes, floods, tsunamis, and some forest fires and insect infestations are processes or events that are not caused by humans, but may have serious consequences for humans and the environment. These events are not preventable, and their precise timing, location, and magnitude are not predictable. However, some precautions can be taken to reduce the damage.

APPLYING GEOGRAPHY TO INTERPRETATION OF THE PAST

Space, environment, and chronology are three different points of view that can be used to study history. Events take place within **geographic contexts**. If the world is flat, then transportation choices are vastly different from those that would be made in a round world, for example. Invasions of Russia from the west have normally failed because of the harsh winter conditions, the vast distances that inhibit steady supply lines, and the number of rivers and marshes to be crossed, among other factors. Any invading or defending force anywhere must make choices based on consideration of space and environmental factors. For instance, lands may be too muddy or passages too narrow for certain equipment. Geography played a role in the building of the Panama Canal because the value of a shorter transportation route had to outweigh the costs of labor, disease, political negotiations, and equipment, not to mention a myriad of other effects from cutting a canal through an isthmus and changing a natural land structure as a result.

APPLYING GEOGRAPHY TO INTERPRETATION OF THE PRESENT AND PLANS FOR THE FUTURE

The decisions that individual people as well as nations make that may **affect the environment** have to be made with an understanding of spatial patterns and concepts, cultural and transportation connections, physical processes and patterns, ecosystems, and the impact, or "footprint," of people on the physical environment. Sample issues that fit into these considerations are recycling programs, loss of agricultural land to further urban expansion, air and water pollution, deforestation, and ease of transportation and communication. In each of these areas, present and future uses have to be balanced against possible harmful effects. For example, wind is a clean and readily available resource for electric power, but the access roads to and noise of wind turbines can make some areas unsuitable for livestock pasture. Voting citizens need to have an understanding of **geographical and environmental connections** to make responsible decisions.

CULTURAL STUDIES

CULTURE

A **culture** is a comprehensive style of living that is developed in a society and maintained from generation to generation. Culture is manifested in a group's traditions, rituals, language, social norms, technology, and economic structures. Broadly speaking, culture is everything that is learned by a member of a particular society, though it may include things that an individual learns but which are never made explicit either in the individual's mind or in his or her social interactions. For this reason, many sociologists feel it is difficult to properly study one's own culture; they suggest that only the unclouded eyes of a foreign observer can perceive a society's most fundamental values.

SOCIOLOGY, PSYCHOLOGY, AND ANTHROPOLOGY

There are three branches of cultural studies known as psychology, sociology, and anthropology. Each of these categories deals with some form of studying humans and human behavior. **Anthropology** is the most material of the branches, as it deals with studying past and present ways of life for humans. It is an intersection between history, geography, technology, and art. Anthropology is the broadest of cultural studies and contains overlap with countless other disciplines. **Sociology** deals with social interaction and the cultures of human civilizations. Often, sociologists bring ethical, political, and historical matters into question. Sociology largely derives its viewpoints from principles of human interaction and external matters of life. **Psychology,** on the other hand, focuses mainly on the internal workings of the mind and the mental and biological processes involved in thinking.

MATERIAL CULTURE

A society's **material culture** is the set all of the physical objects that the people of that society have either created or to which they assign cultural meaning. Hence, material culture may include objects like books, jewelry, buildings, and furniture; but it may also include natural areas if those areas are assigned significance by the members of the society. As an example of this latter kind of material culture, a sociologist might point to the Native American society, in which the land itself held immense cultural value. Along with **verbal culture**, material culture makes up the sum total of what sociologists have at their disposal for study.

NONMATERIAL CULTURE

Nonmaterial culture is all of a society's customs, beliefs, political structures, languages, and ways of using material objects. In the United States, for instance, the emphasis placed on religious freedom and individual liberty might be considered an example of nonmaterial culture. The boundary between material and nonmaterial culture is never altogether clear; how, for instance, should one separate the American flag and

Social Studies

what it stands for, namely the idea of freedom? **Values** and **norms**, as opposed to the physical things that are used to express values and norms, are what make up a society's nonmaterial culture. Typically, nonmaterial culture is more difficult to change than material culture, and its change is more difficult to observe.

VALUES

The **values** of a culture are its highest ideals. In the United States, for example, we would say that freedom and equality are two of our most important values. Values are usually very general concepts. They may be complementary, as for example the values of hard work and material success seem to go together. Values are quite fluid, and a major focus of sociology is observing how they change over time. Values may come into conflict with one another, which can create social conflict and disorganization. An example of this is the conflict in mid-twentieth-century America between the values of equal rights and segregation; ultimately, it was clear that only one of these values could remain.

SANCTIONS

In sociological terms, **sanctions** are any rewards or consequences given to an individual or group to pursue or renounce a certain course of behavior. Sanctions may be positive, as when a reward is promised for something done properly, or negative, as when a punishment is promised for something done improperly. Although the most common use of the word refers to *international economic pressures* (as in, for instance, the economic restrictions placed on Iraq during the 1990s), all societies place sanctions on their members in order to elicit approved behavior. People who uphold the values and norms of the society are rewarded with preferential treatment from their fellows, while those who transgress can be punished socially, economically, or legally.

NORMS

Norms are specific rules regulating behavior in a culture. Norms may or may not be directly codified in the law of a society, but they are intended to encourage behavior that promotes the society's values. Taking again the example of the United States, one might say that treating men and women equally is a social norm, insofar as equality between the sexes is a value aspired to by our culture. Norms, then, depend on values for their justification, and values depend on norms for their enactment. Norms may vary greatly from society to society, such that the same behavior may be approved or condemned depending on where it is performed. Most of the time, norms are so customary for the members of a society that they are performed automatically.

FORMAL NORMS AND INFORMAL NORMS

Norms may be considered formal or informal, depending on whether they are codified in the laws of the society in which they apply. **Formal norms** are written law; examples of formal norms include the prohibition of murder, the forced payment of taxes, and the sanctity of marriage. **Informal norms**, on the other hand, are unwritten codes of conduct. Examples of informal norms might include the prohibition of spitting in public or the encouragement of deference to women. Typically, a society formalizes the norms which are most important, and for which violators should be punished. Formal norms tend to be much more consistent among different societies than informal norms.

SOCIAL MARKERS, LAWS, AND FOLKWAYS

A **social marker** is any part of behavior that indicates the identity, character, or way of understanding of a particular group of people. Social markers can be laws, folkways, traditions, or other patterns of behavior. **Laws** are simply social norms that have been made explicit and are enforced by the government. There are plenty of norms, though, that are encoded in law but are also internalized-- the prohibition of murder, for instance. **Folkways** are social norms that have become habitual or traditional in a society. In the United States, we are accustomed to tipping a waiter or waitress for their service: that this is so ingrained in our daily life makes it an American folkway.

CULTURAL PLURALISM AND SUBCULTURE

Cultural pluralism exists when multiple distinct cultures exist within the same society after a process of accommodation. These self-contained cultures should not be confused with **subcultures**, which are smaller cultures within a large culture. Subcultures usually have a set of norms and values that are different from those held by the larger society of which they are a member. In the United States, we might consider punk rockers or hippies as subcultures, because they have different values than Americans on the whole, but do not really have a self-sustaining or separate society of their own.

COUNTERCULTURES

A **counterculture** is any group whose values and norms challenge and seek to alter the values and norms of the dominant culture in their society. Although the term when used today evokes memories of the 1960s youth rebellion in Western Europe and the United States, earlier countercultural movements include the Bohemians in nineteenth century France, or even the early Christians. Countercultures typically appear at a time when traditional norms and values are felt to no longer be appropriate or helpful in making sense of the world. As in the case of a social movement, a counterculture tends to have more and stronger adherents at the beginning of its life; once the counterculture's norms have been partially co-opted by the larger society, countercultures tend to lose steam.

DOMINANT CULTURE AND ETHNOCENTRISM

In any society, the **dominant culture** is the group whose norms, values, and behavior patterns are most widespread and influential on the rest of the society. Many nations, including the United States, have laws to restrain the dominant culture from extinguishing minority cultures. **Ethnocentrism** describes the tendency to view one's own cultural patterns as superior and to judge all others only as they relate to one's own. This philosophy has been at the root of some of humanity's worst atrocities, including the Holocaust, which was perpetrated by Germans who believed they must maintain the purity of their race, and colonial conquests, in which Western nations brutally imposed their customs on various indigenous peoples.

World History

WORLD HISTORY
PRE-HISTORICAL AND PRE-MODERN PERIODS

The earliest history of the human race is known as **pre-historical** due to the lack of record keeping. The earliest writing did not appear until the Sumerian civilization in Mesopotamia. In addition to the overt lack of writing from early civilizations, historical records were much more localized than more modern historical records. Ancient history can be broken down many ways, but a common distinction is the **pre-modern period**, including early civilizations such as Egypt, Babylon, and the Greek and Roman Empires. These early civilizations saw invention of technologies such as wood and early metalwork and the domestication of animals. Early civilizations were heavily dependent on agriculture and usually needed access to rivers for a consistent water source. The pre-modern period is viewed as ending with the connection of mainland Europe and some of Africa and Asia by the Greek and Roman Empires. The growth of these empires during this period also saw the worldwide spread of religions such as Judaism and Christianity.

IMPORTANT CONTRIBUTIONS OF THE ANCIENT CIVILIZATIONS OF SUMER, EGYPT, AND INDUS VALLEY

These three ancient civilizations are distinguished by their unique contributions to the development of world civilization:

- **Sumer** used the first known writing system, which enabled the Sumerians to leave a sizeable written record of their myths and religion, advanced the development of the wheel and irrigation, and urbanized their culture.
- **Egypt** was united by the Nile River. Egyptians originally settled in villages on its banks, had a national religion that held their pharaohs as gods, had a central government that controlled civil and artistic affairs, and had writing and libraries.

- The **Indus Valley** was also called Harappan after the city of Harappa. This civilization started in the 3rd and 4th centuries BC and was widely dispersed over 400,000 square miles. It had a unified culture of luxury and refinement, no known national government, an advanced civic system, and prosperous trade routes.

> **Review Video: Early Mesopotamia: The Sumerians**
> Visit mometrix.com/academy and enter code: 939880
>
> **Review Video: Ancient Egypt**
> Visit mometrix.com/academy and enter code: 398041

COMMON TRAITS AND CULTURAL IDENTIFIERS OF THE EARLY EMPIRES OF MESOPOTAMIA, EGYPT, GREECE, AND ROME

These empires all had: a strong military; a centralized government; control and standardization of commerce, money, and taxes; a weight system; and an official language.

- **Mesopotamia** had a series of short-term empires that failed because of their oppression of subject peoples.
- **Egypt** also had a series of governments after extending its territory beyond the Nile area. Compared to Mesopotamia, these were more stable and long-lived because they blended different peoples to create a single national identity.
- **Greece** started as a group of city-states that were united by Alexander the Great and joined to create an empire that stretched from the Indus River to Egypt and the Mediterranean coast. Greece blended Greek values with those of the local cultures, which collectively became known as Hellenistic society.
- **Rome** was an Italian city-state that grew into an empire extending from the British Isles across Europe to the Middle East. It lasted for 1,000 years and became the foundation of the Western world's culture, language, and laws.

> **Review Video: Ancient Greece**
> Visit mometrix.com/academy and enter code: 800829

CHARACTERISTICS OF CHINESE AND INDIAN EMPIRES

While the Chinese had the world's longest lasting and continuous empires, the Indians had more of a cohesive culture than an empire system. Their distinct characteristics are as follows:

- **China** – Since the end of the Warring States period in 221 BC, China has functioned as an empire. Although the dynasties changed several times, the basic governmental structure remained the same into the 20th century. The Chinese also have an extensive written record of their culture which heavily emphasizes history, philosophy, and a common religion.
- **India** – The subcontinent was seldom unified in terms of government until the British empire controlled the area in the 19th and 20th centuries. In terms of culture, India has had persistent institutions and religions that have loosely united the people, such as the caste system and guilds. These have regulated daily life more than any government.

MIDDLE AGES IN EUROPEAN HISTORY

The **Middle Ages**, or Medieval times, was a period that ran from approximately 500-1500 AD. The fall of the Greek and Roman civilizations marks the beginning of this period, allowing for the rise of new independent countries, largely relying on the feudal system of government, with kings who allotted power and territory to governors. During this time, the centers of European civilization moved from the Mediterranean countries to

France, Germany, and England, where strong national governments were developing. Key events of this time include:

- **Roman Catholicism** was the cultural and religious center of medieval life, extending into politics and economics.
- **Knights**, with their systems of honor, combat, and chivalry, were loyal to their king.
- **Peasants**, or serfs, served a particular lord and his lands.
- Many **universities** were established that still function in modern times.
- The **Crusades**, the recurring wars between European Christians and Middle East Muslims, raged over the Holy Lands.
- Charles the Great, or **Charlemagne**, created an empire across France and Germany around 800 AD.
- The **Black Death plague** swept across Europe from 1347-1350, leaving between one third and one half of the population dead.

> **Review Video: The Middle Ages**
> Visit mometrix.com/academy and enter code: 413133
>
> **Review Video: Trade in the Middle Ages**
> Visit mometrix.com/academy and enter code: 650839

PROTESTANT REFORMATION

The dominance of the **Catholic Church** during the Middle Ages in Europe gave it immense power, which encouraged corrupt practices such as the selling of indulgences and clerical positions. The **Protestant Reformation** began as an attempt to reform the Catholic Church, but eventually led to separation from it. In 1517, Martin Luther posted his *Ninety-Five Theses* on the door of a church in Saxony, which criticized unethical practices, various doctrines, and the authority of the pope. Other reformers such as John Calvin and John Wesley soon followed, but disagreed among themselves and divided along doctrinal lines. Consequently, the Lutheran, Reformed, Calvinist, and Presbyterian churches were founded, among others. In England, King Henry VIII was denied a divorce by the pope, so he broke away and established the **Anglican Church**. The Protestant reformation caused the Catholic Church to finally reform itself, but the Protestant movement continued, resulting in a proliferation of new denominations.

RENAISSANCE

Renaissance is the French word for rebirth, and is used to describe the renewal of interest in ancient Greek and Latin art, literature, and philosophy that occurred in Europe, especially Italy, from the 14th through the 16th centuries. Historically, it was also a time of great scientific inquiry, the rise of individualism, extensive geographical exploration, and the rise of secular values.

Notable figures of the Renaissance include:

- **Petrarch** – An Italian scholar, writer, and key figure in northern Italy, which is where the Renaissance started and where chief patrons came from the merchant class
- **Leonardo da Vinci** – Artist and inventor
- **Michelangelo** and **Raphael** – Artists
- **Desiderius Erasmus** – Applied historical scholarship to the New Testament and laid the seeds for the Protestant Reformation
- **Sir Thomas More** – A lawyer and author who wrote *Utopia*

Social Studies

- **Niccolò Machiavelli** – Author of *The Prince* and *Discourses*, which proposed a science of human nature and civil life
- **William Shakespeare** – A renowned playwright and poet

Review Video: The Renaissance
Visit mometrix.com/academy and enter code: 123100

AGE OF DISCOVERY AND COLONIALISM

Throughout world history, there have been several waves of so-called **new imperialism**, in which established countries attempted to **colonize** territories that had not been explored by European nations. This was called the **Age of Discovery** largely because of the overseas exploration, "discovering" new lands, even though many of the explored lands were already populated. This colonialism was largely driven by the desire for increased wealth and resources, though many participants also sought after religious freedoms. Some of the earliest colonization attempts came from Spain and Portugal, who launched expeditions into Africa and Asia. These early colonial missions established the slave trade throughout Europe and for future colonial expansions. Later waves of colonialism included exploration of the **Americas** by Britain, France, and Spain. Other countries, such as China, Japan, and Russia, practiced imperialism in Asia. The process of colonizing many of these territories led to great injustices, such as the slave trade, and the horrific spread of disease and massacres of people groups such as the Aztecs in central Mexico and many Native American tribes in North America.

DECOLONIZATION

Following the powerful race for colonization throughout the world, many of the territories secured by European imperialism fought for their own **freedoms** and **independence**. Supporting these colonial missions was extremely costly and oftentimes, the colonials and the people from the ruling countries had very different priorities, which led to many disagreements. This was the case in the British colonies. Britain enacted many invasive and overcontrolling policies on the 13 established colonies. Tensions grew until the colonials revolted and declared their independence beginning the American Revolutionary War, which would solidify the United States of America as an independent nation. Several other countries worldwide followed suit and eventually secured their own independence. Decolonization largely began in the Americas and ended as late as 1960 in many African countries.

WORLDWIDE ABOLITION OF SLAVERY

Slavery has been accepted in various forms throughout most of known history. Contemporary to the decolonization period, the issue of slavery started to gain attention as an ethical matter worldwide. The movement to end slavery worldwide is known as **abolitionism** and roughly began in the late 1700s, however, anti-slavery sentiment was a slow-moving cause. The profitability of the slave trade and the use of slaves as the primary workforce for much of agriculture and shipping was a huge deterrent to change. In America, slavery was largely left as a states' right until tensions grew, leading into the American Civil War. Slavery was abolished progressively throughout the world, though at varying rates. Eventually, the United Nations adopted a firm doctrine on slavery, known as the Universal Declaration of Human Rights in 1948, which abolished slavery internationally.

INDUSTRIAL REVOLUTION

The **Industrial Revolution** started in England with the construction of the first **cotton mill** in 1733. Other inventions and factories followed in rapid succession. The **steel industry** grew exponentially when manufacturers realized that cheap, abundant English coal could be used instead of wood for melting metals. The **steam engine**, which revolutionized transportation and work power, came next. Around 1830, a factory-based, **technological era** was ushered into the rest of Europe. Society changed from agrarian to urban. A need for cheap, unskilled labor resulted in the extensive employment and abuse of women and children, who worked up to 14 hours a day, six days a week in deplorable conditions. Expanding populations brought crowded, unsanitary conditions to the cities, and the factories created air and water pollution. Societies had to deal with these new situations by enacting **child labor laws** and creating **labor unions** to protect the safety of workers.

Review Video: The Industrial Revolution
Visit mometrix.com/academy and enter code: 372796

PARTICIPANTS OF WORLD WAR I AND WORLD WAR II

World War I, which began in 1914, was fought by the **Allies** including Britain, France, Russia, Greece, Italy, Romania, and Serbia. They fought against the **Central Powers** of Germany, Austria-Hungary, Bulgaria, and Turkey. In 1917, the United States joined the Allies, and Russia withdrew to pursue its own revolution. World War I ended in 1918.

World War II was truly a world war, with fighting occurring on nearly every continent. Germany occupied most of Europe and Northern Africa. It was opposed by the countries of the British Empire, free France and its colonies, Russia, and various national resistance forces. Japan, an **Axis** ally of Germany, had been forcefully expanding its territories in Korea, China, Indonesia, the Philippines, and the South Pacific for many years. When Japan attacked Pearl Harbor in 1941, the United States joined the **Allied** effort. Italy changed from the Axis to the Allied side mid-war after deposing its own dictator. The war ended in Europe in April 1945, and in Japan in August 1945.

IMPORTANCE OF CROSS-CULTURAL COMPARISONS IN WORLD HISTORY INSTRUCTION

It is important to make **cross-cultural comparisons** when studying world history so that the subject is **holistic** and not oriented to just Western civilization. Not only are the contributions of civilizations around the world important, but they are also interesting and more representative of the mix of cultures present in the United States. It is also critical to the understanding of world relations to study the involvement of European countries and the United States in international commerce, colonization, and development. **Trade routes** from ancient times linked Africa, Asia, and Europe, resulting in exchanges and migrations of people, philosophies, and religions, as well as goods. While many civilizations in the Americas thrived, and some became very sophisticated, many were eventually overcome or even erased by **European expansion**. The historic isolation of China and the modern industrialization of Japan have had huge impacts on their relations with the rest of the world. The more students understand this history and its effects on the modern world, the better they will able to function in their own spheres.

Economics

ECONOMICS
EFFECTS ECONOMY CAN HAVE ON PURCHASING DECISIONS OF CONSUMERS

The **economy** plays an important role in how careful consumers are when using their resources. It also affects what they perceive as needs as opposed to what they perceive as wants. When the economy is doing well, unemployment figures are low, which means that people can easily attain their basic necessities. As a result, consumers are typically more willing to spend their financial resources. Consumers will also be more willing to spend their resources on products and services that are not necessary to their survival, but are instead products and services that they enjoy having and believe increase their quality of life. On the other hand, when the economy is in a slump, consumers are much more likely to cut back on their spending because they perceive a significantly higher risk of being unable to acquire basic necessities due to a lack of financial resources.

COMMON TERMINOLOGY IN ECONOMICS
- **Supply** is the amount of a product or service available to consumers.

- **Demand** is how much consumers are willing to pay for the product or service. These two facets of the market determine the price of goods and services. The higher the demand, the higher the price the supplier will charge; the lower the demand, the lower the price.
- **Scarcity** is a measure of supply. Demand is high when there is a scarcity, or low supply, of an item.
- **Choice** is related to scarcity and demand in that when an item in demand is scarce, consumers have to make difficult choices. They can pay more for an item, go without it, or go elsewhere for the item.
- **Money** is the cash or currency available for payment.
- **Resources** are the items one can barter in exchange for goods. Money is the cash reserves of a nation, while resources are the minerals, labor force, armaments, and other raw materials or assets a nation has available for trade.
- **Taxes** are legally required payments to the government for income, goods bought, or property owned. Taxes are categorized as direct or indirect.
- **Tariffs** are taxes specifically imposed on imports from another country.

EFFECTS OF ECONOMIC DOWNTURN OR RECESSION

When a **recession** happens, people at all levels of society feel the economic effects. For example:

- High **unemployment** results because businesses have to cut back to keep costs low, and may no longer have the work for the labor force they once did.
- **Mortgage rates** go up on variable-rate loans as banks try to increase their revenues, but the higher rates cause some people who cannot afford increased housing costs to sell or suffer foreclosure.
- **Credit** becomes less available as banks try to lessen their risk. This decreased lending affects business operations, home and auto loans, etc.
- **Stock market prices** drop, and the lower dividends paid to stockholders reduce their income. This is especially hard on retired people who rely on stock dividends.
- **Psychological depression and trauma** may occur in those who suffer bankruptcy, unemployment, or foreclosure during a depression.

ECONOMIC EFFECTS OF ABUNDANT NATURAL RESOURCES

The **positive economic aspects** of abundant natural resources are an increase in **revenue and new jobs** where those resources have not been previously accessed. For example, the growing demand for oil, gas, and minerals has led companies to venture into new regions.

The **negative economic aspects** of abundant natural resources are:

- **Environmental degradation**, if sufficient regulations are not in place to counter strip mining, deforestation, and contamination.
- **Corruption**, if sufficient regulations are not in place to counter bribery, political favoritism, and exploitation of workers as greedy companies try to maximize their profits.
- **Social tension**, if the resources are privately owned such that the rich become richer and the poor do not reap the benefits of their national resources. Class divisions become wider, resulting in social unrest.
- **Dependence**, if income from the natural resources is not used to develop other industries as well. In this situation, the economy becomes dependent on one source, and faces potential crises if natural disasters or depletion take away that income source.

ECONOMICS AND KINDS OF ECONOMIES

Economics is the study of the buying choices that people make, the production of goods and services, and how our market system works. The two kinds of economies are command and market. In a **command economy**, the government controls what and how much is produced, the methods used for production, and the distribution of goods and services. In a **market economy**, producers make decisions about methods and distribution on their own. These choices are based on what will sell and bring a profit in the marketplace. In a market economy, consumers ultimately affect these decisions by choosing whether or not to buy certain goods and services. The United States has a market economy.

MARKET ECONOMY

The five characteristics of a **market economy** are:

- **Economic freedom** – There is freedom of choice with respect to jobs, salaries, production, and price.
- **Economic incentives** – A positive incentive is to make a profit. However, if the producer tries to make too high a profit, the consequences might be that no one will purchase the item at that price. A negative incentive would be a drop in profits, causing the producer to decrease or discontinue production. A boycott, which might cause the producer to change business practices or policies, is also a negative economic incentive.
- **Competition** – There is more than one producer for any given product. Consumers thereby have choices about what to buy, which are usually made based on quality and price. Competition is an incentive for a producer to make the best product at the best price. Otherwise, producers will lose business to the competition.
- **Private ownership** – Production and profits belong to an individual or to a private company, not to the government.
- **Limited government** – Government plays no role in the economic decisions of its individual citizens.

FACTORS OF PRODUCTION AND TYPES OF MARKETS THAT CREATE ECONOMIC FLOW

The factors of **production** are:

- **Land** – This includes not only actual land, but also forests, minerals, water, etc.
- **Labor** – This is the work force required to produce goods and services, including factors such as talent, skills, and physical labor.
- **Capital** – This is the cash and material equipment needed to produce goods and services, including buildings, property, tools, office equipment, roads, etc.
- **Entrepreneurship** – Persons with initiative can capitalize on the free market system by producing goods and services.

The two types of markets are factor and product markets. The **factor market** consists of the people who exchange their services for wages. The people are sellers and companies are buyers. The **product market** is the selling of products to the people who want to buy them. The people are the buyers and the companies are the sellers. This exchange creates a circular economic flow in which money goes from the producers to workers as wages, and then flows back to producers in the form of payment for products.

ECONOMIC IMPACT OF TECHNOLOGY

At the start of the 21st century, the role of **information and communications technologies** (ICT) grew rapidly as the economy shifted to a knowledge-based one. Output is increasing in areas where ICT is used intensively, which are service areas and knowledge-intensive industries such as finance; insurance; real estate; business services; health care; environmental goods and services; and community, social, and personal services. Meanwhile, the economic share for manufacturers is declining in medium- and low-technology industries such as chemicals, food products, textiles, gas, water, electricity, construction, and transport and communication services. Industries that have traditionally been high-tech, such as aerospace, computers, electronics, and pharmaceuticals are remaining steady in terms of their economic share. Technology has become the strongest factor in determining **per capita income** for many countries. The ease of technology investments as compared to industries that involve factories and large labor forces has resulted in more foreign investments in countries that do not have natural resources to call upon.

Social Studies

Chapter Quiz

Ready to see how well you retained what you just read? Scan the QR code to go directly to the chapter quiz interface for this study guide. If you're using a computer, simply visit the bonus page at **mometrix.com/bonus948/praxeems7001** and click the Chapter Quizzes link.

Science

Transform passive reading into active learning! After immersing yourself in this chapter, put your comprehension to the test by taking a quiz. The insights you gained will stay with you longer this way. Scan the QR code to go directly to the chapter quiz interface for this study guide. If you're using a computer, simply visit the bonus page at **mometrix.com/bonus948/praxeems7001** and click the Chapter Quizzes link.

Earth Science

GEOLOGY
EARTH SYSTEM SCIENCE

The complex and interconnected dynamics of the continents, atmosphere, oceans, ice, and life forms are the subject of Earth system science. These interconnected dynamics require an interdisciplinary approach that includes chemistry, physics, biology, mathematics, and applied sciences in order to study the Earth as an integrated system and determine (while considering human impact and interaction) the past, present, and future states of the Earth. Scientific inquiry in this field includes exploration of:

- Extreme weather events as they pertain to a changing climate
- Earthquakes and volcanic eruptions as they pertain to tectonic shifts
- Losses in biodiversity in relation to the changes in the Earth's ecosystems
- Causes and effects in the environment
- The Sun's solar variability in relation to the Earth's climate
- The atmosphere's increasing concentrations of carbon dioxide and aerosols
- Trends in the Earth's systems in terms of changes and their consequences

TRADITIONAL EARTH SCIENCE DISCIPLINES

Modern science is approaching the study of the Earth in an integrated fashion that sees the Earth as an interconnected system that is impacted by humankind and, therefore, must include social dimensions. Traditionally, though, the following were the Earth science disciplines:

- **Geology** – This is the study of the origin and structure of the Earth and of the changes it has undergone and is in the process of undergoing. Geologists work from the crust inward.
- **Meteorology** – This is the study of the atmosphere, including atmospheric pressure, temperature, clouds, winds, precipitation, etc. It is also concerned with describing and explaining weather.
- **Oceanography** – This is the study of the oceans, which includes studying their extent and depth, the physics and chemistry of ocean waters, and the exploitation of their resources.
- **Ecology** – This is the study of living organisms in relation to their environment and to other living things. It is the study of the interrelations between the different components of the ecosystem.

GEOLOGICAL ERAS

Geologists divide the history of the Earth into units of time called eons, which are divided into **eras**, then into **periods**, then into **epochs** and finally into **ages**. Dates are approximate of course, and there may be variations of a few million years. (Million years ago is abbreviated as Ma.) Some of the most commonly known time periods are:

- **Hadean Eon** – About 4.5 to 3.8 billion years ago
- **Archaean Eon** – 3.8 to 2.5 billion years ago

- **Proterozoic Eon** – 2.5 billion to 542 Ma
- **Phanerozoic Eon** – 542 Ma to the present
  - **Paleozoic Era** – 542 Ma to 251 Ma
    - ❖ **Cambrian Period** – 542 to 488 Ma
    - ❖ **Ordovician Period** – 488 to 443 Ma
    - ❖ **Silurian Period** – 443 to 416 Ma
    - ❖ **Devonian Period** – 416 to 359 Ma
    - ❖ **Carboniferous Period** – 359 to 290 Ma
    - ❖ **Permian Period** – 290 to 252 Ma
  - **Mesozoic Era** – 252 to 65 Ma
    - ❖ **Triassic Period** – 252 to 200 Ma
    - ❖ **Jurassic Period** – 200 to 150 Ma
    - ❖ **Cretaceous Period** – 150 to 65 Ma
  - **Cenozoic Era** – 65 Ma to the present
    - ❖ **Paleogene Period** – 65 to 28 Ma
    - ❖ **Neogene Period** – 28 to 2 Ma
    - ❖ **Quaternary Period** – about 2 Ma to the present

DEVELOPMENT OF LIFE ON EARTH ACCORDING TO TIME PERIODS

The evolution of life on Earth is believed to have occurred as follows:

- Igneous rocks formed. (Hadean Eon)
- The continents formed. (Archaean Eon)
- The first multi-cellular creatures such as hydras, jellyfish, and sponges appeared about 600 Ma.
- Flatworms, roundworms, and segmented worms appeared about 550 Ma.
- Moss, arthropods, octopus, and eels appeared. (Cambrian Period)
- Mushrooms, fungi, and other primitive plants appeared; sea animals began to use calcium to build bones and shells. (Ordovician Period)
- Fish with jaws appeared. (Silurian Period)
- Fish developed lungs and legs (frogs) and went on land; ferns appeared. (Devonian period)
- Reptiles developed the ability to lay eggs on land and pine trees appeared. (Carboniferous Period)
- Dinosaurs dominated the land during the Triassic and Jurassic Periods.
- Flying insects, birds, and the first flowering plants appeared; dinosaurs died out. (Cretaceous Period)
- Mammals evolved and dominated; grasses became widespread. (50 Ma)
- Hominids appeared more than 2 Ma.

HYDROSPHERE AND HYDROLOGIC CYCLE

The **hydrosphere** is anything on Earth that is related to water, whether it is in the air, on land, or in a plant or animal system. A water molecule consists of only two atoms of hydrogen and one of oxygen, yet it is what makes life possible. Unlike any other planets that have been discovered, Earth is able to sustain water in a liquid state most of the time. Water vapor and ice are of no use to living organisms. The **hydrologic cycle** is the journey water takes as it proceeds through different forms. Liquid surface water evaporates to form the gaseous state of a cloud, and then becomes liquid again in the form of rain. This process takes about 10 days. This cycle is for surface water only: rivers, lakes, groundwater, ocean surface, etc. Water in the deep ocean and in the heart of glaciers is typically sequestered from the cycle for many thousands of years.

> **Review Video: Hydrologic Cycle**
> Visit mometrix.com/academy and enter code: 426578

AQUIFERS

An **aquifer** is an underground water reservoir formed from groundwater that has infiltrated from the surface by passing through the soil and permeable rock layers to whereever the rock layer is impermeable. The section of permeable layers with water present is called the zone of saturation, and the area above that (with no water) is the zone of aeration. There are two types of aquifers. In one, the water is under pressure (**confined**) as the supply builds up between layers of impermeable rocks and has to move back towards the surface, resulting in a spring or artesian well. The second type of aquifer is called "**unconfined**" because it has room to expand and contract, and the water has to be pumped out. The highest level of the aquifer is called the water table. If water is pumped out of the aquifer such that the water table dips in a specific area, that area is called a cone of depression.

BIOSPHERE

Biosphere is the term used by physical geographers to describe the living world of trees, bugs, and animals. It refers to any place where life exists on Earth, and is the intersection of the hydrosphere, the atmosphere, the land, and the energy that comes from space. The biosphere includes the upper areas of the atmosphere where birds and insects can travel, areas deep inside caves, and hydrothermal vents at the bottom of the ocean.

Factors that affect the biosphere include:

- The **distance and tilt** between the Earth and the Sun – This produces temperatures that are conducive to life and causes the seasons.
- **Climate, daily weather, and erosion** – These change the land and the organisms on and in it.
- Earthquakes, tornadoes, volcanoes, tsunamis, and other **natural phenomena** – These all change the land.
- **Chemical erosion** – This changes the composition of rocks and organic materials.
- **Biological erosion** – This is bacteria and single-celled organisms breaking down organic and inorganic materials.

ECOLOGICAL SYSTEM AND BIOME

An **ecological system**, or ecosystem, is the community of all the living organisms in a specific area interacting with non-living factors such as temperature, sunlight, atmospheric pressure, weather patterns, wind, types of nutrients, etc. An ecosystem's development depends on the energy that passes in and out of it. The boundaries of an ecosystem depend on the use of the term, whether it refers to an ecosystem under a rock or in a valley, pond, or ocean.

A **biome** is a general ecosystem type defined by the plants and animals that live there and the local climate patterns. Examples include tropical rainforests or savannas, deserts, grasslands, deciduous forests, tundra, woodlands, and ice caps. There can be more than one type of biome within a larger climate zone. The transition area between two biomes is an ecotone, which may have characteristics of both biomes.

EROSION

Erosion is the process that breaks down matter, whether it is a rock that is broken into pebbles or mountains that are blown by wind and rained on until they become hills. . The erosion of land by weather or breaking waves is called **denudation**. **Mass wasting** is the movement of masses of dirt and rock from one place to another. This can occur in two ways: **mechanical** (such as breaking a rock with a hammer) or **chemical** (such as pouring acid on a rock to dissolve it). If the material changes color, it indicates that a break down was chemical in nature. Whatever is broken down must go somewhere, so erosion eventually builds something up. For example, an eroded mountain ends up in a river that carries the sediment towards the ocean, where it builds up and creates a wetland or delta at the mouth of the river.

Science

CLIMATES

Scientists have determined the following different types of **climates**:

- Polar (ice caps)
- Polar (tundra)
- Subtropical (dry summer)
- Subtropical (dry winter)
- Subtropical (humid)
- Subtropical (marine west coast)
- Subtropical (Mediterranean)
- Subtropical (wet)
- Tropical (monsoon)
- Tropical (savannah/grasslands)
- Tropical (wet)

Several factors make up and affect climates. These include:

- Temperature
- Atmospheric pressure
- The number of clouds and the amount of dust or smog
- Humidity
- Winds

The moistest and warmest of all the climates is that of the tropical rainforest. It has daily convection thunderstorms caused by the surface daytime heat and the high humidity, which combine to form thunderclouds.

> **Review Video: Climates**
> Visit mometrix.com/academy and enter code: 991320

LAYERS OF THE EARTH

The Earth has several distinct layers, each with its own properties:

- **Crust** – This is the outermost layer of the Earth that is comprised of the continents and the ocean basins. It has a variable thickness (35-70 km in the continents and 5-10 km in the ocean basins) and is composed mostly of alumino-silicates.
- **Mantle** – This is about 2900 km thick, and is made up mostly of ferro-magnesium silicates. It is divided into an upper and lower mantle. Most of the internal heat of the Earth is located in the mantle. Large convective cells circulate heat, and may cause plate tectonic movement.
- **Core** – This is separated into the liquid outer core and the solid inner core. The outer core is 2300 km thick (composed mostly of nickel-iron alloy), and the inner core (almost entirely iron) is 12 km thick. The Earth's magnetic field is thought to be controlled by the liquid outer core.

COMPOSITION OF EARTH'S ATMOSPHERE

The Earth's atmosphere is 79% nitrogen, 20% oxygen, and 1% other gases. The oxygen was originally produced almost entirely by algae-type plants. The atmosphere has four layers:

- **Troposphere** – This is the layer closest to the Earth where all weather takes place. It is the region that contains rising and falling packets of air. Air pressure at sea level is 0.1 atmospheres, but the top of the troposphere is about 10% of that amount.

- **Stratosphere** – In this layer, air flow is mainly horizontal. The upper portion has a thin layer of concentrated ozone (a reactive form of oxygen) that is largely responsible for absorbing the Sun's ultraviolet rays.
- **Mesosphere** – This is the coldest layer. Temperatures drop to -100°C at the top.
- **Thermosphere** – This is divided into the lower ionosphere and the higher exosphere. This layer is very thin and has many ionized atoms with a net electrical charge. The aurora and Van Allen Belts are here. This layer also absorbs the most energetic photons from the Sun and reflects radio waves, enabling long distance radio communication.

> **Review Video: Earth's Atmosphere**
> Visit mometrix.com/academy and enter code: 417614

PALEONTOLOGY

Paleontology is the study of prehistoric plant and animal life through the analysis of **fossil remains**. These fossils reveal the ecologies of the past and the path of evolution for both extinct and living organisms. A historical science, paleontology seeks information about the identity, origin, environment, and evolution of past organisms and what they can reveal about the past of the Earth as a whole. Paleontologists seek to explain causes rather than conduct experiments to observe effects. It is related to the fields of biology, geology, and archaeology, and is divided into several sub-disciplines concerned with the types of fossils studied, the process of fossilization, and the ecology and climate of the past. Paleontologists also help identify the composition of the Earth's rock layers by the fossils that are found, thus identifying potential sites for oil, mineral, and water extraction.

DETERMINING THE ORDER IN WHICH GEOLOGIC EVENTS OCCURRED USING THE ROCK RECORD

The **Law of Superposition** logically assumes that the bottom layer of a series of sedimentary layers is the oldest, unless it has been overturned or older rock has been pushed over it. In addition, igneous intrusions can cut through or flow above already present rocks (e.g., lava flows). This is a further indication that the lower rock layers are older. Another guideline for the rock record is that **rock layers** are older than the folds and faults in them because the rocks must exist before they can be folded or faulted. If a rock contains **atomic nuclei**, reference tables of the half-lives of commonly used radio isotopes can be used to match the decay rate of known substances to the nuclei in a rock, and thereby determine its age. Ages of rocks can also be determined from **contact metamorphism**, the re-crystallization of pre-existing rocks due to changes in physical and chemical conditions, such as heat, pressure, and chemically active fluids that might be present in lava or polluted waters.

MATCHING ROCKS AND GEOLOGIC EVENTS IN ONE PLACE WITH THOSE OF ANOTHER

Geologists physically follow rock layers from one location to another by a process called "walking the outcrop." Geologists walk along the outcropping to see where it goes and what the differences and similarities of the neighboring locations they cross are. Similar rock **types** or **patterns** of rock layers that are similar in terms of thickness, color, composition, and fossil remains tell geologists that two locations have a similar geologic history. Fossils are found all over the Earth, but are from a relatively **small time period** in Earth's history. Therefore, fossil evidence helps date a rock layer, regardless of where it occurs. **Volcanic ash** is a good time indicator since ash is deposited quickly over a widespread area. Matching the date of an eruption to the ash allows for a precise identification of time. Similarly, the **meteor impact** at the intersection of the Cretaceous and Tertiary Periods left a time marker. Wherever the meteor's iridium content is found, geologists are able to date rock layers.

SEQUENCING THE EARTH'S GEOLOGIC HISTORY FROM THE FOSSIL AND ROCK RECORD

Reference tables are used to match specimens and time periods. For example, the fossil record has been divided into time units of the Earth's history. Rocks can therefore be dated by the fossils found with them. There are also reference tables for dating plate motions and mountain building events in geologic history. Since humans have been around for a relatively short period of time, **fossilized human remains** help to affix a

Science

217

date to a location. Some areas have missing **geologic layers** because of erosion or other factors, but reference tables specific to a region will list what is complete or missing. The theory of **uniformitarianism** assumes that geologic processes have been the same throughout history. Therefore, the way erosion or volcanic eruptions happen today is the same as the way these events happened millions of years ago because there is no reason for them to have changed. Therefore, knowledge about current events can be applied to the past to make judgments about events in the rock record.

REVEALING CHANGES IN EARTH'S HISTORY BY THE FOSSIL AND ROCK RECORDS

Fossils can show how animal and plant life have changed or remained the same over time. For example, fossils have provided evidence of the existence of dinosaurs even though they no longer roam the Earth, and have also been used to prove that certain insects have been around for hundreds of millions of years. Fossils have been used to identify four basic eras: **Proterozoic**, the age of primitive life; **Paleozoic**, the age of fishes; **Mesozoic**, the age of dinosaurs; and **Cenozoic**, the age of mammals. Most ancient forms of life have disappeared, and there are reference tables that list when this occurred. Fossil records also show the evolution of certain life forms, such as the horse from the eohippus. However, the majority of changes do not involve evolution from simple to complex forms, but rather an increase in the variety of forms.

MOUNTAINS

A **mountain** is a portion of the Earth that has been raised above its surroundings by volcanic action or tectonic plate movement. Mountains can be made of any type of rock and most lie along active plate boundaries. There are two major mountain systems. The **Circum-Pacific** encircles the entire Pacific Ocean, from New Guinea up across Japan and the Aleutians and down to southern South America. The **Alpine-Himalaya** stretches from northern Africa across the Alps and to the Himalayas and Indonesia. **Orogeny** is the term for the process of natural mountain formation. Therefore, physical mountains are orogens. **Folded mountains** are created through the folding of rock layers when two crustal plates come together. The Alps and Himalayas are folded mountains. The latter was formed by the collision of India with Asia. **Fault-block mountains** are created from the tension forces of plate movements. These produce faults that vertically displace one section to form a mountain. **Dome mountains** are created from magma pushing up through the Earth's crust.

VOLCANOES AND VOLCANIC MOUNTAINS

Volcanoes are classified according to their activity level. An **active** volcano is in the process of erupting or building to an eruption; a dormant volcano has erupted before and may erupt again someday, but is not currently active; and an **extinct** volcano has died out volcanically and will not erupt ever again. Active volcanoes endanger plant and animal life, but lava and ash add enriching minerals to the soil. There are three types of volcanic mountains:

- **Shield volcanoes** are the largest volcanic mountains because of a repeated, viscous lava flow from small eruptions over a long period of time that cause the mountain to grow.
- **Cinder cone volcanoes**, or linear volcanoes, are small in size, but have massive explosions through linear shafts that spread cinders and ash around the vent. This results in a cone-shaped hill.
- **Composite volcanoes** get their name from the mix of lava and ash layers that build the mountain.

SUBDIVISIONS OF ROCK

The three major subdivisions of rock are:

- **Igneous** (magmatites) – This type is formed from the cooling of liquid magma. In the process, minerals crystallize and amalgamate. If solidification occurs deep in the Earth (plutonic rock), the cooling process is slow. This allows for the formation of large crystals, giving rock a coarse-grained texture (granite). Quickly cooled magma has a glassy texture (obsidian).

- **Metamorphic** – Under conditions of high temperature and pressure within the Earth's crust, rock material melts and changes structure, transitioning or metamorphosing into a new type of rock with different minerals. If the minerals appear in bands, the rock is foliated. Examples include marble (unfoliated) and slate (foliated).
- **Sedimentary** – This is the most common type of rock on Earth. It is formed by sedimentation, compaction, and then cementation of many small particles of mineral, animal, or plant material. There are three types of sedimentary rocks: clastic, clay, and sand that came from disintegrated rocks; chemical (rock salt and gypsum), formed by evaporation of aqueous solutions; and biogenic (coal), formed from animal or plant remnants.

> **Review Video: Igneous, Sedimentary, and Metamorphic Rocks**
> Visit mometrix.com/academy and enter code: 689294

GLACIERS

Glaciers start high in the mountains, where snow and ice accumulate inside a cirque (a small semicircular depression). The snow becomes firmly packed into masses of coarse-grained ice that are slowly pulled down a slope by gravity. Glaciers grow with large amounts of snowfall and retreat (diminish) if warm weather melts more ice than can be replaced. Glaciers once covered large areas of both the northern and southern hemispheres with mile-thick ice that carved out valleys, fjords, and other land formations. They also moved plants, animals, and rocks from one area to another. There were two types of glaciers: **valley**, which produced U-shaped erosion and sharp-peaked mountains; and **continental**, which moved over and rounded mountain tops and ridges. These glaciers existed during the ice ages, the last of which occurred from 2.5 million years ago to 12,000 years ago.

EARTH SCIENCE AND WEATHER
LAYERS ABOVE THE SURFACE OF EARTH

The **ozone layer**, although contained within the stratosphere, is determined by ozone (O_3) concentrations. It absorbs the majority of ultraviolet light from the Sun. The ionosphere is part of both the exosphere and the thermosphere. It is characterized by the fact that it is a plasma, a partially ionized gas in which free electrons and positive ions are attracted to each other, but are too energetic to remain fixed as a molecule. It starts at about 50 km above Earth's surface and goes to 1,000 km. It affects radio wave transmission and auroras. The ionosphere pushes against the inner edge of the Earth's magnetosphere, which is the highly magnetized, non-spherical region around the Earth. The homosphere encompasses the troposphere, stratosphere, and mesosphere. Gases in the homosphere are considered well mixed. In the heterosphere, the distance that particles can move without colliding is large. As a result, gases are stratified according to their molecular weights. Heavier gases such as oxygen and nitrogen occur near the bottom of the heterosphere, while hydrogen, the lightest element, is found at the top.

> **Review Video: Earth's Atmosphere**
> Visit mometrix.com/academy and enter code: 417614

TROPOSPHERIC CIRCULATION

Most weather takes place in the **troposphere**. Air circulates in the atmosphere by convection and in various types of "cells." Air near the equator is warmed by the Sun and rises. Cool air rushes under it, and the higher, warmer air flows toward Earth's poles. At the poles, it cools and descends to the surface. It is now under the hot air, and flows back to the equator. Air currents coupled with ocean currents move heat around the planet, creating winds, weather, and climate. Winds can change direction with the seasons. For example, in Southeast Asia and India, summer monsoons are caused by air being heated by the Sun. This air rises, draws moisture

Science

from the ocean, and causes daily rains. In winter, the air cools, sinks, pushes the moist air away, and creates dry weather.

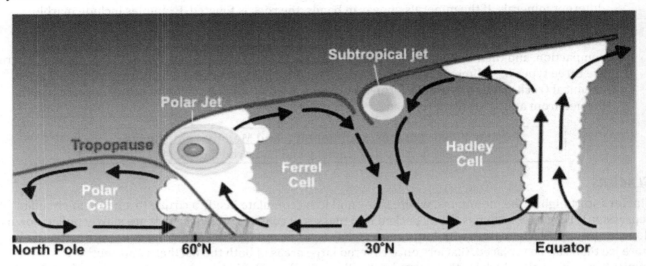

COMMON WEATHER PHENOMENA AND EQUIPMENT TO MEASURE THEM

Common **atmospheric conditions** that are frequently measured are temperature, precipitation, wind, and humidity. These weather conditions are often measured at permanently fixed **weather stations** so weather data can be collected and compared over time and by region. Measurements may also be taken by ships, buoys, and underwater instruments. Measurements may also be taken under special circumstances. Common instruments used and measurements taken include:

- A **thermometer** for measuring temperature
- A **barometer** for measuring barometric/air pressure
- A **hygrometer** for measuring humidity
- An **anemometer** for measuring wind speed
- A **weather vane** for measuring wind direction
- A **rain gauge** for measuring precipitation

WEATHER, CLIMATE, AND METEOROLOGY

Meteorology is the study of the atmosphere, particularly as it pertains to forecasting the weather and understanding its processes. **Weather** is the condition of the atmosphere at any given moment. Most weather occurs in the troposphere and includes changing events such as clouds, storms, and temperature, as well as more extreme events such as tornadoes, hurricanes, and blizzards. **Climate** refers to the average weather for a particular area over time, typically at least 30 years. Latitude is an indicator of climate. Changes in climate occur over long time periods.

WINDS AND GLOBAL WIND BELTS

Winds are the result of air moving by convection. Masses of warm air rise, and cold air sweeps into their place. The warm air also moves, cools, and sinks. The term "prevailing wind" refers to the wind that usually blows in an area in a single direction. **Dominant winds** are the winds with the highest speeds. Belts or bands that run latitudinally and blow in a specific direction are associated with **convection cells. Hadley cells** are formed directly north and south of the equator. The **Farrell cells** occur at about 30° to 60°. The jet stream runs between the Farrell cells and the polar cells. At the higher and lower latitudes, the direction is easterly. At mid latitudes, the direction is westerly. From the North Pole to the south, the surface winds are Polar High Easterlies, Subpolar Low Westerlies, Subtropical High or Horse Latitudes, North-East Trade winds, Equatorial

Low or Doldrums, South-East Trades, Subtropical High or Horse Latitudes, Subpolar Low Easterlies, and Polar High.

RELATIVE HUMIDITY, ABSOLUTE HUMIDITY, AND DEW POINT TEMPERATURE

Humidity refers to water vapor contained in the air. The amount of moisture contained in air depends upon its temperature. The higher the air temperature, the more moisture it can hold. These higher levels of moisture are associated with higher humidity. **Absolute humidity** refers to the total amount of moisture air is capable of holding at a certain temperature. **Relative humidity** is the ratio of water vapor in the air compared to the amount the air is capable of holding at its current temperature. As temperature decreases, absolute humidity stays the same and relative humidity increases. A hygrometer is a device used to measure humidity. The **dew point** is the temperature at which water vapor condenses into water at a particular humidity.

PRECIPITATION

After clouds reach the dew point, **precipitation** occurs. Precipitation can take the form of a liquid or a solid. It is known by many names, including rain, snow, ice, dew, and frost. **Liquid** forms of precipitation include rain and drizzle. Rain or drizzle that freezes on contact is known as freezing rain or freezing drizzle. **Solid or frozen** forms of precipitation include snow, ice needles or diamond dust, sleet or ice pellets, hail, and graupel or snow pellets. Virga is a form of precipitation that evaporates before reaching the ground. It usually looks like sheets or shafts falling from a cloud. The amount of rainfall is measured with a rain gauge. Intensity can be measured according to how fast precipitation is falling or by how severely it limits visibility. Precipitation plays a major role in the water cycle since it is responsible for depositing much of the Earth's fresh water.

CLOUDS

Clouds form when air cools and warm air is forced to give up some of its water vapor because it can no longer hold it. This vapor condenses and forms tiny droplets of water or ice crystals called clouds. Particles, or aerosols, are needed for water vapor to form water droplets. These are called **condensation nuclei**. Clouds are created by surface heating, mountains and terrain, rising air masses, and weather fronts. Clouds precipitate, returning the water they contain to Earth. Clouds can also create atmospheric optics. They can scatter light, creating colorful phenomena such as rainbows, colorful sunsets, and the green flash phenomenon.

HIGH, MIDDLE, AND LOW CLOUD TYPES

Most clouds can be classified according to the altitude of their base above Earth's surface. **High clouds** occur at altitudes between 5,000 and 13,000 meters. **Middle clouds** occur at altitudes between 2,000 and 7,000 meters. **Low clouds** occur from the Earth's surface to altitudes of 2,000 meters. Types of high clouds include cirrus (Ci), thin wispy mare's tails that consist of ice; cirrocumulus (Cc), small, pillow-like puffs that often appear in rows; and cirrostratus (Cs), thin, sheet-like clouds that often cover the entire sky. Types of middle clouds include altocumulus (Ac), gray-white clouds that consist of liquid water; and altostratus (As), grayish or blue-gray clouds that span the sky. Types of low clouds include stratus (St), gray and fog-like clouds consisting of water droplets that take up the whole sky; stratocumulus (Sc), low-lying, lumpy gray clouds; and nimbostratus (Ns), dark gray clouds with uneven bases that indicate rain or snow. Two types of clouds,

Science

cumulus (Cu) and cumulonimbus (Cb), are capable of great vertical growth. They can start at a wide range of altitudes, from the Earth's surface to altitudes of 13,000 meters.

AIR MASSES

Air masses are large volumes of air in the troposphere of the Earth. They are categorized by their temperature and by the amount of water vapor they contain:

- **Arctic** and **Antarctic** air masses are cold
- **Polar** air masses are cool
- **Tropical** and **equatorial** air masses are hot
- **Maritime** and **monsoon** air masses are moist and unstable
- **Continental** and **superior** air masses are dry

WEATHER FRONTS AND WEATHER MAPS

A **weather front** is the area between two differing masses of air that affects weather. Movement of a front is influenced by the jet stream and other high winds as well as the type of front; cold fronts move up to twice as fast as warm ones. It is in the turbulent frontal area that weather events take place, both commonplace and dramatic. This area also creates temperature changes. Weather phenomena include rain, thunderstorms, high winds, tornadoes, cloudiness, clear skies, and hurricanes. Different fronts can be plotted on weather maps using a set of designated symbols. Surface weather maps can also include symbols representing clouds, rain, temperature, air pressure, and fair weather.

SPACE SCIENCE

ASTRONOMY

Astronomy is the scientific study of celestial objects and their positions, movements, and structures. *Celestial* does not refer to the Earth by itself, but does include its movement through space. Other celestial objects include the Sun, the Moon, planets, satellites, asteroids, meteors, comets, stars, galaxies, the universe, and other space phenomena. The term astronomy has its roots in the Greek words *astro* and *nomos*, which means "laws of the stars."

> **Review Video: Astronomy**
> Visit mometrix.com/academy and enter code: 640556

UNIVERSE

ORIGIN

The **universe** can be said to consist of everything and nothing. The universe contains all of space, matter, energy, and time. There are likely still phenomena that have yet to be discovered. The universe can also be thought of as nothing, since a vast portion of the known universe is empty space. It is believed that the universe is expanding. The **Big Bang** is a core part of a theory developed to explain the origin of the universe. It is widely accepted among astronomers, though there are other theories regarding the origin of the universe, such as the **Steady-State theory** and the **Creationist theory**. According to the Big Bang model, all the matter in the universe was once in one place. This matter underwent a huge explosion that spread it into space. Galaxies formed from, this material and the universe is still expanding.

STRUCTURE

What can be seen of the universe is believed to be at least 93 billion light years across. To put this into perspective, the Milky Way galaxy is about 100,000 light years across. Our view of matter in the universe is that it forms into clumps which become stars, galaxies, clusters of galaxies, superclusters, and the Great Wall of galaxies. **Galaxies** consist of stars, some with planetary systems. Some estimates state that the universe is about 13 billion years old. It is not considered dense and is believed to consist of 73% dark energy, 23% cold dark matter, and 4% regular matter. Cosmology is the study of the universe. Interstellar medium (ISM) is the gas and dust in the interstellar space between a galaxy's stars.

Review Video: Dark Matter
Visit mometrix.com/academy and enter code: 251909

GALAXIES

Galaxies consist of stars, stellar remnants, and dark matter. **Dwarf galaxies** contain as few as 10 million stars, while giant galaxies contain as many as 1 trillion stars. Galaxies are gravitationally bound, meaning that stars, star systems, other gases, and dust orbit the galaxy's center. The Earth exists in the **Milky Way galaxy** and the nearest galaxy to ours is the **Andromeda galaxy**. Galaxies can be classified by their visual shape into elliptical, spiral, irregular, and starburst galaxies. It is estimated that there are more than 100 billion galaxies in the universe ranging from 1,000 to 100,000 parsecs in diameter. Galaxies can be megaparsecs apart. Intergalactic space consists of a gas with an average density of less than one atom per cubic meter. Galaxies are organized into clusters which form superclusters. Dark matter may account for up to 90% of the mass of galaxies. Dark matter is still not well understood.

PLANETS

In order of their distance from the Sun (closest to furthest away), the **planets** are: Mercury, Venus, Earth, Mars, Jupiter, Saturn, Uranus, and Neptune (Pluto is now considered to be a dwarf planet). All the planets revolve around the Sun, which is an average-sized star in the spiral Milky Way galaxy. They revolve in the same direction in nearly circular orbits. If the planets were viewed by looking down from the Sun, they would rotate in a counter-clockwise direction. All the planets are in, or near, the same plane, called the ecliptic, and their axis of rotation is nearly perpendicular to the ecliptic. The only exception is Uranus, which is tipped on its side.

TERRESTRIAL PLANETS, JOVIAN PLANETS, AND MASS OF PLANETS

The **Terrestrial Planets** are: Mercury, Venus, Earth, and Mars. These are the four planets closest to the Sun. They are called terrestrial because they all have a compact, rocky surface similar to the Earth's. Venus, Earth, and Mars have significant atmospheres, but Mercury has almost no atmosphere.

The **Jovian Planets** are: Jupiter (the largest planet), Saturn, Uranus, and Neptune. They are called Jovian (Jupiter-like) because of their huge sizes in relation to that of the Earth, and because they all have a gaseous nature like Jupiter. Although gas giants, some or all of the Jovian Planets may have small, solid cores.

The Sun represents 99.85% of all the matter in our solar system. Combined, the planets make up only 0.135% of the mass of the solar system, with Jupiter having twice the mass of all the other planets combined. The

Science

remaining 0.015% of the mass comes from comets, planetary satellites, asteroids, meteoroids, and interplanetary medium.

DEFINITION OF PLANET

On August 24, 2006, the International Astronomical Union redefined the criteria a body must meet to be classified as a planet, stating that the following conditions must be met:

- "A planet orbits around a star and is neither a star nor a moon."
- "Its shape is spherical due to its gravity."
- "It has 'cleared' the space of its orbit."

A **dwarf planet** such as Pluto does not meet the third condition. Small solar system bodies such as asteroids and comets meet only the first condition.

SOLAR SYSTEM

The **solar system** developed about 4.6 billion years ago out of an enormous cloud of dust and gas circling around the Sun. Four rocky planets orbit relatively close to the Sun. Their inside orbits are separated from the outside orbits of the four, larger gaseous planets by an asteroid belt. Pluto, some comets, and several small objects circle in the Kuiper belt outside Neptune's orbit. The Oort cloud, composed of icy space objects, encloses the planetary system like a shell.

EARTH'S MOON

The Moon is the closest celestial body to Earth. Its proximity has allowed it to be studied since the invention of the telescope. As a result, its landforms have been named after astronomers, philosophers, and other scholars. Its surface has many craters created by asteroids since it has no protective atmosphere. These dark lowlands looked like seas to early astronomers, so many have been given names like the Sea of Tranquility, even though there is virtually no water on the Moon except possibly in its polar regions. These impact craters and depressions actually contain solidified lava flows. The bright highlands were thought to be continents, and were named terrae. The rocks of the Moon have been pounded by asteroids so often that there is a layer of rubble and dust called the regolith. Also, because there is no protective atmosphere, temperatures on the Moon vary widely, from 265°F to -255°F.

EARTH'S SUN AND OTHER STARS

A **star** begins as a cloud of hydrogen and some heavier elements drawn together by their own mass. As the matter coalesces due to its own gravity, it begins to rotate. Once there is sufficient mass, the core heats up to several million degrees Fahrenheit, which causes the hydrogen atoms to lose their shells and their nuclei to fuse. This releases enormous amounts of energy, generates an outward pressure that is balanced by the pull of gravity, and enables the star to become stable. At this point the star is in a stage called the **main sequence**. This is the stage our Sun is in, and it will remain in this stage until its supply of hydrogen fuel runs out. Stars are not always alone like our Sun, and may exist in pairs or groups. The hottest stars shine blue-white; medium-hot stars like our Sun glow yellow; and cooler stars appear orange. The Sun is an **average star** in terms of mass, light production, and size. All stars, including our Sun, have a **core** where fusion happens; a photosphere (surface) that produces sunspots (cool, dark areas); a red **chromosphere** that emits solar (bright) flares and shooting gases; and a **corona**, the transparent area only seen during an eclipse.

Review Video: The Sun
Visit mometrix.com/academy and enter code: 699233

COMETS, ASTEROIDS, AND METEOROIDS

Comets are celestial bodies composed of dust, rock, frozen gases, and ice. Invisible until they near the Sun, comets emit volatile components in jets of gas and dust when exposed to the Sun's heat. The **coma** is the comet's fog-like envelope that glows as it reflects sunlight and releases radiation. **Solar winds** blow a comet away from the Sun and give it a tail of dust or electrically charged molecules. Each orbit of a comet causes it to lose matter until it breaks up or vaporizes into the Sun.

Asteroids are irregularly-shaped boulders, usually less than 60 miles in diameter, that orbit the Sun. Most are made of graphite; about 25% are silicates, or iron and nickel. Collisions or gravitational forces can cause them to fly off and possibly hit a planet.

Meteoroids are fragments of asteroids of various sizes. If they come through Earth's atmosphere, they are called meteors or shooting stars. If they land on Earth, they are called meteorites, and create craters on impact (the Barringer Crater in Arizona).

Life Science

BIOLOGY

SUBFIELDS OF BIOLOGY

There are a number of subfields of biology:

- **Zoology** – The study of animals
- **Botany** – The study of plants
- **Biophysics** – The application of the laws of physics to the processes of organisms and the application of the facts about living things to human processes and inventions
- **Biochemistry** – The study of the chemistry of living organisms, including diseases and the pharmaceutical drugs used to cure them
- **Cytology** – The study of cells
- **Histology** – The study of the tissues of plants and animals
- **Organology** – The study of tissues organized into organs
- **Physiology** – The study of the way organisms function, including metabolism, the exchange of matter and energy in nutrition, the senses, reproduction and development, and the work of the nervous system and brain
- **Genetics** – The study of heredity as it relates to the transmission of genes
- **Ethology** – The study of animal behavior
- **Ecology** – The study of the relationship of living organisms to their environments
- **Taxonomy** – The study of the classification of living things

CLASSIFICATION OF LIFE FORMS

All living creatures can be classified based on their characteristics. Carolus Linnaeus, who is said to be the first taxonomist, created the first hierarchical classification system in 1735. He considered every living creature to be a plant or an animal, so his system started with the two **kingdoms** of plants and animals (plus a kingdom of non-living things). Each kingdom was further divided into levels of class, order, genus, and species. He also developed **binomial nomenclature**, an approach to naming species that is still in use today. Since then, as taxonomists have learned more about species' natural history and genetics, more-complex classification systems have been developed. They continue to be changed and refined, especially when it comes to single-celled creatures. For this reason, there are currently many different systems that do not agree with one another. For example, some systems use kingdoms as the top level, while others use domains, empires, or superkingdoms. One popular way to classify living things uses three domains and six kingdoms:

- Domain Bacteria
  - **Kingdom Eubacteria**—single celled prokaryotes with little internal complexity, contains peptidoglycan. Members have just one chromosome, reproduce asexually, may have flagella, and are very simple in form.
- Domain Archaea
  - **Kingdom Archaebacteria**—single celled prokaryotes with little internal complexity, does not contain peptidoglycan. Members have just one chromosome, reproduce asexually, may have flagella, and are very simple in form.
- Domain Eukarya
  - **Kingdom Protista**—single celled eukaryotes with greater internal complexity than Bacteria or Archaea. They have a true nucleus surrounded by a membrane that separates it from the cytoplasm. Most are one-celled and have no complex tissues like plants.
  - **Kingdom Fungi**—single celled or multicellular with considerable variation and complexity. Members have no chlorophyll, so they don't make their own food like plants. They reproduce using spores. Fungi are made up of filaments called hyphae that, in larger fungi, can interlace to form a tissue called mycelium.
  - **Kingdom Plantae**—multicellular with great variation and complexity, rigid cell walls. This group consists of organisms that have chlorophyll and make their own food. Plants have differentiated tissues and reproduce either sexually or asexually.
  - **Kingdom Animalia**—multicellular with much variation and complexity, cell membrane. This group consists of organisms that move around and have to feed on existing organic material.

> **Review Video: Kingdom Animalia**
> Visit mometrix.com/academy and enter code: 558413
>
> **Review Video: Kingdom Fungi**
> Visit mometrix.com/academy and enter code: 315081
>
> **Review Video: Kingdom Plantae**
> Visit mometrix.com/academy and enter code: 710084

CHARACTERISTICS OF INVERTEBRATES

Invertebrates are animals with no internal skeletons. They can be divided into three groups:

1. **Marine Invertebrates** – Members of this group live in oceans and seas. Marine invertebrates include sponges, corals, jellyfish, snails, clams, octopuses, squids, and crustaceans, none of which live on the surface.
2. **Freshwater Invertebrates** – Members of this group live in lakes and rivers. Freshwater invertebrates include worms on the bottom, microscopic crustaceans, and terrestrial insect larvae that live in the water column, but only where there is no strong current. Some live on the surface of the water.

3. **Terrestrial Invertebrates** – Members of this group live on dry ground. Terrestrial invertebrates include insects, mollusks (snails, slugs), arachnids, and myriapods (centipedes and millipedes). Terrestrial invertebrates breathe through a series of tubes that penetrate into the body (trachea) and deliver oxygen into tissues. Underground terrestrial invertebrates are generally light-colored with atrophied eyes and no cuticle to protect them from desiccation. They include worms that live underground and in caves and rock crevices. This group also includes insects such as ants that create colonies underground.

CHARACTERISTICS OF VERTEBRATE GROUPS

The **vertebrates**, animals with an internal skeleton, are divided into four groups:

1. **Fish** – This group is the most primitive, but is also the group from which all other groups evolved. Fish live in water, breathe with gills, are cold-blooded, have fins and scales, and are typically oviparous, which means they lay eggs. Fish typically have either cartilaginous skeletons (such as rays and sharks) or bony skeletons.
2. **Amphibians** – The skin of animals in this group is delicate and permeable, so they need water to keep it moist. Amphibians are oviparous. The young start out in water with gills, but the adults use lungs.
3. **Reptiles and birds** – The skin of animals in this group has very hard, horn-like scales. Birds have exchanged scales for feathers. Most reptiles and all birds are oviparous, although birds care for their eggs and reptiles do not. Members have a cloaca, an excretory and reproductive cavity that opens to the outside. Reptiles are cold-blooded, but birds are warm-blooded.
4. **Mammals** – Mammals have bodies covered with fur; are warm-blooded; are viviparous, meaning they give birth to live young. The young are fed with milk from female mammary glands; and are tetrapods (four-legged). Most live on the ground (except marine mammals like whales and dolphins) and a few fly (bats).

HUNTERS AND PREY ANIMALS

The interaction between **predators** and their **prey** is important to controlling the balance of an ecosystem. **Hunters** are **carnivorous** animals at the top of the ecological pyramid that eat other animals. Hunters tend to be territorial, leaving signs to warn others to stay out or risk a fight. Hunters are equipped to capture with claws, curved beaks, spurs, fangs, etc. They try to use a minimum amount of energy for each capture, so they prey upon the more vulnerable (the old, ill, or very young) when given a choice. Predators never kill more than they can eat. Some hunters have great speed, some stalk, and some hunt in groups. **Prey** animals are those that are captured by predators for food. They are usually **herbivores** further down the ecological pyramid. Prey animals have special characteristics to help them flee from predators. They may hide in nests or caves, become totally immobile to escape detection, have protective coloration or camouflage, have warning coloration to indicate being poisonous, or have shells or quills for protection.

LIFE PROCESSES THAT ALL LIVING THINGS HAVE IN COMMON

Living things share many **processes** that are necessary to survival, but the ways these processes and interactions occur are highly diverse. Processes include those related to:

- **Nutrition** – the process of obtaining, ingesting, and digesting foods; excreting unused or excess substances; and extracting energy from the foods to maintain structure.
- **Transport** (circulation) – the process of circulating essential materials such as nutrients, cells, hormones, and gases (oxygen and hydrogen) to the places they are needed by moving them through veins, arteries, and capillaries. Needed materials do not travel alone, but are "piggybacked" on transporting molecules.
- **Respiration** – the process of breathing, which is exchanging gases between the interior and exterior using gills, trachea (insects), or lungs.
- **Regulation** – the process of coordinating life activities through the nervous and endocrine systems.

Science

- **Reproduction and growth** – the process of producing more of one's own kind and growing from birth to adulthood. The more highly evolved an animal is, the longer its growth time is.
- **Locomotion** (in animals) – the process of moving from place to place in the environment by using legs, flight, or body motions.

ORGANISMS THAT INTERFERE WITH CELL ACTIVITY

Viruses, bacteria, fungi, and other parasites may infect plants and animals and interfere with normal life functions, create imbalances, or disrupt the operations of cells.

- **Viruses** – These enter the body by inhalation (airborne) or through contact with contaminated food, water, or infected tissues. They affect the body by taking over the cell's protein synthesis mechanism to make more viruses. They kill the host cell and impact tissue and organ operations. Examples of viruses include measles, rabies, pneumonia, and AIDS.
- **Bacteria** – These enter the body through breaks in the skin or contaminated food or water, or by inhalation. They reproduce rapidly and produce toxins that kill healthy host tissues. Examples include diphtheria, bubonic plague, tuberculosis, and syphilis.
- **Fungi** – These feed on healthy tissues of the body by sending rootlike tendrils into the tissues to digest them extracellularly. Examples include athlete's foot and ringworm.
- **Parasites** – These enter the body through the skin, via insect bites, or through contaminated food or water. Examples include tapeworms, malaria, or typhus.

HYDROCARBONS AND CARBOHYDRATES

Carbon is an element found in all living things. Two types of carbon molecules that are essential to life are hydrocarbons and carbohydrates. **Hydrocarbons**, composed only of hydrogen and carbon, are the simplest organic molecules. The simplest of these is methane, which has one carbon atom and four hydrogen atoms. Methane is produced by the decomposition of animal or vegetable matter, and is part of petroleum and natural gas. **Carbohydrates** are compounds made of hydrogen, carbon, and oxygen. There are three types of these macromolecules (large molecules):

1. **Sugars** are soluble in water and, although they have less energy than fats, provide energy more quickly.
2. **Starches**, insoluble in water, are long chains of glucose that act as reserve substances. Potatoes and cereals are valuable foods because they are rich in starch. Animals retain glucose in their cells as glycogen, a special type of starch.
3. **Cellulose**, composed of glucose chains, makes up the cells and tissues of plants. It is one of the most common organic materials.

LIPIDS, PROTEINS, AND NUCLEIC ACIDS

Besides hydrocarbons and carbohydrates, there are three other types of carbon molecules that are essential to life: lipids, proteins, and nucleic acids. **Lipids** are compounds that are insoluble or only partially soluble in water. There are three main types: fats, which act as an energy reserve for organisms; phospholipids, which are one of the essential components of cell membranes; and steroids such as cholesterol and estrogen, which are very important to metabolism. **Proteins** are complex substances that make up almost half the dry weight of animal bodies. These molecules contain hydrogen, carbon, oxygen, and other elements, chiefly nitrogen and sulfur. Proteins make up muscle fibers and, as enzymes, act as catalysts. **Nucleic acids** are large molecules (polymers) composed of a large number of simpler molecules (nucleotides). Each one has a sugar containing five carbons (pentose), a phosphorous compound (phosphate group), and a nitrogen compound (nitrogenated base). Nucleic acids facilitate perpetuation of the species because they carry genetic information as DNA and RNA.

228

CELL

The **cell** is the basic organizational unit of all living things. Each component within a cell has a function that helps organisms grow and survive. There are many different types of cells, and they are unique to each type of organism. The one thing that all cells have in common is a **membrane**, which is comparable to a semi-permeable plastic bag. The membrane is composed of phospholipids. There are also some **transport holes**, which are proteins that help certain molecules and ions move in and out of the cell. The cell is filled with a fluid called **cytoplasm** or cytosol. Within the cell are a variety of **organelles**, groups of complex molecules that help a cell survive, each with its own unique membrane that has a different chemical makeup from the cell membrane. The larger the cell, the more organelles it will need to live.

> **Review Video: Difference Between Plant and Animal Cells**
> Visit mometrix.com/academy and enter code: 115568
>
> **Review Video: Cell Structure**
> Visit mometrix.com/academy and enter code: 591293

NUCLEUS AND MITOCHONDRIA IN EUKARYOTIC CELLS

Eukaryotic cells have a nucleus, a big dark spot floating somewhere in the center that acts like the brain of the cell by controlling eating, movement, and reproduction. A **nuclear envelope** surrounds the nucleus and its contents, but allows RNA and proteins to pass through. **Chromatin**, made up of DNA, RNA, and nuclear proteins, is present in the nucleus. The nucleus also contains a nucleolus made of RNA and protein. **Mitochondria** are very small organelles that take in nutrients, break them down, and create energy for the cell through a process called cellular respiration. There might be thousands of mitochondria depending on the cell's purpose. A muscle cell needs more energy for movement than a cell that transmits nerve impulses, for example. Mitochondria have two membranes: a **cover** and the **inner cristae** that folds over many times to increase the surface work area. The fluid inside the mitochondria, the matrix, is filled with water and enzymes that take food molecules and combine them with oxygen so they can be digested.

> **Review Video: Mitochondria**
> Visit mometrix.com/academy and enter code: 444287

CHLOROPLASTS OF PLANT CELLS

Chloroplasts, which make plants green, are the food producers of a plant cell. They differ from an animal cell's mitochondria, which break down sugars and nutrients. **Photosynthesis** occurs when the energy from the sun hits a chloroplast and the chlorophyll uses that energy to combine carbon dioxide and water to make sugars and oxygen. The nutrition and oxygen obtained from plants makes them the basis of all life on earth. A chloroplast has two membranes to contain and protect the inner parts. The **stroma** is an area inside the chloroplast where reactions occur and starches are created. A **thylakoid** has chlorophyll molecules on its surface, and a stack of thylakoids is called a granum. The stacks of sacs are connected by **stromal lamellae**, which act like the skeleton of the chloroplast, keeping all the sacs a safe distance from each other and maximizing the efficiency of the organelle.

PASSIVE AND ACTIVE TRANSPORT

Passive transport within a cell does not require additional energy or active work. For example, when there is a large concentration difference between the outside and the inside of a cell, the pressure of the greater concentration, not energy, will move molecules across the lipid bilayer into the cell. Another example of passive transport is osmosis, which is the movement of water across a membrane. Too much water in a cell can cause it to burst, so the cell moves ions in and out to help equalize the amount of water. **Active transport** is when a cell uses energy to move individual molecules across the cell membrane. **Proteins** embedded in the lipid bilayer do most of the transport work. There are hundreds of different types of proteins because they are

Science

specific. For instance, a protein that moves glucose will not move calcium. The activity of these proteins can be stopped by inhibitors or poisons, which can destroy or plug up a protein.

Review Video: Passive Transport: Diffusion and Osmosis
Visit mometrix.com/academy and enter code: 642038

MITOTIC CELL REPLICATION

Mitosis is the duplication of a cell and all its parts, including the DNA, into two identical daughter cells. There are five phases in the life cycle of a cell:

1. **Prophase** – This is the process of duplicating everything in preparation for division.
2. **Metaphase** – The cell's different pieces align themselves for the split. The DNA lines up along a central axis and the centrioles send out specialized tubules that connect to the centromere. The centromere has two strands of a chromosome (condensed DNA) attached to it.
3. **Anaphase** – Half of the chromosomes go one way and half go another.
4. **Telophase** – When the chromosomes get to the side of the cell, the cell membrane closes in and splits the cell into two pieces. This results in two separate cells, each with half of the original DNA.
5. **Interphase** – This is the normal state of the cell, or the resting stage between divisions. During this stage, the cell duplicates nucleic acids in preparation for the next division.

Review Video: Mitosis
Visit mometrix.com/academy and enter code: 849894

MICROBES

Microbes are the smallest, simplest, and most abundant organisms on earth. Their numbers are incalculable, and a microscope is required to see them. There is a huge variety of microbes, including bacteria, fungi, some algae, and protozoa. Microbes can be harmful or helpful.

Microbes can be **heterotrophic** (eat other things) or **autotrophic** (make food for themselves). They can be solitary or colonial, sexual or asexual. Examples include mold, a multi-cellular type of fungus, and yeasts, which are single-celled (but may live in colonies). A **mushroom** is a fungus that lives as a group of strands underground called hyphae that decompose leaves or bark on the ground. When it reproduces, it develops a mushroom whose cap contains spores. **Mold** is a type of zygote fungi that reproduces with a stalk, but releases zygospores. **Good bacteria** can be those that help plants absorb the nitrogen needed for growth or help grazing animals break down the cellulose in plants. Some **bad bacteria** are killed by the penicillin developed from a fungus.

ROOTS, STEMS, AND LEAVES

Roots are structures designed to pull water and minerals from soil or water. In large plants such as trees, the roots usually go deep into the ground to not only reach the water, but also to support and stabilize the tree. There are some plant species that have roots above ground, and there are also plants called epiphytes that live in trees with their roots clinging to the branches. Some roots, like carrots and turnips, serve as food. Roots are classified as **primary** and **lateral** (like a trunk and branches). The **apical meristem** is the tip of a root or shoot that helps the plant increase in length. **Root hairs** are fuzzy root extensions that help with the absorption of water and nutrients. The majority of the plant above ground is made up of the stems (trunk and branches) and leaves. **Stems** transport food and water and act as support structures. **Leaves** are the site for photosynthesis, and are connected to the rest of the plant by a vascular system.

GYMNOSPERMS, CYCADS, AND CONIFERS

Gymnosperms are plants with vascular systems and seeds but no flowers (flowers are an evolutionary advancement). The function of the seed is to ensure offspring can be produced by the plant by providing a protective coating that lets the plant survive for long periods until it germinates. It also stores food for the new plant to use until it can make its own. Seeds can be spread over a wide area. **Cycads** are sturdy plants with big, waxy fronds that make them look like ferns or palms. They can survive in harsh conditions if there is warm weather. For reproduction, they have big cones located in the center of the plant. The female plant grows a fruit in the middle of the stem. **Conifers** are trees that thrive in northern latitudes and have cones. Examples of conifers are pine, cedar, redwood, and spruce. Conifers are evergreens because they have needles that take full advantage of the sun year-round. They are also very tall and strong because of the chemical substance xylem in their systems.

ANGIOSPERMS

Angiosperms are plants that have flowers. This is advantageous because the plant's seeds and pollen can be spread not only by gravity and wind, but also by insects and animals. Flowers are able to attract organisms that can help pollinate the plant and distribute seeds. Some flowering plants also produce fruit. When an animal eats the fruit, the plant seeds within will be spread far and wide in the animal's excrement. There are two kinds of angiosperm seeds: monocotyledons (monocots) and dicotyledons (dicots). A **cotyledon** is the seed leaf or food package for the developing plant. **Monocots** are simple flowering plants such as grasses, corn, palm trees, and lilies. They always have three petals on their flowers, and their leaves are long strands (like a palm frond). A **dicot** has seeds with two cotyledons, or two seed leaves of food. Most everyday flowers are dicots with four or five petals and extremely complex leaves with veins. Examples include roses, sunflowers, cacti, and cherry trees.

ARTHROPODS

Arthropods have a number of unique characteristics:

- They have an **exoskeleton** (outside instead of inside).
- They **molt**. As the arthropod grows, it must shed its old shell and grow a new one.
- They have several **legs**, which are jointed.
- Their advanced **nervous systems** allow for hunting, moving around, finding a mate, and learning new behaviors for adaptation.
- They develop through **metamorphosis**. As arthropods develop, they change body shape. There are two types of metamorphosis:
  - *Complete* – The entire body shape changes. An example is butterflies, which change from worm-like larvae to insects with wings.
  - *Gradual* – The arthropod starts off small with no wings, and then molts and grows wings. Example: Grasshoppers.

Arthropods include spiders, crustaceans, and the enormous insect species (26 orders) called uniramians. Ranging from fleas to mosquitoes, beetles, dragonflies, aphids, bees, flies, and many more, uniramians have exoskeletons made of chitin, compound eyes, complex digestive systems, and usually six legs. This group is extremely diverse. Some can fly, some have toxins or antennae, and some can make wax, silk, or honey.

REPTILES

One group of vertebrates is the **reptiles**. This group includes:

- **Crocodilia** – This is a group of reptiles that can grow quite large, and includes alligators and crocodiles. Normally found near the water in warmer climates, Crocodilia might be more closely related to birds than other reptiles.
- **Squamata** – This is the order of reptiles that includes snakes and lizards. Snakes are special because they have no legs and no ears. They feel vibrations, smell with their tongues, have specialized scales, and can unhinge their jaws to swallow prey that is larger than they are. Like snakes, lizards have scales, but they differ in that they have external ear openings and eyelids. Most lizards have legs, can dig, can climb trees, and can grab things.

Science

- **Chelonia** – This is the order of reptiles that includes turtles and tortoises. It is a special group because its members have shells. Different varieties live in forests, water, and deserts, or anywhere the climate is warm enough. They also live a long time, up to hundreds of years. Turtles are typically found near water and tortoises on land, even dry areas.

REPRODUCTION IN MAMMALS

When classified according to how they reproduce, there are three types of mammals:

1. **Monotremes** are rare mammals that lay eggs. These were the first mammals, and are more closely related to reptiles than other mammals are. The only monotremes are the duck-billed platypus and four species of spiny anteater (echidna).
2. **Marsupials** are special mammals. They give birth to live young, but the babies mature in pouches, where they are carried and can feed on milk. Many are found in Australia. The isolation of this island continent prevented placental mammals from taking hold. Examples of marsupials include kangaroos, possums, and koalas.
3. **Placental mammals** give birth from the females' placenta to live young. The young may be able to walk immediately, or they may need to be carried. They are still dependent on parental care for at least a short time. Placental mammals are the dominant form of mammals. Members of this group include cetaceans such as whales and dolphins, which are mammals that evolved but returned to the ocean.

RESPIRATORY SYSTEM

The **respiratory system** exchanges gases with the environment. Amphibians exchange gases through their moist skin, and fish use gills, but mammals, birds, and reptiles have lungs. The human respiratory system is made up of the nose, mouth, pharynx, trachea, and two lungs. The purpose of the respiratory system is to bring oxygen into the body and expel carbon dioxide. The respiratory system can inhale viruses, bacteria, and dangerous chemicals, so it is vulnerable to toxins and diseases such as pneumonia, which causes the lungs to fill with fluid until they cannot take in enough oxygen to support the body. **Emphysema**, often caused by smoking tobacco, destroys the tissues in the lungs, which cannot be regenerated. The respiratory system interacts with the **digestive system** in that the mouth and pharynx are used to swallow food and drink, as well as to breathe. It interacts with the circulatory system in that it provides fresh oxygen through blood vessels that pass through the lungs. This oxygen is then carried by the circulatory system throughout the body.

> **Review Video: Respiratory System**
> Visit mometrix.com/academy and enter code: 783075

SKELETAL SYSTEM

The human body has an **endoskeleton**, meaning it is inside the body. It is made up of bones instead of the hard plate of exoskeletons or fluids in tubes, which comprise the hydrostatic system of the starfish. The purpose of the skeleton is to support the body, provide a framework to which the muscles and organs can connect, and protect the inner organs. The skull protects the all-important brain and the ribs protect the internal organs from impact. The skeletal system interacts with the muscular system to help the body move, and softer cartilage works with the calcified bone to allow smooth movement of the body. The skeletal system also interacts with the circulatory system in that the marrow inside the bones helps produce both white and red blood cells.

> **Review Video: Skeletal System**
> Visit mometrix.com/academy and enter code: 256447

NERVOUS SYSTEM

The **nervous system** is divided into two parts: the **central nervous system** (brain and spinal cord) and the **peripheral nervous system** (a network of billions of neurons of different types throughout the entire body). The neurons are connected end to end, and transmit electrical impulses to each other. **Efferent neurons** send impulses from the central system to the limbs and organs. **Afferent neurons** receive sensory information and transmit it back to the central system. The nervous system is concerned with **senses and action**. In other words, it senses something and then acts upon it. An example is a predator sensing prey and attacking it. The nervous system also automatically senses activity inside the body and reacts to stimuli. For example, the first bite of a meal sets the whole digestive system into motion. The nervous system **interacts** with every other system in the body because all the tissues and organs need instruction, even when individuals are not aware of any activity occurring. For instance, the endocrine system is constantly working to produce hormones or adrenaline as needed.

> **Review Video: Function of the Nervous System**
> Visit mometrix.com/academy and enter code: 708428

GENETICS, GENES, AND CHROMOSOMES

Genetics is the science devoted to the study of how characteristics are transmitted from one generation to another. In the 1800s, Gregor Mendel outlined the three laws of heredity that explain how genetics works. Genes are the hereditary units of material that are transmitted from one generation to the next. They are capable of undergoing mutations, can be recombined with other genes, and can determine the nature of an organism, including its color, shape, and size. **Genotype** is the genetic makeup of an individual based on one or more characteristics, while phenotype is the external manifestation of the genotype. For example, genotype determines hair color genes, whereas phenotype is the actual color of the hair observed. **Chromosomes** are the structures inside the nucleus of a cell made up primarily of deoxyribonucleic acid (DNA) and proteins. The chromosomes carry the genes. The numbers vary according to the species, but they are always the same for each species. For example, the human has 46 chromosomes, and the water lily has 112.

> **Review Video: Chromosomes**
> Visit mometrix.com/academy and enter code: 132083

MENDEL'S CONTRIBUTIONS TO GENETICS

Johann Gregor Mendel is known as the father of **genetics**. Mendel was an Austrian monk who performed thousands of experiments involving the breeding of the common pea plant in the garden of his monastery. Mendel kept detailed records including seed color, pod color, seed type, flower color, and plant height for eight years and published his work in 1865. Unfortunately, his work was largely ignored until the early 1900s. Mendel's work showed that genes come in pairs and that dominant and recessive traits are inherited independently of each other. His work established the law of segregation, the law of independent assortment, and the law of dominance.

DARWIN'S CONTRIBUTIONS TO THE THEORY OF EVOLUTION

Charles Darwin's theory of evolution by natural selection is the unifying concept in biology today. From 1831 to 1836, Darwin traveled as a naturalist on a five-year voyage on the *H.M.S. Beagle* around the tip of South America and to the Galápagos Islands. He studied finches, took copious amounts of meticulous notes, and collected thousands of plant and animal specimens. He collected 13 species of finches each with a unique bill for a distinct food source, which led him to believe, due to similarities between the finches, that the finches shared a common ancestor. The similarities and differences of fossils of extinct rodents and modern mammal fossils led him to believe that the mammals had changed over time. Darwin believed that these changes were the result of random genetic changes called mutations. He believed that mutations could be beneficial and eventually result in a different organism over time. In 1859, in his first book, *On the Origin of Species*, Darwin proposed that natural selection was the means by which adaptations would arise over time. He coined the term "natural selection" and said that it is the mechanism of evolution. Because variety exists among individuals of a species, he stated that those individuals must compete for the same limited resources. Some would die, and others would survive. According to Darwin, evolution is a slow, gradual process. In 1871, Darwin published his second book, *Descent of Man, and Selection in Relation to Sex*, in which he discussed the evolution of man.

Science

CONTRIBUTION TO GENETICS MADE BY ALFRED HERSHEY AND MARTHA CHASE

Alfred Hershey and Martha Chase did a series of experiments in 1952 known as the **Hershey-Chase experiments**. These experiments showed that deoxyribonucleic acid (DNA), not protein, is the genetic material that transfers information for inheritance. The Hershey-Chase experiments used a bacteriophage, a virus that infects bacteria, to infect the bacteria *Escherichia coli.* The bacteriophage T2 is basically a small piece of DNA enclosed in a protein coating. The DNA contains phosphorus, and the protein coating contains sulfur. In the first set of experiments, the T2 was marked with radioactive phosphorus-32. In the second set of experiments, the T2 was marked with radioactive sulfur-35. For both sets of experiments, after the *E. coli* was infected by the T2, the *E. coli* was isolated using a centrifuge. In the first set of experiments, the radioactive isotope (P-32) was found in the *E. coli*, showing that the genetic information was transferred by the DNA. In the second set of experiments, the radioactive isotope (S-35) was not found in the *E. coli*, showing that the genetic information was not transferred by the protein as was previously thought. Hershey and Chase conducted further experiments allowing the bacteria from the first set of experiments to reproduce, and the offspring was also found to contain the radioactive isotope (P-32) further confirming that the DNA transferred the genetic material.

ECOLOGY

AUTOTROPHS, PRODUCERS, HERBIVORES, CARNIVORES, OMNIVORES, AND DECOMPOSERS

Energy flows in one direction: from the sun, through photosynthetic organisms such as green plants (producers) and algae (autotrophs), and then to herbivores, carnivores, and decomposers. **Autotrophs** are organisms capable of producing their own food. The organic molecules they produce are food for all other organisms (heterotrophs). **Producers** are green plants that manufacture food by photosynthesis. **Herbivores** are animals that eat only plants (deer, rabbits, etc.). Since they are the first animals to receive the energy captured by producers, herbivores are called primary consumers. **Carnivores**, or secondary consumers, are animals that eat the bodies of other animals for food. Predators (wolves, lions, etc.) kill other animals, while scavengers consume animals that are already dead from predation or natural causes (buzzards). **Omnivores** are animals that eat both plants and other animals (humans). **Decomposers** include saprophytic fungi and bacteria that break down the complex structures of the bodies of living things into simpler forms that can be used by other living things. This recycling process releases energy from organic molecules.

ABIOTIC FACTORS AND BIOTIC FACTORS

Abiotic factors are the physical and chemical factors in the environment that are nonliving but upon which the growth and survival of living organisms depends. These factors can determine the types of plants and animals that will establish themselves and thrive in a particular area. Abiotic factors include:

- Light intensity available for photosynthesis
- Temperature range
- Available moisture
- Type of rock substratum
- Type of minerals
- Type of atmospheric gases
- Relative acidity (pH) of the system

Biotic factors are the living components of the environment that affect, directly or indirectly, the ecology of an area, possibly limiting the type and number of resident species. The relationships of predator/prey, producer/consumer, and parasite/host can define a community. Biotic factors include:

- Population levels of each species
- The food requirements of each species
- The interactions between species
- The wastes produced

HOW PLANTS MANUFACTURE FOOD

Plants are the only organisms capable of transforming **inorganic material** from the environment into **organic matter** by using water and solar energy. This transformation is made possible by chloroplasts, flat structures inside plant cells. **Chloroplasts**, located primarily in leaves, contain chlorophyll (the pigment capable of absorbing light and storing it in chemical compounds), DNA, ribosomes, and numerous enzymes. Chloroplasts are surrounded by a membrane. The leaves of plants are the main producers of oxygen, which helps purify the air. The **chlorophyll** in chloroplasts is responsible for the light, or luminous, phase of photosynthesis. The energy it absorbs breaks down water absorbed through the roots into hydrogen and oxygen to form ATP molecules that store energy. In the dark phase, when the plant has no light, the energy molecules are used to attach carbon dioxide to water and form glucose, a sugar.

PRODUCERS, CONSUMERS, AND DECOMPOSERS

The **food chain**, or food web, is a series of events that happens when one organism consumes another to survive. Every organism is involved in dozens of connections with others, so what happens to one affects the environment of the others. In the food chain, there are three main categories:

- **Producers** – Plants and vegetables are at the beginning of the food chain because they take energy from the sun and make food for themselves through photosynthesis. They are food sources for other organisms.
- **Consumers** – There are three levels of consumers: the organisms that eat plants (primary consumers, or herbivores); the organisms that eat the primary consumers (secondary consumers, or carnivores); and, in some ecosystems, the organisms that eat both plants and animals (tertiary consumers, or omnivores).
- **Decomposers** – These are the organisms that eat dead things or waste matter and return the nutrients to the soil, thus returning essential molecules to the producers and completing the cycle.

> **Review Video: Food Webs**
> Visit mometrix.com/academy and enter code: 853254

SYSTEM OF CLASSIFICATION FOR LIVING ORGANISMS

The main characteristic by which living organisms are classified is the degree to which they are **related**, not the degree to which they resemble each other. The science of classification is called **taxonomy**. This classification is challenging since the division lines between groups is not always clear. Some animals have characteristics of two separate groups. The current system of taxonomy involves placing an organism into a **domain** (Bacteria, Archaea, and Eukarya), and then into a **kingdom** (Eubacteria, Archaeabacteria, Protista, Fungi, Plantae, and Animalia). The kingdoms are divided into phyla, then classes, then orders, then families, and finally genuses and species. For example, the family cat is in the domain of eukaryotes, the kingdom of animals, the phylum of chordates, the class of mammals, the order of carnivores, the family of felidae, and the genus of felis. All species of living beings can be identified with Latin scientific names that are assigned by the worldwide binomial system. The genus name comes first, and is followed by the name of the species. The family cat is *felis domesticus*.

> **Review Video: Biological Classification Systems**
> Visit mometrix.com/academy and enter code: 736052

PROPERTIES THAT CONTRIBUTE TO EARTH'S LIFE-SUSTAINING SYSTEM

Life on earth is dependent on:

- All three states of **water** – gas (water vapor), liquid, and solid (ice)
- A variety of forms of **carbon**, the basis of life (carbon-based units)
- In the atmosphere, carbon dioxide, in the forms of methane and black carbon soot, produces the **greenhouse effect** that provides a habitable atmosphere.

Science

- The earth's **atmosphere and electromagnetic field**, which shield the surface from harmful radiation and allow useful radiation to go through.
- The **earth's relationship to the sun and the moon**, which creates the four seasons and the cycles of plant and animal life.
- The combination of **water, carbon, and nutrients** that provides sustenance for life and regulates the climate system in a habitable temperature range with non-toxic air.

Physical Science

PHYSICS

LAWS OF THERMODYNAMICS

The **laws of thermodynamics** are generalized principles dealing with energy and heat.

- The **zeroth law** of thermodynamics states that two objects in thermodynamic equilibrium with a third object are also in equilibrium with each other. Being in thermodynamic equilibrium basically means that different objects are at the same temperature.
- The **first law** deals with conservation of energy. It states that neither mass nor energy can be destroyed; only converted from one form to another.
- The **second law** states that the entropy (the amount of energy in a system that is no longer available for work or the amount of disorder in a system) of an isolated system can only increase. The second law also states that heat is not transferred from a lower-temperature system to a higher-temperature one unless additional work is done.
- The **third law** of thermodynamics states that as temperature approaches absolute zero, entropy approaches a constant minimum. It also states that a system cannot be cooled to absolute zero.

> **Review Video: Laws of Thermodynamics**
> Visit mometrix.com/academy and enter code: 253607

HEAT AND TEMPERATURE

Heat is energy transfer (other than direct work) from one body or system to another due to thermal contact. Everything tends to become less organized and less orderly over time (**entropy**). In all energy transfers, therefore, the overall result is that the energy is spread out uniformly. This transfer of heat energy from hotter to cooler objects is accomplished by conduction, radiation, or convection. **Temperature** is a measurement of an object's stored heat energy. More specifically, temperature is the average kinetic energy of an object's particles. When the temperature of an object increases and its atoms move faster, kinetic energy also increases. Temperature is not energy since it changes and is not conserved. Thermometers are used to measure temperature.

MASS, WEIGHT, VOLUME, DENSITY, AND SPECIFIC GRAVITY

- **Mass** — Mass is a measure of the amount of substance in an object.
- **Weight** — Weight is a measure of the gravitational pull of Earth on an object.
- **Volume** — Volume is a measure of the amount of space occupied. There are many formulas to determine volume. For example, the volume of a cube is the length of one side cubed (a^3) and the volume of a rectangular prism is length times width times height ($l \times w \times h$). The volume of an irregular shape can be determined by how much water it displaces.
- **Density** — Density is a measure of the amount of mass per unit volume. The formula to find density is mass divided by volume (D = m/V). It is expressed in terms of mass per cubic unit (e.g., grams per cubic centimeter $\frac{g}{cm^3}$).
- **Specific gravity** — This is a measure of the ratio of a substance's density compared to the density of water.

THERMAL CONTACT

Thermal contact refers to energy transferred to a body by a means other than work. A system in thermal contact with another can exchange energy with it through the process of heat transfer. Thermal contact does not necessarily involve direct physical contact. **Heat** is energy that can be transferred from one body or system to another without work being done. Everything tends to become less organized and less useful over time (entropy). In all energy transfers, therefore, the overall result is that the heat is spread out so that objects are in thermodynamic equilibrium and the heat can no longer be transferred without additional work.

MODELS FOR FLOW OF ELECTRIC CHARGE

Models that can be used to explain the **flow of electric current, potential, and circuits** include water, gravity, and roller coasters. For example, just as a mass can have a potential for energy based on its location, so can a charge within an electrical field. Just as a force is required to move an object uphill, a force is also required to move a charge from a low to high potential. Another example is water. Water does not flow when it is level. If it is lifted to a point and then placed on a downward path, it will flow. A roller coaster car requires work to be performed to transport it to a point where it has potential energy (the top of a hill). Once there, gravity provides the force for it to flow (move) downward. If either path is broken, the flow or movement stops or is not completed.

ATOMIC STRUCTURES

MAGNETIC FIELDS

The motions of subatomic structures (nuclei and electrons) produce a **magnetic field**. It is the direction of the spin and orbit that indicates the direction of the field. The strength of a magnetic field is known as the **magnetic moment**. As electrons spin and orbit a nucleus, they produce a magnetic field. Pairs of electrons that spin and orbit in opposite directions cancel each other out, creating a net magnetic field of zero. Materials that have an unpaired electron are magnetic. Those with a weak attractive force are referred to as paramagnetic materials, while ferromagnetic materials have a strong attractive force. A diamagnetic material has electrons that are paired and, therefore, does not typically have a magnetic moment. There are, however, some diamagnetic materials that have a weak magnetic field.

ELECTRIC CHARGES

The attractive force between the electrons and the nucleus is called the **electric force**. A positive (+) charge or a negative (−) charge creates a field of sorts in the empty space around it, which is known as an **electric field**. The direction of a positive charge is away from the electric field and the direction of a negative charge is towards it. An electron within the force of the field is pulled towards a positive charge because an electron has a negative charge. A particle with a positive charge is pushed away, or repelled, by another positive charge. Like charges repel each other and opposite charges attract. Lines of force show the paths of charges. The **electric force** between two objects is directly proportional to the product of the charge magnitudes and inversely proportional to the square of the distance between the two objects. **Electric charge** is measured with the unit Coulomb (C). It is the amount of charge moved in one second by a steady current of one ampere (1C = 1A × 1s).

ELECTRIC CURRENT MOVEMENT THROUGH CIRCUITS

Electric current is the sustained flow of electric charge along a path in a circuit. This differs from a static electric charge, which is a constant non-moving charge rather than a continuous flow. The **rate of flow of electric charge** is expressed using the ampere (amp or A) and can be measured using an ammeter. A current of 1 ampere means that 1 coulomb of charge passes through a given area every second. Electric charges typically only move from areas of high electric potential to areas of low electric potential. To get charges to flow into a high potential area, you must connect it to an area of higher potential by introducing a battery or other voltage source.

SIMPLE CIRCUITS

Movement of electric charge along a path between areas of high electric potential and low electric potential, with a resistor or load device between them, is the definition of a **simple circuit**. It is a closed conducting path between the high and low potential points, such as the positive and negative terminals on a battery. One example of a circuit is the flow from one terminal of a car battery to the other. The electrolyte solution of water and sulfuric acid provides work in chemical form to start the flow. A frequently used classroom example of circuits involves using a D cell (1.5 V) battery, a small light bulb, and a piece of copper wire to create a circuit to light the bulb.

> **Review Video: Resistance of Electric Currents**
> Visit mometrix.com/academy and enter code: 668423

MAGNETS

A **magnet** is any object or material, such as iron, steel, or magnetite (lodestone), that can affect another substance within its **field of force** that has like characteristics. Magnets can either attract or repel other substances. Magnets have two **poles**: north and south. Like poles repel and opposite poles (pairs of north and south) attract. The magnetic field is a set of invisible lines representing the paths of attraction and repulsion. Magnetism can occur naturally, or ferromagnetic materials can be magnetized. Certain matter that is magnetized can retain its magnetic properties indefinitely and become a permanent magnet. Other matter can lose its magnetic properties. For example, an iron nail can be temporarily magnetized by stroking it repeatedly in the same direction using one pole of another magnet. Once magnetized, it can attract or repel other magnetically inclined materials, such as paper clips. Dropping the nail repeatedly will cause it to lose its charge.

> **Review Video: Magnets**
> Visit mometrix.com/academy and enter code: 570803

MAGNETIC FIELDS, CURRENT, AND MAGNETIC DOMAINS

A **magnetic field** can be formed not only by a magnetic material, but also by electric current flowing through a wire. When a coiled wire is attached to the two ends of a battery, for example, an electromagnet can be formed by inserting a ferromagnetic material such as an iron bar within the coil. When electric current flows through the wire, the bar becomes a magnet. If there is no current, the magnetism is lost. A **magnetic domain** occurs when the magnetic fields of atoms are grouped and aligned. These groups form what can be thought of as miniature magnets within a material. This is what happens when an object like an iron nail is temporarily magnetized. Prior to magnetization, the organization of atoms and their various polarities are somewhat random with respect to where the north and south poles are pointing. After magnetization, a significant percentage of the poles are lined up in one direction, which is what causes the magnetic force exerted by the material.

MOTION AND DISPLACEMENT

Motion is a change in the location of an object and is the result of an unbalanced net force acting on the object. Understanding motion requires an understanding of three basic quantities: displacement, velocity, and acceleration.

When something moves from one place to another, it has undergone **displacement**. Displacement along a straight line is a very simple example of a vector quantity. If an object travels from position $x = -5$ cm to $x = 5$ cm, it has undergone a displacement of 10 cm. If it traverses the same path in the opposite direction, its displacement is -10 cm. A vector that spans the object's displacement in the direction of travel is known as a displacement vector.

> **Review Video: <u>Displacement in Physics</u>**
> Visit mometrix.com/academy and enter code: 236197

GRAVITATIONAL FORCE

Gravitational force is a universal force that causes every object to exert a force on every other object. The gravitational force between two objects can be described by the formula, $F = Gm_1m_2/r^2$, where m_1 and m_2 are the masses of two objects, r is the distance between them, and G is the gravitational constant, $G = 6.672 \times 10^{-11}$ N m^2/kg^2. In order for this force to have a noticeable effect, one or both of the objects must be extremely large, so the equation is generally only used in problems involving planetary bodies. For problems involving objects on the earth being affected by earth's gravitational pull, the force of gravity is simply calculated as $F = mg$, where g is 9.81 m/s^2 toward the ground.

> **Review Video: <u>Newton's Law of Gravitation</u>**
> Visit mometrix.com/academy and enter code: 709086

NEWTON'S FIRST TWO LAWS OF MOTION

NEWTON'S FIRST LAW

An object at rest or in motion will remain at rest or in motion unless acted upon by an external force.

This phenomenon is commonly referred to as **inertia**, the tendency of a body to remain in its present state of motion. In order for the body's state of motion to change, it must be acted on by an unbalanced force.

> **Review Video: <u>Newton's First Law of Motion</u>**
> Visit mometrix.com/academy and enter code: 590367

NEWTON'S SECOND LAW

An object's acceleration is **directly proportional** to the net force acting on the object and **inversely proportional** to the object's mass.

This law is generally written in equation form $F = ma$, where F is the net force acting on a body, m is the mass of the body, and a is its acceleration. Note that since the mass is always a positive quantity, the acceleration is always in the same direction as the force.

> **Review Video: <u>Newton's Second Law of Motion</u>**
> Visit mometrix.com/academy and enter code: 737975

SIMPLE MACHINES

Simple machines include the inclined plane, lever, wheel and axle, and pulley. These simple machines have no internal source of energy. More complex or compound machines can be formed from them. Simple machines provide a mechanical advantage to make it easier to accomplish a task. The **inclined plane** enables a force less than the object's weight to be used to push an object to a greater height. A **lever** enables a multiplication of force. The wheel and axle allows for movement with less resistance. Single or double **pulleys** allow for easier

Science

239

direction of force. The wedge and screw are forms of the inclined plane. A **wedge** turns a smaller force working over a greater distance into a larger force. The **screw** is similar to an incline that is wrapped around a shaft.

FRICTION

Friction is a force that arises as a **resistance to motion** where two surfaces are in contact. The maximum magnitude of the frictional force (f) can be calculated as $f = F_c\mu$, where F_c is the contact force between the two objects and μ is a coefficient of friction based on the surfaces' material composition. Two types of friction are static and kinetic. To illustrate these concepts, imagine a book resting on a table. The force of its weight (W) is equal and opposite to the force of the table on the book, or the normal force (N). If we exert a small force (F) on the book, attempting to push it to one side, a frictional force (f) would arise, equal and opposite to our force. At this point, it is a **static frictional force** because the book is not moving. If we increase our force on the book, we will eventually cause it to move. At this point, the frictional force opposing us will be a **kinetic frictional force**. Generally, the kinetic frictional force is lower than static frictional force (because the frictional coefficient for static friction is larger), which means that the amount of force needed to maintain the movement of the book will be less than what was needed to start it moving.

SOUND

Sound is a pressure disturbance that moves through a medium in the form of mechanical waves, which transfer energy from one particle to the next. Sound requires a medium to travel through, such as air, water, or other matter since it is the chain reaction of collisions that transfers energy to adjacent particles, not the actual movement of particles over a great distance. Sound is transferred through the movement of particles, which can be atoms or molecules. Waves of sound energy move outward in all directions from the source. Sound waves consist of compressions (particles are forced together) and rarefactions (particles move farther apart and their density decreases). A wavelength consists of one compression and one rarefaction. Different sounds have different wavelengths. Sound is a form of kinetic energy.

PITCH, LOUDNESS, SOUND INTENSITY, TIMBRE, AND OSCILLATION

Pitch — Pitch is the quality of sound determined by frequency. For example, a musical note can be tuned to a specific frequency. A, for instance, has a frequency of 440 Hz, which is a higher frequency than middle C. Humans can detect frequencies between about 20 Hz to 20,000 Hz.

Loudness — Loudness is a human's perception of sound intensity.

Sound intensity — Sound intensity is measured as the sound power per unit area and can be expressed in decibels.

Timbre — This is a human's perception of the type or quality of sound.

Oscillation — This is a measurement, usually of time, against a basic value, equilibrium, or rest point.

DOPPLER EFFECT

The **Doppler effect** refers to the effect the relative motion of the source of the wave and the location of the observer has on waves. The Doppler effect is easily observable in sound waves. What a person hears when a train approaches or a car honking its horn passes by are examples of the Doppler effect. The pitch of the sound is different not because the *emitted frequency* has changed, but because the *received frequency* has changed. The frequency is higher (as is the pitch) as the train approaches, the same as emitted just as it passes, and lower as the train moves away. This is because the wavelength changes. The Doppler effect can occur when an observer is stationary, and can also occur when two trains approach and pass each other. **Electromagnetic waves** are also affected in this manner. The motion of the medium can also affect the wave. For waves that do not travel in a medium, such as light waves, it is the difference in velocity that determines the outcome.

WAVES

Waves have energy and can transfer energy when they interact with matter. Although waves transfer energy, they do not transport matter. The two basic categories of waves are mechanical and electromagnetic. Mechanical waves are a disturbance of matter that transfers energy from one particle to an adjacent particle. There are many types of mechanical waves, including sound, seismic, and water. **Electromagnetic waves can transmit energy through a vacuum like visible light, microwaves, and radio waves**. A **transverse wave** provides a good illustration of the features of a wave, which include crests, troughs, amplitude, and wavelength.

ELECTROMAGNETIC SPECTRUM

The electromagnetic spectrum is defined by frequency (f) and wavelength (λ). Frequency is typically measured in hertz and wavelength is usually measured in meters. Because light travels at a fairly constant speed, frequency is inversely proportional to wavelength, a relationship expressed by the formula $f = c/\lambda$, where c is the speed of light (about 3.0×10^8 m/s). Frequency multiplied by wavelength equals the speed of the wave; for electromagnetic waves, this is the speed of light, with some variance for the medium in which it is traveling. Electromagnetic waves include (from largest to smallest wavelength) radio waves, microwaves, infrared radiation (radiant heat), visible light, ultraviolet radiation, x-rays, and gamma rays. The energy of electromagnetic waves is carried in packets that have a magnitude inversely proportional to the wavelength. Radio waves have a range of wavelengths, from about 10^{-3} to 10^5 meters, while their frequencies range from 10^3 to about 10^{11} Hz.

> **Review Video: Electromagnetic Spectrum**
> Visit mometrix.com/academy and enter code: 771761

VISIBLE LIGHT

Visible light is defined as the portion of the electromagnetic spectrum that stimulates the human retina. It is absorbed and emitted by electrons, atoms, and molecules that move from one energy level to another. Visible

Science

light interacts with matter through molecular electron excitation (which occurs in the human retina) and through plasma oscillations (which occur in metals). Visible light is between ultraviolet and infrared light on the spectrum. The wavelengths of visible light cover a range from 380 nm (violet) to 760 nm (red). Different wavelengths correspond to different colors.

> **Review Video: Light**
> Visit mometrix.com/academy and enter code: 900556

REFLECTION AND REFRACTION

Reflection is the rebounding of a light wave from a surface back toward the medium from where it came. A light wave that hits a reflecting surface at a 90-degree angle retraces its original path back to its source. Striking the surface at any other angle results in reflection of the wave at an angle in the opposite direction. Reflectance is the amount of light a material reflects; metals have high reflectance. The smoother a surface, the higher its reflectance. **Refraction is the change in the direction of a light wave as it passes between transparent mediums with different optical densities**. This results in a change in the wave's velocity. The ratio of the sine of the angle of the incoming ray to the sine of the angle of refraction is equal to the ratio of the speed of light in the original medium to the speed of light in the refracting medium.

$$\frac{\sin \theta_{in}}{\sin \theta_{ref}} = \frac{v_{in}}{v_{ref}}$$

> **Review Video: Reflection, Transmission, and Absorption of Light**
> Visit mometrix.com/academy and enter code: 109410

CHEMISTRY

PAST ATOMIC MODELS AND THEORIES

There have been many revisions to theories regarding the structure of **atoms** and their **particles**. Part of the challenge in developing an understanding of matter is that atoms and their particles are too small to be seen. It is believed that the first conceptualization of the atom was developed by **Democritus** in 400 B.C. Some of the more notable models are the solid sphere or billiard ball model postulated by John Dalton, the plum pudding or raisin bun model by J.J. Thomson, the planetary or nuclear model by Ernest Rutherford, the Bohr or orbit model by Niels Bohr, and the electron cloud or quantum mechanical model by Louis de Broglie and Erwin Schrodinger. Rutherford directed the alpha scattering experiment that discounted the plum pudding model. The shortcoming of the Bohr model was the belief that electrons orbited in fixed rather than changing ecliptic orbits.

> **Review Video: Atomic Models**
> Visit mometrix.com/academy and enter code: 434851

MODELS OF ATOMS

Atoms are extremely small. A hydrogen atom is about 5×10^{-8} mm in diameter. According to some estimates, five trillion hydrogen atoms could fit on the head of a pin. **Atomic radius** refers to the average distance between the nucleus and the outermost electron. Models of atoms that include the proton, nucleus, and electrons typically show the electrons very close to the nucleus and revolving around it, similar to how the Earth orbits the sun. However, another model relates the Earth as the nucleus and its atmosphere as electrons, which is the basis of the term "**electron cloud**." Another description is that electrons swarm around the nucleus. It should be noted that these atomic models are not to scale. A more accurate representation would be a nucleus with a diameter of about 2 cm in a stadium. The electrons would be in the bleachers. This model is similar to the not-to-scale solar system model. In reference to the periodic table, atomic radius increases as energy levels are added and decreases as more protons are added (because they pull the electrons closer to the nucleus). Essentially, atomic radius increases toward the left and toward the bottom of the periodic table.

STRUCTURE OF ATOMS

All matter consists of **atoms**. Atoms consist of a nucleus and electrons. The **nucleus** consists of protons and neutrons. The properties of these are measurable; they have mass and an electrical charge. The nucleus is positively charged due to the presence of protons. **Electrons** are negatively charged and orbit the nucleus. The nucleus has considerably more mass than the surrounding electrons. Atoms can bond together to make **molecules**. Atoms that have an equal number of protons and electrons are electrically neutral. If the number of protons and electrons in an atom is not equal, the atom has a positive or negative charge and is an ion.

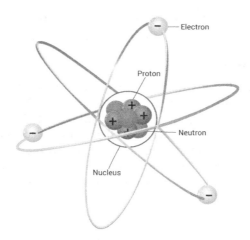

ATOMIC NUMBER, NEUTRONS, NUCLEON, AND ELEMENT

- **Atomic number** (proton number) — The atomic number of an element refers to the number of protons in the nucleus of an atom. It is a unique identifier. It can be represented as Z. Atoms with a neutral charge have an atomic number that is equal to the number of electrons.
- **Neutrons** — Neutrons are the uncharged atomic particles contained within the nucleus. The number of neutrons in a nucleus can be represented as "N."
- **Nucleon** — This refers collectively to both neutrons and protons.
- **Element** — An element is matter with one particular type of atom. It can be identified by its atomic number or the number of protons in its nucleus. There are approximately 118 elements currently known, 94 of which occur naturally on Earth. Elements from the periodic table include hydrogen, carbon, iron, helium, mercury, and oxygen.

MOLECULES

Electrons in an atom can orbit different levels around the nucleus. They can absorb or release energy, which can change the location of their orbit or even allow them to break free from the atom. The outermost layer is the **valence layer**, which contains the valence electrons. The valence layer tends to have or share eight electrons. **Molecules** are formed by a chemical bond between atoms, a bond that occurs at the valence level. Two basic types of bonds are covalent and ionic. A **covalent bond** is formed when atoms share electrons. An **ionic bond** is formed when an atom transfers an electron to another atom. A cation or positive ion is formed when an atom loses one or more electrons. An anion or negative ion is formed when an atom gains one or more electrons. A **hydrogen bond** is a weak bond between a hydrogen atom of one molecule and an

243

electronegative atom (such as nitrogen, oxygen, or fluorine) of another molecule. The **Van der Waals force** is a weak force between molecules. This type of force is much weaker than actual chemical bonds between atoms.

> **Review Video: Molecules**
> Visit mometrix.com/academy and enter code: 349910
>
> **Review Video: Anion, Cation, and Octet Rule**
> Visit mometrix.com/academy and enter code: 303525
>
> **Review Video: Ionic Bonding**
> Visit mometrix.com/academy and enter code: 116546

INTERACTION OF ATOMS TO FORM COMPOUNDS

Atoms interact by **transferring** or sharing the electrons furthest from the nucleus. Known as the outer or **valence electrons**, they are responsible for the chemical properties of an element. **Bonds** between atoms are created when electrons are paired up by being transferred or shared. If electrons are transferred from one atom to another, the bond is ionic. If electrons are shared, the bond is covalent. Atoms of the same element may bond together to form molecules or crystalline solids. When two or more different types of atoms bind together chemically, a compound is made. The physical properties of compounds reflect the nature of the interactions among their molecules. These interactions are determined by the structure of the molecule, including the atoms they consist of and the distances and angles between them.

MATTER

Matter refers to substances that have mass and occupy space (or volume). The traditional definition of matter describes it as having three states: solid, liquid, and gas. These different states are caused by differences in the distances and angles between molecules or atoms, which result in differences in the energy that binds them. **Solid** structures are rigid or nearly rigid and have strong bonds. Molecules or atoms of **liquids** move around and have weak bonds, although they are not weak enough to readily break. Molecules or atoms of **gases** move almost independently of each other, are typically far apart, and do not form bonds. The current definition of matter describes it as having four states. The fourth is **plasma**, which is an ionized gas that has some electrons that are described as free because they are not bound to an atom or molecule.

> **Review Video: States of Matter**
> Visit mometrix.com/academy and enter code: 742449

MOST ABUNDANT ELEMENTS IN THE UNIVERSE AND ON EARTH

Aside from dark energy and dark matter, which are thought to account for all but four percent of the universe, the two most abundant elements in the universe are **hydrogen** (H) and **helium** (He). After hydrogen and helium, the most abundant elements are oxygen, neon, nitrogen, carbon, silicon, and magnesium. The most abundant isotopes in the solar system are hydrogen-1 and helium-4. Measurements of the masses of elements in the Earth's crust indicate that oxygen (O), silicon (Si), and aluminum (Al) are the most abundant on Earth. Hydrogen in its plasma state is the most abundant chemical element in stars in their main sequences but is relatively rare on planet Earth.

ENERGY TRANSFORMATIONS

The following are some examples of energy transformations:

- **Electric to mechanical**: Ceiling fan
- **Chemical to heat**: A familiar example of a chemical to heat energy transformation is the internal combustion engine, which transforms the chemical energy (a type of potential energy) of gas and oxygen into heat. This heat is transformed into propulsive energy, which is kinetic. Lighting a match and burning coal are also examples of chemical to heat energy transformations.

- **Chemical to light**: Phosphorescence and luminescence (which allow objects to glow in the dark) occur because energy is absorbed by a substance (charged) and light is re-emitted comparatively slowly. This process is different from the one involved with glow sticks. They glow due to chemiluminescence, in which an excited state is created by a chemical reaction and transferred to another molecule.
- **Heat to electricity**: Examples include thermoelectric, geothermal, and ocean thermal.
- **Nuclear to heat**: Examples include nuclear reactors and power plants.
- **Mechanical to sound**: Playing a violin or almost any instrument
- **Sound to electric**: Microphone
- **Light to electric**: Solar panels
- **Electric to light**: Light bulbs

RELATIONSHIP BETWEEN CONSERVATION OF MATTER AND ATOMIC THEORY

Atomic theory is concerned with the characteristics and properties of atoms that make up matter. It deals with matter on a *microscopic level* as opposed to a *macroscopic level*. Atomic theory, for instance, discusses the kinetic motion of atoms in order to explain the properties of macroscopic quantities of matter. John Dalton (1766-1844) is credited with making many contributions to the field of atomic theory that are still considered valid. This includes the notion that all matter consists of atoms and that atoms are indestructible. In other words, atoms can be neither created nor destroyed. This is also the theory behind the conservation of matter, which explains why chemical reactions do not result in any detectable gains or losses in matter. This holds true for chemical reactions and smaller-scale processes. When dealing with large amounts of energy, however, atoms can be destroyed by nuclear reactions. This can happen in particle colliders or atom smashers.

> **Review Video: John Dalton**
> Visit mometrix.com/academy and enter code: 565627

DIFFERENCE BETWEEN ATOMS AND MOLECULES

Elements from the periodic table such as hydrogen, carbon, iron, helium, mercury, and oxygen are **atoms**. Atoms combine to form molecules. For example, two atoms of hydrogen (H) and one atom of oxygen (O) combine to form one molecule of water (H_2O).

CHEMICAL AND PHYSICAL PROPERTIES

Matter has both physical and chemical properties. **Physical properties** can be seen or observed without changing the identity or composition of matter. For example, the mass, volume, and density of a substance can be determined without permanently changing the sample. Other physical properties include color, boiling point, freezing point, solubility, odor, hardness, electrical conductivity, thermal conductivity, ductility, and malleability. **Chemical properties** cannot be measured without changing the identity or composition of matter. Chemical properties describe how a substance reacts or changes to form a new substance. Examples of chemical properties include flammability, corrosivity, oxidation states, enthalpy of formation, and reactivity with other chemicals.

CHEMICAL AND PHYSICAL CHANGES

Physical changes do not produce new substances. The atoms or molecules may be rearranged, but no new substances are formed. Phase changes or changes of state such as melting, freezing, and sublimation are physical changes. For example, physical changes include the melting of ice, the boiling of water, sugar dissolving into water, and the crushing of a piece of chalk into a fine powder. **Chemical changes** involve a chemical reaction and do produce new substances. When iron rusts, iron oxide is formed, indicating a chemical change. Other examples of chemical changes include baking a cake, burning wood, digesting a cracker, and mixing an acid and a base.

Science

PHYSICAL AND CHEMICAL PROPERTIES AND CHANGES

Both physical changes and chemical reactions are everyday occurrences. **Physical changes** do not result in different substances. For example, when water becomes ice it has undergone a physical change, but not a chemical change. It has changed its form, but not its composition. It is still H_2O. **Chemical properties** are concerned with the constituent particles that make up the physicality of a substance. Chemical properties are apparent when **chemical changes** occur. The chemical properties of a substance are influenced by its electron configuration, which is determined in part by the number of protons in the nucleus (the atomic number). Carbon, for example, has 6 protons and 6 electrons. It is an element's outermost valence electrons that mainly determine its chemical properties. Chemical reactions may release or consume energy.

> **Review Video: Chemical and Physical Properties of Matter**
> Visit mometrix.com/academy and enter code: 717349

ELEMENTS, COMPOUNDS, SOLUTIONS, AND MIXTURES

- **Elements** — These are substances that consist of only one type of atom.
- **Compounds** — These are substances containing two or more elements. Compounds are formed by chemical reactions and frequently have different properties than the original elements. Compounds are decomposed by a chemical reaction rather than separated by a physical one.
- **Solutions** — These are homogeneous mixtures composed of two or more substances that have become one.
- **Mixtures** — Mixtures contain two or more substances that are combined but have not reacted chemically with each other. Mixtures can be separated using physical methods, while compounds cannot.

HEAT, ENERGY, WORK, AND THERMAL ENERGY

- **Heat** — Heat is the transfer of energy from a body or system as a result of thermal contact. Heat consists of random motion and the vibration of atoms, molecules, and ions. The higher the temperature is, the greater the atomic or molecular motion will be.
- **Energy** — Energy is the capacity to do work.
- **Work** — Work is the quantity of energy transferred by one system to another due to changes in a system that is the result of external forces, or macroscopic variables. Another way to put this is that work is the amount of energy that must be transferred to overcome a force. Lifting an object in the air is an example of work. The opposing force that must be overcome is gravity. Work is measured in joules (J). The rate at which work is performed is known as power.
- **Thermal energy** — Thermal energy is the energy present in a system due to temperature.

TYPES OF ENERGY

Some discussions of energy consider only two types of energy: **kinetic energy** (the energy of motion) and **potential energy** (which depends on relative position or orientation). There are, however, other types of energy. **Electromagnetic waves**, for example, are a type of energy contained by a field. Another type of potential energy is electrical energy, which is the energy it takes to pull apart positive and negative electrical charges. **Chemical energy** refers to the manner in which atoms form into molecules, and this energy can be released or absorbed when molecules regroup. **Solar energy** comes in the form of visible light and non-visible light, such as infrared and ultraviolet rays. **Sound energy** refers to the energy in sound waves.

> **Review Video: Potential and Kinetic Energy**
> Visit mometrix.com/academy and enter code: 491502

CHEMICAL REACTIONS

Chemical reactions measured in human time can take place quickly or slowly. They can take fractions of a second or billions of years. The rates of chemical reactions are determined by how frequently reacting atoms and molecules interact. Rates are also influenced by the temperature and various properties (such as shape) of the reacting materials. **Catalysts** accelerate chemical reactions, while inhibitors decrease reaction rates. Some types of reactions release energy in the form of heat and light. Some types of reactions involve the transfer of either electrons or hydrogen ions between reacting ions, molecules, or atoms. In other reactions, chemical bonds are broken down by heat or light to form reactive radicals with electrons that will readily form new bonds. Processes such as the formation of ozone and greenhouse gases in the atmosphere and the burning and processing of fossil fuels are controlled by radical reactions.

> **Review Video: Understanding Chemical Reactions**
> Visit mometrix.com/academy and enter code: 579876
>
> **Review Video: Catalysts**
> Visit mometrix.com/academy and enter code: 288189

READING CHEMICAL EQUATIONS

Chemical equations describe chemical reactions. The reactants are on the left side before the arrow. The products are on the right side after the arrow. The arrow is the mark that points to the reaction or change. The coefficient is the number before the element. This gives the ratio of reactants to products in terms of moles.

The equation for making water from hydrogen and oxygen is $2H_{2(g)} + O_{2(g)} \rightarrow 2H_2O_{(l)}$. The number 2 before hydrogen and water is the coefficient. This means that there are 2 moles of hydrogen and 2 of water. There is 1 mole of oxygen. This does not need to have the number 1 before the symbol for the element. For additional information, the following subscripts are often included to indicate the state of the substance: (g) stands for gas, (l) stands for liquid, (s) stands for solid, and (aq) stands for aqueous. Aqueous means the substance is dissolved in water. Charges are shown by superscript for individual ions, not for ionic compounds. Polyatomic ions are separated by parentheses. This is done so the kind of ion will not be confused with the number of ions.

> **Review Video: The Process of a Reaction**
> Visit mometrix.com/academy and enter code: 808039

BALANCING EQUATIONS

An **unbalanced equation** is one that does not follow the **law of conservation of mass**, which states that matter can only be changed, not created or destroyed. If an equation is unbalanced, the numbers of atoms indicated by the stoichiometric coefficients on each side of the arrow will not be equal. Start by writing the formulas for each species in the reaction. Count the atoms on each side and determine if the number is equal. Coefficients must be whole numbers. Fractional amounts, such as half a molecule, are not possible. Equations can be balanced by adjusting the coefficients of each part of the equation to the smallest possible whole number coefficient. $H_2 + O_2 \rightarrow H_2O$ is an example of an unbalanced equation. The balanced equation is $2H_2 + O_2 \rightarrow 2H_2O$, which indicates that it takes two moles of hydrogen and one of oxygen to produce two moles of water.

> **Review Video: Balancing Chemical Equations**
> Visit mometrix.com/academy and enter code: 341228

PERIODIC TABLE

The **periodic table** groups elements with similar chemical properties together. The grouping of elements is based on **atomic structure**. It shows periodic trends of physical and chemical properties and identifies families of elements with similar properties. It is a common model for organizing and understanding elements. In the periodic table, each element has its own cell that includes varying amounts of information presented in symbol form about the properties of the element. Cells in the table are arranged in **rows** (periods) and **columns** (groups or families). At minimum, a cell includes the symbol for the element and its atomic number.

Science

The cell for hydrogen, for example, which appears first in the upper left corner, includes an "H" and a "1" above the letter. Elements are ordered by atomic number, left to right, top to bottom.

SOLUTIONS

A solution is a homogeneous mixture, meaning that it is uniform in composition. Solutions consist of a solute (the substance that is dissolved) and a solvent (the substance that does the dissolving). For example, in sugar water the solvent is the water and the solute is the sugar. The intermolecular attraction between the solvent and the solute is called solvation. **Hydration** refers to solutions in which water is the solvent. Solutions are formed when the forces between the molecules of the solute and the solvent are as strong as the forces holding the solute together. An example is that salt (NaCl) dissolves in water to create a solution. The Na^+ and the Cl^- ions in salt interact with the molecules of water and vice versa to overcome the intramolecular forces of the solute.

MIXTURES, SUSPENSIONS, COLLOIDS, EMULSIONS, AND FOAMS

A **mixture** is a combination of two or more substances that are not bonded. **Suspensions** are mixtures of heterogeneous materials. Particles in suspensions are usually larger than those found in true solutions. Dirt mixed vigorously with water is an example of a suspension. The dirt is temporarily suspended in water, but it settles to the bottom of the container once the mixing is ceased. A mixture of large (1 nm to 500 nm) particles is called a **colloidal suspension**. The particles are termed dispersants and the dispersing medium is similar to the solvent in a solution. Sol refers to a liquid or a solid that also has solids dispersed through it, such as milk or gelatin. An aerosol spray is a colloid suspension of gas and the solid or liquid being dispersed. An **emulsion** refers to a liquid or a solid that has small droplets of another liquid dispersed through it. A **foam** is a liquid that has gas dispersed through it.

PH

The **potential of hydrogen** (pH) is a measurement of the concentration of hydrogen ions in a substance in terms of the number of moles of H^+ per liter of solution. All substances fall between 0 and 14 on the pH scale. A lower pH indicates a higher H^+ concentration, while a higher pH indicates a lower H^+ concentration. Pure water has a neutral pH, which is 7. Anything with a pH lower than water (<7) is considered acidic. Anything with a pH higher than water (>7) is a base. Drain cleaner, soap, baking soda, ammonia, egg whites, and sea water are common bases. Urine, stomach acid, citric acid, vinegar, hydrochloric acid, and battery acid are acids. A pH indicator is a substance that acts as a detector of hydrogen or hydronium ions. It is halochromic, meaning it changes color to indicate that hydrogen or hydronium ions have been detected.

PROPERTIES OF ACIDS

When they are dissolved in aqueous solutions, some properties of **acids** are that they conduct electricity, change blue litmus paper to red, have a sour taste, react with bases to neutralize them, and react with active metals to free hydrogen. A **weak acid** is one that does not donate all of its protons or disassociate completely. **Strong acids** include hydrochloric, hydriodic, hydrobromic, perchloric, nitric, and sulfuric. They ionize completely. **Superacids** are those that are stronger than 100 percent sulfuric acid. They include fluoroantimonic, magic, and perchloric acids. Acids can be used in pickling, a process used to remove rust and corrosion from metals. They are also used as catalysts in the processing of minerals and the production of salts and fertilizers. Phosphoric acid (H_3PO_4) is added to sodas and other acids are added to foods as preservatives or to add taste.

> **Review Video: Properties of Acids and Bases**
> Visit mometrix.com/academy and enter code: 645283

PROPERTIES OF BASES

When they are dissolved in aqueous solutions, some properties of **bases** are that they conduct electricity, change red litmus paper to blue, feel slippery, and react with acids to neutralize their properties. A **weak base** is one that does not completely ionize in an aqueous solution, and usually has a low pH. **Strong bases** can free protons in very weak acids. Examples of strong bases are hydroxide compounds such as potassium, barium, and lithium hydroxides. Most are in the first and second groups of the periodic table. A **superbase** is extremely strong compared to sodium hydroxide and cannot be kept in an aqueous solution. Superbases are organized into organic, organometallic, and inorganic classes. Bases are used as insoluble catalysts in heterogeneous reactions and as catalysts in hydrogenation.

PROPERTIES OF SALTS

Some properties of **salts** are that they are formed from acid base reactions, are ionic compounds consisting of metallic and nonmetallic ions, dissociate in water, and are comprised of tightly bonded ions. Some common salts are sodium chloride (NaCl), sodium bisulfate ($NaHSO_4$), potassium dichromate ($K_2Cr_2O_7$), and calcium chloride ($CaCl_2$). Calcium chloride is used as a drying agent, and may be used to absorb moisture when freezing mixtures. Potassium nitrate (KNO_3) is used to make fertilizer and in the manufacturing of explosives. Sodium nitrate ($NaNO_3$) is also used in the making of fertilizer. Baking soda [sodium bicarbonate ($NaHCO_3$)] is a salt, as are Epsom salts [magnesium sulfate ($MgSO_4$)]. Salt and water can react to form a base and an acid. This is called a **hydrolysis reaction**.

UNIQUE PROPERTIES OF WATER

The important properties of water (H_2O) are high polarity, hydrogen bonding, cohesiveness, adhesiveness, high specific heat, high latent heat, and high heat of vaporization. Water is vital to life as we know it. The reason is that water is one of the main parts of many living things.

Water is a liquid at room temperature. The high specific heat of water means that it does not easily break its hydrogen bonds. Also, it resists heat and motion. This is why it has a high boiling point and high vaporization point.

Most substances are denser in their solid forms. However, water is different because its solid-state floats in its liquid state. Water is cohesive. This means that it is drawn to itself. It is also adhesive. This means that it draws in other molecules. If water will attach to another substance, the substance is said to be hydrophilic. Because of its cohesive and adhesive properties, water makes a good solvent. Substances with polar ions and molecules easily dissolve in water.

KINETIC THEORY OF GASES

The **kinetic theory of gases** assumes that gas molecules are small compared to the distances between them and that they are in constant random motion. The attractive and repulsive forces between gas molecules are

Science

249

negligible. Their kinetic energy does not change with time as long as the temperature remains the same. The higher the temperature is, the greater the motion will be. As the temperature of a gas increases, so does the kinetic energy of the molecules. In other words, gas will occupy a greater volume as the temperature is increased and a lesser volume as the temperature is decreased. In addition, the same amount of gas will occupy a greater volume as the temperature increases, but pressure remains constant. At any given temperature, gas molecules have the same average kinetic energy. The **ideal gas law** is derived from the kinetic theory of gases.

> **Review Video: <u>Ideal Gas vs. Real Gas</u>**
> Visit mometrix.com/academy and enter code: 619477

ORGANIC COMPOUNDS

Two of the main characteristics of organic compounds are that they generally include carbon and are formed by covalent bonds. Carbon can form long chains, double and triple bonds, and rings. While inorganic compounds tend to have high melting points, organic compounds tend to melt at temperatures below 300° C. They also tend to boil, sublimate, and decompose below this temperature. Unlike inorganic compounds, they are not very water-soluble. Organic molecules are organized into functional groups based on their specific atoms, which helps determine how they will react chemically. A few groups are alkanes, nitro, alkenes, sulfides, amines, and carbolic acids. The hydroxyl group ($-OH$) consists of alcohols. These molecules are polar, which increases their solubility. By some estimates, there are more than 16 million organic compounds.

> **Review Video: <u>Organic Compounds</u>**
> Visit mometrix.com/academy and enter code: 264922

HYDROGEN BONDS

Hydrogen bonds are weaker than covalent and ionic bonds and refer to the type of attraction in an electronegative atom such as oxygen, fluorine, or nitrogen. Hydrogen bonds can form within a single molecule or between molecules. A water molecule is **polar**, meaning it is partially positively charged on one end (the hydrogen end) and partially negatively charged on the other (the oxygen end). This is because the hydrogen atoms are arranged around the oxygen atom in a close tetrahedron. Hydrogen is **oxidized** (its number of electrons is reduced) when it bonds with oxygen to form water. Hydrogen bonds tend not only to be weak but also short-lived. They also tend to be numerous. Hydrogen bonds give water many of its important properties, including its high specific heat and high heat of vaporization, its solvent qualities, its adhesiveness and cohesiveness, its hydrophobic qualities, and its ability to float in its solid form. Hydrogen bonds are also an important component of proteins, nucleic acids, and DNA.

INORGANIC COMPOUNDS

The main trait of inorganic compounds is that they generally lack carbon. Inorganic compounds include mineral salts, alloys, non-metallic compounds such as phosphate, and metal complexes. A metal complex has a central atom (or ion) bonded to surrounding ligands (molecules or anions). The ligands sacrifice the donor atoms (in the form of at least one pair of electrons) to the central atom. Many inorganic compounds are ionic, meaning they form ionic bonds rather than share electrons. They may have high melting points because of this. They may also be colorful, but this is not an absolute identifier of an inorganic compound. Salts, which are inorganic compounds, are an example of inorganic bonding of cations and anions. Some examples of salts are magnesium chloride ($MgCl_2$) and sodium oxide (Na_2O). Oxides, carbonates, sulfates, and halides are classes of inorganic compounds. They are typically poor conductors, are very water soluble, and crystallize easily. Minerals and silicates are also inorganic compounds.

Scientific Inquiry and Impact

SCIENTIFIC INQUIRY AND LAB SAFETY

COMPONENTS OF SCIENTIFIC EXPERIMENTATION

- A **hypothesis** is a tentative supposition about a phenomenon (or a fact or set of facts) made in order to examine and test its logical or empirical consequences through investigation or methodological experimentation.
- A **theory** is a scientifically proven, general principle offered to explain phenomena. A theory is derived from a hypothesis and verified by experimentation and research.
- A **scientific law** is a generally accepted conclusion about a body of observations to which no exceptions have been found. Scientific laws explain things, but do not describe them.
- A **control** is a normal, unchanged situation used for comparison against experimental data.
- **Constants** are factors in an experiment that remain the same.
- **Independent variables** are factors, traits, or conditions that are changed in an experiment. A good experiment has only one independent variable so that the scientist can track one thing at a time. The independent variable changes from experiment to experiment.
- **Dependent variables** are changes that result from variations in the independent variable.

SCIENCE AS A SERIES OF PROCESSES

Science is not just the steps of experimentation. While the process of posing a question, forming a hypothesis, testing the hypothesis, recording data, and drawing a conclusion is at the heart of **scientific inquiry**, there are other processes that are important as well. Once the scientist has completed the testing of a hypothesis and possibly come up with a theory, the scientist should then go through the process of getting feedback from colleagues, publishing an article about the work in a peer-reviewed journal, or otherwise reporting the results to the scientific community, replicating the experiment for verification of results (by the original scientist or others), and developing new questions. Science is not just a means of satisfying curiosity, but is also a process for developing technology, addressing social issues, building knowledge, and solving everyday problems.

DRAWING CONCLUSIONS AFTER EXPERIMENTS

Conclusions are based on data analysis and background research. The scientist has to take a hard look at the results of an experiment and check the accuracy of the data to draw preliminary conclusions. These should be compared to the background research to find out if the preliminary conclusion can be supported by previous research experiments. If the results do not support the hypothesis, or if they are contrary to what the background research predicted, then further research is needed. The focus should be on finding a reason for the different results. Finally, the scientist provides a discussion of findings that includes a summary of the results of the experiment, a statement as to whether the hypothesis was proven or disproven, a statement of the relationship between the independent and dependent variable, a summary and evaluation of the procedures of the experiment (including comments about successes and effectiveness), and suggestions for changes/modifications in procedures for further studies.

STEPS OF THE SCIENTIFIC METHOD

The steps of the **scientific method** are as follows:

1. The scientific method begins with, and absolutely depends upon, the **observation** of objective, unbiased data. Any prejudice or bias in the observed data nullifies its validity. Thus the basic input from the observations must be rigorously screened to ensure objectivity.
2. The development of a **theory or hypothesis** based on objective data is the next step in the scientific method. These theories or hypotheses pose logical expectations that the experiment may yield.
3. Construction of a rigorous and valid **experimental method** designed to test the theories is the next phase of the scientific method. This experimental method must be carefully constructed to give objective, unbiased conclusions based on the hypotheses posited.

Science

4. Careful and statistically correct **analysis and evaluation** of the experimental results make up the next stage.

5. **Modification and replication** of the experiment must then follow to provide a statistically accurate demonstration of the validity of the hypothesis. Equivalent results must be shown from a number of repetitions of the experiment.

Review Video: The Scientific Method
Visit mometrix.com/academy and enter code: 191386

STEPS OF THE SCIENTIFIC INQUIRY

Scientific inquiry is the impetus and catalyst for all scientific research and experimentation. It grows from questions about the observed world and gives us a template with which to apply the scientific method. Steps in scientific inquiry include the following principles:

- Determination of the content and scope of the questions to be investigated is the first step. These may range from simple to extremely complex questions to be explored by scientists.
- The design, strategy, and method of the inquiry are then carefully considered, and a model for the inquiry is constructed.
- The formulation of theories and models based on the careful observation of objective, unbiased data then follows. This formulation is derived from the scope of the scientific inquiry and the questions to be investigated.
- Analysis of possible alternative conclusions drawn from the models and results of experimentation follows.
- Postulating a theory or constructing a scientific statement based on conclusions is the next logical step.
- Defending the scientific statement against alternative hypotheses is a critical function of scientific inquiry.
- Defense of the theory or conclusion against critical analysis is the final step in the process.

SCIENCE

Science is a method of acquiring and obtaining knowledge. It is the process of gaining reliable information about the real world, including the explanation of phenomena. It is the development of a body of knowledge about observable phenomena, using the best capabilities humans have at their disposal. The process of organizing and classifying knowledge, through objective observation and evaluation, is a major goal of science. Science can be considered *reliable*, but it is not *infallible*. The limits of human knowledge are constantly growing, often making yesterday's science obsolete and simplistic. Science is thus never fixed; it is always subject to change as new information is gained and synthesized with existing knowledge. Ultimately, science is the sum total of knowledge in any period of time, based on the current abilities of man to understand the world of phenomena, verifiable by observable data.

LIMITATIONS OF SCIENCE

There are clear **limits** on what science can explain. The demand for objectivity both strengthens knowledge we gain from scientific experiments and limits what we can explore. Beyond the realm of scientific inquiry are such questions as "Why does anything exist?" or "What is the meaning of life?" These are subjective questions that do not lend themselves easily to scientific inquiry. These questions, and others like them, come from within, and their conclusions, not validated by science, shape the very fabric of a society. They attempt to give meaning to what may be viewed as chaos.

Periodically, science will impact these **subjective conclusions** with new evidence. For example, the theory of evolution is regarded as blasphemy by many religious fundamentalists. These conflicts may cause great upheavals in society, leaving many to wonder how science and religious belief can be reconciled. Ultimately, observation of the external world must stand as the true test of science.

HYPOTHETICO-DEDUCTIVE PROCESS

The **hypothetico-deductive process** states that to have an idea and then formulate a hypothesis are essentially creative processes, driven by eons of human experience. Statements about reality are the logical conclusions of observed experience. Such creative propositions are the basis for scientific inquiry. Empirical evidence must then validate these hypotheses. Creative inspiration and scientific validation are interdependent aspects of scientific inquiry. New observations often are the catalyst for creative new theories. Science thus proceeds through creative thinking and scientific validation. There are criticisms of the hypothetico-deductive process: The problem of deduction points out that the original hypothesis may be proved wrong in the future, thus invalidating all subsequent conclusions. The problem of induction, building a theory from generalizations, is that any generalization may be proved wrong by future objective observations. The hypothetico-deductive process, and its problems, is a fascinating subject to philosophers of science.

HYPOTHESIS

It is important to form a **hypothesis** in order to make a tentative explanation that accounts for an unbiased observation. To be scientific, the hypothesis must be testable through experimentation. Careful construction of the experiment provides that predictions derived from the hypothesis are valid. The hypothesis must be formulated in a manner designed to provide a framework for evaluating the results of an experiment. In many scientific experiments, a hypothesis is posited in negative terms because scientists may accept logically plausible ideas until they are proven false. It is more difficult to prove that a hypothesis is true because its validity must be proven in all possible situations under endless variable conditions. Scientists tend to construct hypotheses for testing by creating experiments that might prove them false. If they succeed in proving it false, the hypothesis must be modified or discarded.

BASIC SCIENCE AND APPLIED SCIENCE

Basic science and applied science share many attributes but are generally motivated by different influences:

- **Basic science** is spurred on by scientific inquiry, the human need to explain the observed physical world. It may have no specific goal, but is mankind's response to questions that arise from human curiosity and interest. It is usually an attempt to explain the laws of nature by using the scientific method.
- **Applied science** has a specific practical goal or application: It is designed to solve a problem. Industry and government are institutions that use applied science regularly.

Thus, basic and applied science share many qualities, including scientific inquiry and the scientific method. The goals of each can be very different. It should be pointed out that basic science very often provides results that have uses in applied science.

BENEFITS OF BASIC SCIENCE

Although **basic science** may have no stated goal or target, it provides many benefits to society:

- Basic science contributes greatly to human understanding and culture, enriching society in many ways.
- Basic science has been responsible for major breakthroughs that have great social and economic impact.
- Basic science provides derivative solutions that can be used in applied science. For example, basic science was critical to the development of the space program, from which countless valuable applications have been derived.
- Basic science contributes to education and research across the broad spectrum of society.

MEASURING, ORGANIZING, AND CLASSIFYING DATA

Measuring data is a crucial part of the scientific process. Measurements are most useful if they are quantified—expressed in numbers. Measuring is the process of determining variables such as time, space, and temperature of objects and processes in precise numbers. The metric system is the universal standard of

Science

measurement in science. Data must be **organized** in a practical, useful manner to be valuable. Scientists use graphs, charts, tables, and other organizational tools to make data more useful. Data must then be **classified**—grouped into organizational schemes for easy access and use. These schemes attempt to organize the maximum amount of useful data in a format that scientists can use. Although these steps may be less glamorous than other areas of science, they are essential.

SCIENTIFIC LAWS

Scientific principles must meet a high standard to be classified as laws; scientific laws are identified as follows:

- **Scientific laws** must be true, not just probable. A highly probable principle may still be proven false.
- Laws are statements of patterns found in nature.
- Laws may have a universal form but be stated conditionally. For example, the statement "All living human beings breathe," may be restated "If a thing is a living human being it must breathe."
- Laws refer to a general, not a particular, class.
- Laws have purely qualitative predicates.
- Laws must have a formal language of expression to be fully understood. Such a language does not exist now.
- Laws may be probabilistic. For example, a law may state "Eight percent of all dogs are terriers."

COMMON CRITICISMS OF THE DEDUCTIVE MODEL

The **deductive model** of the scientific method has the following criticisms:

- The deductive model fails to make logical distinctions among explanations, predictions, and descriptions of things to be explained.
- The deductive model is restrictive: It excludes most scientific examples.
- The deductive model is too inclusive: It admits data that cannot be explained.
- The deductive model requires an account of cause, law, and probability, which are basically unsound.
- The deductive model leaves out the elements of context, judgment, and understanding.

PREDICTION

These are the two widely accepted definitions of **scientific prediction**:

1. In the language of science, prediction is stating in advance the outcome from testing a theory or hypothesis in a controlled experiment. Based on objective observation of data, scientists move from observation of facts to a general explanation, or hypothesis, which must be confirmed by testing through experimentation.
2. Another definition of prediction favored by scientific philosophers is the ability of a hypothesis to lead to deductions of scientific statements that could not be anticipated when the hypothesis was posited. In this sense, prediction means what the scientist can verify from what he or she has deduced from the hypothesis.

LABORATORY SAFETY

The following basic rules should be supplemented by standards appropriate to individual laboratories:

- Hazardous areas must be identified and warnings posted regarding risks.
- A hazard containment plan must be in effect and readily available.
- Safe control of airflow must be maintained at all times.
- Safe work practices must be taught to all who work in the lab.
- Proper maintenance of laboratory equipment must be enforced.
- Safe storage of hazardous material must be implemented.
- Procedures for safe disposal of hazardous wastes must be followed at all times.
- An updated emergency procedure manual must be available.

- A complete emergency first aid kit should be accessible at all times.
- Regular education on the basics of lab safety should be implemented.

VERIFICATION AND CONFIRMATION OF DATA IN VALID SCIENCE

A critical distinction should be made between confirmation and verification of scientific data. **Verification** establishes once and for all the truth of the statement. **Confirmation** is the testing of claims to see how true they are. For a claim to be testable, an experiment must be devised to ensure the validity of the results. A claim can only be confirmed when we know the conditions for verification. A claim confirmation is always relative to the testing procedures. Test results must always be objective and observable. Actually, no factual claim can ever be verified because there is always the possibility of new evidence appearing that proves the claim false. A scientific law must also be confirmed by making predictions based on unbiased, observable data.

SCIENTIFIC MEASUREMENT AND UNIT SYSTEMS

The basis of quantitative measurement is the **unit system**. In order to properly describe how large, how heavy, or how hot something is, it is necessary to have some reference unit. The most commonly used unit system in the world is the **SI**, short for the Systeme International d'Unites, although the English system is still in popular use in the United States. In SI, there are base units and derived units. Derived units may be stated as some combination of the base units. The SI base units for length, mass, time, temperature, and electric current are meter (m), kilogram (kg), second (s), kelvin (K), and ampere (A), respectively. Some common derived units are newtons ($kg \, m/s^2$) and pascals ($kg/(m \, s^2)$). Most SI units can be scaled up or down by adding a prefix. To alter a unit by 10^3, 10^6, or 10^9, add a prefix of kilo (k), mega (M), or giga (G). For instance, a kilometer (km) is 10^3 meters. To change the unit by a factor of 10^{-3}, 10^{-6}, or 10^{-9}, add a prefix of milli (m), micro (µ), or nano (n). For instance, a microsecond (µs) is 10^{-6} seconds. It is important to note that the SI base unit kilogram has already employed a prefix to scale up the smaller unit, gram (g). *Order of magnitude* is a concept that deals with the comparison between two values. If one value differs from the other by a factor of 10^n, it may be said that it differs by n orders of magnitude. Other SI base units include the mole and the candela. Some lesser used prefixes include: hecto (h), 10^2; deca (da), 10^1; deci (d), 10^{-1}; and centi (c), 10^{-2}.

DATA COLLECTION AND ANALYSIS

In order to take **data measurements** from their experimental setups, scientists will often use measurement devices wired to a computer running data-acquisition software. This allows them to take numerous readings per second if necessary. Once the data is collected, it will often be organized using a spreadsheet, such as Microsoft Excel. This multipurpose program contains several options for displaying the data in graphs or charts, as well as tools for performing statistical analyses or linear regressions. Linear regression is a technique used to determine whether gathered data fits a particular trend or equation. It attempts to fit a common line or curve equation to the data set. A very important concept to understand when taking data is that of **significant figures**. Significant figures, or significant digits, indicate how precisely a quantity is known. Each non-zero digit is always significant. A zero is significant if either: 1) it is to the right of both a non-zero digit and the decimal point; or 2) it is between two other significant digits. For instance, 1.0230 has five significant figures while 0.0230 has only three because the trailing zero is the only zero to the right of both a non-zero and the decimal. When multiplying (or dividing), the product (quotient) has as many significant figures as the factor (dividend or divisor) with the fewest. When adding (or subtracting), the sum (difference) should be rounded to the highest final decimal place of the involved terms. For example, $3.4 + 56.78 = 60.18$ rounded to three significant figures is 60.2.

INTERPRETATION AND DRAWING OF CONCLUSIONS FROM DATA PRESENTED IN TABLES, CHARTS, AND GRAPHS

One of the reasons data are so often plotted on graphs is that this format makes it much easier to see **trends** and draw **conclusions**. For instance, on a simple position vs. time graph, the slope of the curve indicates the object's velocity at each point in time. If the curve becomes level, this means the object is not moving. In a simple velocity vs. time graph, the slope of the curve indicates the object's acceleration at each point in time. Additionally, the area contained under the curve indicates the total distance traveled. For instance, if the object is traveling at a constant 5 m/s for 10 s, the velocity vs. time graph will be a straight line at $y = 5$ between $x = 0$ and $x = 10$. The area under this curve is $(5 \text{ m/s})(10 \text{ s}) = 50$ m. Thus, the object traveled 50 meters. Nearly any type of quantity may be graphed, so it is important to always check the axis labels to ensure that you know what the graph represents and what units are being used.

DATA ERRORS AND ERROR ANALYSIS

No measurements are ever 100% accurate. There is always some amount of **error** regardless of how careful the observer or how good the equipment. The important thing for the scientist to know is how much error is present in a given measurement. Two commonly misunderstood terms regarding error are accuracy and precision. **Accuracy** is a measure of how close a measurement is to the true value. **Precision** is a measure of how close repeated measurements are to one another. Error is usually quantified using a confidence interval and an uncertainty value. For instance, if the quantity is measured as 100 ± 2 on a 95% confidence interval, this means that there is a 95% chance that the actual value falls between 98 and 102. When looking for the uncertainty in a derived quantity such as density, the errors in the constituent quantities, mass and volume in this case, are propagated to the derived quantity. The percent uncertainty in the density, U_ρ/ρ, can be found by the equation:

$$\frac{U_\rho}{\rho} = \sqrt{\left(\frac{U_m}{m}\right)^2 + \left(\frac{U_V}{V}\right)^2}$$

SCIENCE, TECHNOLOGY, AND SOCIETY
DEBATE OVER SCIENCE AND ETHICS

Debates over issues paramount to **science and ethics** are rarely resolved unambiguously. Ethical conclusions should be based on reason, logic, and accepted principles that represent a consensus of current thinking on a question. Education and debate are important in clarifying issues and allowing intelligent participation in a democratic process. Deciding issues of science and society usually requires an examination of individual cases. Generalizations in these areas tend to lead to extreme positions that exclude mainstream opinions. There are no blanket solutions to most problems involving science, technology, and societal ethics.

MAJOR EFFECTS OF IMPROVEMENTS IN SCIENTIFIC AND TECHNOLOGICAL KNOWLEDGE ON HUMAN AND OTHER LIFE

Since the Industrial Revolution, **technological improvements** to agricultural production have made agriculture productive on an industrial scale, while advances in medical knowledge have brought about the cures for many diseases. People in many parts of the world live longer and enjoy a higher standard of living than ever before. However, this progress does not come without a price. The effects on the **environment** of industrialization are almost exclusively negative. Monoculture farming practices resulting from industrialization mean that farming no longer exists as a closed ecosystem; the chemical fertilizers that create record crop yields have changed the nutrient environment, and the waste products of industrial agriculture pollute the water rather than fertilizing the soil. Increased travel creates dangerous carbon dioxide emissions and depletes the earth's limited store of fossil fuels. Water pollution means limited access to potable water, and deforestation has begun to change the makeup of ecosystems and cause the extinction of many species. Through the increased contact made available by improved technology, however, humans are also collaborating on solutions to these new problems.

> **Review Video: Industrialization**
> Visit mometrix.com/academy and enter code: 893924

MAJOR ENERGY ISSUES

Since the Industrial Revolution, **energy** for industrialized human needs has come from fossil fuels, particularly coal and petroleum, but increased use means that this source of fuel is quickly being depleted, in addition to causing pollution. The search for **alternative, safe sources** of energy for an increasingly industrialized world population is therefore increasingly important to scientists. An ideal source of energy would be efficient, renewable, and sustainable. Various sources of alternative energy have been proposed, including wind, water, solar, nuclear, geothermal, and biomass, but thus far none have been made practically available on a large scale. Some, such as wind and water, blight the landscape, while the conversion methods for other sources, such as solar and biomass, are still relatively inefficient. The scientific community is still unclear on the best way to harness the power of photosynthesis and biomass for energy needs in a way that would allow a large-scale energy industry to use it. Scientists remain at work studying the long-term solutions to an increasingly urgent problem for humanity.

CONTROVERSIES SURROUNDING USE OF NUCLEAR POWER

Nuclear fission power, while sustainable, has a host of attendant controversial problems. Among them is the incredibly dangerous transportation and long-term storage of its radioactive waste products, for which there is still no safe long-term solution. The effects on those environments and creatures that come in contact with nuclear waste are still largely unknown. In addition, nuclear materials can be used in weaponry, and accidents at nuclear power plants like the one at Chernobyl can be devastating for thousands of years. Scientists continue their study of the process of **nuclear fusion**, hoping that if humans can learn to harness the energy produced by smashing atoms rather than splitting them, the attendant problems of nuclear waste storage will be minimized.

> **Review Video: Nuclear Fusion**
> Visit mometrix.com/academy and enter code: 381782

EFFECTS OF INCREASED PRODUCTION OF CONSUMER GOODS AFTER INDUSTRIAL REVOLUTION

Electric-based, industrial production of **manufactured goods** has led to an increase in the standard of living for many, especially those in the industrialized world. Consumer goods are produced more cheaply than ever before, since the means of production is not as dependent on the physical abilities of human beings. Scientific advancements have led to a huge number of new synthetic materials from which goods can be made, including plastics and nylon. However, this increased production damages the **environment**. Waste products are now created of which humans can make no use, a new phenomenon. Trash created from these new products is buried in landfills, where it has no access to the air, water, and sunlight that are a necessary part of biodegradation; trash made from some synthetic materials does not biodegrade at all. While some waste products can be recycled, many byproducts of industrial manufacturing are hazardous, with no safe way to dispose of them. The long-term sustainability of the environment as a result of massively increased consumer production is an issue of increasing urgency for scientists.

ISSUES CONCERNING MANAGEMENT OF RENEWABLE RESOURCES

Natural resources can be divided into two types, renewable and non-renewable. **Renewable resources** include plants and animals, along with water, air, and soil. A pre-industrial earth was a self-sustaining system, maintaining a natural balance among plants, animals, and non-living elements in which waste products from one natural process were the fuel for another. Modern humans have intervened in this process in a way that upsets the natural balance of life. Humans have introduced non-native species from one part of the world to another, resulting in the devastation of local populations. Industrial-scale buildings can create disasters for local ecosystems, ruining habitats for animal populations. Humans remove an increasing amount of the world's resources for industrial use, too quickly for nature to recover from easily. Renewable resources must be carefully managed to maintain a balanced ecosystem; over-harvesting of forests or over-hunting of animal populations can be devastating. Pollution of the air and water with chemical pollutants has far-reaching effects on the ecosystems of the earth, including the depletion of the ozone layer that protects life on earth from ultraviolet rays. The removal of forests, which produce the earth's oxygen, further depletes the ozone layer.

Science

ISSUES CONCERNING MANAGEMENT OF NON-RENEWABLE RESOURCES

Non-renewable resources include minerals, which are created naturally over millions of years. The industrialized world extracts minerals for fuel as well as for use in electronic equipment and medicine. Increased human extraction of non-renewable resources has endangered their availability, and over-mining has created other ecological problems, including runoff and water pollution. The use of fossil fuels for energy and transportation causes air pollution and is unsustainable. Fossil fuels cannot be replaced once depleted, and they are being depleted at an increasing rate. The need to find a sustainable alternative to the use of non-renewable fossil fuels is imperative.

> **Review Video: Renewable and Nonrenewable Resources**
> Visit mometrix.com/academy and enter code: 840194

RECENT APPLICATIONS OF SCIENCE AND TECHNOLOGY TO HEALTH CARE, THE ENVIRONMENT, AGRICULTURE, AND INFORMATION TECHNOLOGY

Scientific and technological developments have led to the widespread availability of **technologies** heretofore unheard of, including cellular phones, satellite-based applications, and a worldwide network of connected computers. Some notable recent applications include:

- **Health care**: Antibiotics, genetic screening for diseases, the sequencing of the human genome. Issues include problems with health care distribution on an increasingly industrialized planet.
- **The environment**: Computerized models of climate change and pollution monitoring. Issues include increased pollution of the water, air, and soil, and the over-harvesting of natural resources with mechanized equipment.
- **Agriculture**: Genetic improvements in agricultural practices, including increased output on the same amount of arable land. Issues include unknown environmental effects of hybrid species, cross-pollination with organic species, and pollution caused by synthetic chemical fertilizers.
- **Information technology**: New Internet-based industries, increased worldwide collaboration, and access to information. Issues include the depletion of natural resources for electronics production.

SOCIAL IMPACTS OF RECENT DEVELOPMENTS IN SCIENCE AND TECHNOLOGY

Recent **developments in science and technology** have had both positive and negative effects on human society. The issue of sustainable growth is an increasingly important one, as humans realize that the resources they use are not unlimited. Genetic research into diseases, stem cell research, and cloning technology have created great controversies as they have been introduced, and an increasing number of people reject the morality of scientific practices like animal testing in the pursuit of scientific advancement. In addition, an increasingly technology-based world has produced a new social inequality based on access to computers and Internet technology. These issues are beginning to be debated at all levels of human government, from city councils to the United Nations. Does science provide the authoritative answer to all human problems, or do ethics carry weight in scientific debates as well? Ultimately, humans must weigh the competing needs of facilitating scientific pursuits and maintaining an ethical society as they face new technological questions.

HUMAN IMPACTS ON ECOSYSTEMS

Human impacts on ecosystems take many forms and have many causes. They include widespread disruptions and specific niche disturbances. Humans practice many forms of environmental manipulation that affect plants and animals in many biomes and ecosystems. Many human practices involve the consumption of natural resources for food and energy production, the changing of the environment to produce food and energy, and the intrusion on ecosystems to provide shelter. These general behaviors include a multitude of specific behaviors, including the use and overuse of pesticides, the encroachment upon habitat, over hunting and over fishing, the introduction of plant and animal species into non-native ecosystems, not recycling, and the introduction of hazardous wastes and chemical byproducts into the environment. These behaviors have led to a number of consequences, such as acid rain, ozone depletion, deforestation, urbanization, accelerated species loss, genetic abnormalities, endocrine disruption in populations, and harm to individual animals.

GREENHOUSE EFFECT

The **greenhouse effect** refers to the naturally occurring and necessary process of **greenhouse gasses**, ozone, carbon dioxide, water vapor, and methane, trapping infrared radiation that is reflected toward the atmosphere. This is actually beneficial in that warm air is trapped. Without the greenhouse effect, it is estimated that the temperature on Earth would be 30 degrees less on average. The problem lies in human activity generating more greenhouse gases than are necessary. Excess greenhouse gases cause more infrared radiation to become trapped, which increases the temperature at the Earth's surface. The practices that increase the amount of greenhouse gases are the burning of natural gas and oil, farming practices that result in the release of methane and nitrous oxide, factory operations that produce gases, and deforestation practices that decrease the amount of oxygen available to offset greenhouse gases. Population growth also increases the volume of gases released.

IMPACT

Rising temperatures may lead to an increase in sea levels as polar ice melts, lower amounts of available fresh water as coastal areas flood, and species extinction as habitats change. They'll also cause increases in certain diseases and a decreased standard of living for humans. Less fresh water and losses of habitat for humans and other species can also lead to decreased agricultural production and food supply shortages. Increased desertification leads to habitat loss for humans and certain other species. Decreases in animal populations from losses of habitat and increased hunting by other species can lead to extinction. Increases in severe weather, such as huge sustained snowstorms, may also occur at unlikely latitudes. Even though global warming results in weather that is drier and warmer overall, it still gets cold enough to snow. There may be more moisture in the atmosphere due to evaporation. **Global warming** may cause the permanent loss of glaciers and permafrost. There might also be increases in air pollution and acid rain.

IMPACT OF SCIENCE AND TECHNOLOGY ON ENVIRONMENT AND HUMAN AFFAIRS

Since the industrial revolution, science and technology have had a profound impact on **human affairs**. There has been a rapid increase in the number of discoveries in many fields. Many major and minor discoveries have led to a great improvement in the quality of life of many people. This includes longer life spans because of better nutrition, increased access to medical care, and a decrease in workplace health hazards. Not all problems, such as health hazards and poor nutrition, have been solved, and many still exist in one form or another. For example, even though there are means to recycle, not every business does so because of economic factors. These advances, while improving the lives of many humans, have also taken their toll on the environment. A possible solution may arise when the carrying capacity for humans on Earth is reached. The population will decline, and solutions will have to be found. Otherwise, an immediate halt or decrease in the human behaviors that are causing environmental damage will need to happen.

PURPOSE OF STUDYING INTERACTIONS AMONG HUMANS, NATURAL HAZARDS, AND THE ENVIRONMENT

In science class, students will learn that the **human population** on earth can be affected by various factors from both their natural environments and from the technologies they use in their daily lives. These factors can be positive or negative, so students need to learn how to prepare for, respond to, and evaluate the consequences of environmental occurrences over a long period of time. Natural disasters are a negative experience, but so are human-made disasters such as pollution and deforestation. Students need to understand that science is involved in the interactions between the human population, natural hazards, and the environment. They should know that the aim of science is to make these interactions **balanced and positive**. Science is a discipline that can help find ways to increase safety during and remediate destruction after natural disasters. Science can also advance technology and transportation in an environmentally safe manner, prevent and cure diseases, and remediate the effects of pollution and resource depletion.

Science

SUBJECTS COVERED IN PERSONAL HEALTH PORTION OF SCIENCE CLASS

Among the personal and social perspectives of science are the issues of **personal and public health care**. In this area, students learn such things as:

- The importance of regular **exercise** to the maintenance and improvement of health
- The need for **risk assessment** and educated decisions to prevent injuries and illnesses because of the potential for accidents and the existence of hazards
- The risk of illness and the social and psychological factors associated with the use of **tobacco products**
- The dangers of abusing **alcohol and other drug substances**, including addiction and damage to body functions
- The energy and nutrition values of various **foods**, their role in growth and development, and the requirements of the body according to variable factors
- The complexities of **human sexuality** and the dangers of sexually transmitted infections
- The relationship between **environmental and human health**, and the need to monitor soil, water, and air standards

RISK AND BENEFIT ANALYSIS AS STUDIED IN PERSONAL AND SOCIAL PERSPECTIVES OF SCIENCE

Risk analysis considers the type of hazard and estimates the number of people who might be exposed and the number likely to suffer consequences. The results are used to determine options for reducing or eliminating risks. For example, the Center for Disease Control must analyze the risk of a certain new virus strain causing a pandemic, how many people and what age groups need to be vaccinated first, and what precautions can be taken to guard against the spread of the disease. **Risk and benefit analysis** involves having students consider the dangers of natural (major storms), chemical (pollution), biological (pollen and bacteria), social (occupational safety and transportation), and personal (smoking, dieting, and drugs) hazards. Students then use a systematic approach to think critically about these hazards, apply probability estimates to the risks, and compare them to estimated and perceived personal and social benefits.

INTERACTIONS OF SCIENCE AND TECHNOLOGY WITH SOCIETY

The interactions of science and technology with society include:

- **Scientific knowledge** and the procedures used by scientists influence the way many people think about themselves, others, and the environment.
- **Technology** influences society through its products and processes. It influences quality of life and the ways people act and interact. Technological changes are often accompanied by social, political, and economic changes. Science and technology contribute enormously to economic growth and productivity. The introduction of the cell phone into society is a perfect example of technology influencing society, quality of life, human interaction, and the economy.
- **Societal challenges** often inspire questions for scientific research, and social priorities often influence research priorities through the availability of research funding.

Science and technology have been advanced through the contributions of many different people in a variety of cultures during different time periods in history. Scientists and engineers work in colleges, businesses and industries, research institutes, and government agencies, touching many lives in a variety of settings.

Chapter Quiz

Ready to see how well you retained what you just read? Scan the QR code to go directly to the chapter quiz interface for this study guide. If you're using a computer, simply visit the bonus page at **mometrix.com/bonus948/praxeems7001** and click the Chapter Quizzes link.

Science

Praxis Practice Test #1

Want to take this practice test in an online interactive format?
Check out the bonus page, which includes interactive practice questions and much more: **mometrix.com/bonus948/praxeems7001**

Teaching Reading

1. Which activity would be most appropriate to teach decoding of CVCe words?

   a.   Covering parts of the word
   b.   Chunking
   c.   Building word families
   d.   Blending

2. A classroom teacher observes that a new ELL student consistently omits the /h/ sound in words. Of these, what is the first factor the teacher should consider?

   a.   The student may have an articulation disorder.
   b.   The student may be a native Spanish speaker.
   c.   The student may need a hearing assessment.
   d.   The student may have a respiratory problem.

3. Which of the following questions requires students to make an inference about a fictional text?

   a.   Did the author support her points with strong evidence?
   b.   How do you think the character felt when she said that?
   c.   What do you think will happen next?
   d.   Does this character remind you of any characters in other books you have read?

4. A third-grade student has difficulties with decoding and struggles to read grade-level texts independently. Which statement is likely to be true based on this information?

   a.   The student will benefit from additional implicit phonics instruction.
   b.   The student will also struggle with phonological awareness.
   c.   The student will also struggle with fluency and comprehension.
   d.   The student likely has a language processing disorder and requires further evaluation.

5. What statement is most accurate regarding the context(s) wherein students develop literacy?

   a.   Students develop literacy by reading, writing, listening, and speaking.
   b.   Students develop literacy by reading, writing, and listening to speech.
   c.   Students develop literacy by reading and writing only.
   d.   Students develop literacy only by reading.

6. A student is able to:

- apply strategies to comprehend the meanings of unfamiliar words
- supply definitions for words with several meanings such as *crucial, criticism,* and *witness*
- reflect on her background knowledge in order to decipher a word's meaning

These features of effective reading belong to which category?

a. Word recognition
b. Vocabulary
c. Content
d. Comprehension

7. Mr. Clark is conducting a daily phonics lesson. Today, the class is focusing on the *st* consonant blend. Students first repeatedly produce the sound the blend makes. They then search for *st* words within the classroom. Which approach to phonics instruction is Mr. Clark demonstrating?

a. Implicit
b. Explicit
c. Whole language
d. Analytical

8. Assessment results often inform instructional practices. At what point should teachers begin teaching the stages of composition?

a. They should start teaching the stages of composition only after children have learned to form letters.
b. They should start teaching the stages of composition only after children have learned to spell words with reliable success.
c. They should start teaching the stages of composition only once children can generate full sentences.
d. They should start teaching the stages of composition concurrently as these writing skills develop.

9. When assessing error patterns in a student's reading, which is most detrimental to reading proficiency?

a. Substitution of "control" for "contrariness"
b. Substitution of "resistant" for "recalcitrant"
c. Substituting a noun, not a verb, for a noun
d. Substituting for errors informed by context

10. Which of the following is the cognitive or learning objective of an assignment that asks students to "describe," "explain," "summarize," "restate," "classify," or "review" material they have read?

a. Knowledge recall
b. Application
c. Comprehension
d. Evaluation

11. Olivia, a first-grade student, has a reading intervention plan to improve her decoding of CVCe words. In addition to working with the teacher in a small group each day, Olivia's teacher gives her 10 new CVCe words to decode each Friday. The number of words read correctly is recorded on a graph, and the teacher notes any improvement made from the previous weeks. Which type of assessment is the teacher demonstrating?

a. Progress monitoring
b. Screening assessment
c. Summative assessment
d. Norm-referenced assessment

12. Among these forms of electronic media, which have the highest level of formality?

a. Online news articles
b. Online blogs
c. Emails
d. All are the same

13. After only two or three months into 1st grade, a new substitute teacher gives grades in the 80s to a student who had been receiving 100s from the regular teacher before the teacher had to take emergency leave. The substitute deducts points when the student occasionally reverses a letter or number, or misspells words like *biscuit, butterfly,* and *swallowed*. Which of the following most accurately describes this scenario?

    a. The regular teacher should not have given 100s; the substitute grades errors more thoroughly.
    b. The student should be evaluated for possible dyslexia because she reverses letters and numbers.
    c. The student's writing is developmentally appropriate; the substitute's grading is inappropriate.
    d. The student's occasional reversals are not important, but the misspellings need interventions.

14. At the beginning of each month, Mr. Yi has Jade read a page or two from a book she hasn't seen before. He notes the total number of words in the section and the number of times she leaves out or misreads a word. If Jade reads the passage with less than 3% error, Mr. Yi is satisfied that Jade is:

    a. Reading with full comprehension
    b. Probably bored and should try a more difficult book
    c. Reading at her independent reading level
    d. Comfortable with the syntactical meaning

15. Which example best demonstrates a student learning in his zone of proximal development?

    a. Being taught to apply a new decoding strategy while reading a book that contains some words that are new to the student
    b. Casually practicing reading using a reading passage that the student is very familiar with
    c. Listening to an audio version of a story in place of reading the written text because it is too difficult to read independently
    d. Pairing up a stronger student with a struggling reader to model use of a comprehension strategy

16. A class is reading *The Heart Is a Lonely Hunter*. The teacher asks students to write a short paper explaining the story's resolution. She is asking them to locate and discuss the story's:

    a. Outcome
    b. Highest or most dramatic moment
    c. Plot
    d. Lowest point

17. It is the beginning of the school year. To determine which second-grade students might need support, the reading teacher wants to identify those who are reading below grade level. She works with students one at a time. She gives each child a book at a second-grade reading level and asks the child to read out loud for two minutes. Which students will need reading support?

    a. Only students who read fewer than 100 words in the time given
    b. All students who read fewer than 200 words in the time given
    c. All students who read more than 100 words in the time given
    d. Only students who read more than 200 words in the time given

18. A third-grade science teacher gives her students one hour to read an article about penguins, take notes on important information, and use the notes to write a three-paragraph expository essay. At the end of the hour, Joshua only has his notes completed. The teacher examines his notes, part of which are shown below.

> Penguins are animals that live in the Southern Hemisphere.
>
> Many people believe that penguins live in the Arctic, but that is not true.
>
> Penguins in Antarctica huddle together to stay warm. They take turns standing on the outside of the huddle, where it is colder.
>
> Penguins' feathers help protect them from the water and cold air.
>
> Penguins live in groups called colonies.

Which strategy would be most helpful for the teacher to focus on with Joshua to prepare him for similar tasks?

a. Grouping the notes into three sections to correspond with the paragraphs of the essay
b. Selecting only a few facts to record before moving on to the essay
c. Using drawings rather than words
d. Recording only key words and phrases rather than sentences

19. Which of the following strategies would not be helpful in building the word-identification skills of emergent readers?

a. Allowing for invented spelling in written assignments or in-class work.
b. Reinforcing phonemic awareness while reading aloud.
c. Using dictionaries to look up unfamiliar words.
d. Studying and reviewing commonly used sight words at the students' ability level.

20. Which of the following students may need extra instruction and evaluation with respect to oral language skills?

a. Rosa: whose first language is Spanish. Rosa speaks with a distinct accent and can be difficult to understand when speaking about a new or unfamiliar topic.
b. Greer: who avoids oral assignments when possible. He avoids speaking up in class and only responds when called upon.
c. Ashley: who often has trouble answering questions in class. Her responses are often off-topic. She also struggles with oral presentations, seeming to present a string of unrelated facts.
d. Brett: who frequently becomes loud and disruptive whenever group work is assigned. He often becomes involved in heated discussions with classmates when discussing ideas.

21. Elizabeth, a sixth-grade student, is researching Hellen Keller's life before writing a biographical report about her. The report will include information about both her childhood and adulthood, along with information about how she learned to communicate over time. When selecting books to use as sources and while writing her own report, which type of text structure would best fit her purposes?

a. Cause and effect
b. Time-order
c. Compare and contrast
d. Descriptive

22. An understanding of the meanings of prefixes and suffixes such as *dis, mis, un, re, able,* and *ment* are important for:

a. Reading comprehension
b. Word recognition
c. Vocabulary building
d. Reading fluency

23. Which of the following examples best demonstrates teacher scaffolding?

a. A teacher gives students a mixture of building materials and challenges them to construct the tallest tower possible in 15 minutes.

b. A teacher reads a book related to the current science unit aloud because it is too difficult for students to read independently.

c. A teacher gives students time to self-select books related to their interests from the classroom library.

d. A teacher uses picture cards to pre-teach vocabulary before students read a new book independently.

24. What is orthographic processing?

a. The ability to separate spoken words into component sounds

b. Understanding the predictable sound each letter makes

c. Recognizing letter patterns that make up words or word parts

d. Understanding spoken words

25. The teacher and her students brainstorm a list of talents, skills, and specialized knowledge belonging to members of the class. Some of the items on the list include how to make a soufflé, how to juggle, and how to teach a dog to do tricks. One student knows a great deal about spiders, and another knows about motorcycles. The teacher asks the students to each write an essay about something they are good at or know a great deal about. What kind of essay is she asking the students to produce?

a. Cause and effect

b. Compare/contrast

c. Expository

d. Argumentative

26. Some experts maintain that teaching reading comprehension entails not only the application of skills but also the process of actively constructing meaning. They describe this process as interactive, strategic, and adaptable. Which of the following descriptions best applies to the interactive aspect of this process?

a. The process involves the text, the reader, and the context in which reading occurs.

b. The process involves readers using a variety of strategies in constructing meaning.

c. The process involves readers changing their strategies to read different text types.

d. The process involves changing strategies according to different reasons for reading.

Refer to the following for questions 27–28:

A teacher is concerned about three of her students. While they are enthusiastic about writing, they do not always recognize letters, confusing *b*, *d*, and *p*, or *e* and *o*. They do, however, know which sounds go with certain letters when they are orally drilled. When they write, they appear to be attempting letter–sound associations.

"Now I'm writing *M*," the teacher heard one boy say as he scripted a large *N* in the upper right corner of his paper. He studied it for a moment and added, "Nope, it needs another leg." The student then wrote an *I* beside the *N*. "There," he said. "Now you are an *M*. I can write the word *man* because now I have *M*." The child then moved to the lower left corner of the paper. "M-A-N," he said to himself, slowly pronouncing each sound. "I already have that *M*. Here is where the rest of the word goes." He turned the paper sideways and wrote *N*.

The second child sang to herself as she gripped the crayon and scribbled lines here and there on her paper. Some of the lines resembled letters, but few actually were. Others were scribbles. As she "wrote," she seemed to be making up a story and seemed to believe she was writing the story down.

The third child didn't vocalize at all while he worked. He gripped the paper and carefully wrote the same letter over and over and over. Sometimes the letter was large, sometimes tiny. He turned the paper in every direction so that sometimes the letter was sideways or upside down. Sometimes he flipped it backward. "What are you writing?" the teacher asked him. "My name," the child told her. The teacher then realized the letter was, indeed, the first letter of his name. She gently told him he had done a fine job of writing the first letter of his name. Did he want her to help him write the rest of it? "Nope," he cheerfully told her, "it's all here." He pointed at one of the letters and "read" his full name. He pointed at another letter and again seemed to believe it represented all the sounds of his name.

27. In the above example, the emergent writers are demonstrating their understanding that letters symbolize predictable sounds, that words begin with an initial sound/letter, and that by "writing," they are empowering themselves by offering a reader access to their thoughts and ideas. The next three stages the emergent writers will pass through in order will most likely be:
- a. Scripting the end-sound to a word (KT=cat), leaving space between words, writing from the top left to the top right of the page and top to bottom
- b. Scripting the end-sound to a word (KT=cat), writing from the top left to the top right of the page and from top to bottom, separating the words from one another with a space between
- c. Leaving space between the initial letters that represent words, writing from the top left to the top right of the page and from top to bottom, scripting the final sound of each word as well as the initial sound (KT=cat)
- d. Drawing a picture beside each of the initial sounds to represent the entire word, scripting the end-sound to a word (KT=cat), scripting the interior sounds that compose the entire word (KAT=cat)

28. At what point should the kindergarten teacher in the above example offer the three children picture books and ask them to read to her?
- a. When the three children are all able to script initial sounds, end sounds, and interior sounds.
- b. As each child reaches the stage in which he or she can script initial sounds, end sounds, and interior sounds, the teacher should ask only that child to read to her.
- c. As each child reaches the stage in which he habitually writes from the top to the bottom of the page, moving left to right.
- d. From the first day of school onward

29. Which of the following linguistic domains does NOT play a role in decoding unfamiliar words when reading?
- a. Syntactic
- b. Semantic
- c. Graphophonic
- d. Pragmatic

30. A teacher takes a running record while Charlie, a second grader, reads a new text. Part of the running record is shown below.

> home
> The witch's house was deep in the woods, hidden behind some
> grumpy
> trees. A grouchy cat guarded the entrance to the house, hissing
> omission
> loudly when any strangers approached. Nobody had dared to go
>
> near it in years.

Which strategy would be most appropriate for the teacher to focus on during the next guided reading session?

  a. Using semantic cues
  b. Using syntactic cues
  c. Omissions
  d. Self-corrections

31. A second-grade class is listening to a read-aloud of a fictional text about Thanksgiving Day in America. One student has recently moved to America and is unfamiliar with the holiday. Which of the following options is the most effective way for the teacher to address this issue with the student?

  a. Ask the student to retell the story after listening to it to assess comprehension.
  b. Provide background information on Thanksgiving before reading, relating it to traditions the student is familiar with.
  c. Provide the student with a written outline of the key elements in the story before reading.
  d. After reading, describe the key features of the story and holiday again with different language than what was used in the book.

32. A teacher has a student in her class who is not very motivated to write because he finds it difficult. She observes he has a highly visual learning style, does not like reading books but loves graphic novels, and has considerable artistic drawing talent and interest. Which of the following instructional strategies would best address his individual needs, strengths, and interests?

  a. Giving him audio recordings to accompany and guide his writing homework
  b. Letting him complete all assignments by drawing pictures instead of writing
  c. Having him draw the pictures and write accompanying text in graphic novels
  d. Providing and assigning him to view animated videos on the topic of writing

33. Which of the following relates primarily to how sounds are represented in a text?

  a. Syntactic
  b. Semantic
  c. Graphophonic
  d. Pragmatic

34. The first-grade teacher wants her class to understand that stories have a certain order. She reads them a story, then orally reviews how each event that happened in the story caused the next event to happen. To reinforce the lesson, the teacher should:

   a. Give each child a piece of drawing paper that has been folded in half and then in half again, creating four boxes, along with a piece that has not been folded. The teacher should then ask the students to draw a cartoon about the story. Each of the first four boxes will show the events in order. The second page is to show how the story ends.

   b. Give each child a piece of drawing paper and ask the students to draw the most important scene.

   c. Give each child a piece of drawing paper and ask the students to draw the story's beginning on the front of the page and ending on the back.

   d. Give each child a piece of drawing paper that has been folded in half and then in half again, creating four boxes, along with a piece that has not been folded. The teacher should then ask the students to draw a cartoon about anything they want. She reminds them to put their story cartoons in proper order.

35. The pairs of words *sea* and *see*, *fair* and *fare*, are called:

   a. Homophones

   b. Antonyms

   c. Homographs

   d. Twin words

36. Silent reading fluency can best be assessed by:

   a. Having the student retell or summarize the material to determine how much was understood.

   b. Giving a written test that covers plot, theme, character development, sequence of events, rising action, climax, falling action, and outcome. A student must test at a 95% accuracy rate to be considered fluent at silent reading.

   c. Giving a three-minute Test of Silent Contextual Reading Fluency four times a year. The student is presented with text in which spaces between words and all punctuation have been removed. The student must divide one word from another with slash marks, as in the example: The/little/sailboat/bobbed/so/far/in/the/distance/it/looked/like/a/toy. The more words a student accurately separates, the higher her silent reading fluency score.

   d. Silent reading fluency cannot be assessed. It is a private act between the reader and the text and does not invite critique.

37. Research indicates that developing oral language proficiency in emergent readers is important because:

   a. Proficiency with oral language enhances students' phonemic awareness and increases vocabulary.

   b. The more verbally expressive emergent readers are, the more confident they become. Such students will embrace both Academic and Independent reading levels.

   c. It encourages curiosity about others. With strong oral language skills, students begin to question the world around them. The more they ask, the richer their background knowledge.

   d. It demonstrates to students that their ideas are important and worth sharing.

38. A teacher has concerns that a standardized test she is required to give does not accurately measure what it is designed to measure. The test claims to measure students' abilities to make inferences, yet there are no questions that directly address this skill. The teacher has concerns with which aspect of the standardized test?

   a. Validity

   b. Reliability

   c. Bias

   d. Objectivity

39. What is the primary result of using sentences that vary in their length and complexity?

  a.   It gives the main theme.
  b.   It eliminates unnecessary details.
  c.   It replaces complex terms with simpler words.
  d.   It improves the readability.

40. Which text should a teacher choose in order to practice the skills of previewing and reviewing information?

  a.   A poem
  b.   A chapter from the students' science class textbook
  c.   A library book of each student's own choosing
  d.   A short story from language arts class

41. Cause and effect, compare and contrast, and time order are all examples of what?

  a.   Literary devices
  b.   Literary elements
  c.   Genres
  d.   Text structures

42. Which of the following activities best demonstrates a multisensory approach to teaching letter formation?

  a.   Locating words containing a certain letter in a book
  b.   Tracing prewritten letters on paper with a pencil
  c.   Identifying letters on flashcards
  d.   Writing letters in shaving cream

43. Which of the following linguistic domains relates primarily to the meanings of words?

  a.   Graphophonic
  b.   Semantic
  c.   Syntactic
  d.   Pragmatic

44. Of the following examples, which one is NOT an open-ended question?

  a.   "When does the climax of this story occur?"
  b.   "Is this expression a simile or a metaphor?"
  c.   "How are similes and metaphors different?"
  d.   "What are some reasons we have poetry?"

45. Which statement accurately reflects a principle regarding self-questioning techniques for increasing student reading comprehension?

  a.   Asking only what kinds of "expert questions" fit the text's subject matter
  b.   Asking only those questions that the text raises for the individual student
  c.   Asking how each text portion relates to chapter main ideas is unnecessary
  d.   Asking how the text information fits with what the student already knows

46. Abi, a fifth-grader, is reading aloud to his teacher during one-on-one reading time. His teacher uses this time to evaluate ongoing fluency and comprehension skills. Following today's reading, Abi's teacher determines that he needs practice with words that begin with digraphs. Which of the following sets of words would most likely be part of this assignment?

   a.   Chicken, Shells, That
   b.   Were, Frame, Click
   c.   Sponge, Think, Blank
   d.   Packed, Blistered, Smoothed

47. Character maps, fact and opinion charts, 5Ws charts, and webs are all examples of what?

   a.   Literary elements
   b.   Genres
   c.   Text features
   d.   Graphic organizers

48. What is the purpose of targeted instruction?

   a.   Deliver instructions that are precise, clear, and direct so that students understand exactly what is expected.
   b.   Accurately rank a group of learners from low achievers to high achievers so that the teacher knows from the beginning of the school year which students have less ability and will therefore need support.
   c.   Teach students how to take information from a text and reorganize it into bulleted lists.
   d.   Assess and target areas needing improvement as well as areas of greatest strength for each student to ensure that all members of a class are receiving instruction tailored to their specific needs.

49. If a student has a writing assignment, which of the following is true regarding his or her audience?

   a.   The student need not identify the audience because it is the teacher.
   b.   The student should consider the readers' purpose for reading and response to the writing.
   c.   The student should know his or her writing purpose and not be concerned with a reader's purposes.
   d.   The student can develop an audience profile but assume the main audience is the teacher.

50. A fourth-grade student struggles to decode several words in her science textbook, including *organism*, *conclusion*, and *prediction*. Which strategy would best help the student decode these and other similar words?

   a.   Using context clues to select words that make sense in the sentences
   b.   Slowly stretching out the letter sounds
   c.   Blending the phonemes
   d.   Looking for known word parts, such as prefixes and suffixes

51. Which of the following factors affects ELL students' English-language literacy development?

   a.   A Chinese student's L1 is not written alphabetically like English is.
   b.   A Spanish student's L1 is more phonetically regular than English is.
   c.   Neither one of these has any effects on L2 literacy development.
   d.   Both factors affect L2 literacy development but in different ways.

52. Phonological awareness activities are:

   a.   Oral
   b.   Visual
   c.   Tactile
   d.   Semantically based

53. Which of the following choices will be most important when designing a reading activity or lesson for students?

    a. Selecting a text
    b. Determining the number of students participating
    c. Analyzing the point in the school year at which the lesson is given
    d. Determining a purpose for instruction

54. A second-grade teacher wants to help her students enrich their vocabulary. She's noticed that their writing journals are filled with serviceable but unexciting verbs such as "said" and "went," and general rather than specific nouns. The most effective lesson would involve:

    a. Suggesting students use a thesaurus to replace common words with more unusual words
    b. Suggesting students add an adjective to each noun
    c. Brainstorming a list of verbs that mean ways of talking or ways of going, then adding them to the word wall along with some nouns that specify common topics
    d. Suggesting students look up the meanings of boring words and consider another way to express them

55. A kindergarten teacher pronounces a series of word pairs for her students. The students repeat the pairs. Some of the pairs rhyme (*see/bee*) and some of the pairs share initial sounds but do not rhyme (*sit, sun*). The students help her separate the word pairs into pairs that rhyme and pairs that do not. Once the students are able to distinguish between two words that rhyme and two words that do not, the teacher says a word and asks them to provide a rhyme. When she says *cat* a child responds with *fat*. When she says *sing* a child offers *thing*. How does this strictly oral activity contribute to the children's ability to read?

    a. It doesn't. Oral activities must have a written component to be useful to emergent readers.
    b. It is helpful in that it demonstrates how different sounds are made with different letters.
    c. It actually discourages children from reading. By emphasizing orality over literacy, the teacher is suggesting to the children that reading is not an important skill.
    d. Being able to identify rhyme is an important element of phonological awareness.

56. In which of the following sentences would it be most appropriate to suggest that a first-grade student use the "sound it out" strategy to decode the underlined word?

    a. The child started to <u>tear</u> the wrapping paper off the gift.
    b. The <u>chain</u> on the swing was squeaky.
    c. The kitten was hiding behind the <u>curtain</u>.
    d. The dolphin swam across the <u>ocean</u>.

57. Prekindergarten students tell their teacher, Mr. Clark, that they want to write about their field trip to the zoo. Mr. Clark writes down the students' sentences on chart paper, and then reads them back to the class, pointing to each word and modeling appropriate fluency. After reading the story multiple times, Mr. Clark invites the students to read with him. Which type of interaction is Mr. Clark demonstrating?

    a. Language experience approach
    b. Writing workshop
    c. Trait-based writing
    d. Modeled writing

58. A kindergarten teacher is administering a reading assessment to her students. She dictates some CVC words and asks students to write them down on paper. The words she dictates are *cat* and *cot*. One student writes the following responses on her paper.

bhp
wpi

Which skill should the teacher focus on first with this student?

a. Phonological awareness
b. Alphabetic principle
c. Phonics generalizations
d. Blending

59. Which of the following words has exactly three syllables?

a. House
b. Relentless
c. Beauty
d. Destructible

60. A student is reading a fictional book and has difficulty decoding the word *maple*. Which spelling pattern could the teacher explain to help the student decode this word and similar words in the future?

a. Vowel digraph pairs
b. R-controlled vowels
c. Closed syllables
d. Open syllables

61. Which of the following genres is most important for children just beginning to become readers in grades K, 1, and 2?

a. Alphabet books, wordless picture books, and easy-to-read books
b. Legends and tall tales
c. Biographies and informational books
d. Chapter books and fantasy books

62. Which assessment will determine a student's ability to identify initial, medial, blended, final, segmented, and manipulated "units"?

a. Phonological awareness assessment
b. High-frequency word assessment
c. Reading fluency assessment
d. Comprehension quick-check

63. Kindergarten students learn one new letter and its corresponding sound each week. They participate in songs and chants that include repetitive use of the letter name and sound. Which concept are students practicing?

a. Alphabetic principle
b. Concepts of print
c. Phonological awareness
d. Automaticity

64. A teacher asks students to close their eyes while she reads a descriptive, fictional text aloud. When she is done reading, students draw pictures of the story's setting and share their pictures with the class. Which reading strategy are students practicing?

    a. Predicting
    b. Inferring
    c. Summarizing
    d. Visualizing

65. Collaborative Strategic Reading (CSR) is a teaching technique that depends on two teaching practices. These practices are:

    a. Cooperative learning and reading comprehension
    b. Cooperative reading and metacognition
    c. Reading comprehension and metacognition
    d. Cooperative learning and metacognition

66. A teacher is introducing a new phonics skill to her students. She begins with explicit instruction on the skill, followed by modeling. Which instructional component should come next?

    a. Independent practice
    b. Guided practice
    c. Generalization
    d. Feedback

67. The most effective strategy for decoding irregular sight words is:

    a. Segmenting sight words into syllables. Beginning readers are understandably nervous when encountering a long word that isn't familiar. Blocking off all but a single syllable at a time renders a word manageable and allows the reader a sense of control over the act of reading.
    b. Word families. By grouping the sight word with similar words, patterns emerge.
    c. A phonemic approach. When students understand the connection between individual words and their sounds, they will be able to sound out any sight word they encounter.
    d. None; irregular sight words cannot be decoded. Readers must learn to recognize these as whole words on sight.

68. A student participating in a reading assessment uses information from illustrations in the text he or she is reading to support reading performance. The student is using which kind of cue?

    a. A visual cue
    b. A meaning cue
    c. A structural cue
    d. A graphophonic cue

69. A teacher wants to determine a student's accuracy and reading rate in order to determine if a text is in the student's frustration, instructional, or independent reading level. Which of the following assessments should she use?

    a. Authentic assessment task
    b. Rubric
    c. Guided reading observation
    d. Running record

70. A third grader knows he needs to write from left to right and from top to bottom on the page. He knows what sounds are associated with specific letters. He can recognize individual letters and can hear word families. He correctly identifies prefixes, suffixes, and homonyms, and his reading comprehension is very good. However, when he is asked to write, he becomes very upset. He has trouble holding a pencil, his letters are very primitively executed, and his written work is not legible. He most likely has:

a. Dysgraphia
b. Dyslexia
c. Dyspraxia
d. Nonverbal learning disorder

71. A fifth-grader has prepared a report on reptiles, which is something he knows a great deal about. He rereads his report and decides to make a number of changes. He moves a sentence from the top to the last paragraph. He crosses out several words and replaces them with more specific words. He circles key information and draws an arrow to show another place the information could logically be placed. He is engaged in:

a. Editing
b. Revising
c. First editing, then revising
d. Reviewing

72. A student is having difficulties comprehending the content-related vocabulary words in his science textbook, even with the available context clues. Which text feature could the teacher direct the student to use to best assist with this difficulty?

a. Table of contents
b. Headings
c. Index
d. Glossary

73. Which of the following exercises would be the most appropriate tool for helping students evaluate the effectiveness of their own spoken messages?

a. Discuss written and oral assignments in class before completing them. Once the assignments are completed, the teacher meets individually with each student to discuss the content and effectiveness of each student's work.
b. Instruct students to present oral reports in class, which are then "graded" by classmates. A score of 1-10 is assigned based on students' perception of the reports' clarity. The students' average scores determine the effectiveness of each report.
c. Ask each student to prepare an oral report and a content quiz that highlights the report's main idea. The student then uses classmates' scores on the reviews to determine the report's effectiveness.
d. Put students into groups of three. Two students complete a role-playing assignment based on prompts provided by the teacher. The third student gives constructive feedback on how the other two can refine and clarify their speech.

74. Round-robin reading refers to the practice of allowing children to take turns reading portions of a text aloud to the rest of the group during class. Which of the following statements is LEAST true about this practice?

a. Students have the chance to practice reading aloud with this strategy.
b. This practice is ineffective in its use of time, leaving students who are not reading aloud to become bored or daydream.
c. Round-robin reading lacks the creativity or engaging qualities that will interest students in building literacy skills.
d. This practice helps students feel comfortable with reading aloud due to continuous practice and encouragement from the teacher and peers.

75. A student encounters a multisyllabic word. She's not sure if she's seen it before. What should she do first? What should she do next?

a. Locate familiar word parts, then locate the consonants
b. Locate the consonants, then locate the vowels
c. Locate the vowels, then locate familiar word parts
d. Look it up in the dictionary, then write down the meaning

76. Which of the following is correct regarding phonological awareness in kindergarteners?

a. Children with delayed language development have benefited from phonological awareness training.
b. Researchers into instruction in phonological awareness advise against using SLPs and their methods.
c. Phonological awareness in kindergarteners requires changing phonemes in words to change meaning.
d. Phonological awareness instruction for kindergarteners involves only the individual phoneme level.

77. Arthur writes a paper. One classmate identifies ideas and words that resonated with her when she read it. Another describes how reading the paper changed his thinking. A third asks Arthur some questions about what he meant by certain statements in the paper. A fourth suggests that a portion of the paper needs more supporting information. Which of the following is taking place?

a. A portfolio assessment
b. A writing workshop
c. A holistic scoring
d. A peer review

78. A struggling reader has difficulty comprehending vocabulary words when they are encountered in unfamiliar texts. She frequently uses a dictionary to look up the unknown words. While this helps her figure out the meanings of the words, it interrupts her fluency and affects comprehension. Her teacher, Mr. Palmer, would like to teach her other strategies she can use instead that will minimize the disruptions to her fluency and increase her comprehension. Which strategy would likely be most effective?

a. Quickly asking a classmate for the meanings of the words
b. Creating a list of the unknown words and looking them up later
c. Trying to determine the meanings of the words from context clues
d. Skipping over the words she does not know as long as the sentences make sense

79. Among the following, which is NOT a common academic standard for kindergarten students in decoding and identifying words?

a. Showing knowledge that letter sequences correspond to phoneme sequences
b. Understanding that word sounds and meanings change along with word letters
c. Decoding monosyllabic words using initial and final consonant and vowel sounds
d. Matching letters to consonant sounds; reading simple, monosyllabic sight words

80. Students in a fifth-grade class are breaking the word *invisible* into its component parts. They identify the prefix *in-*, the root *vis*, and the suffix *-ible*, along with the meanings of each part. What type of activity is being demonstrated?

    a. Miscue analysis
    b. Structural analysis
    c. Syllabification
    d. Decoding

Mathematics

1. If the midpoint of a line segment graphed on the xy-coordinate plane is $(3, -1)$ and the slope of the line segment is -2, which of these is a possible endpoint of the line segment?

    a. $(-1,1)$
    b. $(0,-5)$
    c. $(7,1)$
    d. $(5,-5)$

2. What is the value of the underlined digit in 8,<u>7</u>06?

    a. 70
    b. 700
    c. 7
    d. 7,000

3. A dress is marked down 45%. The cost, after taxes, is $39.95. If the tax rate is 8.75%, what was the original price of the dress?

    a. $45.74
    b. $58.61
    c. $66.79
    d. $72.31

4. Solve $\frac{x-2}{x-1} = \frac{x-1}{x+1} + \frac{2}{x-1}$.

    a. $x = 2$
    b. $x = -5$
    c. $x = 1$
    d. No solution

5. Amy saves $450 every 3 months. How much does she save after 3 years?

    a. $4,800
    b. $5,200
    c. $5,400
    d. $5,800

6. Which of the following equations may be used to convert $0.\overline{8}$ to a fraction?

    a. $9x = 80$
    b. $90x = 8$
    c. $9x = 8$
    d. $99x = 80$

7. A man standing on a flat, level surface casts a shadow that is 6.2 ft in length. The man is 5.8 ft tall. Which of the following best represents the distance from the top of his head to the end of the shadow?

    a. 7 ft
    b. 7.5 ft
    c. 8 ft
    d. 8.5 ft

8. Which of the following best describes an isosceles triangle?

    a. A triangle with no sides of equal measurement and one obtuse angle
    b. A triangle with three sides of equal measurement
    c. A triangle with two sides of equal measurement and at least two acute angles
    d. A triangle with one right angle and two non-congruent acute angles

Refer to the following for question 9:

The box-and-whisker plot displays student test scores by class period.

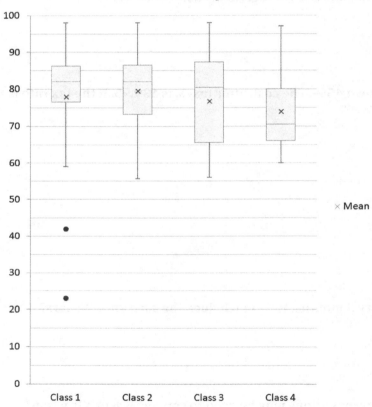

9. Which of the following statements is true of the data?

    a. The mean better reflects student performance in class 1 than the median.
    b. The mean test score for class 1 and 2 is the same.
    c. The median test score for class 1 and 2 is the same.
    d. The median test score is above the mean for class 4.

10. Which of the following correctly compares the sets of rational and irrational numbers?

    a.   The set of rational numbers is a subset of the set of irrational numbers.
    b.   The set of irrational numbers is a subset of the set of rational numbers.
    c.   The sets of irrational and rational numbers are disjoint.
    d.   The sets of irrational and rational numbers are equal.

11. A random sample of 90 students at an elementary school were asked these three questions:

    Do you like carrots?
    Do you like broccoli?
    Do you like cauliflower?

The results of the survey are shown below. If these data are representative of the population of students at the school, which of these is most probable?

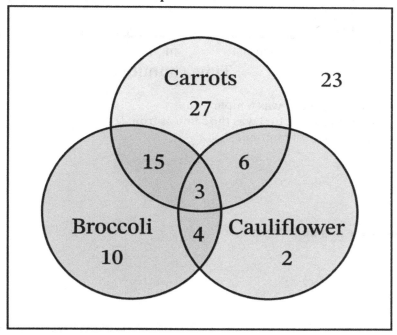

    a.   A student chosen at random likes broccoli.
    b.   Given a student chosen at random likes carrots, they will also like at least one other vegetable.
    c.   Given a student chosen at random likes cauliflower and broccoli, they will also like carrots.
    d.   A student chosen at random does not like carrots, broccoli, or cauliflower.

12. What linear equation includes the data in the table below?

x	y
-3	1
1	-11
3	-17
5	-23
9	-35

    a. $y = -3x - 11$
    b. $y = -6x - 8$
    c. $y = -3x - 8$
    d. $y = -12x - 11$

13. Aaron goes on a run every morning down the straight country road that he lives on. The graph below shows Aaron's distance from home at times throughout his morning run. Which of the following statements is (are) true?

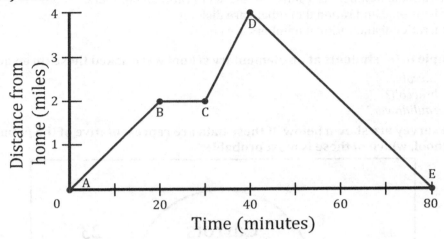

I. Aaron's average running speed was 6 mph.
II. Aaron's running speed from A to B was the same as from D to E.
III. Aaron ran a total distance of four miles.

a. I only
b. II only
c. I and II
d. I, II, and III

14. How many diagonals are in a dodecagon?

a. 12
b. 24
c. 54
d. 108

15. Elementary teachers in one school surveyed their students and discovered that 15% of their students have iPhones. Which of the following correctly states 15% in fraction, decimal, and ratio equivalents?

a. $\frac{3}{20}$, 0.15, 3 : 20
b. $\frac{3}{25}$, 0.15, 3 : 25
c. $\frac{15}{10}$, 1.5%, 15 : 10
d. $\frac{2}{1}$, 1.5%, 2 : 1

16. Robert buys a car for \$24,210. The price of the car has been marked down by 10%. What was the original price of the car?

a. \$25,900
b. \$26,300
c. \$26,900
d. \$27,300

17. Given this stem and leaf plot, what are the mean and median?

Stem	Leaf	
1	6	8
2	0	1
3	4	
4	5	9

   a.   Mean = 28 and median = 20
   b.   Mean = 29 and median = 20
   c.   Mean = 29 and median = 21
   d.   Mean = 28 and median = 21

18. What is the correct solution for x in the following system of equations?

$$\begin{cases} x - 1 = y \\ y + 3 = 7 \end{cases}$$

   a. $x = 6$
   b. $x = 5$
   c. $x = 4$
   d. $x = 8$

19. What is the approximate area of the shaded region between the circle and the square in the figure shown below? Use 3.14 for π.

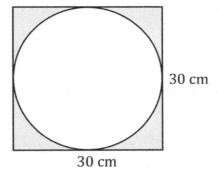

30 cm

30 cm

   a.   177 cm^2
   b.   181 cm^2
   c.   187 cm^2
   d.   193 cm^2

20. If a, b, and c are even integers and $3a^2 + 9b^3 = c$, which of these is the largest number which must be factor of c?

   a.   2
   b.   3
   c.   6
   d.   12

21. Quentin sets aside 10% of his monthly salary to save for a car. If his monthly salary is $2,450, how much will he set aside each month?

    a. $2.45
    b. $24.50
    c. $245
    d. $2,450

22. Ms. Chen is instructing her students on divisibility rules. Which of the following rules can be used to determine if a number is divisible by 6?

    a.   The last digit of the number is divisible by 2 or 3.
    b.   The number ends in 6.
    c.   The number is divisible by 2 and 3.
    d.   The last two digits of the number are divisible by 6.

23. A cylindrical carrot stick is sliced with a knife. Which of the following shapes is NOT a possible cross section?

    a.   Circle
    b.   Rectangle
    c.   Ellipse
    d.   Triangle

24. Mr. Amad draws a line with a slope of $-\frac{2}{3}$ on the white board through three points. Which of the sets could possibly be these three points?

    a. $(-6, -2), (-7, -4), (-8, -6)$
    b. $(-4, 7), (-8, 13), (-6, 10)$
    c. $(-3, -1), (-6, 1), (0, -3)$
    d. $(-2, -3), (-1, -3), (0, -3)$

25. Which of the following equations demonstrates the associative property of multiplication?

    a. $2(3 + 4) = 2(3) + 2(4)$
    b. $(3 \times 6) \times 2 = (4 \times 3) \times 3$
    c. $(2 \times 3) \times 4 = 2 \times (3 \times 4)$
    d. $6 \times 4 = 4 \times 6$

26. Kayla rolls a die and tosses a coin. What is the probability she gets an even number and heads?

    a. $\frac{1}{6}$
    b. $\frac{1}{4}$
    c. $\frac{1}{3}$
    d.   1

27. Which of these is NOT a net of a cube?

a.   b.   c.   d.

   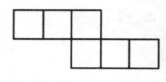

28. Tom needs to buy ink cartridges and printer paper. Each ink cartridge costs \$30. Each ream of paper costs \$5. He has \$100 to spend. Which of the following inequalities may be used to find the combinations of ink cartridges and printer paper that he may purchase?

   a. $30c + 5p \leq 100$
   b. $30c + 5p < 100$
   c. $30c + 5p > 100$
   d. $30c + 5p \geq 100$

29. Kyra sets aside $\frac{1}{3}$ of her income to pay rent and utilities at her apartment. If the monthly cost of rent and utilities is \$1,050, what is her monthly salary?

   a. \$3,150
   b. \$3,225
   c. \$3,750
   d. \$4,050

30. Hannah spends at least \$16 on 4 packages of coffee. Which of the following expresses this relationship in terms of the cost of a package of coffee, p?

   a. $16 \geq 4p$
   b. $16 < 4p$
   c. $16 > 4p$
   d. $16 \leq 4p$

31. Eli rolls a six-sided die and tosses a coin. What is the probability that he gets a prime number or tails?

   a. $\frac{1}{4}$

   b. $\frac{1}{3}$

   c. $\frac{1}{2}$

   d. $\frac{3}{4}$

32. Given that x is a prime number and the greatest common factor of x and y is greater than 1, compare the two quantities.

Quantity A	Quantity B
y	the least common multiple of x and y

   a. Quantity A is greater.
   b. Quantity B is greater.
   c. The two quantities are the same.
   d. The relationship cannot be determined from the given information.

33. Which of the following formulas may be used to represent the sequence 8, 13, 18, 23, 28, ...?

   a. $a_n = 5n + 3; n \in \mathbb{N}$
   b. $a_n = n + 5; n \in \mathbb{N}$
   c. $a_n = n + 8; n \in \mathbb{N}$
   d. $a_n = 5n + 8; n \in \mathbb{N}$

34. In a pack of 20 jelly beans, there are two licorice- and four cinnamon-flavored jelly beans. What is the probability of choosing a licorice jelly bean followed by a cinnamon jelly bean?

   a. $\frac{2}{5}$
   b. $\frac{8}{20}$
   c. $\frac{2}{95}$
   d. $\frac{1}{50}$

35. Elijah pays a $30 park entrance fee plus $4 for every ticket he buys. Which of the following equations correctly represents his total cost y in terms of the number of tickets x?

   a. $y = 30x + 4$
   b. $y = 34x$
   c. $y = 4x + 30$
   d. $y = 34x + 30$

36. The ratio of employee wages and benefits to all other operational costs of a business is $2:3$. If a business's total operating expenses are $130,000 per month, how much money does the company spend on employee wages and benefits?

   a. $43,333.33
   b. $86,666.67
   c. $52,000.00
   d. $78,000.00

37. If 1 inch on a map represents 60 feet, how many yards apart are two points if the distance between the points on the map is 10 inches?

   a. 1,800
   b. 600
   c. 200
   d. 2

38. Sophia is at the market buying fruit for her family of four. Kiwifruit is only sold in packages of three. If Sophia would like each family member to have the same number of kiwifruits, which of the following approaches can Sophia use to determine the fewest number of kiwifruits she should buy?

   a. Sophia needs to determine the greatest common multiple of 3 and 4.
   b. Sophia needs to determine the least common multiple of 3 and 4.
   c. Sophia needs to determine the least common divisor of 3 and 4.
   d. Sophia needs to determine the greatest common divisor of 3 and 4.

39. Which of the following represents an inversely proportional relationship?

   a. $y = 3x$
   b. $y = \frac{1}{3}x$
   c. $y = \frac{3}{x}$
   d. $y = 3x^2$

40. A dress is marked down by 20% and placed on a clearance rack, on which is posted a sign reading, "Take an extra 25% off already reduced merchandise." What fraction of the original price is the final sale price of the dress?

 a. $\frac{2}{5}$

 b. $\frac{9}{20}$

 c. $\frac{3}{5}$

 d. $\frac{11}{20}$

Social Studies

1. Of the following economists, who advocated government intervention to prevent and remedy recessions and depressions?

 a. Adam Smith
 b. John Maynard Keynes
 c. Friedrich Hayek
 d. Milton Friedman

2. Which of the following will result if two nations use the theory of comparative advantage when making decisions of which goods to produce and trade?

 a. Each nation will make all of their own goods.
 b. Both nations will specialize in the production of the same specific goods.
 c. Each nation will specialize in the production of different specific goods.
 d. Neither nation will trade with one another.

3. How long can members of the Federal Judiciary serve?

 a. Four years
 b. Eight years
 c. For life
 d. Six years

4. Which of the following statements is false regarding the Puritans?

 a. In terms of their theology, the Puritans were considered Calvinists.
 b. Many Puritans agreed with radical views that criticized the Swiss Calvinists.
 c. Many of those identified as Calvinists opposed the Puritans.
 d. The Restoration and the Uniformity Act reunified the Puritan movement and the Church of England.

5. How must inferior courts interpret the law?

 a. According to the Supreme Court's interpretation
 b. According to the Constitution
 c. However they choose
 d. According to the political climate

6. Social dialects typically emerge when

 a. a particular group is isolated from the rest of society due to class, race, age, or gender differences.
 b. a group of new immigrants is assimilated into society.
 c. two social groups that share a common language become geographically isolated.
 d. specialized jargons develop in certain industries and academic disciplines.

285

7. The idea that the purpose of the American colonies was to provide Great Britain with raw materials and a market for its goods is an expression of:

a. Free trade
b. Most favored nation status
c. Mercantilism
d. Laissez-faire capitalism

8. The social scientists most likely to study the role of kinship relationships within a cultural group are:

a. Economists
b. Political scientists
c. Psychologists
d. Anthropologists

9. Which of the following was NOT an immediate effect of rapid urban growth in the 1800s?

a. Poor sanitation conditions in the cities
b. Epidemics of diseases in the cities
c. Inadequate police and fire protection
d. Widespread urban political corruption

10. What is the main reason that tropical regions near the Equator tend to experience relatively constant year-round temperatures?

a. They are usually located near the ocean.
b. The angle at which sunlight hits them remains relatively constant throughout the year.
c. They are located along the "Ring of Fire."
d. They do not have seasons.

11. Which of the following empires still existed following the armistice ending World War I?

a. The Austro-Hungarian Empire
b. The Ottoman Empire
c. The German Empire
d. The British Empire

12. A filibuster is used to delay a bill. Where can a filibuster take place?

a. The House of Representatives
b. The Senate
c. Committees
d. The Supreme Court

13. Which of the following exemplifies the multiplier effect of large cities?

a. The presence of specialized equipment for an industry attracts even more business.
b. The large population lowers the price of goods.
c. Public transportation means more people can commute to work.
d. A local newspaper can afford to give away the Sunday edition.

14. The Trail of Tears was:

a. The forced removal of British soldiers after the American Revolution
b. The forced evacuation of Cherokee peoples into Oklahoma
c. The forced evacuation of freed slaves from the South after the Civil War
d. The tears of Betsy Ross while she sewed the first American flag

15. Among the following, which is correct regarding some essential geography concepts?

a. An example of absolute location is urban vs. rural land prices.
b. Relative location equals the latitude and longitude of a place.
c. Product and land prices are affected by geographical distance.
d. Achievability relates to surface conditions and never changes.

16. Which type of chart is best at representing the cycle of demographic transition?

a. Pie chart
b. Political map
c. Line graph
d. Flow-line map

17. What is the main difference between a primary election and a caucus?

a. A primary election is privately run by political parties, and a caucus is held by local governments.
b. Caucuses are always held on the same day, but the dates of state primaries vary.
c. A caucus is privately run by political parties, and a primary is an indirect election run by state and local governments.
d. Primary elections are all held on the same date, but the dates of caucuses vary.

18. How are members of the Federal Judiciary chosen?

a. They are elected by voters.
b. They are appointed by the president and confirmed by the House of Representatives.
c. They are chosen by a committee.
d. They are appointed by the president and confirmed by the Senate.

19. Which of the following is most likely to benefit from inflation?

a. A bond investor who owns fixed-rate bonds
b. A retired widow with no income other than fixed Social Security payments
c. A person who has taken out a fixed-rate loan
d. A local bank who has loaned money out at fixed rate

20. After the Civil War, urban populations increased. This growth was likely due to:

a. An increased reliance on agriculture
b. The Industrial Revolution
c. Prohibition
d. Slavery persisting in some areas

21. Power divided between local and central branches of government is a definition of what term?

a. Bicameralism
b. Checks and balances
c. Legislative oversight
d. Federalism

22. During the decolonization of the Cold War years, which of the following events occurred chronologically latest?

a. The Eastern Bloc and Satellite states became independent from the Soviet Union.
b. Canada became totally independent from British Parliament via the Canada Act.
c. The Bahamas, in the Caribbean, became independent from the United Kingdom.
d. The Algerian War ended, and Algeria became independent from France.

23. **Which of the following conquistadores unwittingly gave smallpox to the indigenous peoples and destroyed the Aztec empire in Mexico?**
    a. Vasco Núñez de Balboa
    b. Juan Ponce de León
    c. Hernán Cortés
    d. Álvar Núñez Cabeza de Vaca

24. **During the early Medieval period in Europe, before the 5th century, where were the main centers of literacy found?**
    a. They were in the homes of the wealthy.
    b. They were in the churches and monasteries.
    c. They were in the local artisan and craft guilds.
    d. There were no centers of literacy.

25. **Which of the following soil types has the smallest grains?**
    a. Sand
    b. Silt
    c. Clay
    d. Loam

26. **Which of the following are the leading producers of petroleum in Latin America?**
    a. Argentina and Bolivia
    b. Mexico and Guatemala
    c. Brazil and Venezuela
    d. Columbia and Uruguay

27. **The presidential veto of legislation passed by Congress illustrates which principal in American government?**
    a. Checks and balances
    b. Federal regulation
    c. Freedom of speech
    d. Separation of church and state

28. **The Yellow River Valley began to emerge as a cultural center during the:**
    a. Shang Dynasty
    b. Neolithic Era
    c. Xia Dynasty
    d. Paleolithic Era

29. **Congressional elections are held every _____ years.**
    a. four
    b. two
    c. six
    d. three

30. **Which Italian Renaissance figure was best known as a political philosopher?**
    a. Dante Alighieri
    b. Leonardo Da Vinci
    c. Francesco Petrarca
    d. Niccolò Machiavelli

31. The first amendment guarantees all below except:

a.   Freedom of assembly
b.   The right to bear arms
c.   Freedom of the press
d.   The right to speak freely

32. What is true regarding survey findings about family differences among American socioeconomic and racial groups?

a.   Cultural and demographic factors influence disagreement styles more than parental stress does.
b.   Low-socioeconomic young children have no more development/behavior problems than others.
c.   Data have shown more violence in African-American families, followed by Latino and then white families.
d.   Socioeconomically disadvantaged children have more problems and receive more help for these.

33. The primary expense for most state and local governments is:

a.   Emergency medical services
b.   Transportation services
c.   Police and fire departments
d.   Education

34. Which of the following statements is NOT true about the Gilded Age in America?

a.   The Gilded Age was the era of the "robber barons" in the business world.
b.   The Gilded Age got its name from the excesses of the wealthy upper class.
c.   The Gilded Age had philanthropy Carnegie called the "Gospel of Wealth".
d.   The Gilded Age is a term whose origins have not been identified clearly.

35. On which type of map are different countries represented in different colors, with no two adjacent countries sharing a color?

a.   Physical map
b.   Political map
c.   Climate map
d.   Contour map

36. Of the following, which person or group was NOT instrumental in advancement of civil rights and desegregation during the 1940s and 1950s?

a.   The President
b.   The Supreme Court
c.   The Congress
d.   The NAACP

37. Which of the following is NOT a true statement regarding the Louisiana Purchase?

a.   Jefferson sent a delegation to Paris to endeavor to purchase only the city of New Orleans from Napoleon.
b.   Napoleon, anticipating US intrusions into Louisiana, offered to sell the US the entire Louisiana territory.
c.   The American delegation accepted Napoleon's offer, though they were only authorized to buy New Orleans.
d.   The Louisiana Purchase, once it was completed, increased the territory of the US by 50% overnight.

38. On a topographic map, an area where the contour lines are very close together indicates which of the following?

  a. A stream is present.
  b. The slope is very gentle.
  c. The slope is very steep.
  d. The area surrounds a depression.

39. All else being equal, which of the following locations is likely to have the coolest climate?

  a. A city located at 6,000 feet above sea level
  b. A city located at 500 feet above sea level
  c. A city that receives less than 10 inches of precipitation per year
  d. A city that receives more than 50 inches of precipitation per year

40. Which of the following is NOT one of the demographic variables?

  a. Fertility
  b. Diversity
  c. Mortality
  d. Migration

41. To be President of the United States, one must meet these three requirements:

  a. The President must be college educated, at least 30 years old, and a natural citizen.
  b. The President must be a natural citizen, have lived in the US for 14 years, and have a college education.
  c. The President must be a natural citizen, be at least 35 years old, and have lived in the US for 14 years.
  d. The President must be at least 30 years old, be a natural citizen, and have lived in the US for 14 years.

42. The Andes Mountain Range is located on which continent?

  a. North America
  b. South America
  c. Australia
  d. Asia

43. Guaranteed rights enumerated in the Declaration of Independence, possessed by all people, are referred to as:

  a. Universal rights
  b. Unalienable rights
  c. Voting rights
  d. Peoples' rights

44. Which entity in American government is the closest to direct democracy?

  a. The Electoral College
  b. The House of Representatives
  c. Committees within the Senate
  d. The Supreme Court

45. Who negotiates treaties?

  a. The President
  b. The House of Representatives
  c. Ambassadors
  d. The Senate

46. John Maynard Keynes advocated what?

a. Supply-side economics
b. Demand-side economics
c. Laissez faire economics
d. The Laffer Curve

47. As a form of government, what does oligarchy mean?

a. Rule by one
b. Rule by a few
c. Rule by law
d. Rule by many

48. The bubonic plague spread through Europe in which of the following ways?

a. It spread along rivers and through contaminated drinking water.
b. It was carried by birds that migrated south during the winter.
c. It spread along trade routes, carried by infected animals and people on ships.
d. It was carried by travelers on religious pilgrimages.

49. Which of the following is NOT correct regarding assumptions of mercantilism?

a. The money and the wealth of a nation are identical properties.
b. In order to prosper, a nation should try to increase its imports.
c. In order to prosper, a nation should try to increase its exports.
d. Economic protectionism by national governments is advisable.

50. The Supreme Court has nine members. How is this number determined?

a. It is outlined in the Constitution.
b. Congress determines the number.
c. The President determines the number.
d. The Court decides on the number.

51. Which of the following statements correctly describes totemism?

a. It is a Native American practice in which a totem pole is worshipped.
b. It is the Chinese practice of asking ancestors for guidance in daily life.
c. It is associated with the East Asian concept of filial piety.
d. It characterizes clans in which members believe they are all descendants of a common ancestor, often an animal.

52. Virginian _____ advocated a stronger central government and was influential at the Constitutional Convention.

a. Benjamin Franklin
b. James Madison
c. George Mason
d. Robert Yates

53. Which of the following statements is NOT true regarding English expansionism in the 16th century?

a. England's defeat of the Spanish Armada in 1588 brought a decisive end to their war with Spain.
b. King Henry VIII's desire to divorce Catherine of Aragon strengthened English expansionism.
c. Queen Elizabeth's support for the Protestant Reformation strengthened English expansionism.
d. Sir Francis Drake and other English sea captains plundered the goods that the Spaniards took from indigenous peoples.

54. Criminal cases are tried under:

I. State law
II. Federal law
III. Civil court

a. I and III
b. II only
c. I only
d. I and II

55. After completing a unit focused on the human characteristics of places and regions, a fourth-grade class will create an original settlement in a real or imagined region. Students will be asked to determine the population of the area, choose economic activities based on the natural physical characteristics of the region, decide on a political system, and establish a culture. This instructional activity is an example of which of the following assessment approaches?

a. Total participation activity
b. Formative assessment
c. Project-based summative assessment
d. Benchmark assessment

Science

1. Which of the following statements correctly compares rocks and minerals?

a. Minerals may contain traces of organic compounds, while rocks do not.
b. Rocks are classified by their formation and the minerals they contain, while minerals are classified by their chemical composition and physical properties.
c. Both rocks and minerals can be polymorphs.
d. Both rocks and minerals may contain mineraloids.

2. After a science laboratory exercise, some solutions remain unused and are left over. What should be done with these solutions?

a. Dispose of the solutions according to local disposal procedures.
b. Empty the solutions into the sink and rinse with warm water and soap.
c. Ensure the solutions are secured in closed containers and throw away.
d. Store the solutions in a secured, dry place for later use.

3. Which of the following situations would result in the generation of new crust?

a. Two crustal plates converge.
b. Two crustal plates move apart.
c. Two crustal plates slide past one another.
d. A crustal plate is pushed down into the mantle.

4. Which of the following sources of fresh water is unavailable for human use?

a. Rivers
b. Estuaries
c. Aquifers
d. Glaciers

5. Which of the following statements about heat transfer is NOT true?

a. As the energy of a system changes, its thermal energy must change or work must be done.
b. Heat transfer from a warmer object to a cooler object can occur spontaneously.
c. Heat transfer can never occur from a cooler object to a warmer object.
d. If two objects reach the same temperature, energy is no longer available for work.

6. A tapeworm lives within another organism and feeds off the nutrients that are ingested by that organism. At times, this can cause the organism to experience malnutrition or death. This is an example of what type of relationship?

a. Predator/prey
b. Symbiosis
c. Parasite/host
d. Producer/consumer

7. Which part of a flower collects pollen?

a. Style
b. Stigma
c. Petals
d. Sepals

8. How are organisms, such as snakes, cacti, and coyotes, able to survive in harsh desert conditions?

a. Over thousands of years, these organisms have developed adaptations to survive in arid climates.
b. These organisms migrate out of the desert during the summer months, only living in the desert for a portion of the year.
c. Snakes, cacti, and coyotes work together to find sources of food and water.
d. Snakes, cacti, and coyotes are all aquatic species that live in ponds and rivers during the hot day.

9. Which of the following diseases has been eradicated by immunization?

a. Polio
b. Mumps
c. Measles
d. Smallpox

10. What will happen to light waves as they hit a convex lens?

a. They will be refracted and converge.
b. They will be refracted and diverge.
c. They will be reflected and converge.
d. They will be reflected and diverge.

11. Which of the following is a source of nonrenewable energy?

a. Solar power
b. Wind power
c. Wood
d. Coal

12. Elements on the periodic table are arranged into groups and periods and ordered according to all of the following EXCEPT:

a. Atomic number
b. Refractive index
c. Reactivity
d. Number of protons

13. Which of the following is needed for an experiment to be considered successful?

  a. A reasonable hypothesis
  b. A well-written lab report
  c. Data that others can reproduce
  d. Computer-aided statistical analysis

14. Which of the following terms describes an intrusion of magma injected between two layers of sedimentary rock, forcing the overlying strata upward to create a dome-like form?

  a. Sill
  b. Dike
  c. Laccolith
  d. Caldera

15. The stream of charged particles that escape the Sun's gravitational pull is best described by which of the following terms?

  a. Solar wind
  b. Solar flare
  c. Solar radiation
  d. Sunspots

16. Scientists often form hypotheses based on particular observations. Which of the following is NOT true of a good hypothesis?

  a. A good hypothesis is complex.
  b. A good hypothesis is testable.
  c. A good hypothesis is logical.
  d. A good hypothesis predicts future events.

17. When an animal takes in more energy than it uses over an extended time, the extra chemical energy is stored as:

  a. Fat
  b. Starch
  c. Protein
  d. Enzymes

18. The most recently formed parts of the Earth's crust can be found at:

  a. Subduction zones
  b. Compressional boundaries
  c. Extensional boundaries
  d. Mid-ocean ridges

19. When two tectonic plates are moving laterally in opposing directions, this is called a(n):

  a. Transform boundary
  b. Compressional boundary
  c. Oppositional boundary
  d. Lateral boundary

20. A gas is held in a closed container and held at constant temperature. What is the effect of increasing the volume of the container by 3 times?

  a. The pressure is tripled.
  b. The pressure increases by one-third.
  c. The pressure decreases to one-third.
  d. The pressure remains constant.

21. The electrolysis of water is an example of which of the following?

   a.   An adiabatic process
   b.   A chemical change
   c.   A synthesis reaction
   d.   Reverse osmosis

22. Two species of finches are able to utilize the same food supply, but their beaks are different. They are able to coexist on an island because of:

   a.   Niche overlap
   b.   Character displacement
   c.   Resource partitioning
   d.   Realized niches

23. Where are the reproductive organs of a plant?

   a.   Style
   b.   Stigma
   c.   Flowers
   d.   Sepals

24. Which type of nuclear process features atomic nuclei splitting apart to form smaller nuclei?

   a.   Fission
   b.   Fusion
   c.   Decay
   d.   Ionization

25. Which of the following words is NOT connected to the process of mountain building?

   a.   Folding
   b.   Faulting
   c.   Transform
   d.   Convergent

26. Which of the following is considered a non-renewable resource?

   a.   Glass
   b.   Wood
   c.   Cattle
   d.   Soil

27. If an atom has a neutral charge, what must be true of the atom?

   a.   The nucleus contains only neutrons and no protons.
   b.   The atomic mass is equal to the number of neutrons.
   c.   The atomic number is equal to the number of neutrons.
   d.   The atomic number is equal to the number of electrons.

28. In a food chain, where does energy go after the secondary consumer dies?

   a.   Back to the Sun
   b.   To the producers
   c.   Into the air, becoming wind
   d.   To decomposers

29. What part of a plant system responds to stimuli by releasing water via transpiration, except during adverse conditions like a drought when it closes up to prevent the plant from dehydration?

   a. Pith
   b. Stomata
   c. Guard cells
   d. Sepals

30. Which of the following would not be used as evidence for evolution?

   a. Fossil record
   b. DNA sequences
   c. Anatomical structures
   d. Reproductive habits

31. Which of the following is an example of a trace fossil?

   a. A mouse jaw
   b. A footprint
   c. A shark tooth
   d. A cast of a skull

32. Which of the following is a serious direct impact of climate change?

   a. Soil erosion
   b. Deforestation
   c. Water pollution
   d. Increase in average sea level

33. Which of the following are formed when the plasma membrane surrounds a particle outside of the cell?

   a. Golgi bodies
   b. Rough endoplasmic reticulum
   c. Secretory vesicles
   d. Endocytic vesicles

34. Where is the type of RNA that carries and positions amino acids for further assembly located in the cell?

   a. Cytoplasm
   b. Nucleus
   c. Ribosome
   d. Mitochondria

35. What laboratory practice can increase the accuracy of a measurement?

   a. Repeating the measurement several times
   b. Calibrating the equipment each time you use it
   c. Using metric measuring devices
   d. Reading the laboratory instructions before the lab

36. What term is used to describe two waves that are out of phase as they come together to produce a new wave?

   a. Incomplete interference
   b. Distorted interference
   c. Constructive interference
   d. Destructive interference

Praxis Practice Test #1

37. In insects whose life cycles include an incomplete metamorphosis, which stage of the metamorphosis does not take place?

    a. The egg
    b. The larva
    c. The imago
    d. The pupa

38. Which of the following describes the physical or non-biological part of the carbon cycle?

    a. Phytoplankton use carbon dioxide and other nutrients to produce carbohydrates and oxygen.
    b. Cold water dissolves atmospheric carbon dioxide, stores it, and releases it back out to the atmosphere as needed.
    c. Carbon dioxide is dissolved in sea water and is broken up to free carbon for use by marine life.
    d. Warm, surface water dissolves carbon dioxide where it is converted to nitrogen and phosphorus for use by marine life.

39. Which of the following animal structures is NOT paired to its correct function?

    a. Muscle System – controls movement through three types of muscle tissue
    b. Nervous System – controls sensory responses by carrying impulses away from and toward the cell body
    c. Digestive System – breaks down food for absorption into the blood stream where it is delivered to cells for respiration
    d. Circulatory System – exchanges gases with the environment by delivering oxygen to the bloodstream and releasing carbon dioxide

40. What type of change occurs when a liquid transitions to a gas?

    a. A phase change
    b. A chemical change
    c. Sublimation
    d. Condensation

41. What is the scientific definition of work?

    a. The amount of energy used to accomplish a job
    b. The force used to move a mass over a distance
    c. The amount of energy used per unit of time
    d. Energy stored in an object due to its position

42. In which of the following scenarios is work NOT applied to the object?

    a. Mario moves a book from the floor to the top shelf.
    b. A book drops off the shelf and falls to the floor.
    c. Mario pushes a box of books across the room.
    d. Mario balances a book on his head.

43. According to Ohm's Law, how are voltage and current related in an electrical circuit?

    a. Voltage and current are inversely proportional to one another.
    b. Voltage and current are directly proportional to one another.
    c. Voltage acts to oppose the current along an electrical circuit.
    d. Voltage acts to decrease the current along an electrical circuit.

44. How does adding a solute to a liquid solvent affect the vapor pressure of the liquid?

a. The vapor pressure increases by an amount proportional to the amount of solute.
b. The vapor pressure increases by an amount proportional to the amount of solvent.
c. The vapor pressure decreases by an amount proportional to the amount of solute.
d. The amount of solute present in a liquid solvent does not have any effect on vapor pressure.

45. A man accidentally drops his wallet in a swimming pool. He can see his wallet at the bottom of the pool. He jumps in to retrieve it, but the wallet is not where it appeared to be. What is the reason for the optical illusion?

a. The reflection of sunlight off of the water disrupted his view.
b. Light is refracted as it enters the water, changing the wallet's apparent location.
c. The current at the bottom of the pool caused the wallet to move.
d. The heat from the Sun has impaired the man's vision.

46. Which of the following is the major way in which carbon is released into the environment?

a. Transpiration
b. Respiration
c. Fixation
d. Sedimentation

47. What causes the motion of glaciers?

a. Gravity
b. Erosion
c. Wind
d. Temperature change

48. How does the loss of biodiversity directly impact the environment and society?

a. Increase of access to raw materials
b. Increase of access to clean water
c. Decrease of food supply
d. Decrease of vulnerability to natural disasters

49. What is true about erosion on the surface of the Earth?

a. Erosion causes rock, dirt, and sand to be destroyed.
b. Erosion causes rock, dirt, and sand to change form and location.
c. Erosion occurs via mechanical processes, but not chemical ones.
d. Erosion breaks down rather than building up areas of the Earth.

50. What drives weather systems to move west to east in the mid-latitudes?

a. The prevailing westerlies
b. The prevailing easterlies
c. The trade winds
d. The doldrums

Answer Key and Explanations for Test #1

Teaching Reading

1. C: Word families are an effective strategy for teaching CVCe words. Once students have determined the sound made by the last three letters using knowledge of the silent *e* rule, they can identify other rhyming words within the same family by changing the first letter. This increases the number of words they can easily decode. Because these words have a silent letter that affects the vowel sound, covering parts of the word, chunking, and blending are not as effective.

2. B: In the Spanish language, the letter h is typically silent. Because the student is an ELL and the USA has many people—both immigrants and those born here—whose first and/or only language is Spanish, this is the first factor to consider among the choices. An articulation disorder (A) is possible, but the teacher should not assume this first with an ELL student. (An SLP evaluation can determine the difference.) While a hearing assessment (C) is always a good idea, if /h/ omission were due to hearing loss the student would likely omit or distort other unvoiced fricatives like /f/, /s/, /ʃ/, and /θ/. If the student had a breathing problem (D), other symptoms would occur in addition to not articulating /h/.

3. B: Inferring requires readers to use clues rather than explicit evidence to determine the author's meaning. Choice B requires students to use the character's statements to infer how he or she felt at the time. Choice A requires students to evaluate the writing. Choice C requires students to make a prediction. Choice D requires students to make a text-to-text connection.

4. C: Decoding, fluency, and comprehension are interrelated. The student is likely spending a lot of mental energy trying to decode unknown words, leaving little energy left to focus on comprehension. Additionally, repeatedly stopping to decode words interrupts fluency. This may cause the reader to struggle to make connections between the disjointed words and sentences. Implicit phonics instruction is not the best intervention option, as research has shown that systematic and explicit phonics instruction is most effective. Additionally, there is not enough information available to determine the cause of the student's decoding difficulties. Therefore, it cannot be assumed that it is related to a lack of phonological awareness skills or a language processing disorder.

5. A: Students develop literacy within multiple contexts by learning to listen to, speak, read, and write language. Therefore, it is inaccurate to say that only reading, writing, and listening (B) are activities for developing literacy. Literacy development is not confined to reading and writing (C) as some non-educators may believe. Some may even have the mistaken impression that reading is the only activity important for literacy development (D). However, literacy develops through all activities using language.

6. B: Strategizing in order to understand the meaning of a word, knowing multiple meanings of a single word, and applying background knowledge to glean a word's meaning are all ways in which an effective reader enhances vocabulary. Other skills include an awareness of word parts and word origins, the ability to apply word meanings in a variety of content areas, and a delight in learning the meanings of unfamiliar words.

7. B: Explicit phonics instruction uses a part-to-whole approach. Mr. Clark's students first learn the *st* blend in isolation before applying it to whole words. Implicit phonics instruction, also referred to as whole language or analytical phonics, uses a whole-to-part approach. Students recognize whole words by sight before breaking them down into individual phonemes.

8. D: Teachers should instruct children in the stages of composition at the same time they are developing skills for forming letters (A), spelling words (B), and generating sentences (C) rather than waiting until after they have developed them. The multifaceted approach allows for more practice in all skills and can help reduce overloading instruction into just one element of language development.

299

9. A: The type or pattern of error most damaging to reading proficiency is substituting words with similar appearances or spelling but completely different meanings, because this shows a lack of reading for meaning. Substituting synonyms (B) shows some comprehension of word meaning. Substituting like parts of speech (C) shows some comprehension of grammar and syntax. Substituting correct words or closer approximations for errors based on information from the sentence context (D) shows skills in both reading for meaning and self-correction.

10. C: Choice C is correct, since the verbs mentioned in the question all refer to interpreting information in one's own words—which involves the cognitive objective of comprehension. Tasks targeting knowledge recall (A) would ask students to name, label, list, define, repeat, memorize, order, or arrange material. Tasks targeting application (B) would ask students to calculate, solve, practice, operate, sketch, use, prepare, illustrate, or apply material. Tasks targeting evaluation (D) would ask students to judge, appraise, evaluate, conclude, predict, score, or compare material.

11. A: Progress monitoring is a type of assessment used to track students' progress towards certain goals over time. When students are receiving reading interventions, frequent progress monitoring should be done to assess their progress and determine if the interventions are succeeding. Screening is done initially to determine if students are at risk for academic difficulties, and it is done at greater intervals, such as the start of each school year. Summative assessment occurs at the end of a unit of study or other larger unit of instruction. Norm-referenced tests compare students' performances to the performances of sample groups of similar students, while progress monitoring is done to assess students' progress towards their own personal goals.

12. A: News articles published on the internet are more formal in their content and language than blogs (B), which are written from a more personal, less journalistic perspective. News articles are also more formal than emails (C), which can be even more casual than blogs as they involve communications between individuals rather than writing intended for larger audiences like blogs and news articles. Hence, these are not all the same in formality level (D).

13. C: It is normal for students to reverse letters and numbers occasionally not only in 1st grade but through the end of 2nd grade. Thus, they do not indicate possible dyslexia (B) at this age. The words cited are above 1st-grade spelling level, particularly so early in the school year, so misspelling them is normal, should not be marked incorrect, and does not require intervention (D). Also, teachers should not deduct points for misspelling in written compositions unless the misspelled words are included in weekly class spelling lists. First-graders are frequently in transitional phases of writing when phonetic spelling is not only common but desirable. The student's writing is developmentally appropriate; the substitute's grading is inappropriate. Hence choice A is incorrect.

14. C: When reading independently, students are at the correct level if they read with at least 97% accuracy.

15. A: According to Vygotsky, activities in the zone of proximal development are ones that students are almost able to complete independently, but they require some scaffolding. The activities are not too easy or too difficult, but just challenging enough to allow some growth to occur. Reading books at the instructional level with teacher guidance is an example of an activity in the zone of proximal development. Choices B and D represent activities that are easy for the student. Choice C demonstrates a way to make a text accessible for a student when it is too difficult for the student to read independently.

16. A: Story action can be analyzed in terms of rising action, story climax, falling action, and resolution. Rising action consists of those events that occur before and lead up to the story's most dramatic moment, or climax. The climax occurs toward the end of the book, but rarely, if ever, right at the end. Following the climax, the consequences of that dramatic moment are termed "falling action." The story reaches resolution with the outcome of the falling action.

17. A: At the beginning of the school year, second-grade students should be able to read 50–80 words per minute. By the time they are well into the school year, second-grade level reading is tracked at 85 words per minute.

18. D: To allow Joshua more time and energy to focus on his essay, he can record only key words and phrases in his notes rather than writing complete sentences. This will also make it easier for him to locate the key information in his notes when he is ready to add it to his essay. Grouping notes into categories and using visuals can be beneficial, but based on Joshua's notes, recording the key words and phrases is the most pressing need. Recording only a few facts may not provide enough information to complete an entire three-paragraph essay, so it would be more helpful to record additional facts in a more concise manner.

19. A: Emergent readers are those who are not yet reading fluently (with appropriate speed and accuracy). Choice B refers to the practice of reviewing relationships between letters and sounds, which is vital to building reading skills. Choice C would help students build vocabulary retention by requiring them to find unfamiliar words in the dictionary. This practice causes the student to analyze and retain spelling of unfamiliar words, as well as reinforces dictionary/reference skills. Choice D addresses the fact that many words in the English language are irregularly spelled and cannot be decoded with conventional phonetic instruction. While invented spelling described in Choice A may be permitted in emergent readers, this practice is not likely to build specific reading skills.

20. C: Oral language skills can be distinguished from specific speech characteristics exhibited by some children. Many students like Rosa, whose first language is not English, will speak with an accent and may be less clear when speaking about a topic that is unfamiliar. In fact, even those who are not English Language Learners may exhibit difficulty speaking on new topics. Greer may avoid oral assignments or speaking in class for a number of reasons, such as self-consciousness. This student could be helped by evaluating oral language skills in a one-on-one environment or by introducing peer scaffolding to help reduce anxiety. Brett's demeanor in group assignments may also be due to social characteristics rather than oral skills; it would be important to evaluate his skills in various contexts. Ashley, however, shows marked problems communicating orally both in class discussion and in prepared assignments. She would benefit from specific instruction related to presenting ideas orally.

21. B: Because Elizabeth will be including facts about all stages of Helen Keller's life, as well as how she learned to communicate over time, a time-order, or chronological, text structure is the best fit. Time-order text structures tell the key points about the topic in sequential order. The other options could be used to share information about her life, but they would not be as logical of a fit for this type of biographical report, as they may weave back and forth between different time periods to show relationships between events.

22. A: Prefixes and suffixes are important for reading comprehension because they change the meanings of the root word to which they are attached. A student who understands that *un* means "not" will be able to decipher the meanings of words such as *unwanted, unhappy,* or *unreasonable.*

23. D: Scaffolding occurs when teachers provide assistance to help students accomplish tasks that they are almost able to complete independently. In this example, the teacher introduces words that may be challenging to students to enable them to read the text independently. Choice A does not specify what role, if any, the teacher will play in assisting students with the building challenge, so no scaffolding is demonstrated. In choice B, the teacher is reading a book that is too difficult for students to read independently, meaning the task is out of students' zone of proximal development. Choice C represents an independent activity that students complete without any assistance.

24. C: Orthographic processing refers to recognizing letter patterns that make up words or word parts. For example, a student may see the word *sight* and immediately recognize the *ight* pattern. The ability to separate spoken words into component sounds is a part of phonological awareness. Alphabetic principle is the understanding that each letter makes a predictable sound. Receptive language involves understanding spoken words.

25. C: Expository essays are any type of essay in which the writer is providing meaningful information about a topic for the purpose of informing. Most of the topics listed in the example include informational tasks, explaining the process of doing something, such as baking or juggling. Expository essays can use various organizational schemes to help structure the information, such as by comparing and contrasting two things. An expository essay is different from an argumentative essay in that it is not trying to convince the reader of anything, but only trying to inform. Similarly, the purpose of a descriptive essay is to show detail, but not necessarily to inform about how something works.

26. A: The process of actively constructing meaning from reading is interactive, in that it involves the text itself, the person reading it, and the setting in which the reading is done. These three elements influence each other, and this is the concept indicated by the term *interactive* in the question, so choice A is correct. Choice B is a better definition of the *strategic* aspect of the process. Choices C and D are better definitions of the *adaptable* aspect of the process.

27. A: The next three stages are scripting the end-sound to a word (KT=cat), leaving space between words, and writing from the top left to the top right of the page and from top to bottom. Each of these steps is progressively more abstract. Scripting the end-sound to a word helps a young writer recognize that words have beginnings and endings. This naturally leads to the willingness to separate words with white space so that they stand as individual entities. Once this step is reached, the child realizes that in English, writing progresses from left to right and from the top of the page to the bottom.

28. D: The teacher should encourage all students to "read" picture books from the first day of school. Talking about the pictures from page to page gives young readers the idea that books are arranged sequentially. Pictures also offer narrative coherence and contextual clues. Emergent readers who are encouraged to enjoy books will more readily embrace the act of reading. Holding a book and turning pages gives young readers a familiarity with them.

29. D: Decoding unfamiliar words when reading primarily involves understanding the structure, meaning, and the relationship between letters and sounds. Syntactic (e.g. syntax) refers to word order and sentence structure, which is necessary to interpret the meaning of phrases in context. Semantics refers to word meaning and has a very direct role in decoding meaning when encountering word roots. Graphophonic refers to written words and how the written form corresponds to the oral form of a word. To adequately read and recognize unfamiliar words, a reader needs to be able to sound out and possible recognize patterns that they have encountered elsewhere. With each of these systems activated, readers are able to succeed when encountering many unfamiliar words. However, the pragmatic domain, which deals with the use of language in social contexts and the rules for effective communication, does not directly contribute to the process of decoding written words.

30. D: Charlie did not acknowledge any errors, but instead kept reading after each one. Proficient readers recognize when something does not look right, sound right, or make sense, and they try again until they find the correct words. The teacher can prompt Charlie to stop and question himself when he makes errors until he begins recognizing and self-correcting them on his own. Because Charlie's errors both make sense and sound right in the sentences, he is already using both semantic and syntactic cues. The student only omitted one minor word, which did not change the meaning of the sentence.

31. B: Readers rely on prior knowledge and existing schemata to make sense of newly encountered texts. Therefore, texts that are more closely related to students' existing cultural schemata are more easily comprehended. To increase the likelihood of comprehension, the teacher should provide the student with background information on Thanksgiving before reading the book. Relating it to familiar traditions will also assist with activating the student's prior knowledge. Choice A does not provide any scaffolding to the student

302

to assist with comprehension. Choice C offers some scaffolding in the form of a written outline, but it is less likely to be effective than an interactive discussion about the topic and the connection to the student's own cultural traditions. Choice D waits until after the book is read to offer additional information, even though it would be more beneficial to introduce the topic before reading.

32. C: Because this student loves reading graphic novels and has both talent and enjoyment in drawing, having him create his own graphic novels is a good way to motivate him to write by using his visual style, ability, and interest to access writing activity. Giving audio recordings (A) to a highly visual student is not as appropriate to his strengths and interests. Letting him substitute drawing pictures for all writing assignments (B) would address his strengths and interests but not his needs for learning to write. Having him watch animated videos about writing (D) would suit his visual learning style but would not give him the actual writing practice he needs.

33. C: Graphophonic cues are based on the speech sounds in words and their alphabetic representations in print, so choice C is correct. Syntactic cues (A) are based on how words are arranged and ordered to create meaningful phrases, clauses and sentences. Semantic cues (B) are based on the meanings of morphemes and words and how they combine to create additional meanings. Pragmatic cues (D) are based on the readers' purposes for reading and their understanding of how textual structures function in the texts that they read.

34. A: The teacher should give each child a piece of drawing paper that has been folded in half and then in half again, creating four boxes, along with a piece that has not been folded. The teacher should then ask the students to draw a cartoon about the story. Each of the first four boxes will show the events in order. The second page is to show how the story ends. When a child is able to visually see the way a familiar story has unfolded, that child can find causal or thematic connections in the action that increases her comprehension of the story overall. Asking the class to draw a single picture or to draw the beginning and end doesn't sufficiently demonstrate the importance of order to meaning. While some first-graders may be able to create their own cartoon stories that demonstrate a logical series of events, many first-graders are not yet ready to organize thought into a linear progression.

35. A: Homophones. Homophones are a type of homonym that sound alike but are spelled differently and have different meanings. Other examples are *two*, *to*, and *too* and *their*, *they're*, and *there*.

36. C: Silent reading fluency can be monitored over time by giving the Test of Silent Contextual Reading Fluency (TSCRF) four times a year. A similar assessment tool is the Test of Silent Word Reading Fluency (TOSWRF), in which words of increasing complexity are given as a single, undifferentiated, and unpunctuated strand. As with the TSCRF, three minutes are given for the student to separate each word from the next. *Itwillcannotschoolbecomeagendaconsistentphilosophysuperfluous* is an example of such a strand.

37. A: Proficiency with oral language enhances students' phonemic awareness and increases vocabulary. Understanding that words are scripted with specific letters representing specific sounds is essential to decoding a text. Students cannot effectively learn to read without the ability to decode. An enhanced vocabulary supports the act of reading; the larger an emergent reader's vocabulary, the more quickly he will learn to read. He will be able to decode more words, which he can organize into word families and use to decode unfamiliar words.

38. A: A test is valid if it measures what it is designed to measure. If a test claims to measure a student's ability to make inferences, then the questions on the test should require students to use this skill. Reliability refers to ensuring that there is consistency in test results over time and between participants. Bias refers to ensuring that the test does not put any participants at a disadvantage. Objectivity refers to ensuring that all tests are scored in the same manner without being affected by any outside influences or bias.

39. D: Mixing longer, more complex sentences in with shorter, more direct ones is the ideal way of writing for a general audience. If all sentences are short, the reader will quickly be bored, and will also find reading the piece unpleasant. If all sentences are long, the reader will lose focus and often have to go back and reread things again. Mixing up sentences by length and complexity avoids these extremes, and keeps the reader engaged and focused.

40. B: Previewing and reviewing are skills that assist in learning detailed or large amounts of information. Using these concepts, students learn skills such as skimming and outlining to get an idea of what the text is about before actually reading it. After reading, the students learn to review the information they learned and compare it to their initial previews. This method is particularly helpful when individuals are reading in order to learn new information, as they would be when reading their science texts.

41. D: Text structure refers to how a text is organized. Different text structures are used depending on the purpose for writing, and cause/effect, compare/contrast, and time-order text structures are all commonly used in nonfiction texts. Literary devices are techniques authors use in their writing to set a certain mood, emphasize a point, convey a description, or more. Literary elements refer to parts of texts, such as characters, setting, plot, conflict, and resolution. Genres refer to specific categories of texts, such as fantasies.

42. D: While all of these options can assist students with learning letter formation, writing letters in shaving cream best represents a multisensory approach. It involves movement, touch, and sight.

43. B: Semantics is the branch of linguistics that deals with meaning. The semantic system in language includes all aspects of language use that carries meaning. Semantics include words, phrases, sentences, and further contexts that help to convey meaning. Semantics are involved in both receptive and expressive language processes. Choice A is incorrect because the graphophonic system is largely related to the sounds of a language and their written representations. Graphophonics study the relationship between phonics and orthography (writing system). Choice C is incorrect because the syntactic system refers primarily to sentence structure, word order, and other elements of grammar. Syntax does impact meaning, but in a more indirect way than semantics. Choice D is incorrect because pragmatics refers to practical application of language in a variety of contexts. For example, pragmatics is interested in language shifts between social and academic contexts. In reading, this involves being aware of how writers use language to convey moods and draw out more subtle implications.

44. B: This is an example of a closed question because the student can only answer "simile" or "metaphor" without needing to elaborate unless asked to explain the answer. In contrast, choice C is an open-ended question because the student must both define simile and metaphor and explain the difference between them. Choice A is an open-ended literature question because the student cannot answer with yes, no, or some other single word or short phrase; he or she has to describe the action or events in a story that represent its climax, which requires understanding story structure, story elements, knowing the definition of a story's climax, reading the story, and understanding it. Choice D is a very open-ended question, as students have considerable latitude in giving the reasons each of them perceives for having poetry.

45. D: When students ask themselves how the information in a text they are reading fits with what they already know, they are relating the text to their own prior knowledge, which increases their reading comprehension. Students should not only ask themselves what kinds of "expert questions" fit the subject matter of the text (A)—e.g., classification, physical, and chemical properties are typical question topics in science; genre, character, plot, and theme are typical of literature questions; sequence, cause-and-effect, and comparison-contrast questions are typical of history—but also what questions the material brings up for them personally (B). It is necessary and important for students to ask themselves continually how each text portion relates to its chapter's main ideas (C) as they read to optimize their reading comprehension and retention.

46. A: It is important to evaluate specific reading skills, such as phonemic awareness, in a variety of contexts. Reading aloud with Abi allowed his teacher to notice that he consistently misread words beginning with digraphs. Digraphs are sounds in which two distinct letters, when combined, produce a single third sound (e.g., when s and h produce the -sh sound). Blends are words in which two letters produce a third sound which is a combination of both sounds put together (e.g., *b* and *l* combined to make *b*). The only set of words consisting only of digraphs is choice A.

47. D: Character maps, fact and opinion charts, 5Ws charts, and webs are all examples of graphic organizers, which are used to help students organize and visualize information, concepts, and relationships. Literary elements are components of fictional stories, such as characters and settings. Genres are categories of texts, such as biographies and fairy tales. Text features are parts of nonfiction texts, such as headings and graphics, that are used to organize the text and provide additional information.

48. D: Targeted instruction is achieved by assessing areas needing improvement as well as areas of greatest strength for each student, and adjusting instruction to target those areas. This helps to ensure that all members of a class are receiving instruction tailored to their specific needs.

49. B: Students should always target an audience, perform an audience analysis, and develop an audience profile to determine what they should include in or omit from their writing. Even though the assigning teacher may be the only one to read the writing, students still need to identify an audience (A) and should not write as if the teacher is the main audience (D). In addition to knowing their purpose for writing before beginning, students should also consider what purpose their writing will meet for their readers (C) and how it is likely to be used.

50. D: Multisyllabic words often contain smaller parts that students recognize, such as prefixes, roots, and suffixes. Identifying these known parts can help students figure out the words. Context clues can help students guess words that make sense, but students should be able to apply word analysis skills to cross check their guesses and ensure they are selecting the correct words. Stretching out the sounds and blending the phonemes are helpful strategies for decoding shorter words with predictable spelling patterns. However, these strategies are less reliable for decoding multisyllabic words with more complex spelling patterns.

51. D: The concept in question is known as language transfer, also known as L1 interference, in which language features from the first language affects the acquisition of a second language. This is particularly noteworthy in language features that exist in one language, but not in the other. For instance, in English, plural nouns are usually marked by adding -*s* to the end of the word, whereas Chinese does not make use of a plural indicator. This grammatical feature, therefore, is commonly difficult to accurately acquire. Regarding the options in the question, the Chinese written language is ideographic rather than alphabetic (A)—that is, its written symbols represent concepts visually rather than being letters representing speech sounds. Also, the fact that Spanish is much more phonetically regular than English (B) (i.e., many more words are pronounced the same way as they are spelled than in English) contributes different effects to ELL students' English-language literacy development. Therefore, choice C is incorrect.

52. A: Phonological awareness refers to an understanding of the sounds a word makes. While phonological awareness leads to fluent reading skills, activities designed to develop an awareness of word sounds are, by definition, oral.

53. D: It is impossible to include every text desired into the language curriculum—there are simply too many good books, stories, poems, speeches, and media available. Teachers must first think about what skills their students need to acquire, as well as what skills they have already mastered. In designing activities for class, a good teacher will start first with the purpose for instruction. For example, purposes of reading can include: reading for information, reading for enjoyment, understanding a message, identifying main or supporting ideas, or developing an appreciation for artistic expression/perception. Once the purpose or intended learning outcome has been identified, the teacher will have a much better idea of which texts, strategies, and activities will support that purpose.

54. C: The most effective lesson would be brainstorming a list of verbs that mean ways of talking or ways of going, then adding them to the word wall along with some nouns that specify common topics. Second graders aren't developmentally ready for a thesaurus; most will believe that any words in a particular list are interchangeable. For example, a student who wrote *my little sister walks like a baby* might find the verbs *strut, sidle,* and *amble* in the thesaurus. None of these verbs would be an appropriate substitution. Supplementing a noun with an adjective often results in flat writing: *There's a tree in my yard* might become *There's a nice tree in my big yard.* Adjectives such as *pretty, fun, cute, funny,* and so forth don't add much in terms of meaning, but they are the adjectives younger writers reach for first. A more specific noun is both more meaningful and more interesting. *There's a weeping willow in my yard* is evocative.

55. D: Young children use language in a solely oral way. Oral language is composed of separate sounds that are represented in written form by the alphabet. In order to read, a child must first have a sense of the sounds that are used in English (phonological awareness). By helping children hear the difference between rhyming and non-rhyming words, the teacher is preparing them to make the transition to sound–letter association and word families.

56. B: The word *chain* contains a common consonant digraph, *ch*; and two vowels together, *ai*, which make the /ā/ sound. Recognizing these patterns will make the word easy to sound out. In choice A, the two vowels in *tear* do not make the /ē/ sound, as would likely be expected. The sound produced by *ain* in *curtain* makes it more difficult for a first grader to sound out, as does the sound of the *c* in *ocean*.

57. A: In the language experience approach, students decide on a story they want to tell and dictate it to a teacher, who writes the words down on paper. The teacher then reads the story back multiple times, modeling appropriate fluency. Students are then invited to join in reading the story. In writing workshop, students work on independent writing pieces following the stages of the writing process. They may all be involved in different stages at different times. Trait-based writing teaches students to consider the traits of good writing, such as word choice, throughout the writing process. During modeled writing, teachers think aloud as they record their thoughts on paper or on the board.

58. B: The student's responses include random strings of letters that do not correlate with the sounds in the spoken words. Additionally, she has represented the /c/ sound at the beginning of each word differently in her responses. Understanding that letters make predictable sounds is part of the alphabetic principle. Her three-letter responses indicate that she has some phonological awareness skills. She knows there are three sounds in each word, but she is not aware of which letters are used to represent each sound. Teaching phonics generalizations will be more helpful after the student has developed an awareness of the alphabetic principle and consistently matches letters to their sounds.

59. B: A syllable is a unit of pronunciation with one uninterrupted sound. Students can be taught to clap or tap to determine the number of syllables in a word. *Relentless* has three syllables: *re-lent-less*. Choice A has one syllable, choice C has two syllables, and choice D has four syllables.

60. D: The word *maple* begins with an open syllable, spelled *ma*. Open syllables end with a vowel and usually have a long vowel sound. Knowing this will help the student decode this word and other words with open syllables. This word does not contain any vowel digraph pairs, r-controlled vowels, or closed syllables. Vowel digraph pairs consist of two vowels that together make one sound. R-controlled vowels consist of a vowel before the letter *r*. Closed syllables end with a consonant and usually have a short vowel sound.

61. A: Alphabet books, wordless picture books, and easy-to-read books all promote skills important for children beginning to become readers. The other genres are more suitable for older children with well-developed reading skills.

62. A: The words in this question prompt are most often used to refer to *sounds* made while reading. Initial/onset, medial, and final sounds are decoded in the beginning, middle, and end of words. When a teacher needs to assess an emergent or struggling reader's ability to differentiate between sounds in words, he or she may use a phonological awareness assessment. This tool will provide the teacher with information about the student's current ability to decode or encode words.

63. A: Alphabetic principle is the understanding that each letter of the alphabet makes a predictable sound. Students are practicing this by repeating the letter name and sound each week. Concepts of print are conventions used to convey meaning in text. Examples include knowing how to hold a book and track text correctly. Phonological awareness is the ability to identify and manipulate sounds in words. It does not involve letter/sound relationships. Automaticity refers to the ability to recognize whole words quickly and effortlessly.

64. D: When readers visualize, they use the clues and details in the stories to form mental pictures in their minds. When students draw a setting based on how they imagined it from the description in the story, they are visualizing. Predicting refers to making guesses about the text before reading. Inferring refers to using clues in the story to determine the meaning when it is not explicitly stated. Summarizing refers to retelling the main events of the story.

65. A: Cooperative learning occurs when a group of students at various levels of reading ability have goals in common. Reading comprehension is achieved through reading both orally and silently, developing vocabulary, a reader's ability to predict what will occur in a piece of writing, a reader's ability to summarize the main points in a piece of writing, and a reader's ability to reflect on the text's meaning and connect that meaning to another text or personal experience.

66. B: Typically, guided practice follows modeling. Independent practice and application would then follow the guided practice, and generalization would come last. Feedback should be provided throughout multiple levels of instruction, particularly during the practice phases.

67. D: None; irregular sight words cannot generally be decoded. Readers must learn to recognize these as whole words on sight. They either have irregular spelling or do not follow typical phonic patterns, so an attempt at decoding may ultimately mislead the reader. Segmenting them into syllables or using a phonemic approach are ineffective strategies to aid a reader in recognizing a sight word because these approaches depend on rules a sight word doesn't follow. Word families group words that share common patterns of consonants and vowels. The spelling of those words is, therefore, regular because they follow a predictable pattern. Sight words that are irregular, do not follow a predictable pattern, and must be instantaneously recognized for writing fluency. Decoding is not useful.

68. B: Although the illustrations themselves are visual images, using the information available from them to inform reading is not using a visual cue (A). Word appearance and length, familiar-looking phrases, and word-initial letters or phonemes—i.e., visual aspects of the verbal text itself—are examples of visual cues. Because the student uses information from illustrations, he or she uses a meaning cue (B). A structural cue (C) would involve using knowledge of syntax (sentence structure) to inform correct reading. A graphophonic cue (D) would involve using knowledge of sound-to-letter correspondences.

69. D: When completing a running record, a teacher records the number of words the student reads correctly out of the total number of words in the text. This is used to calculate the accuracy rate, which helps to determine if the text is at the student's frustration, instructional, or independent reading level. Authentic assessment tasks provide opportunities for students to complete reading and writing activities while solving real-world problems rather than opportunities to calculate the accuracy rate when reading a text. Rubrics are used to evaluate students' performances based on multiple criteria on assignments and assessments, but they are not used to calculate accuracy rate, either. Guided reading observations may help the teacher determine if a text is much too easy or much too difficult for a student to read independently, but without the running record, the exact accuracy rate cannot be determined.

70. A: Individuals with dysgraphia have difficulty with the physical act of writing. They find holding and manipulating a pencil problematic. Their letters are primitively formed, and their handwriting is illegible.

71. B: Revision (literally, *re+vision*) is the act of "seeing again." When revising, writers examine what they have written in order to improve the meaning of the work. Fine-tuning word choices, moving information to another location, and adding or deleting words are all acts of revision.

307

72. D: A glossary contains an alphabetized list of important vocabulary words found in a text, along with their meanings. It is similar to a dictionary. It would be the most helpful text feature for a student to use to determine the meanings of the content-related vocabulary words in the text. The table of contents helps the reader identify which pages contain which topics in the text. Headings help the reader determine the main idea of each section of the text. The index is an alphabetized list of topics in the text, along with the page numbers on which they can be found.

73. C: Each answer can be an effective tool in teaching students to build oral language skills. The question makes clear that the objective is to help students evaluate their own oral language skills, which will assist them in both spoken and written assignments. The only answer choice that involves the students evaluating their own message is choice C. When the students prepare a review/quiz based upon important information, they will be more able to speak specifically to that information. When classmates complete the review, each student can identify any patterns in the questions' answers that give clues as to how well those main ideas were communicated. In this way, the student can evaluate how effective the oral presentation was, without relying on classmates or the teacher.

74. D: Round-robin reading is a common practice in language arts classes and has been for many years. In this process, students take turns reading aloud for their peers. Other students are asked to follow along silently in their texts while a peer is reading. This strategy does provide a way for students to read texts in class and include as many students as possible, which is often the intended outcome. However, this process often creates a boring atmosphere, since only one student at a time is actively engaged. While that student is reading, other students may become distracted by their own thoughts, other school work, or off-task interaction with each other. All of these issues subvert the intended outcome of the process. There is rarely enough time for each student to practice reading aloud to build students' reading fluency or comprehension in significant ways.

75. C: She should locate the vowels, then locate familiar word parts. Syllables are organized around vowels. In order to determine the syllables, this student should begin by locating the vowels. It's possible to have a syllable that is a single vowel (*a/gain*). It isn't possible to have a syllable that is a single consonant. Once the word has been broken into its component syllables the reader is able to study the syllables to find ones that are familiar and might give her a clue as to the word's meaning, such as certain prefixes or suffixes.

76. A: Multiple research studies have found that teaching phonological awareness skills to kindergarteners with delayed language development has enhanced their language development. Researchers also recommend involving speech-language pathologists (SLPs) and their instructional methods as effective in teaching phonological awareness skills (B). Phonological awareness involves being able to recognize and change phonemes (speech sounds) without any reference to meanings (C) of words, syllables, or morphological units. Researchers and others instructing kindergarteners in phonological awareness skills have provided training at both the individual phoneme level (identifying and differentiating phonemes, matching initial and final phonemes, deleting phonemes, blending phonemes, etc.) and above (D) the phoneme level (syllable, word, and rhyme awareness).

77. D: This description matches that of a typical peer review, so choice D is correct. In a peer review, writers read a peer's paper and then identify values in it, describe it, ask questions about it, and suggest points for revision. These types of feedback have been identified by experts as helpful for writing. Choices A and C are incorrect because these types of reviews are not typically collaborative. For a portfolio assessment (A), the teacher collects finished work products from a student over time, eventually assembling a portfolio of work. Holistic scoring (C) is a method of scoring a piece of writing for overall quality (evaluating general elements such as focus, organization, support, and conventions) rather than being overly concerned with any individual aspect of writing. While a writing workshop (B) may be collaborative, it may or may not include a peer review session, and the main motivation for attending a writing workshop is generally not for the peer feedback but for professional guidance, as from a coach or editor, and to build a professional network.

78. C: Using context clues can help the reader determine the meanings of many unknown words quickly and also contribute to reading comprehension. Asking a classmate for the meanings of words may work in the short term, but it does not help the reader develop independent reading strategies, and there may not always be another person present while reading. Looking up the unknown words later may result in the student missing words that are critical to the meaning of the text, negatively affecting comprehension. Similarly, while skipping over the unknown words may result in sentences that appear to make sense, the missing words may play important roles in the meaning.

79. C: Decoding monosyllabic words by referring to the initial and final consonant, short vowel, and long vowel sounds represented by their letters is a common academic standard for 1st-grade students. Typical academic standards for kindergarten students include demonstrating knowledge of letter-sound correspondences; understanding the alphabetic principle; matching letters to their corresponding consonant (and short vowel) sounds; and reading simple, monosyllabic sight words, i.e., high-frequency words.

80. B: Students are analyzing the structure of the word by identifying the prefix, root, and suffix. Miscue analysis refers to analyzing reading errors to determine patterns in the strategies that students are using. Syllabification refers to breaking words into syllables. Because the suffix -*ible* has two syllables, and students are focusing on the meanings of the word parts, they are not focused on syllabification. Decoding is the process of translating graphemes into phonemes, or letters into sounds. In this example, students are focusing on identifying the word parts and their meanings rather than on simply decoding and reading the word.

Mathematics

1. D: The point $(5, -5)$ lies on the line segment that has a slope of -2 and passes through $(3, -1)$. If $(5, -5)$ is one of the endpoints of the line segment, then the other would be $(1, 3)$.

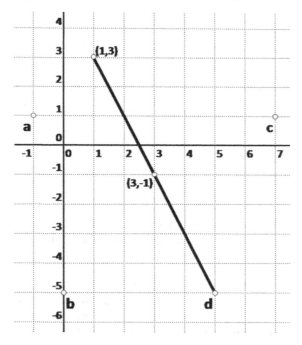

2. B: The place value is assigned by the position of the digit. The places to the left of the decimal are ones, tens, hundreds, then thousands, respectively. Since the digit 7 is in the third place to the left of the implied decimal, it's in the hundreds place. The value of this digit is 7×100, which is 700.

3. C. The original price may be modeled by the equation:

$$(x - 0.45x) + 0.0875(x - 0.45x) = \$39.95$$

This simplifies to $0.598125x = \$39.95$. Dividing each side of the equation by the coefficient of x gives $x \approx$ $66.79.

4. B: Notice that $x = 1$ results in a zero in the denominator, so choice C cannot be correct since $x \neq 1$. To solve, subtract $\frac{2}{x-1}$ from both sides, then cross-multiply.

$\dfrac{x-2}{x-1} = \dfrac{x-1}{x+1} + \dfrac{2}{x-1}$	Write out the original equation.
$\dfrac{x-4}{x-1} = \dfrac{x-1}{x+1}$	Subtract $\dfrac{2}{x-1}$ from both sides.
$(x+1)(x-4) = (x-1)(x-1)$	Cross multiply.
$x^2 - 3x - 4 = x^2 - 2x + 1$	Multiply the binomials on both sides.
$-3x - 4 = -2x + 1$	Subtract x^2 from both sides.
$-4 = x + 1$	Add $3x$ to both sides.
$-5 = x$	Subtract 1 from both sides.

5. C: There are 36 months in 3 years. Since Amy saves \$450 every 3 months, the following proportion can be written to find the amount she saves in 36 months: $\frac{450}{3} = \frac{x}{36}$. Cross multiplying gives you the equation $3x = 16{,}200$, which can be solved for x. Dividing both sides of the equation by 3 gives $x = 5{,}400$.

6. C: The repeating decimal may be converted to a fraction by writing:

$$10x = 8.\overline{8}$$
$$-\quad x = 0.\overline{8}$$

which simplifies as $10x - x = 8.\overline{8} - 0.\overline{8}$, or $9x = 8$.

7. D: The Pythagorean theorem may be used to find the diagonal distance from the top of his head to the base of the shadow. Using the following equation, we can determine this distance, c: $5.8^2 + 6.2^2 = c^2$. Thus, $c \approx 8.5$. The distance is approximately 8.5 ft.

8. C: Triangles can be classified as scalene, isosceles, or equilateral. Scalene triangles have no equal side measurements and no equal angle measurements. Isosceles triangles have two sides of equal measurement and two angles of equal measurement. Equilateral triangles have three sides of equal measurement and three angles of equal measurement. A right triangle is isosceles only if its two acute angles are congruent.

9. C: The line through the center of the box represents the median. The median test score for classes 1 and 2 is 82.

Note that for class 1, the median is a better representation of the data than the mean. There are two low outliers, points which lie outside of two standard deviations from the mean, which bring down the average test score. In cases such as this, the mean is not the best measure of central tendency.

10. C: The set of irrational numbers is separate from the set of rational numbers. A rational number cannot be irrational, and an irrational number cannot be rational.

11. B: Determine the probability of each option.

For choice A, this is the total number of students in the broccoli circle of the Venn diagram divided by the total number of students surveyed:

$$\frac{10 + 4 + 3 + 15}{90} = \frac{32}{90} \approx 35.6\%$$

For choice B, this is the total number of students in the carrots circle and also in at least one other circle divided by the total number in the carrots circle:

$$\frac{15 + 3 + 6}{15 + 3 + 6 + 27} = \frac{24}{51} \approx 47.1\%$$

For choice C, this is the number of students in the intersection of all three circles divided by the total number in the overlap of the broccoli and cauliflower circles:

$$\frac{3}{3 + 4} = \frac{3}{7} \approx 42.9\%$$

For choice D, this is the number of students outside of all the circles divided by the total number of students surveyed:

$$\frac{23}{90} \approx 25.6\%$$

Since choice B has the highest percentage, it is the choice that is most probable.

12. C: Using the points $(-3,1)$ and $(1,-11)$, the slope may be written as $m = \frac{-11-1}{1-(-3)}$ or $m = -3$. Substituting the slope of –3 and the x- and y-values from the point $(-3,1)$, into the slope-intercept form of an equation gives $1 = -3(-3) + b$, which simplifies to $1 = 9 + b$. Subtracting 9 from both sides of the equation gives $b = -8$. Thus, the linear equation that includes the data in the table is $y = -3x - 8$.

13. C: Aaron ran four miles from home and then back again, so he ran a total of eight miles. Therefore, statement III is false. Statements I and II, however, are both true. Since Aaron ran eight miles in eighty minutes, he ran an average of 1 mile every 10 minutes, or 6 miles every 60 minutes, which is 6 mph. He ran two miles from point A to B in 20 minutes, which is a rate of 1 mile per 10 minutes, and four miles from D to E in 40 minutes, which is also a rate of 1 mile per 10 minutes, so his running speed between both sets of points was the same.

14. C: To find the number of diagonals in a polygon, use the formula $\frac{n(n-3)}{2}$, where n is the number of sides on the polygon. A dodecagon has 12 sides, so substitute 12 for n and simplify.

$$\frac{12(12 - 3)}{2} = \frac{12(9)}{2} = \frac{108}{2} = 54$$

Therefore, a dodecagon has 54 diagonals.

15. A: To convert a percentage to a fraction, remove the percent sign and place the number over 100. That means 15% can be written as $\frac{15}{100}$, which reduces to $\frac{3}{20}$. To convert a percentage to a decimal, remove the percent sign and move the decimal two places to the left. To convert a percentage to a ratio, first write the percentage as a fraction, and then rewrite the fraction as a ratio.

16. C: The original price may be represented by the equation $24{,}210 = x - 0.10x$ or $24{,}210 = 0.9x$. Dividing both sides of the equation by 0.9 gives $x = 26{,}900$.

17. C: The mean is the average of the data and can be found by dividing the sum of the data by the number of data: $\frac{16+18+20+21+34+45+49}{7} = 29$. The median is the middle data point when the data are ranked numerically. The median is 21.

18. B: The equation $y + 3 = 7$ is solved by subtracting 3 from both sides to yield $y = 4$. Substituting $y = 4$ into $x - 1 = y$ yields $x - 1 = 4$. Adding 1 to both sides of this equation yields $x = 5$.

19. D: The area of the square is $A = s^2 = (30 \text{ cm})^2 = 900 \text{ cm}^2$. The area of the circle is $A = \pi r^2 = (3.14)(15 \text{ cm})^2 \approx 707 \text{ cm}^2$. The area of the shaded region is equal to the difference between the area of the square and the area of the circle, or $900 \text{ cm}^2 - 707 \text{ cm}^2$, which equals 193 cm^2.

20. D: Since a and b are even integers, each can be expressed as the product of 2 and an integer. So, if we let $a = 2x$ and $b = 2y$, then $3(2x)^2 + 9(2y)^3 = c$.

$$3(4x^2) + 9(8y^3) = c$$
$$12x^2 + 72y^3 = c$$
$$12(x^2 + 6y^3) = c$$

Since c is the product of 12 and some other integer, 12 must be a factor of c. Incidentally, the numbers 2, 3, and 6 must also be factors of c since each is also a factor of 12.

21. C: The amount he saves is equal to $0.1 \times \$2{,}450$. Thus, he saves $245.

22. C: A number that is divisible by 6 is divisible by 2 and 3. A number is divisible by 2 if it is even, and it is divisible by 3 if the sum of the digits is divisible by 3. For example, the number 12 is divisible by 2 and 3, so it is also divisible by 6.

23. D: The cross section of a cylinder will never be a triangle.

24. C: The slope of a line can be found using any two points and the formula slope $= \frac{y_2 - y_1}{x_2 - x_1}$. The only points that give a slope of $-\frac{2}{3}$ are $(-3, -1)$, $(-6, 1)$, and $(0, -3)$.

$$\frac{1 - (-1)}{-6 - (-3)} = \frac{2}{-3} = -\frac{2}{3}$$

$$\frac{-3 - 1}{0 - (-6)} = \frac{-4}{6} = -\frac{2}{3}$$

25. C: The associative property of multiplication states that when three or more numbers are multiplied, the product is the same regardless of the way in which the numbers are grouped (i.e., where parentheses are inserted or removed). Choice C shows that the product of 2, 3, and 4 is the same with two different groupings of the factors. Choice A demonstrates the distributive property. Choice B shows grouping, but the factors are different. Choice D demonstrates the commutative property of multiplication. Therefore, the correct choice is C.

26. B: The probability may be written as $P(E \text{ and } H) = P(E) \times P(H)$. The probability of rolling an even number on a die is $E = \frac{3}{6} = \frac{1}{2}$. The probability of a coin landing on heads is $H = \frac{1}{2}$. Substituting the probability of each event gives $P(E \text{ and } H) = \frac{1}{2} \times \frac{1}{2} = \frac{1}{4}$.

27. B: A cube has six square faces. The arrangement of these faces in a two-dimensional figure is a net of a cube if the figure can be folded to form a cube. If choice B is folded, the bottom square in the second column will overlap the fourth square in the top row, so the figure does not represent a net of a cube. The other figures represent three of the eleven possible nets of a cube.

28. A: The inequality will be less than or equal to, since he may spend $100 or less on his purchase.

29. A: Kyra's monthly salary may be modeled as $\frac{1}{3}x = 1,050$. Multiplying both sides of the equation by 3 gives $x = 3,150$.

30. D: Since Hannah spends at least $16, the relation of the cost of a package of coffee to the minimum cost may be written as $4p \geq 16$. Alternatively, the inequality may be written as $16 \leq 4p$.

31. D: Let $P(T)$ represent the probability of getting tails on the coin toss. We can see that $P(T) = \frac{1}{2}$. Let $P(P)$ be the chance of getting a prime number on the die. Of the possible outcomes (1 through 6), three are prime (2, 3, and 5), so $P(P) = \frac{3}{6} = \frac{1}{2}$.

Since $P(P)$ and $P(T)$ are not mutually exclusive, $P(P \text{ or } T) = P(P) + P(T) - P(P \text{ and } T)$. Because the events are independent, $P(P \text{ and } T) = P(P) \times P(T)$. Substituting the probability of each event gives $P(P \text{ or } T) = \frac{1}{2} + \frac{1}{2} - \left(\frac{1}{2} \times \frac{1}{2}\right) = \frac{1}{2} + \frac{1}{2} - \frac{1}{4} = \frac{3}{4}$.

32. C: If x is a prime number and the greatest common factor of x and y is greater than 1, the greatest common factor of x and y must be x. The least common multiple of two numbers is equal to the product of those numbers divided by their greatest common factor. So, the least common multiple of x and y is $\frac{xy}{x} = y$. Therefore, the two quantities are the same.

33. A: The sum of 3 and the product of each term number and 5 equals the term value. For example, for term number 4, the value is equal to $5(4) + 3$, or 23.

34. C: To find the probability of an event, divide the number of favorable outcomes by the total number of outcomes. When there are two events in which the first depends on the second, multiply the first ratio by the second ratio. In the first part of the problem, the probability of choosing a licorice jelly bean is two out of twenty possible outcomes, or $\frac{2}{20}$. Then, because one jelly bean has already been chosen, there are four cinnamon beans out of a total of 19, or $\frac{4}{19}$. By multiplying the two ratios and dividing by a common denominator, one arrives at the final probability of $\frac{2}{95}$.

35. C: Elijah's total cost is $30 plus $4 times the number of tickets. Rewriting this in mathematical notation (using y for total cost and x for the number of tickets) gives $y = 30 + 4x$, which is equivalent to choice C.

36. C: When you have a ratio, you can find the fraction that each part of the ratio is of the whole by dividing a part by the sum of the parts. Since the ratio of wages and benefits to other costs is $2:3$, the amount of money spent on wages and benefits is $\frac{2}{2+3} = \frac{2}{5}$ of total operational costs.

$$\frac{2}{5} \times \$130,000 = \$52,000$$

37. C: Start by setting up a proportion to solve: $\frac{1 \text{ inch}}{60 \text{ feet}} = \frac{10 \text{ inches}}{x \text{ feet}}$. When the numbers are cross-multiplied, you get $x = 600$. Now we need to convert 600 feet to yards. There are 3 feet in 1 yard, so divide 600 by 3 to find the number of yards between the two points: $600 \div 3 = 200$. Therefore, the two points are 200 yards apart.

38. B: Sophia needs to find multiples of 3 (3, 6, 9, 12, 15, ...) and multiples of 4 (4, 8, 12, 16, ...) and find the least common multiple between them, which is 12. The greatest common divisor of 3 and 4 is 1. The least common divisor between two numbers is always 1. The greatest common multiple can never be determined. Therefore, the correct answer is choice B.

39. C: An inversely proportional relationship is written in the form $y = \frac{k}{x}$; thus, the equation $y = \frac{3}{x}$ shows that y is inversely proportional to x.

40. C: When the dress is marked down by 20%, the cost of the dress is 80% of its original price. Since a percentage can be written as a fraction by placing the percentage over 100, the reduced price of the dress can be written as $\frac{80}{100}x$, or $\frac{4}{5}x$, where x is the original price. When discounted an extra 25%, the dress costs 75% of the reduced price. This results in the expression $\frac{75}{100}\left(\frac{4}{5}x\right)$, which can be simplified to $\frac{3}{4}\left(\frac{4}{5}x\right)$, or $\frac{3}{5}x$. So the final price of the dress is three-fifths of the original price.

Social Studies

1. B: Keynesian economics is based on the notion that governments can effectively stimulate economic growth through taxation, adjustment of interest rates, and the funding of public projects. His economic philosophy contrasts sharply with the free-market philosophies of Smith, Hayek, and Friedman.

2. C: When a nation follows the theory of comparative advantage, it specializes in producing the goods and services it can make at a lower opportunity cost and then engages in trade to obtain other goods.

3. C: Article III judges are appointed for life and can retire at 65. They can only be removed from their posts by impeachment in the House and conviction in the Senate. Having judges serve life terms is meant to allow them to serve without being governed by the changing opinions of the public.

4. D: Because the Puritans took on a Reformed theology, they were in this sense Calvinists. However, many Puritans endorsed radical views that criticized such Calvinists as John (Jean) Calvin and Huldrych (Ulrich) Zwingli in Switzerland. Not only were Puritans critical of Calvinists despite their mutual Reformed approaches, reciprocally many Calvinists were opposed to the Puritans as well. The Puritan movement changed less in American colonies than in England during the 1660s. Following the Restoration (1660) and the Uniformity Act (1662) in England, nearly all of the Puritan clergy objected and left the Church of England, thereby creating a dramatic change in the movement in that country. Nevertheless, in America, the Puritans who had emigrated from England continued their original Puritan traditions for a longer time, as they had neither the same Anglican Church as in England nor the legislation restoring earlier church status against which the English Puritans had reacted.

5. A: The Supreme Court interprets the law and the Constitution. The inferior courts are bound to uphold the law as the Supreme Court interprets and rules on it.

6. A: Social dialects typically emerge when a particular group is isolated from the rest of society due to class, race, age, or gender differences. Dialects are language variants, and those that result from geographic isolation are called regional dialects. Assimilation of immigrants includes language acquisition, and thus would not typically produce a new dialect. Jargon is simply the development of a specialized vocabulary, and although it may be unintelligible to outsiders, this is the result of a vocabulary gap, not dialect differences.

7. C: Mercantilism is the economic theory that nations advance the goal of accumulating capital by maintaining a balance of trade such that the value of exports exceeds that of imports. Great Britain maintained colonies to provide an inexpensive source of raw materials while creating markets for the goods manufactured in England. Under free trade, governments refrain from hindering the international exchange of goods and services. Nations that are granted most favored nation status are assured of enjoying equal advantages in international trade. A laissez-faire capitalist economy would theoretically be completely free of government regulation.

8. D: Anthropology is the study of human social relationships and the analysis of cultural characteristics. Economists study how societies use resources and distribute goods. Political science is the study of government and political institutions. Psychologists focus on mental functions and human behavior.

9. D: Political corruption was not an immediate effect of the rapid urban growth during this time. The accelerated growth of cities in America did soon result in services being unable to keep up with that growth. The results of this included deficiencies in clean water delivery and garbage collection, causing poor sanitation. That poor sanitation led to outbreaks of cholera and typhus, as well as typhoid fever epidemics. Police and fire fighting services could not keep up with the population increases, and were often inadequate. With people moving to the cities at such a fast rate, there were also deficits in housing and public transportation.

10. B: Tropical regions near the Equator tend to experience relatively constant temperatures year-round because the angle at which sunlight hits them remains relatively constant throughout the year. In regions that are farther north or south, the angle at which sunlight hits them changes much more drastically due to the changing angle of the Earth's axis relative to the Sun. This results in greater variations in the length of daylight and in temperatures. Tropical regions do have seasons (usually a "wet" season and a "dry" season), but temperature fluctuations are less pronounced than those in regions farther from the Equator.

11. D: Only the British Empire existed following the armistice ending WWI. The Austro-Hungarian Empire, the Ottoman Empire, and the German Empire were all among the Central powers that lost the war. As empires capitulated, armistices and peace treaties were signed and the map of Europe was redrawn as territories formerly occupied by Central powers were partitioned. For example, the former Austro-Hungarian Empire was partitioned into Austria, Hungary, Czechoslovakia, Yugoslavia, Transylvania, and Romania. The Treaty of Lausanne (1923) gave Turkey both independence and recognition as successor to the former Ottoman Empire after Turkey refused the earlier Treaty of Sèvres (1920), and Mustafa Kemal Ataturk led the Turkish Independence War. Greece, Bulgaria, and other former Ottoman possessions became independent. The Lausanne Treaty defined the boundaries of these countries as well as the boundaries of Iraq, Syria, Cyprus, Sudan, and Egypt.

12. B: The House has strict rules that limit debate. A filibuster can only occur in the Senate where senators can speak on topics other than the bill at hand and introduce amendments. A filibuster can be ended by a supermajority vote of 60 senators.

13. A: One example of the multiplier effect of large cities would be if the presence of specialized equipment for an industry attracted even more business. Large cities tend to grow even larger for a number of reasons: they have more skilled workers, they have greater concentrations of specialized equipment, and they have already-functioning markets. These factors all make it easier for a business to begin operations in a large city than elsewhere. Thus, the populations and economic productivity of large cities tend to grow quickly. Some governments have sought to mitigate this trend by clustering groups of similar industries in smaller cities.

14. B: The Trail of Tears was the forcible removal of Native American tribes from their homes in the Southeastern US to Oklahoma. The name came due to the high number of Native Americans who died on the journey.

15. C: One geographical concept is distance. For example, product prices are affected by the cost of transportation, which in turn is affected by how far away raw materials are from the factories that process them, and prices for land closer to highways are higher than for land farther away from them. Location is another geography concept. Absolute location is determined by a place's latitude and longitude, not land prices (A). Relative location is determined by a region's changing characteristics, which surrounding areas can influence; one example is that land costs more in urban than rural areas. Relative location is not determined by latitude and longitude (B). Achievability is related to the accessibility of a geographical area; for example, villages with surrounding forests or swamps are less accessible than those on beaches. The dependency of an area, and hence its achievability, *does* change (D) as its technology, transportation, and economy change.

16. C: The cycle of demographic transition is best illustrated by a line graph. Demographic transition is a phenomenon in which a region's growth rate increases rapidly, peaks, and then decreases slowly over a long time. In the early phase of a region's development, both the birth and death rates are high, which can cause the population to fluctuate. As the people of the region become settled, the growth rate calms down, and the region enters a period of rapid increase. Political maps are better at depicting borders and the locations of cities, while pie charts are better at representing proportions. Flow-line maps are good for illustrating the movement of people, goods, or trends across a physical area.

17. C: Political parties organize their caucus as a private event while an official primary is an indirect election administered by state and local governments. Voters may award delegates to candidates for the national conventions, depending on state laws.

18. D: According to Article III of the Constitution, Justices of the Supreme Court, judges of the courts of appeals and district courts, and judges of the Court of International Trade are appointed by the president with the confirmation of the Senate. The judicial branch of the government is the only one not elected by the people.

19. C: A person who has taken out a fixed-rate loan can benefit from inflation by paying back the loan with dollars that are less valuable than they were when the loan was taken out. In the other examples, inflation harms the individual or entity.

20. B: Growth of industry was concentrated in urban areas, which cyclically drew laborers into cities, growing the population of cities and increasing efficiency and quality in industry.

21. D: Federalists who helped frame the Constitution believed the central government needed to be stronger than what was established under the Articles of Confederation. Anti-federalists were against this and feared a strong federal government. A system of checks and balances was established to prevent the central government from taking too much power.

22. A: The latest occurring decolonization event was the Eastern Bloc and Soviet Satellite states of Armenia, Azerbaijan, Estonia, Georgia, Kazakhstan, Kyrgyzstan, Latvia, Lithuania, Moldova, Russia, Tajikistan, Turkmenistan, Ukraine, and Uzbekistan, which all became independent from the Soviet Union in 1991. (Note: This was the last decolonization of the Cold War years, as the end of the Soviet Union marked the end of the Cold War.) Canada completed its independence from British Parliament via the Canada Act in 1982. In the Caribbean, the Bahamas gained independence from the United Kingdom in 1973. Algeria won its independence from France when the Algerian War of Independence, begun in 1954, ended in 1962.

23. C: Hernán Cortés conquered the Mexican Aztecs in 1519. He had several advantages over the indigenous peoples, including horses, armor for his soldiers, and guns. In addition, Cortés' troops unknowingly transmitted smallpox to the Aztecs, which devastated their population as they had no immunity to this foreign illness. Vasco Núñez de Balboa was the first European explorer to view the Pacific Ocean when he crossed the

Isthmus of Panama in 1513. Juan Ponce de León visited and claimed Florida in Spain's name in 1513. Álvar Núñez Cabeza de Vaca was one of only four men out of 400 to return from an expedition led by Pánfilo de Narváez in 1528 and was responsible for spreading the story of the Seven Cities of Cibola (the "cities of gold").

24. B: During the early Medieval period (or Middle Ages), Europe was characterized by widespread illiteracy, ignorance, and superstition once the unifying influence of the Roman Empire was lost. Few universities, like the university at Constantinople founded in 2 AD and those at Athens, Antioch, and Alexandria around the same time, existed then. Before the 5th and 6th centuries C.E., any education was conducted at cathedral or monastery schools or privately in the homes of wealthy families, which cannot be considered "main centers of literacy." More religious schools were created through Charlemagne's reforms in the 9th century, and early forms of universities began developing in the 11th and 12th centuries.

25. C: Clay soil has the smallest grains. This is somewhat counterintuitive because clay tends to clump together when it is exposed to any moisture. However, the individual constituent parts of clay are finer than grains of sand. In fact, silty soils have smaller grains than sand as well. Loam is a combination of sand, silt, and clay. In most cases, loam is the best soil for agriculture. Most soils are comprised of some mixture of sand, silt, and clay.

26. C: Brazil is the 10th largest producer of oil in the world and the largest in South America. Venezuela is the second largest producer of oil in South America, and has the world's largest oil reserves. Bolivia, Guatemala, and Uruguay are not petroleum-producing nations.

27. A: Presidents may veto legislation passed by both houses of Congress, and in turn Congress can override a presidential veto with a 2/3 majority. These governmental practices are a further manifestation that each branch of government is watched by the other branches and, when necessary, can undo a decision it deems ill-advised or unconstitutional.

28. B: Historians have determined that the Yellow River Valley in China began to develop into a cultural center during the Neolithic Era between c. 12,000–10,000 BC. The Shang Dynasty occurred between c. 1700–1046 BC—still part of the Ancient Era, but very long after the Neolithic era. The Xia Dynasty ruled between circa 2100–1600 BC, preceding the Shang Dynasty but still long after the Neolithic Era. Archaeological evidence exists of Homo erectus in China from more than a million years ago, during the Paleolithic Era, but the Yellow River Valley was not an emergent cultural center that long ago.

29. B: Members of the House are elected for two-year terms. Senators serve six-year terms, but the elections are staggered so roughly one-third of the Senate is elected every two years.

30. D: Niccolò Machiavelli, perhaps best known for his book The Prince, was an Italian Renaissance political philosopher noted for writing more realistic representations and rational interpretations of politics. In The Prince, he popularized the political concept of "the ends justify the means." Dante Alighieri was a great poet famous for his Commedia (additionally labeled Divina by contemporary poet and author Boccaccio, who wrote the Decameron and other works) or Divine Comedy, a trilogy consisting of Inferno, Purgatorio, and Paradiso (Hell, Purgatory, and Heaven). Dante's work helped propel the transition from the Medieval period to the Renaissance. Francesco Petrarca, known in English as Petrarch, was famous for his lyrical poetry, particularly sonnets.

31. B: The first amendment to the Constitution states, "Congress shall make no law respecting an establishment of religion, or prohibiting the free exercise thereof; or abridging the freedom of speech or of the press; or the right of the people peaceably to assemble, and to petition the Government for a redress of grievances." The right to bear arms is guaranteed by the second amendment: "A well-regulated Militia, being necessary to the security of a free State, the right of the people to keep and bear Arms, shall not be infringed."

32. C: Data collected from 2003 show that more than 15% of African-American families had violent conflicts; over 11% of Latino families did; and fewer than 9% of white families did. While researchers concede that cultural and demographic variables can influence styles of disagreement in families, they find parental stress the strongest influence on whether family conflicts become violent (A). The National Survey of Child and Adolescent Well-Being found that children of socioeconomically disadvantaged families have more developmental and behavioral problems than in other groups (B). However, these children were also less likely to receive help with their problems (D). For example, more than 40% of toddlers and more than 68% of preschoolers in contact with the child welfare system had high levels of developmental and behavioral needs; yet fewer than 23% of these children were receiving services to address those needs.

33. D: Free public education has been a US tradition since the 18th century. State constitutions govern the educational issues of each state, although federal, state, and local governments all work together on educational issues.

34. D: It is not true that the Gilded Age is a term whose origins have not been identified clearly. In 1873, Mark Twain and Charles Dudley Warner co-authored a book entitled *The Gilded Age: A Tale of Today*. Twain and Warner first coined this term to describe the extravagance and excesses of America's wealthy upper class, who became richer than ever due to industrialization. Furthermore, the Gilded Age was the era of the "robber barons" such as John D. Rockefeller, Cornelius Vanderbilt, J.P. Morgan, and others. Because they accumulated enormous wealth through extremely aggressive and occasionally unethical monetary manipulations, critics dubbed them "robber barons" because they seemed to be elite lords of robbery. While these business tycoons grasped huge fortunes, some of them—such as Andrew Carnegie and Andrew Mellon—were also philanthropists, using their wealth to support and further worthy causes such as literacy, education, health care, charities, and the arts. They donated millions of dollars to fund social improvements. Carnegie himself dubbed this large philanthropic movement the "Gospel of Wealth." Another characteristic of the Gilded Age was the Beaux Arts architectural style, a neo-Renaissance style modeled after the great architectural designs of the European Renaissance. The Panic of 1893 ended the Gilded Age and began a severe four-year economic depression. The Progressive Era followed these events.

35. B: On a political map, countries are represented in different colors, and countries that share a border are not given the same color. This is so that the borders between countries will be distinct. Political maps are used to illustrate those aspects of a country that have been determined by people: the capital, the provincial and national borders, and the large cities. Political maps sometimes include major physical features like rivers and mountains, but they are not intended to display all such information. On a physical, climate, or contour map, however, the borders between nations are more incidental. Colors are used on these maps to represent physical features, areas with similar climate, etc. It is possible that colors will overrun the borders and be shared by adjacent countries.

36. C: The person or group NOT instrumental in advancing civil rights and desegregation immediately after WWII was Congress. As African American soldiers came home from the war, racial discord increased. President Harry Truman appointed a Presidential Committee on Civil Rights in 1946. This committee published a report recommending that segregation and lynching be outlawed by the federal government. However, Congress ignored this report and took no action. Truman then used his presidential powers to enforce desegregation of the military and policies of "fair employment" in federal civil service jobs. The National Association for the Advancement of Colored People (NAACP) brought lawsuits against racist and discriminatory practices, and in resolving these suits, the Supreme Court further eroded segregation. For example, the Supreme Court ruled that primaries allowing only whites would be illegal, and it ended the segregation of interstate bus lines. The landmark civil rights laws were not passed by Congress until the 1960s.

37. D: The Louisiana Purchase actually increased the US's territory by 100% overnight, not 50%. The Louisiana territory doubled the size of the nation. It is true that Jefferson initially sent a delegation to Paris to see if Napoleon would agree to sell only New Orleans to the United States. It is also true that Napoleon, who expected America to encroach on Louisiana, decided to avoid this by offering to sell the entire territory to the US It is likewise true that America only had authority to buy New Orleans. Nevertheless, the delegation accepted Napoleon's offer of all of Louisiana. Due to his belief in strict interpretation of the Constitution,

Jefferson did require approval from Congress to make the purchase. When his advisors characterized the purchase as being within his purview based on the presidential power to make treaties, Congress agreed.

38. C: On a topographic map, an area where the contour lines are very close together indicates that the slope is very steep. Lines very far apart would indicate a more gradual change in elevation. Contour lines help represent the actual shape of the Earth's surface features and geographic landmarks like rivers, lakes, and vegetation. Topographic maps also show man-made features such as roads, dams, and major buildings. They are based on aerial photography, and the quadrangle maps are produced in various scales. The 7.5-minute quadrangle is very common and provides a 1:24,000 scale, where 1 inch represents 2,000 feet.

39. A: A city located at 6,000 feet above sea level is likely to have a cooler climate, all other things being equal. Since air is less dense at higher altitudes, it holds heat less effectively, and temperatures tend to be lower as a result. Precipitation is not as strong an indicator of temperature. Some areas that receive moderate or large amounts of precipitation are cooler (temperate and continental climates), while some areas that receive lots of precipitation, like the tropics, are warmer.

40. B: Diversity is not one of the demographic variables. Demographers, or those who study population, rely on fertility, mortality, and migration to determine the number of people in a region. The general equation is *Total Population = Original Population + Births – Deaths + Immigration – Emigration*. The natural increase, on the other hand, is calculated only with the number of births and deaths. The diversity of a population may be relevant to subsequent research performed by the demographer, but it is not considered one of the essential three demographic variables.

41. C: The President must be a natural citizen, be at least 35 years old, and have lived in the US for 14 years. There is no education requirement for becoming President. Truman did not have a college education, but most Presidents have had college degrees.

42. B: The Andes mountain range is the world's longest continental mountain range. It lies as a continuous chain of mountains along the western coast of South America.

43. B: "...endowed by their Creator with certain unalienable Rights," is excerpted from the Declaration of Independence. These rights are unable to be taken away from individuals, referring to the colonists' rights that Great Britain could not oppress.

44. B: Direct democracy is a system in which all members of a population vote directly on the issue at hand. A representative democracy refers to a system in which representatives vote on behalf of the population. The House of Representatives, the Senate, and the Electoral College are all representative democracies. The House of Representatives gives weight to population, whereas the Senate and the Electoral College do not. Members of the House of Representatives are elected in proportion to the population of each state. Representation by senators is not based on population and is therefore skewed in electoral weight. The Electoral College can and has contradicted the popular vote in the Presidential election.

45. A: The president has the authority to negotiate and sign treaties. A two-thirds vote of the Senate, however, is needed to ratify a treaty for it to be upheld.

46. B: John Maynard Keynes argued that government could help revitalize a recessionary economy by increasing government spending and therefore increasing aggregate demand. This is known as demand-side economics.

47. B: Oligarchy is defined as the rule by few. An example is aristocracy, which in ancient Greece, was government by an elite group of citizens as opposed to a monarchy. In later times, it meant government by the class of aristocrats, a privileged group, as opposed to democracy. The rule of one is called autocracy. Examples include monarchy, dictatorship, and many others. The rule by law is called a republic. Some examples are constitutional republics, parliamentary republics, and federal republics. The rule by many could apply to democracy, which governs according to the people's votes or to the collective leadership form of socialism, where no one individual has too much power.

48. C: The bubonic plague spread along trade routes, carried by infected animals and people on ships. After reaching Cyprus in 1347, the epidemic followed trade routes to infect the populations of Italy and France. Then, also through trade routes, it traveled north to Germany, England, and eventually Scandinavia and Russia in 1351.

49. B: In order to prosper, a nation should not try to increase its imports. Mercantilism is an economic theory including the idea that prosperity comes from a positive balance of international trade. For any one nation to prosper, that nation should increase its exports but decrease its imports. Exporting more to other countries while importing less from them will give a country a positive trade balance. This theory assumes that money and wealth are identical assets of a nation. In addition, this theory also assumes that the volume of global trade is an unchangeable quantity. Mercantilism dictates that a nation's government should apply a policy of economic protectionism by stimulating more exports and suppressing imports. Some ways to accomplish this task have included granting subsidies for exports and imposing tariffs on imports. Mercantilism can be regarded as essentially the opposite of the free trade policies that have been encouraged in more recent years.

50. B: Congress has the authority to shape the judicial branch. The Supreme Court once operated with only six members. Nine has been the standard number since 1869.

51. D: Totemism characterizes clans in which members believe they are all descendants of a common ancestor, often an animal. This belief characterized societies around the world, although it is most commonly associated with Native Americans.

52. B: James Madison was a close friend of Thomas Jefferson and supported a stronger central government. George Mason and Robert Yates were both against expanding federal authority over the states. Benjamin Franklin was a proponent of a strong federal government, but he was from Massachusetts.

53. A: It is not true that England's defeat of the Spanish Armada in 1588 ended their war with Spain. It did establish England's naval dominance and strengthened England's future colonization of the New World, but the actual war between England and Spain did not end until 1604. It is true that Henry VIII's desire to divorce Catherine of Aragon strengthened English expansionism. Catherine was Spanish, and Henry split from the Catholic Church because it prohibited divorce. Henry's rejection of his Spanish wife and his subsequent support of the Protestant movement angered King Philip II of Spain and destroyed the formerly close ties between the two countries. When Elizabeth became Queen of England, she supported the Reformation as a Protestant, which also contributed to English colonization. Sir Francis Drake, one of the best-known English sea captains during this time period, would attack and plunder Spanish ships that had plundered Native Americans, adding to the enmity between Spain and England. Queen Elizabeth invested in Drake's voyages and gave him her support in claiming territories for England.

54. D: Criminal cases are tried under both state law and federal law. The nature of the crime determines whether it is tried in state court or federal court.

55. C: Summative assessments are typically administered at the end of a lesson or unit to measure students' progress toward achieving academic standards. Such assessments can take several forms, including written exams, essays, or project-based learning opportunities. Project-based summative assessments provide flexibility and student choice in how students demonstrate understanding, as these assessments can be designed to accommodate variances in learning styles, needs, and interests. By using a project-based summative assessment at the end of this unit, the teacher provides an authentic opportunity for students to apply their learning in a relevant, meaningful way for strengthened overall understanding.

Science

. **B:** It is true that rocks are classified by their formation and the minerals they contain, while minerals are classified by their chemical composition and physical properties. Choice A is incorrect because rocks may contain traces of organic compounds. Choices C and D are incorrect because only minerals can be polymorphs and only rocks contain mineraloids.

. **A:** Solutions and compounds used in labs may be hazardous according to state and local regulatory agencies and should be treated with appropriate precaution. Emptying the solutions into the sink and rinsing with warm water and soap does not take into account the hazards associated with a specific solution in terms of vapors or interactions with water, soap, and waste piping systems. Ensuring the solutions are secured in closed containers and throwing them away may allow toxic chemicals into landfills and subsequently into freshwater systems. Storing the solutions in a secured, dry place for later use is incorrect, as chemicals should not be reused due to the possibility of contamination.

. **B:** When two crustal plates move apart, magma welling up could result in the formation of new crust. This has been shown to be occurring on the ocean floor where places of the crust are weaker. The crust spreads apart at these trenches, pushing outward and erupting at the ridges. When two crustal plates converge, sublimation occurs as one plate runs under another pushing it up. Two crustal plates sliding past one another is an example of a transform fault, which does not create new crust. A crustal plate being pushed down into the mantle does not form new crust but perhaps recycles the old one.

. **D:** Glaciers and ice caps are fresh water unavailable for human use as they are frozen. The hydrologic cycle refers to all the water on planet Earth. Some water is in forms that humans do not tend to use, such as oceans (too salty and expensive to desalinate) and glaciers. Water suitable for drinking can be found as surface water and in ground water, which is obtained through wells. Rivers, estuaries, and aquifers are all examples of surface water that are available to humans.

5. **C:** Heat transfer can never occur from a cooler object to a warmer object. While the second law of thermodynamics implies that heat never spontaneously transfers from a cooler object to a warmer object, it is possible for heat to be transferred to a warmer object, given the proper input of work to the system. This is the principle by which a refrigerator operates. Work is done to the system to transfer heat from the objects inside the refrigerator to the air surrounding the refrigerator. All other answer choices are true.

6. **C:** A parasite is an organism that feeds off the nutritional assets of another living thing called the host, which can lead to the host becoming malnourished or dying. Symbiosis occurs when there is a benefit to both organisms. A predator eats its prey. A producer produces food in the form of plant material that is eaten by a consumer.

7. **B:** Flowers are the reproductive organs of a plant. Flowering plants reproduce by sexual reproduction where the gametes join to form seeds. Pollen is sperm. Pollinators help transfer the sperm to the ovule, by way of the stigma. The style is the part of the female reproduction system that transports the sperm between the stigma and the ovary, which are all parts of the pistil. The stigma is the sticky tip of the style on which the pollen lands. Sepals are usually small leaves between or underneath the petals and are not as obvious or as large and colorful as the petals.

8. **A:** Many organisms, especially organisms that live in harsh conditions such as deserts or frozen icy areas, have developed specific adaptations that allow them to survive. For example, cacti are able to expand to store large amounts of water, coyotes absorb some water from their food, and snakes can escape the heat by hiding within rocks.

9. **D:** Smallpox is the only disease that has been eradicated by immunization. Progress has been made in the elimination of measles, mumps, and polio.

10. A: When light waves hit a convex lens, they are refracted and converge. A convex lens curves or bulges with the middle being thicker and the edges thinner. A magnifying glass is an example. Light rays are refracted by different amounts as they pass through the lens. After light rays pass through, they converge at a point called the focus. An object viewed with a magnifying glass looks bigger because the lens bends the rays inward. Choice B would indicate a concave lens as it would cause the light to be refracted and diverge. Light is not reflected in this case, so neither choice C nor D would be applicable.

11. D: Sources of renewable energy include geothermal power, solar energy, and wind power. Sources of nonrenewable energy include nuclear power and fossil fuels like coal, natural gas, and crude oil.

12. B: The refractive index is an optical property which is not related to the organization of the periodic table. Elements on the periodic table are arranged into periods, or rows, according to atomic number, which is the number of protons in the nucleus. The periodic table illustrates the recurrence of properties. Each column, or group, contains elements that share similar properties, such as reactivity.

13. C: For an experiment to be considered successful, it must yield data that others can reproduce. A reasonable hypothesis (A) may be considered part of a well-designed experiment. A well-written lab report (B) and computer-aided statistical analysis (D) may be considered part of an experiment that is reported on by individuals with expertise.

14. C: A laccolith is formed when an intrusion of magma injected between two layers of sedimentary rock forces the overlying strata upward to create a dome-like form. Eventually, the magma cools, the sedimentary rock wears away and the formation is exposed. Sills and dikes are both examples of sheet intrusions, where magma has inserted itself into other rock. Sills are horizontal and dikes are vertical. A caldera is a crater-like feature that was formed from the collapse of a volcano after erupting.

15. A: The stream of charged particles that escape the Sun's gravitational pull is called solar wind. Solar wind is composed primarily of protons and electrons, and these particles are deflected away from the Earth by its magnetic field. When stray particles do manage to enter the atmosphere, they cause the auroras (northern and southern lights) and geomagnetic storms that can affect power grids.

16. A: A good hypothesis is testable and logical, and can be used to predict future events. A good hypothesis is also simple, not complex.

17. A: Long-term energy storage in animals takes the form of fat. Animals also store energy as glycogen, and plants store energy as starch, but these substances are for shorter-term use. Fats are a good storage form for chemical energy because fatty acids bond to glycerol in a condensation reaction to form fats (triglycerides). This reaction, which releases water, allows for the compacting of high-energy fatty acids in a concentrated form.

18. D: The most recently formed parts of the Earth's crust can be found at mid-ocean ridges. New crust forms here when magma erupts from these ridges and pushes preexisting crust horizontally towards the continental plates. Such ridges include the Mid-Atlantic Ridge and the East Pacific Rise.

19. A: When two tectonic plates are moving laterally in opposing directions, this is called a transform boundary. When there is friction at transform boundaries and pressure builds up, it can result in shallow earthquakes (usually at a depth of less than 25 meters). California's San Andreas Fault is an example of a transform boundary.

20. C: The pressure decreases to one-third. A gas in a closed container at constant temperature will decrease in pressure to one-third when the volume of the container is tripled. The ideal gas law is $PV = nRT$ where P is pressure, V is volume, n is the moles of the gas, R is the gas constant, and T is temperature. Dividing by volume gives the following expression for pressure:

$$P = \frac{nRT}{V}$$

Boyle's Law indicates that pressure and volume are inversely proportional. The pressure cannot be increased because that would imply that pressure and volume are directly proportional.

21. B: The electrolysis of water is a chemical change that transforms water into hydrogen and oxygen gases. Synthesis reactions are those that combine reactants to form a product, which is the opposite of what happens when electrolyzing water. Reverse osmosis is a technique often used to purify water by forcing impure water through a semipermeable membrane using a pressure differential.

22. D: Species may theoretically be able to inhabit a particular area, called its fundamental niche. But the presence of competing species may mean that it only occupies part of its niche, called a realized niche.

23. C: Flowers are the reproductive organs of a plant. Flowering plants reproduce by sexual reproduction where the gametes join to form seeds. Pollen is sperm. Pollinators help transfer the sperm to the ovule, the egg. The style is the part of the female reproduction system that transports the sperm between the stigma and the ovary, which are all parts of the pistil. The stigma is the sticky tip of the style on which the pollen lands. Sepals are usually small leaves between or underneath the petals and are not as obvious or as large and colorful as the petals.

24. A: Fission is a nuclear process where atomic nuclei split apart to form smaller nuclei. Nuclear fission can release large amounts of energy, emit gamma rays, and form daughter products. It is used in nuclear power plants and bombs. Choice B, fusion, refers to a nuclear process whereby atomic nuclei join to form a heavier nucleus, such as with stars. This can release or absorb energy depending upon the original elements. Choice C, decay, refers to an atomic nucleus spontaneously losing energy and emitting ionizing particles and radiation. Choice D, ionization, refers to a process by which atoms obtain a positive or negative charge because the number of electrons does not equal that of protons.

25. C: Transform is not connected to the process of mountain building. Orogeny, or mountain building, occurs at the Earth's lithosphere or crust. Folding, or deformation, is a process that occurs to make mountains where two portions of the lithosphere collide. One is subducted and the other is pushed upward forming a mountain. This action produces various types of folding. Faulting can be characterized by a brittle deformation where the rock breaks abruptly (compared with folding). Faulting and fault types are associated with earthquakes and relatively rapid deformation. Convergent is a more general term used to describe plates interacting.

26. A: Glass is manufactured and can be recycled, but is considered a non-renewable resource. Wood is considered a renewable resource because with proper management, an equilibrium can be reached between harvesting trees and planting new ones. Cattle are managed in herds and a balance can be achieved between those consumed and those born. Soil is the result of long-term erosion and includes organic matter and minerals needed by plants. Soil found naturally in the environment is renewed. Crops can be rotated to help maintain a healthy soil composition for farming.

27. D: An atom has a neutral charge if its atomic number is equal to its number of electrons. The atomic number (Z) of an element refers to the number of protons in the nucleus. If an atom has fewer or more electrons than its atomic number, then it will be positively or negatively charged, respectively. Cations are positively charged ions; anions are negatively charged ones.

28. D: After a secondary consumer dies, such as a wolf, its body is partially consumed by decomposers, such as bacteria and fungi. Bacteria and fungi live in soil and digest body tissues of dead organisms, converting them into basic nutrients that plants need to grow. Therefore, after secondary consumers die, their energy is consumed by decomposers, who make nutrients available in the soil for producers to use. *Do not confuse nutrients in the soil with energy that producers get from the Sun to make their own food.*

29. B: A stoma (plural: stomata) is the part of a plant system that responds to stimuli by releasing water via transpiration. It can also close during adverse conditions like a drought to prevent the plant from dehydration. Stomata closure can also be triggered by the presence of bacteria. Pith refers to the central, spongy part of the stem in vascular plants. Guard cells flank stomata and regulate the opening. Sepals are modified leaves that protect the flower bud before it opens.

30. D: Reproductive habits would not be considered evidence for evolution. Usually, how a species reproduces does not support nor add to the body of evidence for the theory of evolution. Reproductive habits might exemplify how any given organism can adapt to changes in its environment as a way to survive. This does not necessarily show evolution. Fossil record is evidence for evolution as it shows evolutionary change of organisms over time. DNA sequences show that organisms that are related evolutionarily also have related gene sequences. Anatomical structures such as having an internal bony structure provide evidence of descent from a common ancestor.

31. B: A trace fossil shows evidence of existence but is not an organism itself. A trace fossil can be contrasted with a body fossil, which has been formed from an organism. Other examples of trace fossils include eggs, nests, burrows, borings, and coprolites (fossilized feces). A mouse jaw and a shark tooth are examples of body fossils. A cast of a skull is a replica and neither a body nor a trace fossil.

32. D: Of these options, the only real direct impact of climate change is the rising sea level. This is due to the melting glaciers and ice sheets. Also, the oceans expand slightly as they get warmer.

33. D: Endocytosis is a process by which cells absorb larger molecules or even tiny organisms, such as bacteria, that would not be able to pass through the plasma membrane. Endocytic vesicles containing molecules from the extracellular environment often undergo further processing once they enter the cell.

34. A: The type of RNA described by the question is transfer RNA (tRNA). The tRNA is found in the cytoplasm and carries and positions amino acids at the ribosome for protein synthesis. There are two other types of RNA. Messenger RNA (mRNA) contains the coding for the amino acid sequence in the protein. The mRNA is first made in the nucleus before traveling through the cytoplasm to a ribosome. Ribosomal RNA (rRNA) is the RNA that is found in the ribosome along with proteins, which allows the mRNA and tRNA to bind for protein synthesis. All three types of RNA originate in the nucleus where they are transcribed from DNA. Mitochondria are organelles that harbor mitochondrial DNA (mtDNA).

35. A: Repeating a measurement several times can increase the accuracy of the measurement. Calibrating the equipment should only be done once for a whole set of measurements. Calibrating for each use will add a source of error and prevent measurements from being able to be compared. None of the other choices are useful strategies to increase the accuracy of a measurement.

36. D: Destructive interference describes two waves that are out of phase as they come together to produce a new wave. Out of phase refers to the crest of one and the trough of another arriving together. Interference, when used to discuss wave phenomenon, is the interaction of two or more waves passing the same point, which could be either destructive or constructive. Incomplete interference and distorted interference are not real terms. Constructive interference refers to wave interference that results in higher peaks than the waves singularly because the waves arrive in phase with one another (the crests arrive together).

37. D: A complete metamorphosis, as butterflies undergo, includes the stages of egg (A), larva (B), pupa (D), and imago (C) or adult form. Insects such as mosquitos, grasshoppers, dragonflies, and cockroaches undergo an incomplete metamorphosis: they do not go through the stage of a pupa, which is typically inactive, does not feed, and stays hidden until the adult (imago) stage. The butterfly pupa, protected by a cocoon, is called a chrysalis. The mosquito pupa is called a tumbler.

38. B: Cold water dissolves atmospheric carbon dioxide, stores it, and releases it back out to the atmosphere as needed. This describes the physical or non-biological part of the carbon cycle. The carbon and nutrient cycles f the ocean are processed in part by the deep currents, mixing, and upwelling that occurs. Carbon dioxide CO_2) from the atmosphere is dissolved into the ocean at the higher latitudes and distributed to the denser eep water. When upwelling occurs, CO_2 is brought back to the surface and emitted into the tropical air.

9. D: The circulatory system and gas exchange with the environment is not paired correctly. It is the espiratory system that exchanges gases with the environment by delivering oxygen to the bloodstream and eleasing carbon dioxide. The circulatory system transports nutrients, gases, hormones, and blood to and away rom cells. The muscle system controls movement through three types of muscle tissue. The nervous system ontrols sensory responses by carrying impulses away from and toward the cell body. The digestive system reaks down food for absorption into the bloodstream where it is delivered to cells for respiration.

0. A: The addition of energy causes a phase change. Phase changes are physical changes, not chemical hanges. While sublimation is an example of a phase change, it occurs when a solid turns directly into a gas vithout passing through the liquid state. Condensation, another phase change, occurs when a gas turns to iquid.

1. B: Work is defined as the force used to move a mass over a distance. The amount of energy used to ccomplish a job is a non-scientific definition of work. The amount of energy used per unit of time is the lefinition of power. Energy stored in an object due to its position is the definition of potential energy.

2. D: Mario balances a book on his head. In this example, work is not applied to the book because the book is not moving. One definition of work is a force acting on an object to cause displacement. In this case, the book vas not displaced by the force applied to it. Mario's head applied a vertical force to the book to keep it in the ame position.

3. B: Ohm's Law states that voltage and current in an electrical circuit are directly proportional to one another. Ohm's Law can be expressed as $V = IR$, where V is voltage, I is current and R is resistance. Voltage is also known as electrical potential difference and is the force that moves electrons through a circuit. For a given amount of resistance, an increase in voltage will result in an increase in current. Resistance and current are nversely proportional to each other. For a given voltage, an increase in resistance will result in a decrease in current.

44. C: The vapor pressure decreases by an amount proportional to the amount of solute. Raoult's law states that the vapor pressure of a solution containing a non-volatile solute is equal to the vapor pressure of the volatile solvent multiplied by its mole fraction, which is basically the proportion of the solution that is made up by solvent. In a liquid, some of the surface particles have higher than average energy and can break away to become a gas, or evaporate. The pressure of this gas right above the surface of the liquid is called the vapor pressure. Increasing the amount of solute in a liquid decreases the number of solvent particles at the surface. Because of this, fewer solvent molecules are able to escape, thus lowering the vapor pressure.

45. B: Light travels faster in air than it can in water. Water molecules are closer together than air particles are, which causes the light to slow down and bend as it enters the water. The bending of light is called refraction and creates the illusion of the wallet being next to where it actually is.

46. B: Carbon is released in the form of CO_2 through respiration, burning, and decomposition.

47. A: Glaciers move because they are incredibly heavy, and the force of gravity slowly pulls them lower. Erosion is a result rather than a cause of glacier movement. Although large glaciers may only move a few inches a year or may not move at all, some valley glaciers in Europe move as much as 600 feet annually. The result is a rounded valley and a trail of rock and soil debris known as a moraine. The Great Lakes in the United States were formed by the passage of glaciers long ago.

48. C: The loss of biodiversity destabilizes ecosystems and impacts society by decreasing the food supply, decreasing the access to raw materials and clean water, and increasing the vulnerability to natural disasters.

49. B: Erosion is the natural process of weather wearing down landforms on the surface of the Earth. It does not cause natural matter like rocks, dirt, and sand to be destroyed (A); rather, it causes them to change in form and location. Erosion can consist of both mechanical processes, e.g., the breaking into pieces of rock, and also chemical processes (C), e.g., the dissolution of rock in water. Erosion both breaks down some areas of the land and builds up others (D) by transporting eroded sediment elsewhere. For example, rivers break down the material of mountains and carry the broken-down sediment downstream, where it accumulates at the mouths of rivers and creates new landforms like deltas and swamps.

50. A: The prevailing westerlies drive weather systems to move west to east in the mid-latitudes. The direction refers to that which the wind is coming from. The polar easterlies that travel from the northeast occur between 90-60 degrees north latitude. The ones from the southeast are between 90-60 degrees south latitude. The trade winds refer to those occurring near the equator in the tropics moving east. The doldrums are also in the tropics, but they refer to an area of low-pressure where frequently the winds are light and unpredictable.

Praxis Practice Tests #2 and #3

To take these additional practice tests, visit our bonus page:
mometrix.com/bonus948/praxeems7001

How to Overcome Test Anxiety

Just the thought of taking a test is enough to make most people a little nervous. A test is an important event that can have a long-term impact on your future, so it's important to take it seriously and it's natural to feel anxious about performing well. But just because anxiety is normal, that doesn't mean that it's helpful in test taking, or that you should simply accept it as part of your life. Anxiety can have a variety of effects. These effects can be mild, like making you feel slightly nervous, or severe, like blocking your ability to focus or remember even a simple detail.

If you experience test anxiety—whether severe or mild—it's important to know how to beat it. To discover this, first you need to understand what causes test anxiety.

Causes of Test Anxiety

While we often think of anxiety as an uncontrollable emotional state, it can actually be caused by simple, practical things. One of the most common causes of test anxiety is that a person does not feel adequately prepared for their test. This feeling can be the result of many different issues such as poor study habits or lack of organization, but the most common culprit is time management. Starting to study too late, failing to organize your study time to cover all of the material, or being distracted while you study will mean that you're not well prepared for the test. This may lead to cramming the night before, which will cause you to be physically and mentally exhausted for the test. Poor time management also contributes to feelings of stress, fear, and hopelessness as you realize you are not well prepared but don't know what to do about it.

Other times, test anxiety is not related to your preparation for the test but comes from unresolved fear. This may be a past failure on a test, or poor performance on tests in general. It may come from comparing yourself to others who seem to be performing better or from the stress of living up to expectations. Anxiety may be driven by fears of the future—how failure on this test would affect your educational and career goals. These fears are often completely irrational, but they can still negatively impact your test performance.

Elements of Test Anxiety

As mentioned earlier, test anxiety is considered to be an emotional state, but it has physical and mental components as well. Sometimes you may not even realize that you are suffering from test anxiety until you notice the physical symptoms. These can include trembling hands, rapid heartbeat, sweating, nausea, and tense muscles. Extreme anxiety may lead to fainting or vomiting. Obviously, any of these symptoms can have a negative impact on testing. It is important to recognize them as soon as they begin to occur so that you can address the problem before it damages your performance.

The mental components of test anxiety include trouble focusing and inability to remember learned information. During a test, your mind is on high alert, which can help you recall information and stay focused for an extended period of time. However, anxiety interferes with your mind's natural processes, causing you to blank out, even on the questions you know well. The strain of testing during anxiety makes it difficult to stay focused, especially on a test that may take several hours. Extreme anxiety can take a huge mental toll, making it difficult not only to recall test information but even to understand the test questions or pull your thoughts together.

Effects of Test Anxiety

Test anxiety is like a disease—if left untreated, it will get progressively worse. Anxiety leads to poor performance, and this reinforces the feelings of fear and failure, which in turn lead to poor performances on subsequent tests. It can grow from a mild nervousness to a crippling condition. If allowed to progress, test anxiety can have a big impact on your schooling, and consequently on your future.

Test anxiety can spread to other parts of your life. Anxiety on tests can become anxiety in any stressful situation, and blanking on a test can turn into panicking in a job situation. But fortunately, you don't have to let anxiety rule your testing and determine your grades. There are a number of relatively simple steps you can take to move past anxiety and function normally on a test and in the rest of life.

Physical Steps for Beating Test Anxiety

While test anxiety is a serious problem, the good news is that it can be overcome. It doesn't have to control your ability to think and remember information. While it may take time, you can begin taking steps today to beat anxiety.

Just as your first hint that you may be struggling with anxiety comes from the physical symptoms, the first step to treating it is also physical. Rest is crucial for having a clear, strong mind. If you are tired, it is much easier to give in to anxiety. But if you establish good sleep habits, your body and mind will be ready to perform optimally, without the strain of exhaustion. Additionally, sleeping well helps you to retain information better, so you're more likely to recall the answers when you see the test questions.

Getting good sleep means more than going to bed on time. It's important to allow your brain time to relax. Take study breaks from time to time so it doesn't get overworked, and don't study right before bed. Take time to rest your mind before trying to rest your body, or you may find it difficult to fall asleep.

Along with sleep, other aspects of physical health are important in preparing for a test. Good nutrition is vital for good brain function. Sugary foods and drinks may give a burst of energy but this burst is followed by a crash, both physically and emotionally. Instead, fuel your body with protein and vitamin-rich foods.

Also, drink plenty of water. Dehydration can lead to headaches and exhaustion, especially if your brain is already under stress from the rigors of the test. Particularly if your test is a long one, drink water during the breaks. And if possible, take an energy-boosting snack to eat between sections.

Along with sleep and diet, a third important part of physical health is exercise. Maintaining a steady workout schedule is helpful, but even taking 5-minute study breaks to walk can help get your blood pumping faster and clear your head. Exercise also releases endorphins, which contribute to a positive feeling and can help combat test anxiety.

When you nurture your physical health, you are also contributing to your mental health. If your body is healthy, your mind is much more likely to be healthy as well. So take time to rest, nourish your body with healthy food and water, and get moving as much as possible. Taking these physical steps will make you stronger and more able to take the mental steps necessary to overcome test anxiety.

Mental Steps for Beating Test Anxiety

Working on the mental side of test anxiety can be more challenging, but as with the physical side, there are clear steps you can take to overcome it. As mentioned earlier, test anxiety often stems from lack of preparation, so the obvious solution is to prepare for the test. Effective studying may be the most important weapon you have for beating test anxiety, but you can and should employ several other mental tools to combat fear.

First, boost your confidence by reminding yourself of past success—tests or projects that you aced. If you're putting as much effort into preparing for this test as you did for those, there's no reason you should expect to fail here. Work hard to prepare; then trust your preparation.

Second, surround yourself with encouraging people. It can be helpful to find a study group, but be sure that the people you're around will encourage a positive attitude. If you spend time with others who are anxious or cynical, this will only contribute to your own anxiety. Look for others who are motivated to study hard from a desire to succeed, not from a fear of failure.

Third, reward yourself. A test is physically and mentally tiring, even without anxiety, and it can be helpful to have something to look forward to. Plan an activity following the test, regardless of the outcome, such as going to a movie or getting ice cream.

When you are taking the test, if you find yourself beginning to feel anxious, remind yourself that you know the material. Visualize successfully completing the test. Then take a few deep, relaxing breaths and return to it. Work through the questions carefully but with confidence, knowing that you are capable of succeeding.

Developing a healthy mental approach to test taking will also aid in other areas of life. Test anxiety affects more than just the actual test—it can be damaging to your mental health and even contribute to depression. It's important to beat test anxiety before it becomes a problem for more than testing.

Study Strategy

Being prepared for the test is necessary to combat anxiety, but what does being prepared look like? You may study for hours on end and still not feel prepared. What you need is a strategy for test prep. The next few pages outline our recommended steps to help you plan out and conquer the challenge of preparation.

STEP 1: SCOPE OUT THE TEST

Learn everything you can about the format (multiple choice, essay, etc.) and what will be on the test. Gather any study materials, course outlines, or sample exams that may be available. Not only will this help you to prepare, but knowing what to expect can help to alleviate test anxiety.

STEP 2: MAP OUT THE MATERIAL

Look through the textbook or study guide and make note of how many chapters or sections it has. Then divide these over the time you have. For example, if a book has 15 chapters and you have five days to study, you need to cover three chapters each day. Even better, if you have the time, leave an extra day at the end for overall review after you have gone through the material in depth.

If time is limited, you may need to prioritize the material. Look through it and make note of which sections you think you already have a good grasp on, and which need review. While you are studying, skim quickly through the familiar sections and take more time on the challenging parts. Write out your plan so you don't get lost as you go. Having a written plan also helps you feel more in control of the study, so anxiety is less likely to arise from feeling overwhelmed at the amount to cover.

STEP 3: GATHER YOUR TOOLS

Decide what study method works best for you. Do you prefer to highlight in the book as you study and then go back over the highlighted portions? Or do you type out notes of the important information? Or is it helpful to make flashcards that you can carry with you? Assemble the pens, index cards, highlighters, post-it notes, and any other materials you may need so you won't be distracted by getting up to find things while you study.

If you're having a hard time retaining the information or organizing your notes, experiment with different methods. For example, try color-coding by subject with colored pens, highlighters, or post-it notes. If you learn better by hearing, try recording yourself reading your notes so you can listen while in the car, working out, or simply sitting at your desk. Ask a friend to quiz you from your flashcards, or try teaching someone the material to solidify it in your mind.

STEP 4: CREATE YOUR ENVIRONMENT

It's important to avoid distractions while you study. This includes both the obvious distractions like visitors and the subtle distractions like an uncomfortable chair (or a too-comfortable couch that makes you want to fall asleep). Set up the best study environment possible: good lighting and a comfortable work area. If background music helps you focus, you may want to turn it on, but otherwise keep the room quiet. If you are using a computer to take notes, be sure you don't have any other windows open, especially applications like social media, games, or anything else that could distract you. Silence your phone and turn off notifications. Be sure to keep water close by so you stay hydrated while you study (but avoid unhealthy drinks and snacks).

Also, take into account the best time of day to study. Are you freshest first thing in the morning? Try to set aside some time then to work through the material. Is your mind clearer in the afternoon or evening? Schedule your study session then. Another method is to study at the same time of day that you will take the test, so that your brain gets used to working on the material at that time and will be ready to focus at test time.

STEP 5: STUDY!

Once you have done all the study preparation, it's time to settle into the actual studying. Sit down, take a few moments to settle your mind so you can focus, and begin to follow your study plan. Don't give in to distractions or let yourself procrastinate. This is your time to prepare so you'll be ready to fearlessly approach the test. Make the most of the time and stay focused.

Of course, you don't want to burn out. If you study too long you may find that you're not retaining the information very well. Take regular study breaks. For example, taking five minutes out of every hour to walk briskly, breathing deeply and swinging your arms, can help your mind stay fresh.

As you get to the end of each chapter or section, it's a good idea to do a quick review. Remind yourself of what you learned and work on any difficult parts. When you feel that you've mastered the material, move on to the next part. At the end of your study session, briefly skim through your notes again.

But while review is helpful, cramming last minute is NOT. If at all possible, work ahead so that you won't need to fit all your study into the last day. Cramming overloads your brain with more information than it can process and retain, and your tired mind may struggle to recall even previously learned information when it is overwhelmed with last-minute study. Also, the urgent nature of cramming and the stress placed on your brain contribute to anxiety. You'll be more likely to go to the test feeling unprepared and having trouble thinking clearly.

So don't cram, and don't stay up late before the test, even just to review your notes at a leisurely pace. Your brain needs rest more than it needs to go over the information again. In fact, plan to finish your studies by noon or early afternoon the day before the test. Give your brain the rest of the day to relax or focus on other things, and get a good night's sleep. Then you will be fresh for the test and better able to recall what you've studied.

331

STEP 6: TAKE A PRACTICE TEST

Many courses offer sample tests, either online or in the study materials. This is an excellent resource to check whether you have mastered the material, as well as to prepare for the test format and environment.

Check the test format ahead of time: the number of questions, the type (multiple choice, free response, etc.), and the time limit. Then create a plan for working through them. For example, if you have 30 minutes to take a 60-question test, your limit is 30 seconds per question. Spend less time on the questions you know well so that you can take more time on the difficult ones.

If you have time to take several practice tests, take the first one open book, with no time limit. Work through the questions at your own pace and make sure you fully understand them. Gradually work up to taking a test under test conditions: sit at a desk with all study materials put away and set a timer. Pace yourself to make sure you finish the test with time to spare and go back to check your answers if you have time.

After each test, check your answers. On the questions you missed, be sure you understand why you missed them. Did you misread the question (tests can use tricky wording)? Did you forget the information? Or was it something you hadn't learned? Go back and study any shaky areas that the practice tests reveal.

Taking these tests not only helps with your grade, but also aids in combating test anxiety. If you're already used to the test conditions, you're less likely to worry about it, and working through tests until you're scoring well gives you a confidence boost. Go through the practice tests until you feel comfortable, and then you can go into the test knowing that you're ready for it.

Test Tips

On test day, you should be confident, knowing that you've prepared well and are ready to answer the questions. But aside from preparation, there are several test day strategies you can employ to maximize your performance.

First, as stated before, get a good night's sleep the night before the test (and for several nights before that, if possible). Go into the test with a fresh, alert mind rather than staying up late to study.

Try not to change too much about your normal routine on the day of the test. It's important to eat a nutritious breakfast, but if you normally don't eat breakfast at all, consider eating just a protein bar. If you're a coffee drinker, go ahead and have your normal coffee. Just make sure you time it so that the caffeine doesn't wear off right in the middle of your test. Avoid sugary beverages, and drink enough water to stay hydrated but not so much that you need a restroom break 10 minutes into the test. If your test isn't first thing in the morning, consider going for a walk or doing a light workout before the test to get your blood flowing.

Allow yourself enough time to get ready, and leave for the test with plenty of time to spare so you won't have the anxiety of scrambling to arrive in time. Another reason to be early is to select a good seat. It's helpful to sit away from doors and windows, which can be distracting. Find a good seat, get out your supplies, and settle your mind before the test begins.

When the test begins, start by going over the instructions carefully, even if you already know what to expect. Make sure you avoid any careless mistakes by following the directions.

Then begin working through the questions, pacing yourself as you've practiced. If you're not sure on an answer, don't spend too much time on it, and don't let it shake your confidence. Either skip it and come back later, or eliminate as many wrong answers as possible and guess among the remaining ones. Don't dwell on these questions as you continue—put them out of your mind and focus on what lies ahead.

e sure to read all of the answer choices, even if you're sure the first one is the right answer. Sometimes you'll nd a better one if you keep reading. But don't second-guess yourself if you do immediately know the answer. our gut instinct is usually right. Don't let test anxiety rob you of the information you know.

you have time at the end of the test (and if the test format allows), go back and review your answers. Be autious about changing any, since your first instinct tends to be correct, but make sure you didn't misread any f the questions or accidentally mark the wrong answer choice. Look over any you skipped and make an ducated guess.

t the end, leave the test feeling confident. You've done your best, so don't waste time worrying about your erformance or wishing you could change anything. Instead, celebrate the successful completion of this test. nd finally, use this test to learn how to deal with anxiety even better next time.

> **Review Video: Test Anxiety**
> Visit mometrix.com/academy and enter code: 100340

Important Qualification

Jot all anxiety is created equal. If your test anxiety is causing major issues in your life beyond the classroom or esting center, or if you are experiencing troubling physical symptoms related to your anxiety, it may be a sign f a serious physiological or psychological condition. If this sounds like your situation, we strongly encourage ou to seek professional help.

How to Overcome Test Anxiety

Additional Bonus Material

Due to our efforts to try to keep this book to a manageable length, we've created a link that will give you access to all of your additional bonus material:

mometrix.com/bonus948/praxeems7001

Made in the USA
Monee, IL
25 April 2025